THE RIDDLE OF GENDER

THE RIDDLE OF
GENDER

Science, Activism, and Transgender Rights

DEBORAH RUDACILLE

Pantheon Books, New York

Grateful acknowledgment is made to BMG Music Publishing
International for permission to use an excerpt from "Something in the
Air" by Thunderclap Newman. Copyright © by Towser Tunes Inc.
(BMI)/Abkco Music Inc./Fabulous Music. All rights for the world on
behalf of Towser Tunes Inc. (BMI) administered by BMG Music
Publishing International (PRS). All rights for the U.S. on behalf of BMG
Music Publishing International (PRS) administered by Careers-BMG
Music Publishing, Inc. (BMI). Reprinted by permission of BMG Music
Publishing International.

Library of Congress Cataloging-in-Publication Data
The riddle of gender : science, activism, and transgender rights /
Deborah Rudacille.
p.   cm.
Includes bibliograpical references and index.
ISBN 0-375-42162-9
1. Transsexualism—United States. 2. Transsexuals—United
States—Interviews. I. Title.
HQ77.95.U6R83 2005   306.76'8—dc22   2004055297

www.pantheonbooks.com

Printed in the United States of America
First Edition
2   4   6   8   9   7   5   3   1

FOR AIDEN

Glory be to God for dappled things—
. . . .
All things counter, original, spare, strange;
Whatever is fickle, freckled (who knows how?)
With swift, slow; sweet, sour; adazzle, dim;
He fathers-forth whose beauty is past change

—*Gerard Manley Hopkins,* "Pied Beauty"

CONTENTS

INTRODUCTION

"And what sort of person might you be?" asked the smiling young man behind the registration desk.

I stared at him for a moment in bafflement and dread, running through a list of potential responses. I was registering for the True Spirit Conference, an annual gathering for transsexual men and their partners and families. It was my first foray into the community, and I was nervous and feeling very much like an outsider; I was sure that people could tell merely by looking at me that I didn't belong.

"Well . . ." I said, preparing to announce that I was a heterosexual woman, a single mother of three, and a science writer, when suddenly I noticed the three options for registration on the page I had just signed: student, low income, and regular.

"Regular," I said, with relief.

"Great," the young man replied, as I filled out a check for ninety dollars and handed it over, my face burning as I realized how close I had come to looking like an idiot.

Nonetheless, throughout the next two days, as I attended sessions and introduced myself to people at the conference, I was asked the same question over and over in varying forms. The answer to the question seemed important to everyone I met. What kind of person are you? Why are you here? Why are you interested in our lives? Not far beneath those questions lurked accusations. Are you here to exploit us? To attack us? To make us look like freaks or deviants? "Just what," one guy said, "is your agenda?" I thought the question fair enough. And since it has been posed, in one form or another, by everyone whom I have interviewed on this subject, I feel that it is right that I begin this book with an answer to it, since it is probably also a question that will be entertained by readers.

I attended the True Spirit Conference in 2001 because I had recently learned that a friend of mine was transitioning from female to male. This baffled me, as I knew nothing at all about transsexuality, transgenderism, gender-queerness, or gender variance, nothing at all about the motivations that would impel a twenty-two-year-old female-bodied person to inject herself with testosterone or undergo a mastectomy or live as a man. I was concerned and confused and I soon learned that I was not alone. Nearly everyone I spoke with about the subject was as confused as I was, and in some cases far more judgmental. "That's crazy," "It's sick," and "That's disgusting" were some of the most extreme comments, together with the pious "It's against God's plan to change your sex" and the pseudoscientific "She needs psychiatric help."

It's important to note that these comments were uttered by people who are more or less comfortable with homosexuality. People who had accepted and embraced gay friends, colleagues, and family members seemed bewildered by transsexuality and its close cousin transvestism, or cross-dressing. The adjective "transgendered"—indicating individuals who either cross the great gender divide or live between the poles of male and female—is recognized, but not, it seems, widely understood. I found this to be no less true of my children's generation than of my own or my parents'. This lack of understanding breeds fear, and fear often gives birth to violence. This was brought home to me most acutely a few months after I learned of my friend's decision to transition, when a transwoman (male-to-female, or MTF, transsexual) was murdered a few blocks from my home.

Walking home from a neighborhood bar, Tacy Ranta was shot by a gang of adolescents and young adults who had been on a crime spree, carjacking and mugging twelve people in the neighborhood over a five-hour period. Although the miscreants robbed everyone, the only person they shot was Ranta. The newspaper reports on the murder focused on Ranta's transsexuality and used the male pronouns of her birth sex when referring to her, even though she had been living as a woman for years and, in the month preceding her murder, had had the sex on her driver's license altered from *M* to *F*.

The murder of Tacy Ranta mere blocks from my home, coming on the heels of my friend's announcement, caused me to confront my basic lack of knowledge and understanding of a group of people who I barely knew existed. I wanted to know more about gender variance, and though this desire was born partly of a desire to understand and support my friend, it was also linked to my own lifelong questioning of gender roles.

I was born in 1958 and grew up in the seventies, when large numbers of women began to challenge the institutions and assumptions that had created their social subordination. I lived through the second wave of feminism and I know that my life has been profoundly affected by the vastly increased opportunities for women and the breakdown of gender stereotypes that were its fruits.

Yet I, like many women, have also felt ambivalent about some of the results of that revolution. I remember very well the patronizing attitudes I encountered from other women when I chose to remain at home with my preschool children during the eighties. The unspoken assumption seemed to be that only a chump would sacrifice her career advancement to take care of babies. Virtues of the traditionally gendered female (modesty, gentleness, and emotional generosity) were scorned by those who viewed them as a pathetic accommodation to the patriarchal status quo. The qualities our culture respects and rewards are the traditionally masculine traits of independence, assertiveness, and enlightened self-interest, and feminism has done nothing to change that. We wanted the best of both worlds; instead it seems sometimes that we have the worst of each. Women have been liberated to become rakes and workaholics, and men have won the freedom to drift aimlessly in a kind of perpetual adolescence. This may be a kind of progress, but it is not the equality between the sexes once envisioned by feminists.

And despite our well-intentioned efforts to melt gender stereotypes with the blowtorch of change, differences remain. As a parent, I have certainly observed what seem to be gender-mediated differences between my daughters and my son throughout their childhood, adolescence, and young adulthood. As toddlers, they played equally happily with the Little Tikes play kitchen, a car, and various other gender-neutral toys that I as a feminist parent provided. But at a certain point, my son and his best friend began to develop an interest in dinosaurs and Godzilla, to manufacture guns and swords out of tree branches, and to engage in the kind of semi-serious wrestling and roughhousing that often produced minor injuries. Yet my son's two trips to the emergency room in early childhood were the result of "accidental" injuries inflicted by his older sister. Clearly, she hadn't heard the news that girls are less aggressive than boys!

On the other hand, from a young age my daughters were far more attuned to social nuances than was my son. While her brother could sit in the same classroom for years with various children and still not know their names, my younger daughter could rattle off not only the names but also the familial and social bonds uniting every child in the elementary school. She and her older sister have always possessed a kind of emotional radar that their more analytical brother lacks. Yet my son, unlike his sisters, remains close to his best friends from elementary and middle school, a challenge to the prevailing wisdom that females have a greater gift for forming long-lasting intimate friendships.

As teenagers, these young men developed an interest in tabletop war games, in which players build and paint fantasy armies and engage in battles based on a complicated set of rules and strategies. I can testify that in my many visits to the Games Workshop, where the armies are purchased and the tournaments played, I have never seen a female player or a female employee—only other mothers like me, anxiously clutching Christmas and birthday lists. Is there a gene for War-Hammer? Doubtful, but there is something—and I don't think the something is culturally inscribed—that causes males to be drawn to ritualized combat, whether in sport, in games, or on film. Yet, after years of watching violent movies, playing violent video games, and directing the clash of armies on plywood battlefields, my son and his friends eagerly participated in the marches against the war in Iraq and were bitterly and vocally opposed to the conflict.

My daughters were completely uninterested in the peace movement or the war itself; for them the political was not at all personal. They are intensely interested in the lives of acquaintances and celebrities, however, and have prodigious memories for who has dated, married, and dumped whom and whose career is foundering because of what ill-advised choices. Their baffled brother finds their interest in the personal lives of strangers incomprehensible: "You don't *know* these people," he is apt to snap when subjected to yet another conversation about the latest juicy celebrity gossip. In *The Essential Difference,* the British psychiatrist Simon Baron-Cohen proposes an explanation for these and other differences in male and female interests and abilities: the average woman has an "empathizing" brain while the average male has a "systematizing" brain. Males are driven to analyze, explore, and construct systems while women tend to identify with other people's thoughts, feelings, and emotions in an attempt to understand and predict behavior. I'll have more to say about Baron-Cohen's hypothesis later, but for now it's enough to point out that it does provide an explanation for the kinds of everyday differences we notice between men and women—and that the hypothesis is viewed as reactionary by those who deny any essential biological difference between male and female brains.

I grew up in a time when increasing numbers of people believed that the differences between males and females were socially constructed, and that if children were raised to understand that there were no essential differences between being born in a male body and being born in a female body, we would all be "free to be"—free of all gender-based boundaries and limitations, free of social stereotypes based on genital distinctions. Boys could cry, and girls could compete; boys could be nurses, homemakers, and teachers (the nurturing professions), and girls could be fighter pilots, police officers, and firefighters (the warrior professions). I am happy to live in a society that has struggled to eradicate limiting beliefs and practices that have kept both men and women from realizing their full potential as human beings. But I have largely abandoned the belief that all the differences we note between men and women are purely a matter of social custom. Some differences run much deeper than custom, the primary one being the deeply felt and ineradicable sense that one is male or female—or neither.

Let's talk about the distinction between gender and sex.

Virginia (neé Charles) Prince, founder of *Transvestia* magazine, famously said that "gender is what's above the neck and sex is what's below the neck." Gender is meta-sex—it's what we make of the difference in our bodies and their reproductive anatomy and capabilities. My female body is made to give birth and to nurture. Your male body is constructed to seed me and to protect our offspring. From an evolutionary perspective, our common goal is to ensure that our children survive until they can reproduce themselves and thus transmit our genes to the next generation. Gender is the cultural tapestry that we weave from those fundamental facts.

But gender differences cannot be rooted in culture alone, because my body (what's below my neck) and my brain (what's above my neck) are not divided by some kind of biological Berlin Wall. The body and the brain are an open city, built on the constant exchange of information. Just after my mother's egg and my father's sperm united, each contributing an X chromosome to my female genotype, skeins of DNA began to uncoil and replicate. Messages traveled between the rapidly multiplying cells that had not yet differentiated into specific organs and tissues, switching genes on and off under instructions from the master template, guiding my development. In the sixth week of pregnancy, the process of sexual differentiation began. The androgynous embryo, which possesses both mullerian and wolffian ducts and thus has the potential to develop either a male or a female reproductive anatomy, accepted its genetic fate, and an exquisitely choreographed dance began, performed by a company of steroid hormones. Because I am an XX person, midway through the second month of pregnancy, the primordial gonad developed into egg-bearing ovaries. My nascent wolffian ducts began to wither away, and the mullerian ducts differentiated into the gothic architecture of the female reproductive system—fallopian tubes, uterus, cervix, vagina. Within a few weeks, ultrasound images revealed a recognizably female external anatomy. Evidence suggests that my brain was prenatally "sexed" as well, though the mechanism by which this process is carried out is less clearly understood. Animal research has provided ample evidence of the organizing effects of hormones on the sexual differentiation of the brain, but the extent to which the animal data can be extrapolated to human development remains hotly contested. The sexual differentiation of the brain is completed after birth, as I learn what sorts of attitudes, behavior, and role my culture expects of me as a female.

In an XY fetus, a different set of chemical messages begins circulating in the second month of pregnancy, based on instructions encoded in the Y chromosome. "Male!" the Y chromosome shouts, and a gene called SRY directs the primitive gonad to form testicles, rather than ovaries. The testicles soon begin to produce androgens, which will masculinize both genitalia and brain. One of the chemical messengers produced by the testicles, mullerian-inhibiting substance (MIS), begins circulating throughout the rapidly dividing cells, barking out orders to arrest the development of a female reproductive anatomy. Testosterone and MIS ensure that the fissure that would otherwise develop into a vagina fuses together to form a scrotum, and that the primary instrument of sexual pleasure (glans penis) develops outside the fleshy mound of the pubis, rather than hidden within it (glans clitoridis). In males, the hormone-driven sexing of the brain is known to continue into the weeks immediately following birth, when the testicles pump out a flood of testosterone at levels that will not be matched until puberty. By that time, the male child will have learned what behaviors and attitudes his family and culture expect him to display; these are based on the presence of male genitals.

The process of prenatal sexual differentiation is complex and multifaceted. An embryo needs more than a Y chromosome to become male; it also needs an androgen receptor gene on the X chromosome to enable it to respond to the androgens its testes are producing. If the androgen receptor gene isn't functioning, the XY fetus will develop female genitalia. Moreover, testosterone (the so-called male hormone) is transformed into estrogen in the brain by an enzyme called aromatase. As researcher Lindsey Berkson has pointed out, "one cheeky irony of life is that how masculine a man is as an adult may be partly the result of his having had optimal amounts of estrogen in his brain at a certain time during his stay in the womb. Amazingly minute differences—parts per trillion or parts per billion of a few sex hormones—literally affect the making of men or women." More often than most people suspect, the "script" of sexual differentiation is altered during pregnancy, producing variation.

Yet we continue to wonder how much of gender performance is cultural and how much is biological. That's the heart of the riddle, the part that really baffles us. And it's that part of the riddle that gender-variant people may ultimately help resolve. My conversations with transgendered, transsexual, and intersexual people over the past few years have helped me understand a number of facts that I had not recognized previously. First, despite the social changes initiated by the second wave of feminism, we as a society still maintain some fairly inflexible strategies for policing the boundaries between the sexes. Each time you relieve yourself in a public place, for example, you implicitly accept the idea that Door Number 1 (women) and Door Number 2 (men) are the only options, and that each person will know precisely to which category he or she belongs, and use the "appropriate" toilet. To most of us, the choice may not seem quite as oppressive as that between the "White" and "Colored" bathrooms that were contested by the civil rights movement, but the significance is the same. A ritual boundary is being enforced, as the opponents of the Equal Rights Amendment recognized when they claimed that the ERA would result in a promiscuous mingling of the sexes in bathrooms.

Similarly, many people pay lip service to the idea that males and females have both a "feminine" and a "masculine" side, and as I finish the final draft of this book, a great deal of attention is being devoted to the rise of the "metrosexual," an urban feminized man. Yet a male-bodied person who expresses his femininity by wearing dresses quickly discovers the limits of social tolerance. Women have more freedom to dress as they please, as I discovered on a rainy night in Washington, D.C., when I attended a support group meeting for cross-dressers. As I sat in the meeting in my sweatshirt and jeans—the only female-bodied person in the room and the only person wearing pants—I realized that little more than a century ago, I would have been just as freakishly attired as the male-bodied people around me in their dresses, high heels, and makeup. According to the social standards of 1902, I, too, was "cross-dressed." Even in 1932 my garb would have been considered suspicious. But because our culture now permits women to wear clothing once thought of as "masculine," my outfit was unremarkable. Not so for the outfits on the people around me. They are defined (and define themselves) as "transgendered" partially because they yearn to express aspects of femininity denied to male-bodied persons by cultural norms. While most male-bodied persons don't seem to feel a desire to wear dresses and use cosmetics, the ones who do so encounter extraordinary social ostracism and violence. The great majority of transgendered people who are the victims of hate crimes are male-bodied persons dressing and living as females.

That doesn't mean that women are free of gender-based limitations and bias. Western women may wear pants, and some may have claimed the right to work, play, and have sex like men, but as any woman of a certain age will be happy to tell you, female cultural power is still largely a function of youth and beauty. Women of all ages spend an inordinate amount of their time and resources maintaining an attractive appearance. Young women are indoctrinated into this feminine cult at a young age, with girls typically beginning to shave, pluck, paint, and perfume at around eleven or twelve years old. Throughout adolescence, girls learn that their perceived value as people is tied to their appearance; they must be fit, fresh-smelling, and fashionably attired in order to lead happy, successful lives. The pressure to maintain a pleasing appearance increases as we age. Few straight men spend as much time on the scale, in the salon, or at the gym as their female counterparts. Why spend so much time, energy, and money to look young, fit, and fertile if being a middle-aged woman is not somehow related to a loss of prestige and power? Middle-aged men seem immune to this pressure. One of my sources—a surgeon transitioning from male to female at age fifty—told me that her spouse simply cannot understand why a successful middle-aged man would surrender his cultural power to assume the lower-caste status of a middle-aged woman. "Who will want you?" she asked, a poignant expression of the creeping sense of invisibility and insignificance many aging women feel.

Male privilege remains a very real phenomenon in our supposedly postfeminist society. Many of the transmen (female-to-male, or FTM, transsexual people) I interviewed noted that, as men, they are treated far more respectfully and deferentially than they were as women. "I get a lot of white male privilege. Oh, my god! I can't even believe that. When I would go into stores before, they had security guards following me around, because I was this sort of big motorcycle leather dyke. Now, they're like, 'Can I help you, sir? Is there anything we can do for you?'" says Tom Kennard, a burly, middle-aged transman. "They will give men power, and you just have to take it. I have to figure out how I can use that power responsibly."

Those who travel in the other direction, from male to female, are conversely aware of the loss of privilege that is an unavoidable consequence of their decision to transition. In giving up their maleness, transwomen often give up high incomes, social status, and, very often, the ability to support themselves in their chosen profession. Transwomen tend to be more visible, and thus less employable, than transmen. They are more often the victims of violence and discrimination, simply because they are seen or "read" in a way that transmen are not. But they also have surrendered the social protections of maleness. Though men can be sexually violated, they are not usually victims of rape except in all-male environments such as prisons. Transwomen seem to be at high risk for rape, however, both before and after their surgical transition. This may be because, as one source told me, transwomen aren't raised with the "dont's" that most natal women absorb from their mothers and other women. These spoken and unspoken prohibitions (don't go home with strange men, don't walk down dark streets by yourself, don't open the door to strangers) circumscribe our lives, but they may also provide some measure of protection. Transwomen learn late the painful lesson most natal women absorb in adolescence: that being a woman automatically confers vulnerability to sexual assault. This is true even if one retains the (hidden) insignia of masculinity, a penis. As a woman, I know intimately the sense of physical vulnerability that transwomen encounter when they assume the social role of women. That sense of shared vulnerability is one of the strongest bonds I have felt with the transwomen I interviewed for this book.

Fear and mistrust of men and masculinity still permeate discussions of gender. Neither women nor individual men appear to trust or think kindly of males as a group, a prejudice that seems justified when one considers the disproportionate propensity of males for committing acts of physical violence and aggression. As I have researched this book, I have learned from transmen just how painful and shocking it is suddenly to be perceived as a threatening figure, purely by virtue of one's maleness. Women may cross to the other side of the street to avoid sharing the sidewalk with you; they stop looking you in the eye. A wall goes up, and those transmen who have lived as lesbians for years before their transitions find that wall particularly disturbing. "It's really upsetting to me that men are perceived as bad," says Tom Kennard. "And I wonder how boys, men who grow up as men, deal with that. How do they internalize that? What does it do to them? Because when I talk to them, they know about this. But they're just like, 'Well, what can you do?'"

Like many of the transmen I interviewed, Kennard had to overcome deep-seated negative feelings about masculine identity and behavior in order to proceed with his transition. He didn't want to be a "man" as manhood is defined in our culture, and yet, he felt that he had no other choice because he was not a woman either. "People say that gender is what's between your ears and not between your legs, but I don't know," he says. "I just didn't belong in the girls' pile. It's sort of an exclusion thing, rather than inclusion. I just felt like I didn't belong over there. If we have a binary system, and there are only two choices, I belong here. And I like being over here. I'm really comfortable being over here."

These observations lead me to the most salient fact that my conversations with transsexual people have illuminated: though the way we express gender is clearly influenced by culture, gender identity itself seems far too deeply embedded to be purely an artifact of culture. There are few benefits to adult sex reassignment, other than the feeling that one's body and social role finally reflect one's inner sense of self. The process of sex reassignment is physically and emotionally grueling, and hugely expensive in terms of money, time, and lost personal relationships. Most of my transsexual sources knew from a very young age (typically before age five) that there was something different about them. Often they spent decades trying to understand the source of that difference and come to terms with the implications of their process of self-discovery. Those who decide to physically change their sex then spend a number of years committed to the process of transition; the outcome is a series of painful surgeries. No one would undertake this arduous quest unless driven to it by acute misery. I have been told by person after person, "It was this or suicide."

Transgendered people who do not surgically transition, who live with bodies at odds with their gender presentation, court even greater risks, enduring the constant threat of discovery and exposure. The penalty for such transgression is often brutal. Many people have heard of the murder of Brandon Teena (née Teena Brandon), the subject of the film *Boys Don't Cry*, but few know that such murders are commonplace. In 2002 alone, twenty-three people in the United States were slain in what appear to have been transgender hate crimes. For example, in October 2002, while at a party, seventeen-year-old Gwen Araujo was dragged into a garage, where she was beaten and strangled by three young men who had discovered that she was male-bodied. Her body was then dumped in the desert. It took two weeks for the other young people present at the party to report the murder. Two months before Gwen Araujo's death, on August 12, 2002, Stephanie Thomas, nineteen, and Ukea Davis, eighteen, were shot to death as they sat in their parked car a block from the apartment they shared in Washington, D.C. Davis and Thomas had lived as women since their early teens, and became close friends after meeting at a support group. Unlike Araujo, whose "secret" was unknown to many of her acquaintances, Thomas and Davis were well known and apparently well liked in the southeast D.C. neighborhood where they grew up. Their openness did not protect them. Each was hit more than ten times in the head and upper body by bullets fired by a passenger in a passing car, which, according to witnesses, turned around and released a second volley of bullets before speeding off. Despite a $10,000 reward for information leading to the arrest and indictment of a suspect, the identity of the killer or killers remains unknown.

A vigil for Thomas and Davis was held a few days after their deaths, ironically at the very same intersection where, in 1995, Tyra Hunter, a transgendered hairdresser, had lain bleeding to death after an automobile accident. Paramedics arrived on the scene immediately after the accident, but while stripping Hunter to assess her condition, they discovered her male genitalia, jumped back in shock, and began to ridicule her. As Hunter lay dying (but still conscious), the EMT team continued to mock her; she died shortly afterward in the ER from blood loss. In 1998, her mother was awarded $2.8 million in damages in a wrongful death lawsuit, based on negligence by the D.C. Fire Department and malpractice by an ER physician. "Tyra's story is surprisingly commonplace and speaks to the fears of most transsexuals [*sic*] who sometimes feel pressured to undergo expensive sexual reassignment surgery and to alter their legal documents specifically to avoid such nightmares," wrote Sarah D. Fox, Ph.D., a neurobiologist and communications director of It's Time, Ohio!, a gay, lesbian, bisexual, and transgender (GLBT) lobby organization, after the verdict was announced. The drive to express an inborn gender identity must be strong indeed to compel individuals such as Teena, Araujo, Thomas, Davis, and Hunter to face the kind of hatred that led to their deaths. Milton Diamond, professor of anatomy and reproductive biology at the University of Hawaii, explains the violence and incomprehension suffered by transgendered people simply: "Nature loves variety. Society hates it."

The transgendered and transsexual people whom I interviewed for this book were kind enough, and courageous enough, to share their stories with me. Most of the individuals whose stories are contained in these pages are "success stories"—they are primarily well-educated, middle-class white Americans whose privileged socioeconomic status contributed to their positive outcomes. In this arena, as in so many others, race, class, and economics play a huge role. Yet even with all their advantages, the individuals profiled in this book grappled with an enigma that might have consumed them, had they not found the courage and strength to endure the struggle, and the support and assistance they required. Each narrative chapter of the book is followed by the edited transcript of an interview, which provides commentary on the chapter preceding it and context for the chapter that follows. This structure will, I hope, reflect something of my own journey as I undertook my research and will enable the reader to recognize what I soon recognized myself—that the larger historical narrative is in fact composed of many individual narratives, each worthy of the telling. I am only sorry that I wasn't able to include all of the stories I heard over the past few years, or the full text of every interview.

Like politics and religion, the issue of nature versus nurture with respect to gender is one that invariably gives rise to passionate debate. I do not expect that this book will convert people who believe that gender differences are grounded entirely in social conditioning; nor do I believe that the book will eradicate the bigotry, discrimination, and violence suffered by transgendered, transsexual, and intersexual people. But I do hope that the narrative history and dialogues within its pages will promote greater understanding and acceptance of a group (or groups) of people who typically want nothing more than to live their lives in peace and be able to enjoy the same civil status and protections granted to others.

I also hope to show that the history contained in these pages is, in a very real sense, a *shared* history. The growing visibility of transsexual, transgendered, and intersexual people has coincided with a radical questioning and reshuffling of traditional sex roles among people who consider themselves normatively gendered. The boundaries of gender were once very clearly drawn in our culture; we are not as far removed from the rigidity and repression of traditional sex roles as we sometimes like to pretend. At the same time we remain baffled by the still unfolding gender revolution; what does it mean to be a man or a woman, and how can we best achieve fulfillment of our identities as man or woman? I entered into the research for this book partly to help myself resolve that ongoing internal debate. Along the way I discovered that each of us has been profoundly affected by the questions posed by the individuals described here, and by the answers that science has provided, and will continue to provide, to the riddle of gender.

THE RIDDLE OF GENDER

One

THE HANDS OF GOD

I certify that Chevalier d'Éon lived with me for approximately three years, that I always considered him to be a woman; however, after his death and upon observation of the corpse discovered that he was a man. My wife certifies the same.

WILLIAM BOUNING, LONDON, 1810

I began the research for this book in the way that I approach every scientific subject that interests me, by searching the literature. I soon discovered that far from being a product of the modern world, gender variance has been documented across cultures and in every epoch of history. Male-bodied persons dressing and living as women and female-bodied persons dressing and living as men were known in ancient Greece and Rome, among Native American tribes prior to the arrival of Europeans, on the Indian subcontinent, in Africa, in Siberia, in eastern Europe, and in nearly every other indigenous society studied by anthropologists. According to historian Vern Bullough, "gender crossing is so ubiquitous, that genitalia by itself has never been a universal nor essential insignia of a lifelong gender." In some of these cultures, cross-gendered persons were considered shamans gifted with extraordinary psychic powers, and they assumed special ceremonial roles. In many religions, the gods themselves can transform their sex at will, cross-dress, or are androgynous. Our Judeo-Christian heritage, founded on a belief in an exclusively male deity, has frowned on such gender fluidity; nonetheless, throughout the Middle Ages and even into the modern era, cross-dressing has been permitted and indeed celebrated at festivals, in clubs, and on the stage.

Moreover, the deathbed discovery of a gender reversal is a far more common occurrence in Western history than one might suspect. Many (though not all) of the persons whose names and stories are known to us today were born female and lived some or all of their lives as men. A few of the better-known individuals in this category include James Barry, British army physician and Inspector-General, died 1865; Charles Durkee Pankhurst, California stagecoach driver, died 1879; Murray Hall, Tammany Hall politician, died 1901; Jack Bee Garland, soldier in the Spanish-American War, died 1936; and Billy Tipton, jazz trumpeter, died 1989. Some of these people were married to women, who publicly expressed shock and amazement when their partners died and were found to be other than what friends and neighbors assumed them to be. It is impossible to know if this shock was real or was feigned for the benefit of a public that was not prepared to accept the alternative explanation—that the widow had lived happily with a female-bodied person who saw himself and was accepted by others (including his wife) as a man. The case of the Chevalier d'Éon, an eighteenth-century aristocrat whose gender was a source of considerable controversy during his lifetime, is a bit more complex, and because it became a public scandal, I will recount it more fully here.

Born in France in 1728, Charles-Geneviève Louis-Auguste-André-Timothée d'Éon de Beaumont lived forty-nine years as a man and thirty-four as a woman. Aristocrat, diplomat, soldier, and spy, d'Éon worked for the French government in both male and female roles, exhibiting such a chameleon-like ability to change from man to woman and back again that contemporary historians remain just as baffled as d'Éon's peers by the chevalier's metamorphoses. Traditional accounts suggest that d'Éon was dispatched on his first diplomatic mission to Russia in female garb to infiltrate the social circle of the Empress Elizabeth. After successfully carrying out this mission, d'Éon returned to France and assumed an unambiguously male role, becoming a captain of dragoons and fighting valiantly in the Seven Years' War. Wounded in battle, d'Éon was named a Knight of St. Louis, and in 1762 was offered a diplomatic assignment at the British royal court. In a letter, the

French king Louis XV congratulated the chevalier on his new post and wrote, "You have served me just as well in women's clothing as you have in the clothes you are now wearing."

While d'Éon was serving as minister plenipotentiary in London, his slight build and pretty features led many to believe that he was in fact a cross-dressed woman. People in England and France began placing wagers on his sex. The London Stock Exchange took bets on his gender, and the amount of money wagered on the chevalier purportedly rose to nearly two hundred thousand pounds in England alone. The fear of kidnapping began to haunt the chevalier, who suspected that those who had wagered large sums of money on the shape of his genitalia might seek to resolve the question by kidnapping and forced exposure. To avert a diplomatic crisis, King Louis XV of France sent a letter to George III of England, stating that d'Éon was a woman. Rather than calming public doubts, this letter created an even greater frenzy. Lawsuits were filed by losing bettors, doctors were called in to testify, and d'Éon was officially declared a woman by an English court. The chevalier responded to this public humiliation with dignity and defiance, writing to a friend, "I am what the hands of God have made me."

In exchange for d'Éon's agreement to live quietly as a woman, the French government granted the chevalier a generous pension. Although agreeing to abandon military dress, d'Éon requested permission to continue wearing the Cross of St. Louis, which as he wrote in a letter to the king "has always been a reward for bravery on the battlefield. Many officers have become priests or politicians and have worn this distinction over their new apparel. Therefore, I do not believe that a brave woman, who was raised in men's clothing by her family, can be denied this right after she has carried out the dangerous duties in a praiseworthy fashion." This request was granted and Mademoiselle d'Éon spent much of the remainder of her life residing in London with a female companion. When d'Éon died in 1810, five men who had known d'Éon were asked to examine the body and record their observations in order to settle definitively the question of d'Éon's sex. All five witnesses testified that the body was anatomically male. The deceased's female companion of many years professed herself shocked to discover that Mademoiselle d'Éon was not the women she had always assumed her to be.

A generation after the Chevalier d'Éon's death, a group of French doctors examined another puzzling corpse—that of a thirty-year-old railroad employee who had committed suicide in a squalid attic room in Paris. Abel Barbin, known for twenty-four years as Adelaide Herculine Barbin (and called Alexina), had been born with a body that appeared female. She was raised in a convent and became a teacher at an all-girl boarding school. Severe pain in her lower abdomen caused Alexina to seek medical assistance while employed at the school. The results of the doctor's examination changed her life forever. "His hand was already slipping under my sheet and coming to a stop at the sensitive place. It pressed upon it several times, as if to find there the solution to a difficult problem. It did not leave off at that point!!! He had found the explanation that he was looking for! But it was easy to see that it exceeded all his expectations!"

The doctor had discovered Alexina's undescended testicles and small penis, though he did not reveal this information to either Alexina or her employer, and instead advised the headmistress of the school to terminate the young schoolmistress. Alexina sought the advice of her bishop, who sent her to a second physician, a researcher, who prepared "a voluminous report, a masterpiece in the medical style, intended to ensure before the courts a petition for rectification." In June 1860, the birth register in Barbin's home district was amended, and the female Alexina became the male Abel—by an act of law, not surgery. Though the body remained the same, the legal person was transformed from female to male. The scandal that ensued when the newspapers and the public discovered that a man had been teaching in an all-girl boarding school condemned Abel to "abandonment, to cold isolation." His life as a man began in pain and confusion and plummeted rapidly into despair. He attempted to make a fresh start in Paris, but, impoverished and alone in a city that granted anonymity if not happiness, Abel was unable to make the transition from convent-bred woman to working man. He committed suicide at the age of thirty, overcome by feelings of isolation and desolation, the sense that he was absolutely alone in the world.

In his journal, Abel predicted that after his death his anomalous body would become a teaching tool and an exemplar of oddity. "When that day comes a few doctors will make a little stir around my corpse; they will shatter all the extinct mechanisms of its impulses, will draw new information from it, will analyze all the mysterious sufferings that were heaped up on a single human being." This premonition was fulfilled as Abel's body was autopsied and the genitals and internal organs probed, studied, and sketched for the edification of future physicians pondering the riddle of "hermaphrodites," individuals whose bodies did not conform to traditional notions of male and female anatomy.

Though the Chevalier d'Éon and Abel Barbin are perhaps the best-known cases of presurgical "sex changes" in Western history, physically intersexual people such as Herculine Barbin and neurologically intersexual people such as the Chevalier d'Éon have always existed. Gender variance thus appears to be a "natural" phenomenon, an example of biological diversity. Professor Milton Diamond of the University of Hawaii, who has studied the phenomenon of intersexuality for more than half a century, argues persuasively that gender variance should be considered neither an anomaly nor a pathology, but a simple variation. "Variety is Nature's way," he told an audience at the International Foundation for Gender Education (IFGE) in March 2003. "How many of us in this room are the same height, weight? We're all part of a great experiment." Unfortunately, society doesn't view gender variance with the same benevolence that it views differences in height and (less benevolently today) weight. "Difference is a dirty word to many," Diamond pointed out.

As contemporary historians and writers have worked to uncover the hidden history of homosexuality, some long-dead individuals who adopted cross-gendered dress and lifestyles have been lauded as gay pioneers. The most famous such case is that of Alan Hart (née Alberta Lucille), a Portland physician who began living as a man after a hysterectomy in 1917. The historian Jonathan Ned Katz identified Hart on the basis of a case study published by the physician who oversaw, and encouraged, Hart's metamorphosis. Katz and the larger gay community promptly proclaimed Hart (who was married to a woman) a lesbian pioneer, and explained Hart's decision to live as a man as an accommodation to social prejudices and coercion by a homophobic physician.

Among gays as well as straights, the complex relationship between sexual orientation and gender identity has thus sometimes been reduced to a simple formula with four variables: male or female, gay or straight. This perspective is shared by members of the (straight) public who believe that a man who wears dresses can't possibly be heterosexual, even if he sleeps with women only, just as some gay Americans believe that a female-bodied person who dresses like a man must be a masculine lesbian. Both gays and straights have a hard time believing that both of these individuals might in fact be heterosexual men. That idea challenges everything that we think we know about sex, gender, and sexual orientation. "Some men are born in female bodies," said Katherine (Kit) Rachlin—a clinical psychologist who has worked with transgendered clients for more than fifteen years—at a conference I attended while beginning research on this book. Like many Americans, gay and straight, I received this statement with certain skepticism. But after having met numerous men born in female bodies and women born in male bodies, I no longer doubt that it is true.

Sexual orientation is invisible, but gender identity is difficult to hide. It's evident in the way we walk, the way we talk, the way we dress, the way we cut our hair. My identity as a woman is clearly visible in hundreds of small and large ways. When you pass me on the street, your brain registers my long hair, makeup, skirt, pocketbook, and painted nails, and renders the verdict "female." Even if I cut my hair short, skipped makeup, and wore jeans and a T-shirt, you would still identify me as a woman by my physique, by my gait, and by the way I related to you, my fellow pedestrian, as I walked by. But what if, when you passed me on the street, you felt a moment of confusion? What if you felt it necessary to turn around and stare at me as I walked away from you? What if you turned to your companion and said, "Was that a guy or a girl?" Would you be reacting to sexual orientation or gender expression?

Many people infer the former from the latter, and believe that "masculine" women and "feminine" men are invariably gay. Feminine males and masculine females are often subject to scorn and derision, as anyone who has spent time on a playground can testify. A boy who rejects rough play and sports, who walks or talks in a way considered effeminate by his peers, is verbally and sometimes physically abused. The rules for girls are a bit looser in childhood. But by middle school, girls who are deemed inappropriately masculine by their peers are also teased and harassed. These prejudices carry through into adult life, and the all-purpose word used by many people to enforce gender conformity is "gay"—even when they are referring not to the person's choice of partner, but to the way he or she expresses gender. It is worth noting that though an increasing number of cities and states have added "sexual orientation" to civil rights legislation, fewer have added riders protecting people whose gender expression makes them targets of discrimination or violence. This lapse is a sign of our continuing failure to understand and acknowledge the distinction between sexual orientation and gender identity, and it has major consequences.

Jillian Weiss, an attorney who has published several articles about the legal issues confronting transgendered and transsexual people, notes that "gender identity is subject to scrutiny in a way that sexual identity [orientation] is not." The letter *M* or *F* affixed to one's birth certificate "publicly identifies us in every area of life, whether it be a license to drive or conduct business, proof of citizenship required to obtain employment, a benefit program such as social security, or filing of income taxes." Biological sex (and therefore gender identity) is thus regulated by the state in a way that sexual orientation is not. Citizens of the United States and most other nations are not required to announce their sexual orientation or to affirm it in legal documents. If you are a woman who decides to begin sleeping with women, it is no one's business but your own. But if you (a female-bodied or intersexual person assigned as female at birth) decide that you are a man and wish to live and be recognized as a man in the world, then you must petition the authorities to *approve* that change. In effect, you must ask the state's permission to live as a man—and present a legitimate (medical) reason for your desire to do so.

Law is based on custom. Deeply rooted assumptions about our bodies keep us locked into the belief that there are only two sexes—male and female—and that the sex of the body is always consistent with the sex of the brain. The equations work like this: Born with a vagina, fe-male. Born with a penis, male. It seems incomprehensible that a child born with a penis could grow up with the certain knowledge that she is a girl, or that a child born with a vagina could be equally convinced that he is a boy. Many people are unwilling to accept that "the hands of God" or Nature could have fashioned human beings whose sense of self is at war with their flesh, or whose gender identity falls somewhere in between the poles of male and female.

Because we live in a culture that expects science to settle questions based in the body, we look to science to tell us what it means to be male and female, how gender identity is formed, and why it is that the sex of the body sometimes seems to be at odds with the sex of the mind. But despite our sophisticated tests, science can still offer no definitive answer to this question, only tantalizing clues. When the governments of England and France attempted to solve the riddle of the Chevalier d'Éon's sex, they called in two doctors to examine the chevalier's body. From the evidence of their eyes (the chevalier appeared to have breasts), the doctors concluded that a woman stood before them. Only at death were the chevalier's genitals examined, and they told a dif-ferent story. Today our tools are vastly more powerful, yet they are no more accurate in predicting gender identity in certain cases than the eyeball test that established the Chevalier d'Éon's or Herculine Barbin's anatomical sex.

"Ordinarily, the purpose of scientific investigation is to bring more clarity, more light into fields of obscurity. Modern researchers, how-ever, delving into 'the riddle of sex,' have actually produced—so far—more obscurity, more complexity. Instead of the two conven-tional sexes with their anatomical differences, there may be up to ten or more separate concepts and manifestations of sex and each could be of vital importance to the individual," the pioneering sexologist Harry Benjamin wrote in 1966. "Here are some of the kinds of sex I have in mind: chromosomal, genetic, anatomical, legal, gonadal, germinal, endocrine (hormonal), psychological and also the social sex, usually based on the sex of rearing."

Benjamin's understanding of the multiplicity of factors that con-tribute to a person's gender identity, and his ability to see that a lack of

agreement among these components is a source of considerable anguish for some people, remains rare. Most people do not consider gender a riddle. Most do not make a distinction between anatomical sex
and gender identity. Nor do they realize that it is possible for a person
to have XY chromosomes yet female-body morphology and genitals
as a result of androgen insensitivity syndrome (AIS), or XX chromosomes yet male-body morphology and genitals as a result of congenital adrenal hyperplasia (CAH). Those are only two of a number of
genetic and endocrine conditions that can create anatomically intersexual people. Once these persons were called hermaphrodites, after
the intersexual offspring of the gods Hermes and Aphrodite. As that
myth indicates, in some cultures, intersexual and transgendered persons have been viewed with reverence and respect.

Our own culture has not been so kind. Intersexual people have been
forced to undergo physically and psychologically traumatic surgeries
to "normalize" their genitalia. The medicalization of intersex conditions has caused tremendous suffering. However, it has also granted
intersexual people legitimacy in the eyes of the medical profession,
lawmakers, and the public. No one accuses intersexual persons of
being mentally ill. Their gender variance is inscribed on their bodies,
in their gonads, genitals, or chromosomes—and so seems "real" because it is a material, measurable entity. The same is not true of transgendered and transsexual persons, who present a baffling enigma to
their families, physicians, and themselves.

Take for example a genitally female, genetically XX girl who tells
her mother at age three that she is a boy, and from her earliest childhood spurns girlish activities, clothing, and behavior. "My whole life
I'm telling my mom, 'I'm not a girl, I'm not a girl, I'm not a girl' and
thinking what the hell is going on here?" says Brad, one of the first employees of the city of San Francisco to take advantage of the new policy of insurance reimbursement for sex reassignment surgery for city
employees. "When you are little, you're kind of androgynous. Both
little boys and little girls are running around, taking their shirts off,
jumping in mud, throwing dirtballs. So if you are a little aggressive
and gened as female, they say you're just a tomboy. But once you get
up to a certain age, like six or seven, it starts separating. And I was like,

'You're pushing me the wrong way. I'm supposed to be over there with the boys; why are you making me go over here with the girls?' You look at your body and you are in the wrong body, and it's a nightmare. You wake up in this nightmare every day and you have to deal with it. And you keep thinking, When am I gonna wake up?"

Brad's description of his early life was echoed by many of the transgendered and transsexual people I interviewed for this book, who struggled for many years to understand their suffering and confusion without being able to put a name on what they were experiencing. Gender variance is not a widely discussed subject, even in medical schools, and as a consequence many physicians, like the general public, know very little about the subject other than what they are able to glean from sensationalist media accounts of cross-dressing and transsexuality. Gender variance still seems to be considered a more suitable topic for late-night talk show jokes than for journals of public health and public policy, even though a recent needs assessment survey in Washington, D.C., estimated that the median life expectancy of a transgendered person in the nation's capital is only thirty-seven years. Poverty, substance abuse, HIV infection, violence, and inadequate health care are the factors behind this statistic. Of the 252 transgendered people surveyed in the district, 29 percent reported no source of income, and another 31 percent reported annual incomes of under ten thousand dollars per year. Half the participants did not have health insurance and 39 percent did not have a doctor, though 52 percent had taken sex hormones at some time in their lives and 36 percent were taking hormones at the time of the study. A number of the respondents were working, or had worked, as commercial sex workers—a consequence of the persistent employment discrimination experienced by many transgendered people.

Though many are far better off materially than the subjects of the Washington, D.C., study, transgendered and transsexual people of every social class and at every income level share many of the same vulnerabilities. Public prejudices make it difficult for visibly transgendered or transsexual people to gain an education, employment, housing, or health care, and acute gender dysphoria leaves people at high risk for drug abuse, depression, and suicide. "You do everything you can possibly do to check out, to get away," says Brad, who at forty-six has been sober for sixteen years. When I asked if his drinking and drug abuse were tied to his confusion about his gender and related traumas, he replied, "Absolutely. Because I couldn't be who I was after so many years of hiding from myself. At that point I didn't really know who I was. It's very much a catch-22, and you're just like, 'Fuck it. I'll just take more drugs. I'll just do more drinking. I'll just do whatever because I can't deal with this.'" Brad began his transition after nearly a decade of sobriety. "Without being clean and sober, I would never have gotten to this point," he says. "I would have been dead."

Though the first scientific study of gender variance was published in Germany nearly a century ago, scientific understanding of the causes of what are today classified as "gender identity disorders" remains sketchy. Did transvestites (people who wear the clothes and sometimes adopt the lifestyle of the other sex) exist before the German sexologist Magnus Hirschfeld introduced them into the clinical literature in 1910? Undoubtedly. But prior to Hirschfeld, transvestites were believed to be a kind of homosexual—a category that itself had been only recently created. (Hirschfeld was the first to note that transvestites were usually heterosexual.) Similarly, though Hirschfeld included case studies of people born male who clearly expressed female gender identities, he didn't identify transsexuals as a separate diagnostic category. British sexologist Havelock Ellis, who had experience with both transvestites and transsexuals, wanted to call members of both groups "eonists," after the Chevalier d'Éon, a nomenclature that never caught on. It remained for the American physician Harry Benjamin to clarify the distinction between transvestism (today called cross-dressing) and transsexuality in his 1966 book, *The Transsexual Phenomenon*, and for a professional organization in Benjamin's name to establish Standards of Care for treatment of transsexuality, in 1980.

More recently, "gender identity disorder" has been created to replace "transsexualism" as a diagnosis in the American Psychiatric Association's *Diagnostic and Statistical Manual of Mental Disorders* (DSM). But science is no more certain today why some people feel so acutely uncomfortable in the sex they were assigned at birth than it was in Hirschfeld's time—nor why their number seems to be increasing.

Statistics on transsexualism and transgenderism are notoriously unreliable; in the case of transgenderism (a broad and variously defined category) they are mere guesswork. However, it is possible to track the number of people requesting sex-reassignment surgery and to make some general estimates of prevalence (the number of cases of a given condition present in a given population during a given time) based on those figures.

According to the fourth edition of the DSM (DSM-IV), about 1 in 10,000 people seek sex-reassignment surgery (SRS) in the United States every year, and approximately 1 in 30,000 men and 1 in 100,000 women will undergo SRS at some point during their lives. This is believed to be a very conservative estimate, based on SRS statistics that are decades old. Professor Lynn Conway of the University of Michigan suggests that the DSM-IV figures are off by at least two orders of magnitude and that "the prevalence of SRS in the U.S. is at least on the order of 1:2500, and may be as much as twice that value. Therefore, the intrinsic prevalence of MtF transsexualism here must be on the order of ~1:500 and may be even larger than that." A group of researchers in the Netherlands recently estimated the prevalence of transsexuality to be 1 in 11,900 males and 1 in 30,400 females; this estimate was based on the number of Dutch citizens seeking services compared with the general population.

Legal scholar Jillian Weiss has pointed out that "gender identity disorders" are probably far more common than previously suspected, on the basis of four general observations. First, unrecognized gender problems are occasionally diagnosed when patients are seen with anxiety, depression, substance abuse, and other psychiatric conditions, which often serve to mask the underlying gender issue. Second, many individuals who meet the diagnostic criteria for "gender identity disorder" never present themselves for treatment (this category includes the great majority of cross-dressers, professional female impersonators, and gender-variant gay people). Third, the intensity of some people's feelings of gender-related discomfort fluctuates throughout their lifetimes, and does not always achieve a sustained "clinical threshold" requiring treatment. Finally, gender-variant behavior among female-bodied persons is "invisible" in a way that gender-variant behavior in male-bodied persons is not. On the most basic level, this is exemplified by the relative ease with which women can don men's clothing.

The number of people self-identifying as transgendered or transsexual and seeking services (hormone therapy and/or surgery) has certainly risen in every decade since Christine Jorgensen brought the issue to the public's attention, in 1952. Gunter Dorner, a German endocrinologist who has devoted his career to studying the effects of hormones on the brain, has postulated a fourfold increase in the incidence of transsexualism over the past forty years in the former East Germany. Is Dorner correct? No one knows. But if various forms of gender variance are indeed on the increase, as seems to be the case, what might be the cause of this phenomenon? Dr. Paul McHugh, former chief of psychiatry at Johns Hopkins School of Medicine and a noted opponent of sex reassignment surgery, believes that gender variance is a fad or a "craze" driven by the media and the Internet. McHugh's views are the flip side of the postmodern "performativity" argument that gender is a cultural construction and that the body is a text upon which individuals are free to inscribe their gender of choice. In this view, gender-queer people are revolutionaries helping to dismantle an oppressive system—and their numbers are increasing, as more and more people challenge the tyranny of the gender binary.

Others believe that greater public tolerance and acceptance, combined with the increased ability to connect with others online and in person, is responsible for the increasing visibility and political activism of gender-variant people. "Twenty or forty or fifty years ago, you couldn't have had a meeting like this one," Professor Milton Diamond told me at the 2003 annual meeting of the International Foundation for Gender Education. The majority of the meeting's participants were cross-dressed men, a group that remains the most heavily closeted of sexual minorities and the most persecuted. "A meeting like this would have been broken up by the police," Diamond said. Then too, he pointed out, "Many of these individuals think that they are the only ones in the world, and they don't think that there is a solution, and when they find a solution or find a safe haven somewhere, they utilize it. Many of these activities are like support groups in their own way. They don't call them that, but that's what they are."

Without denying the influence of social factors in helping more people come out, as a science writer I can't help being interested in biological explanations for what seems to be a pronounced increase in the number of gender-variant people in the world today. An enormous quantity of man-made chemicals has been released into the environment since the chemical revolution began after World War II. According to researchers who have studied their effects, "many of these chemicals can disturb development of the endocrine system and of the organs that respond to endocrine signals in organisms indirectly exposed during prenatal and/or early postnatal life; effects of exposure during development are permanent and irreversible." Some scientists and transpeople argue that the buildup of these endocrine-disrupting chemicals in the environment has begun to produce the same kind of effects on human sexual differentiation that have already been observed in wildlife and laboratory animals. In this view, a previously rare collection of endocrine-mediated anomalies is becoming more common as a result of the bioaccumulation of these chemicals, many of which are stored in fat and transmitted to the developing fetus through the placenta in pregnancy.

The strongest evidence for a possible biological basis for gender variance comes from research on the effects of the drug diethylstilbestrol (DES). DES is a synthetic estrogen developed in 1938. Between 1945 and 1970, DES and other synthetic hormones were prescribed to millions of pregnant women in the mistaken belief that they would help prevent miscarriages. DES was even included in vitamins given to pregnant women, and in animal feed. Use of DES during pregnancy was discontinued in the United States in 1971, when seven young women whose mothers had taken DES during pregnancy were found to be suffering from a rare vaginal cancer. Since then, research on animals and human epidemiological studies have proved that DES causes myriad health problems in both males and females exposed to the drug in the womb, including structural damage to the reproductive system. Animal research has also shown that DES and other estrogenic chemicals affect the development of sex-dimorphic brain structures and behavior in animals. Laboratory animals exposed to hormones at critical stages of development in utero exhibited behaviors associated with the other sex after birth. Only in recent years have some researchers begun to note higher-than-expected rates of transgenderism in DES sons and daughters. The moderators of an online discussion group for the XY children of DES mothers surveyed subscribers in 2002 and discovered that 36.5 percent of the forum's members were either preoperative or postoperative transsexuals, while another 14.3 percent defined themselves as transgendered. An update taken on the five-year anniversary of the group showed that since 1999, between one-quarter and one-third of the members of the DES Sons Network had indicated that gender identity and/or sexuality issues were among their most significant concerns. These data have not yet found their way into the scientific literature, however, and the combined cohort studies of DES children have thus far failed to ask a single question related to gender identity. This epidemiologic failure baffles DES "sons" who are now daughters and who are aware of the increasing public health concerns about chemicals that bind to the estrogen receptor in humans and animals.

"There are millions of us who were exposed to DES. And millions more exposed to DDT, DDE, dioxin, and god knows whatever else is out there that is estrogenic," says Dr. Dana Beyer, a transgendered physician who serves as co-moderator of the DES Sons Network. "You look at DES and say, 'If that can mimic estrogen, there must be other things out there. What are people eating? What are they exposed to in the water supply? Five million people were exposed to DES in this country alone. Globally, there are many millions more. And we're still alive and kicking and suffering from the effects. Plus there probably will be third-generation effects and maybe fourth- and fifth-generation effects."

Efforts to establish the etiology, or cause, of transsexuality and other forms of gender variance have most often focused on psychological rather than organic causes—this is not surprising, since gender identity disorders are classified as psychiatric, not medical, conditions. Many psychiatrists have attempted to root gender nonconformity in an unstable home environment, abusive or disturbed parents, gender confusion in the family, and other social factors. This line of research has not been very successful, however, as relatively few individuals who grow up in disturbed circumstances of any kind exhibit gender anomalies. As early as 1973, a psychologist working with cross-gendered clients noted that "there is no more psychopathology in the transsexual population than in the population at large, although societal response to the transsexual does impose almost insurmountable problems."

For that reason many transgendered people reject "pathologization" and would like to see the gender identity disorders removed from the *Diagnostic and Statistical Manual of Mental Disorders* in the same way that homosexuality was removed from the DSM. Others argue that this step would have disastrous effects for transsexual people. Rusty Moore, a professor at Hofstra University, in New York, says that transsexuality is "a part of human variation just like having a clubfoot is human variation. So people have surgery to correct clubfeet or cleft palate and that gets paid for by medical reimbursement. But in the meantime, until that medical reclassification takes place, our biggest legal protection is what we already have, the DSM. Because that's the only thing that stops the people that are out to get us."

Some who believe that transgenderism and transsexuality are biologically based argue that the condition known as "gender identity disorder" ought to be removed from the DSM and reclassified as a congenital endocrinological disorder. "Somewhere the hormones that are secreted either by the brain or by the testes in response to the brain—the fetal hormonal system—are messed up. The end result is the morphological phenomenon, the brain anatomy or hypothalamic anatomy," says Dr. Dana Beyer. For that reason, "we're thinking of trying to push a new name for this: Benjamin's disorder. So that when a baby is born or when a child is growing up and comes and says, 'You know, Mommy says that I'm a boy, but I think I'm a girl,' the doctor would say, 'Okay, let's rule out Benjamin's disorder.' Let's figure out what's going on here, rather than telling the parents the kid is crazy, delusional. The assumption is that you are psychotic or have some kind of mental abnormality. That's the problem with the DSM. If we can make this a congenital anomaly just like cleft palate and cleft lip, or any of the physical intersex conditions, that shifts everybody's perspective."

In *The Normal and the Pathological*, a study that traces the development of the concept of pathology in medicine, the historian of science Georges Canguilhem pointed out that "an anomaly or mutation is not in itself pathological." Canguilhem carefully delineated the distinction between anomaly and pathology. "An anomaly is a fact of individual variation which prevents two beings from being able to take the place of each other completely," he writes. "But diversity is not disease; the *anomalous* is not the pathological." This concept was articulated in various ways by many of the transgendered people with whom I have spoken over the past three years.

"There's an idea that people have subconsciously inculcated about how gender and the body work, and when someone says, 'I'm doing it a little differently,' it's like 'No, you're wrong.' But no, we're just doing it differently than you," says historian Susan Stryker. "It's a privilege to not have to think about how you are embodied," she says, comparing gender privilege to race privilege and pointing out that normatively gendered people don't have to think about gender "in the same way that white people never have to think about race." According to Stryker, transgendered people must question basic assumptions about what it means to be male or female, and the relation of gender to the body, in the same way that other minority groups must examine and reject the assumptions that create their oppression. "I didn't have the privilege of having my body communicate who I am to other people without some kind of interventions. Transsexuals are subject to a double standard. People say, 'You're essentializing gender because you think it's all in the genitals.' Well, no, I don't. It's about my sense of self, and being able to communicate my sense of self to other people the way everybody else does."

The concept of "gender" as applied to human beings is itself a fairly new concept. Until the middle of the twentieth century, scientists recognized only biological sex, and though a determination of "sex" was usually based on the appearance of the genitals at birth, scientific discoveries complicated this simple picture as early as the eighteenth century. In cases of ambiguous genitalia, the gonads (testicles or ovaries) were used to establish sex until the discovery of Barr bodies (inactivated X chromosomes in female cells) in the mid-twentieth century. Then chromosomes became the new litmus test for sex—but by that point, it had become increasingly clear that there were persons, rare though they might be, whose sense of themselves as men or women was in distinct contrast to the results of chromosome testing. The terms "gender role" and "gender identity" as descriptions of a person's innate sense of self were born in the 1950s, and very quickly the word "gender" became a synonym for sex, although transgendered people today (and throughout history) have made it clear that this is a misconception. Sometimes, they say, the body lies.

CONVERSATION WITH BEN BARRES, M.D., PH.D.

Dr. Barres is Professor of Neurobiology and Developmental Biology at Stanford University. He graduated from the Massachusetts Institute of Technology, obtained an M.D. from Dartmouth Medical School, completed a neurology residency at Cornell, and obtained a Ph.D. from Harvard Medical School. He studies interactions between glia and neurons in the brain, and is internationally known for his work. He is in his late forties, but his bearded baby face makes him look much younger. I interviewed him in his office at Stanford University, which was cluttered in the way a scientist's office is usually cluttered, with books and papers. He was wearing shorts, a T-shirt, and tennis shoes and looked like he had just come from his lab. I asked him to speak from his perspective as both a scientist and a transman.

Q: Do you feel comfortable sharing some of the details of your personal story?

I think that I have the typical story. All the transsexuals I talk to have exactly the same story. It gets boring after a while. As early as I can remember, I thought that I was a boy. I wanted to play with boys' toys, play with my brother and my brother's friends and not my sister. I was always being given girls' toys, like Barbie. But I never wanted to play with dolls. I wanted to go and beat up on boys. I remember one year my brother got Rock 'Em, Sock 'Em Robots, and I was so jealous. And I remember at Halloween I was dressing up as an army man, or I was a football player. And it just seemed so natural to me, but looking back now I think, "My god, what must my parents have been thinking?"

Q: Did they think that you were a tomboy?

I guess so. I remember that I beat up the biggest bully in grade school. Came home with broken glasses from fighting the boys in the street. Got mud all over me and played with trucks. I had a great time. It became a problem only when I got to the age where the boys realized that they shouldn't be playing with girls. It was at some point in grade school, around nine or so, when it became clear that the boys didn't want to play with girls anymore. And I'd go over to my friend's house to play and I remember at one point the parents said, "I don't think that it's right for you to play with him anymore," and I was like "Why not?" I didn't understand it. I was just having a good time playing. You know, if I had been gay, I think that I might have had a lot of hazing from the other boys, about wanting to play with girls, but . . .

Q: The gender rules were looser for girls?

Only up to a certain age, though. At that point it did begin to become quite difficult. I can remember that I wanted to be in the Cub Scouts so bad, and Boy Scouts. Instead I was in the Brownies, and I hated that. We were baking cookies, and I wanted to go camping. I wanted to take shop and auto mechanics. There are a lot of girls who might want to do that stuff, too. I can remember feeling strongly about it and really being distressed, particularly when some of the guys were allowed to take cooking classes. But I've always been the kind of person who has had a lot of interests and can keep myself busy, so I just decided to be by myself rather than playing with my sister's friends or the other girls. I was kind of ostracized growing up. I was never in the "in" group. I was always sort of socially rejected. Because I was different. I really was sort of like that boy in a dress, or something.

I was remembering just the other day something that happened in grade school, or maybe it was in junior high. I remember the Girl Scout leader yelling at me, saying, "Why do you always have to be different, Barbara? Why do you always have to be different?" And she was absolutely at her wits' end. And I remember being shocked by this because I was always the good kid. You know, I always got good grades and I never got in trouble. I wasn't trying to cause any trouble. And I remember being shocked because obviously I had, without even trying, really pissed this teacher off. And then I remember, because she shocked me so much, I started thinking about it and kind of said to myself, "You know, I guess I am doing something kind of different than the other girls." Well, I didn't want to do what they were doing. That was boring.

So that was what it was like growing up, but then you reach puberty. That got really weird, you know, because then you start to get breasts. I really didn't want them, and they just seemed like foreign objects. I wore really loose T-shirts just like I'm doing now so that they wouldn't show. I never did the binding thing, I think because I wasn't that big-chested, and maybe if I had been I would have. Another thing that I noticed in puberty was my incredible discomfort about wearing dresses. I wanted to wear guys' clothes. Ever since I could choose my own clothes, I would always wear jeans and shorts.

The only way to explain it is that I felt very uncomfortable and I didn't understand why. Like when it came time to shave my legs. I didn't want to do that. I felt like a naked chicken or something. And makeup: there was just no way I was going to put on makeup. And jewelry. I was constantly being given jewelry as gifts and being encouraged to, you know, do my hair, but of course I always had my hair cut short. In puberty, it really started to get very weird. I could never dance because that would mean behaving female, and there was no way that I was going to do that. Dating, wearing dresses—guys never asked me out anyway because I think that I was very masculine in my behavior. But, overall, I guess that I had this feeling of just being wrong in my body. I just started to feel very uncomfortable and in fact became uncomfortable for the rest of my life because you have to wear dresses. If you are a doctor, you have to wear a dress to go to the clinic. You have to wear a dress to funerals and weddings. Having to go to my sister's wedding and wear this flowery dress. These are amongst the big traumatic experiences of my life!

And that sort of discomfort (because I've only changed my sex over the past few years) has characterized most of my life. Just this very, very uncomfortable feeling about being female—every aspect of it. But I didn't understand it and I was always very confused about it. When I went to college, I was diagnosed with mullerian agenesis.

They realized that I didn't have a vagina or uterus. I remember the doctors going up and looking for testicles that were undescended, checking my karyotype. They never told me the results of the karyotype, so I just assumed that it was normal. I remember talking to these doctors and they were saying that they were going to construct an artificial vagina, and I never had any say in the matter. They never asked me if I wanted it. I remember thinking, "God, I'm just an interesting case to them." They would come in and they would go out, but they would never ask me how I felt. And I had feelings! I felt very confused about the whole thing, like why are they going to do this, and I really don't feel female, and I didn't think that I particularly wanted a vagina. But on the other hand, I was a girl and I should have a vagina. It didn't seem like there was any choice really. And I had a boyfriend at the time—I'm attracted to men, by the way, weakly, not strongly—so I thought if I'm going to have sex with him, I guess that I should have a vagina. But I never really had an interest in vaginal sex. But they did it anyway.

And then I remember when I was in medical school learning about testicular feminization [the discarded name for androgen insensitivity syndrome, a condition in which the lack of cellular receptors for testosterone and dihydrotestosterone creates a female-body morphology even though the person is of XY chromosomal sex], and that seemed to me to be the thing that explained it all when I learned it in class. I still remember that day etched vividly in my mind. It just explained it. I thought, "Okay, I've always felt like a guy, and I just have testicular feminization and they just didn't tell me." I remember going through the literature when I was in medical school and trying to understand. I assumed that the reason I felt so different about myself was the mullerian agenesis. That's an aspect that a lot of transsexuals don't have—they don't have this physical problem. But for me it was a confounding thing, and a confusing thing. I think it kept me from realizing my transsexuality for a long time. I thought that everything was somehow related to that.

I also knew that my mother had been treated during her pregnancy with an androgen-like drug—not DES, one of the androgenic progesterones. My sister asked the doctor who treated my mother with this hormone many years ago (he's long dead now) and she was told that it was definitely not DES, but rather an "androgenic progesterone." I was never told the exact name. Anyway, I've always assumed that my gender variance was due to that drug, and that's what caused this reproductive defect. But then in fact if you look at the [scientific] literature, there really isn't a correlation between androgen exposure and mullerian agenesis; there is no evidence that mullerian agenesis is caused by hormonal anomalies. And in addition, women who have mullerian agenesis feel like women. They don't have this gender disturbance. And again I found that very confusing.

So, I just thought, "Well, there hasn't been a lot of research, and what do they know anyway?" It was really only after I moved to the Bay Area and read a newspaper article about James Green [a well-known Bay Area transman and activist] that I realized that there was anyone else out there like me. I had never really talked to anybody. I just felt kind of ashamed of it.

Q: Yet you grew up in a time when there was extensive media coverage of celebrity transsexuals like Chris Jorgensen and Renée Richards. You didn't make the connection?

No, I never did. Partly because while I was in high school, college, and medical school, I never read the newspaper. I never watched TV. I was very intense about my studies. I knew a lot about science, but I didn't know a lot about other stuff. I was a typical science geek, and I really had no other interests. It wasn't until I came here [to Stanford] that I started reading the newspaper. I was just very driven. I worked seven days a week, fifteen-hour days, right through training. So I didn't hear a lot about those people.

Then after two years of being here, I got breast cancer, which runs in my family. My mother died of it when she was my age. So when I had breast cancer I remember going to have the surgery, and even though they had picked it up early and it hadn't spread, I begged my doctor to do a bilateral mastectomy, even though only one breast needed to come off. I said to him, "You know my mother died of this. I think it's genetic and I think it would be best to do it [the double mastectomy] as prophylaxis." This was before the [BRCA] gene test was available. It turns out that a couple of years afterward, I did have the gene test and I did test positive. Anyway, I finally did manage to convince him to cut it off, over a lot of objections. This was one of the things that made me feel very comfortable about the gender change later because I remember leaving that doctor's office feeling like this was the best thing that had ever happened to me. And I remembered that when my mother went through it, she just had one breast cut off, and it was so traumatic for her. So incredibly traumatic. And I experienced nothing like that. I was happy to have them cut off. I was relieved. "Relief" is a really good word to describe it.

But at this hospital where I had my surgery, they also did sex changes, and I remember one of the nurses talking about this person who'd changed from male to female, and I remember thinking, "Man, what a pervert. How weird." I think I had the same reaction that everybody else had: "What a bunch of weirdos." And I never related that to me. I don't know what that's about. Here I am, a doctor. I've been confused about my gender my whole life, but I didn't—maybe it's some form of denial—but I still find it fantastic that I didn't make the connection. And then you read this article, and it's like in your face. It was so moving. It was like everything he said was the story of my life. And in the article it mentioned this clinic right down the street and how you need to get this evaluation. So I just contacted them, filled it out, and the next thing you know they were seeing me and saying, "You are a classic case. Would you like to change your sex?"

It was all done very quickly. There was a period of a few weeks where I was pretty stressed because I was thinking, "Do I really want to do this?" And you know, a lot of transsexuals, when they change their sex, they move somewhere and change their entire identity. But I am internationally known, and my whole career rests on my not changing my last name at least. So that was rough, wondering if I would lose my career, lose my job, wondering whether students would still come to my lab. So I thought about it a lot. And I actually talked to some senior people here about what I was thinking about doing, and when they said that they didn't think that it would hurt my career, that made me feel good.

I really felt by that point that life had been so hard on me—I never feel like I really do a good job of explaining what it was like, but I didn't sleep a lot of nights, I was suicidal, life was so uncomfortable. Don't get me wrong, I've really enjoyed my life, but somehow it's like it was split into two parts. The personal part, which has been very uncomfortable, and the professional part that's been a pleasure, that I've really enjoyed. But the personal part was just so uncomfortable that sometimes you think, "I've had enough." It's that distressing.

So, at the time I went to the clinic, I just felt like it was either this or suicide. I didn't see any other alternatives. And it all happened very quickly. Within a few months of being seen, I was on hormones and then within a few months after that, I had my ovaries taken out—which was actually prophylactic surgery for the genetic mutation that I had, although female-to-male transsexuals really should have their ovaries taken out anyway. Then when I came back to work after the oophorectomy, I had begun shaving, and I sent a letter out to a few people in the department letting them know that I was changing my sex. It's amazing how when you are well known, how quickly rumors get around. Really, within a day or two after sending out that letter, everybody around the world knew. Especially with e-mail, you can imagine how quickly the news spread, and of course there was a lot of talk, but after a couple of months it died down. Everyone here at Stanford has been fantastically supportive, from students, my faculty here, the deans.

Q: Your first scientific meeting after transition must've been interesting.

Some people made funny comments about it, but most people just didn't say anything. I'm sure they were shocked. The hardest thing is pronouns. It's very hard for people to switch. Most of them are very good about that, but every once in a while they'll slip, particularly if they've had any alcohol. I have trouble with it myself sometimes. I was just interviewing a young female-to-male transsexual who lost her job when she . . . he announced that he was changing sex and came to talk to me about the possibility of a job here, and throughout the whole interview I kept calling him "her." Once I know, even I do it. And I had to keep checking myself. I don't care if someone accidentally calls me "she." I care if they do it systematically and as a form of harassment. Fortunately, that hasn't happened to me.

I feel like I had this gender issue, I dealt with it, and it's resolved. The most important thing is that I've been happy. I've been so much happier. I enjoy life now.

Q: It seems like FTMs in general choose to transition and then get on with their lives. They don't seem so interested in activism, in being out and politically active as MTFs.

Well, I'm out. I don't hide it. Hiding is why people are so ignorant about transsexuality. That's why it took me so long to figure it out. But I think that males to females are so much more defensive in how they deal with it afterward. It seems to me that not that many males to females remain in the same job that they were in before they changed. For example, a geology professor here at Stanford changed male to female, and she totally changed her research. She does gender studies now. She had a much rougher time [than I]. She had a very difficult time. I think that the medical school is a more accepting environment because we are biologists, familiar with biological variation. Geology is much more of a macho, male-dominated field.

Q: What do you think about gender? Is it in the body or the mind? Is it biological or is it social?

I think that there is something bimodal about gender. Biologically bimodal because it's important for evolution and all species have it. Males and females are designed differently, and it's all under the influence of hormone-driven programs, and if you look at behavior, male and female behavior is different, and I don't think that's all social. In fact, some of the best evidence for that comes from transsexuals. If you look at female-to-male transsexuals and results of their spatial tests before and after testosterone—and hundreds of studies have shown, and everyone agrees, that males and females differ in certain verbal and spatial tests—what's cool about transsexuals is that they are their own control; you can do before-and-after tests. They have the same genes; the only thing that's different is the hormones—and you find that female-to-male transsexuals become more malelike in their spatial abilities after testosterone. So there clearly are some gender-specific things that are controlled by hormones.

So it's a very bimodal thing, but of course in any spectrum there's going to be something in between. I just think that's biology; it's just the way we are. I would think that a lot of transsexuals feel this way because otherwise why do they feel so strongly from the time they are born that there's something wrong? Why can't they just get used to the way they are? That doesn't come from the way society treated me. That comes from deep within. It comes from within. That's my own personal view.

Two

THROUGH SCIENCE TO JUSTICE

Plato was acquainted with persons on the borderline of both emotional worlds, that of man and that of women. "Mixed beings" they are called. But here in my sickly body dwelt two beings, separate from each other, unrelated to each other, hostile to each other, although they had compassion on each other, as they knew that this body had room for only one of them. One of these two beings had to disappear, or else both had to perish.

LILI ELBE (NÉE EINAR WEGENER), BERLIN, 1930

Western science first took notice of cross-gendered people and tried to provide some kind of therapeutic assistance for those who sought it in the first decades of the twentieth century. Much of this work was carried out in Berlin, at the *Institut für Sexualwissenschaft* (Institute for Sexual Science), founded in 1919 by the pioneering physician and activist Magnus Hirschfeld. Housed in a beautiful old building in the heart of Berlin once owned by the violinist Joseph Joachim, the institute served as a doctor's office for Hirschfeld and his colleagues, research facility, library, museum, and lecture hall. Hirschfeld and his staff studied a wide range of sexual behaviors and treated a broad array of clients, acquiring data on the gender identities and sexual practices of more than ten thousand men and women through a tool that Hirschfeld termed a "psychobiological questionnaire."

Few people today recognize Hirschfeld's name, and yet he was one of the most famous scientists in the world during the 1920s. Hirschfeld was the most prominent public figure in the first generation of *sexologists,* biological and social scientists who approached the study of human sexual behavior as a serious scholarly endeavor, best suited to interdisciplinary study. Hirschfeld was born in 1868. Early in his career as a physician he was drawn to the subjects that would become his life's work. Stirred by the international furor over the trial of Oscar Wilde in England, Hirschfeld published a thirty-four-page monograph titled *Sappho und Socrates,* in which he asked, "How can one explain the love of men and women for people of their own sex?" In 1897 Hirschfeld founded the Scientific Humanitarian Committee, a group of scientists and activists who would work tirelessly for the next thirty years for the repeal of Paragraph 175, a German law criminalizing sexual acts between men. The motto of the committee was "through science to justice."

In Hirschfeld's Berlin, two crucial strands of modernity met and mingled. Berlin was a great scientific center in an era when Germany led the world in research, and it was also a place where gay and trans people were visible and in some respects tolerated. At the center of this coupling stood Hirschfeld, a gay man and a scientist, who existed comfortably in both worlds and brought them together in his work. The city of Berlin, "a strange million-headed city like a cuirass," in the words of Hirschfeld's patient Einar Wegener, was the womb that nurtured the budding sexologist. "Berlin, in Hirschfeld's time, changed from a quiet, almost rural Prussian town into the large German capital and hectic metropolis," writes Erwin J. Haeberle, in *The Birth of Sexology,* describing the environment that incubated the study of human sexual behavior. Haeberle notes that Hirschfeld and his contemporaries "lived through the most extraordinary scientific upheavals, technological innovations, cultural breakthroughs, social upheavals and political changes," as Berlin was transformed from the city of Bismarck and Kaiser Wilhelm's imperial residence to the heart of Weimar culture. "All of this had its impact on our pioneers," Haeberle says. "It constituted the climate in which sexology was conceived and could grow."

By the time Hirschfeld moved to Berlin, around the turn of the century, it was home to a growing gay subculture. Though still relatively quiet and discreet, Berlin's gay underground proved a fertile environment for both the man and the researcher. Hirschfeld's biographer Charlotte Wolff describes the city's impact on the young physician.

"During the early years of the twentieth century, Hirschfeld certainly had a field day visiting pubs, hotels and the private houses of homosexuals to see, to learn and to live in an atmosphere which was close to his heart. His homosexuality was still a secret to many but, surely, clear to himself," she says. But Hirschfeld wasn't looking just for sex, love, and acceptance in Berlin's gay bars and clubs. He was looking for research subjects—and attempting to persuade influential people that members of the "third sex" (homosexuals and gender-variant people) posed no threat to the community.

Hirschfeld escorted friends, fellow academics, and foreign writers to the bars. He even brought Dr. H. Kopp, the Kriminalkommissar (chief inspector) for sex offenses of the Berlin police department. Like many others who came into contact with Hirschfeld, Kopp was converted to his view and became a supporter of the Scientific Humanitarian Committee. In fact, the professor and the detective became friends, and many years later Dr. Harry Benjamin, author of *The Transsexual Phenomenon*, the first book-length scientific treatment of transsexuality and sex reassignment, recalled that it was Kopp who introduced him to Hirschfeld. "A couple of times I was invited to accompany Hirschfeld and Kopp, who were good friends, on tours through a few gay bars in Berlin. The most famous was the Eldorado, where mainly transvestites gathered and female impersonators performed. Hirschfeld was well known there and referred to as 'Tante Magnesia.'"

Berlin's reputation as the decadent drag nightclub of the Continent attracted many foreign visitors. Some of the most vivid descriptions of Weimar Berlin and its inhabitants were penned by the writer Christopher Isherwood, who with his friends Wystan and Stephen (the poets W. H. Auden and Stephen Spender) traveled to Berlin in search of the sexual freedom they could not find as gay men at home in England. Isherwood's *The Berlin Stories* formed the basis for the Broadway show (and later film) *Cabaret*. Years later, in his frank memoir, *Christopher and His Kind*, published in 1976, Isherwood reveals the sly artifice behind the city's seedy reputation, the knowing wink that accompanied the perverse erotic invitation. He contrasts the ambience of his favorite gay bar, The Cosy Corner, "plain, homely and unpretentious," with the tourist traps of West End Berlin, "dens of pseudo-vice catering to heterosexual tourists. Here screaming boys in drag and mono-cled, Eton-cropped girls in dinner jackets play-acted the hijinks of Sodom and Gomorrah, horrifying the onlookers and reassuring them that Berlin was still the most decadent city in Europe." Wryly, Isher-wood questions whether or not Berlin's "famous decadence" wasn't simply a public relations ploy, "a commercial line which the Berliners had instinctively developed in their competition with Paris. Paris had long since cornered the straight girl–market, so what was Berlin left to offer its visitors but a masquerade of perversions?" Like many hard-luck ladies, Berlin may have found that offering forbidden sex to strangers put food on the table. Still, the city's winking tolerance of homosexuality and gender diversity was real, not feigned.

This tolerance was surely due in part to the efforts of Hirschfeld and his colleagues, who worked for nearly three decades to increase public and scientific understanding of homosexuality, under the auspices of the Scientific Humanitarian Committee, widely acknowledged as the world's first gay-rights organization. The committee produced the first scientific journal focusing on homosexuality and other sexual variations, the *Yearbook of Intermediate Sexual Stages*, which published articles by all the pioneers of sexology. In 1921, Hirschfeld organized the first International Congress for Sexual Reform on a Sexological Basis, and in 1928, he organized and served as one of the first presi-dents of the World League for Sexual Reform. All of this activity, combined with his heavy schedule of speaking engagements, primar-ily to working-class audiences, bore fruit in the increasing tolerance and acceptance of homosexuality and gender variance in Weimar Germany.

Perhaps the most significant of Hirschfeld's achievements was the founding of the Institute for Sexual Science. Researchers at the insti-tute created the first premarital counseling service in Germany and ad-vised young couples planning to marry on the likelihood of health problems in their children, based upon their genetic history. They studied and treated impotence and venereal disease, intersex and trans-gender conditions, all types of fetishes, and what later came to be called "paraphilias" (disorders of desire). Men who were being prosecuted under Paragraph 175 came to the institute for treatment and lived under the protection of Hirschfeld until their cases came to trial, at which time they were represented by the institute's legal staff. The staff of the institute delivered public presentations in an auditorium decorated with busts of Darwin and the German biologist Ernst Haeckel. Scholars and visitors from around the world came to the institute and carried out research in its library, which contained more than twenty thousand volumes and thirty-five thousand pictures and photographs. Many years later, Christopher Isherwood described the broad impact of the institute: "It was a place of education for the public, its lawmakers and its police."

Hirschfeld's great mission was the reduction of suffering through a scientific understanding of sex, a goal he shared with many prominent physicians and scientists of his time. By proving that homosexuality and gender variance were based in biology, Hirschfeld hoped to bring an end to the persecution of what he called "sexual intermediaries," people who lived somewhere between the boundaries of male and female. "By sexual intermediaries we understand manly-formed women and womanly-formed men at every possible stage or, in other words, men with womanly characteristics, and women with manly ones," Hirschfeld writes in his groundbreaking study of cross-dressing, *Die Transvestiten,* published in Germany in 1910.

In *Die Transvestiten,* Hirschfeld illuminated a previously unstudied phenomenon. Most of Hirschfeld's contemporaries shared the view of earlier researchers such as Carl von Westphal that homosexuality and transvestitism were nearly synonymous. Hirschfeld himself confesses in *Die Transvestiten* that when he first encountered transvestites, or to use the modern term, cross-dressers, he was "inclined to assume that we again had homosexuality before us, perhaps unconscious." He soon found, however, that this was far from the case, "because the main marker of homosexuality, as its root word -homos, or 'same,' indicates, is the direction of the sex drive toward persons of the same sex. We saw in most of our cases that there was not a trace of it; that, on the other hand, there was an even stronger antipathy than normally appears in other heterosexuals."

In other words, Hirschfeld discovered that many of his male cross-dressing subjects were rampantly homophobic and described themselves as sickened by the thought of having sex with another man. Hirschfeld suspected that transvestism was far more common than assumed, though he admitted that he didn't have enough data to make a positive statement about its prevalence. "Whether erotic transvestism is a rare and exceptional phenomenon, or whether it occurs more often than we might at first imagine, more evaluation is needed at this time," he writes, adding that "with regards to homosexuality, for a long time people believed it to be a rarity too, until they gradually recognized its relative frequency."

Hirschfeld quotes his clients extensively in the case studies that introduce the book, and the stories they tell provide some indication of the range of gender variance that Hirschfeld encountered in his practice.

"My sex life is not so great. Whenever I do not have on a dress, I have absolutely none at all. I have intercourse with my wife every six or eight weeks. Otherwise, we live a happy life. Also, I treat my wife very well because I take care of almost all of the housework. . . . Unfortunately, my feminine tendencies also got us into financial trouble. Because the mania for dresses is very great in me, it hardly helps at all when I can get dressed after the day's work. Lately, it is almost impossible for me to fall asleep without putting on a slip. It is a force in me that I cannot withstand. This constant battling against a power that I cannot withstand has already frazzled my nerves. Because I have to use my hands at work, I have to control myself in order to work. Then it suddenly comes over me like a storm, my nerves fail, and I have to leave work, stay at home, which many times costs me my job, because today there are many workers available. . . . When I am permitted to wear dresses permanently, and when I can wear these clothes in front of other women without having to feel degraded, then my life will take a turn for the better." (Case 16)

"As a rule I only cross-dress when my girlfriend is with me; sometimes the urge is so strong that I masturbate in costume. The yearning to feel totally like a woman also leads me to have coitus 'with myself' using wax candles, cigars, and things like that. . . . So the main content of my yearning is to be a woman completely. An extraordinary fascination for me would be to shave myself completely, put on make-up, put on women's clothing; to be sure, truly elegant, the 'last word' but not too loud, underwear fine and silky, narrow shoes, lots of embroidery, artistic hat, in short, to be like a brilliantly entertaining prostitute. . . . I am a good sportsman, marksman, ride well and have proved myself in the military. Nevertheless I feel freer in the company of women and drawn to them as if by an invisible bond." (Case 8)

"When I put on a woman's dress my whole relationship to the external world changes. During this metamorphosis, which extends to how I dress my hair, I have a totally different view into the environment; the outside world affects me differently, finer and gentler, and challenges me to appreciate the delicate and the gentle. Noteworthy is that this effect is so universal that, in cross-dressing, I am repulsed by both beer and smoking, in spite of the fact that I am a lover of both. My greatest desire goes so far as to be able to live untroubled and undistinguished as a woman, and what is worse, what I see in my future is the impossibility of the fulfillment of this yearning." (Case 3)

"I myself, as a child, took every opportunity to wear my sister's clothing, was often beaten for it, mocked and teased, played with girls, and yearned for the time when I would finish school and work as a nanny. I finally stole the clothes of a young woman, and her certificate of domicile and, dressed as a woman, fled to Switzerland, so that for years no one knew where I was. . . ." (Case 13)

"I cannot report anything of much importance from my childhood, only that I had the burning desire that I was really a boy. I often blamed my dear father because I was not a boy, but what could the poor man do? My dear parents made every possible effort to make me into a quiet, gentle being. At age fourteen they sent me to a priest in a boarding house so that I would become totally domesticated, homely, in short a patient sheep. But it failed totally. After three months I disappeared through a window. Not because I committed a crime, but rather because the priest had the audacity to give me a box on the ears and for what? Only because we were having a bit of fun, and when he was away, we danced. Of course, I was the one who incited it. We were, that is to say, nine boarders and we were supposed to do as we were told. But what did such a country priest know about Berlin blood? Well, I made it clear to him many times he should not try to hit a Berliner but continue to pick his country oranges." (Case 15)

Hirschfeld noted certain shared traits in the people he studied. First, and most important, their cross-dressing began at a very young age and was generally lifelong. "In most of the cases we can trace the urge back to their early childhood. It increases during puberty; the conviction becomes even clearer in their awareness at that time, and then remains almost unchanged for their entire life." Second, he found that far from exhibiting symptoms of general pathology or derangement, most of the transvestites he knew appeared to be socially and economically successful people, whose only deviation from the norm lay in their persistent and often compulsive desire to cross-dress. "The transvestites that we have come to know here are intelligent, conscientious people who have diverse interests and a broad education," he writes in *Die Transvestiten*. "In school, almost all of them excelled in motivation, diligence, and especially in their ease of understanding (which many psychiatrists today of course look upon as a slight stigma of degeneration). At present, all of them find themselves in good financial standing and in good jobs in which they have been promoted because of their great energy and proficiency."

To understand the curious nature of that assertion, its generally positive and complimentary tone marred only by the reference to "degeneration," one must know something about the context in which Hirschfeld was working. To the sexologists who came before him and even to his peers, all forms of sexual nonconformity, including homosexuality, were indications of disease. "The pre-sexological era of modern sex research was almost exclusively devoted to the study of people believed to be sick. The sexual manifestations of their sickness were carefully listed, and as a rule, described to degeneration," wrote Erwin A. Haeberle, in *The Birth of Sexology*. The word "degeneracy" had a very specific meaning for Hirschfeld, his predecessors, and his

contemporaries. Degeneracy implied weak or damaged genes, a hered-
itary defect that manifested in conditions as various as alcoholism,
mental retardation, promiscuity, and sexual "disorders" such as homosexuality, transvestism, and fetishism. Today, the word "degeneracy"
connotes a moral failing, but to Hirschfeld and his contemporaries it
referred to an organic defect that should not be passed on to future
generations. Like many physicians of the time, within Germany and
without, Hirschfeld was a eugenicist, concerned not just with individual patients but also with the health of society as a whole. His belief in
eugenics, and more specifically in biological explanations for human
behavior, provided the impetus for his scientific investigations, his
medical practice, and his social activism. Biology, in particular the new
science of endocrinology, promised to explain everything for Hirschfeld and for his contemporaries, including the riddle of sexual intermediaries.

Hirschfeld defined four types of sexual intermediaries. First came
people born with ambiguous genitalia, neither classically male nor
classically female—the clinically intersexual. Next, people with cross-
gendered secondary sexual characteristics, "men with womanly mammary tissue (gynecomastia) and women without such; women with
manly hair, such as manly beard or manly pubes." Into this group
Hirschfeld classed men and women whose body morphology deviated
from the norm. These were the unfortunate men and women who were
more often mocked, harassed, and/or stopped by police when they
were actually wearing the clothes of their biological sex, rather than
when they were cross-dressed. One woman mentioned by Hirschfeld
was actually stopped by police more than a dozen times when dressed
as a woman. Dressed as a man, she encountered no problems at all.

Next came those "persons divergent with regard to their sex drive."
This category included not only homosexuals and bisexuals, but also
masochistic men and those who preferred to adopt the "female" role in
sex with women, and sadistic women and those who adopted the
"male" role in sex with men. So, for example, men attracted to "ener-
getic" women or to women "who are considerably more mature, intellectual and older than themselves" were believed by Hirschfeld to be
expressing a kind of femininity that placed them in the same category

as homosexuals. Similarly, "women betray their manly mixture in a preference for the womanly type of man, very dependent, very youthful, unusually gentle men, in general for such ones who in their traits of behavior and character correspond more to the feminine type."

The final category of sexual intermediary included "men whose feminine emotions and feelings are reflected in their manner of love, their direction of taste, their gestures and manners, their sensitivity, and many times their particular way of writing. Also men who more or less dress themselves as women or live totally as such; on the other side women of manly character, manly ways of dressing and thinking and writing, strong tendency towards manly passions, manly dress, naturally also such women who more or less lead the life of men." These were the people who would eventually be called "transsexual," though there is some dispute about the origin of the term, which some attribute to Hirschfeld and others attribute to the physician David O. Cauldwell, whose perspective on these patients was considerably less positive.

Using the new science of endocrinology to support his theory of intermediaries, Hirschfeld found the work of the Viennese pathologist Eugen Steinach—who transplanted testicles and ovaries into neutered animals of both sexes—especially significant. Noting that that the sexual behavior of the experimental animal was profoundly affected by the type of gonad that Steinach implanted, Hirschfeld concluded that in addition to germ cells (sperm or eggs), testicles and ovaries produced secretions that masculinized or feminized experimental animals irrespective of their birth sex. Extrapolating from the animal data, Hirschfeld concluded that the various forms of gender variance (including homosexuality) were the result of endocrine anomalies. The production of sex hormones in testicles and ovaries would soon be confirmed by endocrinologists, but the second half of Hirschfeld's hypothesis—that homosexuality and other forms of gender variance were the result of endocrine anomalies—has been vigorously contested ever since.

Hirschfeld's theories and the work of his fellow endocrinologists and sexologists fascinated not only fellow physicians but also the general public. "Early in the twentieth century, endocrinology was the shit!" says historian Susan Stryker. "It explained everything. It had this radical view of the body: 'no one is fully man, no one is fully woman.' We're all a mixture of different things, and certain tendencies predominate and that's why homosexuality can be caused by a glandular imbalance. That whole model that people exist on a continuum was Hirschfeld's idea. Among the educated, that was more the model for how things were, part of the destabilizing thrust of modernism—that endocrinological view of gender difference," says Stryker.

In many ways, we are the heirs of that "destabilizing" world view that Hirschfeld and his colleagues sought to anchor in biology. While reading Hirschfeld, I realized with a shock that I would probably qualify as a low-grade intermediary under the Hirschfeld nosology (system of classification). Although I do not have a beard or a male body shape, nor do I desire to be a man, I do exhibit a mix of the natural psychological attributes of absolute "maleness" and "femaleness" identified by Hirschfeld. "Capable, active, enterprising, wandering," in general, men are "active, aggressive, searching," says Hirschfeld, and tend to lack the "grace, gentleness, charm and submissiveness of the woman." "Womanly" women, by contrast, are "receptive, impressionable, sensitive, emotional and more direct than the man while less concerned with the strongly abstract, the racking of one's brains, or even the purely creative and active side of the human psyche." Reading this description, I thought back to my research trip to California at the start of this project, in which I drove alone from hilly San Francisco to the fertile midsection of the state to the desert outside Palm Springs and then back up the coast, to San Diego and Los Angeles via San Juan Capistrano. Along the way I interviewed sources whom I had met over the Internet and through my local contacts. The trip required both "masculine" independence and initiative to get me on the road and keep me there, but also "feminine" receptivity and sensitivity as I asked questions, listened, and empathized with the life stories of my sources. If I had been purely "masculine" or purely "feminine," in the traditional sense, I could not have carried out this work successfully. I should add that I thoroughly enjoyed both aspects of the trip, although, when I returned home, I discovered that my sixteen-year-old daughter had wrecked my new car in my absence! My response to this

debacle was both "masculine" and "feminine"—the empathizing female self was exclusively concerned with my daughter's well-being
(thankfully she was fine), while the analytical male self grimly calcu-
lated the inconvenience and the expense. Like most "mixed" beings
these days, I don't perceive these aspects of my personality as at war
with each other, however, nor do I consider myself transgendered. The
definition of "femininity" has, over the past hundred years, expanded
to include many qualities once coded "masculine," and vice versa.

My research trip and my freedom to define myself as a woman in
any way I choose are in many ways the consequence of a social revolution that began around the time Hirschfeld was initiating his research,
when a "New Woman" appeared to challenge prevailing beliefs about
the essential nature of the sexes. "The nineteenth century had cherished a belief in the separate spheres of femininity and masculinity that
amounted almost to a religious faith," comments the distinguished lit-
erary scholar Elaine Showalter in *Sexual Anarchy*, a study of the fin de
siècle and that era's revolutionary retooling of sex. This faith was
founded, Professor Showalter and other scholars point out, on the icon
of the "womanly woman," the flower of femininity. The womanly
woman was first and foremost a mother and a wife. She was gentle and
soft and self-sacrificing. Her natural place was the home, which she
sought to make a place of comfort and beauty. "Often compared to a
flower, a kitten, or a child, she was modest and pure-minded, unselfish
and meek. She knew her place well; naturally fitted to the common
round of household duties, she could make a home of a hovel by min-
istering to the needs of her husband, either as uncomplaining drudge
or angel on the hearth. Nothing in herself, the littlest and least of all
creation, she achieved greatness not in her own right but in her relat-
edness as daughter and wife," writes historian Patricia Marks. "The
'womanly woman' was one of the nineteenth century's most memo-
rable myths."

The New Woman, who appeared as if by magic on two continents,
Europe and North America, late in the nineteenth century, was an
iconoclastic figure who blasphemed this gospel of femininity. She rejected the cult of maternity and self-sacrifice conceived as elements of
the essential nature of womanhood. She argued for self-determination

and self-fulfillment. She was not exactly a feminist, as her primary goal was not to gain legal or political rights. The defining characteristic trait of the New Woman was her desire to live life on her own terms and her refusal to be defined solely as daughter, wife, or mother. With her masculine thirst for education and work, lack of interest in marriage and motherhood, and demands to be taken seriously as a human being, the New Woman raised disturbing questions about the essential natures of men and women.

In the 1880s, women in England and France were finally granted the right to divorce unfaithful spouses and own property in their own right. Women's colleges were founded in the United States and England, and in France secular secondary public-school and university education was opened to both sexes. Demographic changes also sent large numbers of women into the workforce, with or without an education. When the 1891 British census revealed that there were approximately nine hundred thousand more females than males in the total population, there was a great deal of public hand-wringing about the eventual fate of such "surplus" women, who might never marry or have children. Instead, they became the first generation of Western women to move to urban areas alone to work as shopgirls, teachers, journalists, and secretaries.

These New Women rejected sexual apartheid in word and deed; the visible emblem of their revolt was their mode of dress. Throwing off corsets, bustles, and back-buttoned bodices, the New Woman advocated "rational dress," suitable for work, shopping, and exercise. Her divided skirts permitted free movement but were attacked by conservatives as an attempt to usurp the powers and privileges of men. Trousers or "bifurcated garments" defined masculinity, in the same way that restrictive corsets and crinolines defined femininity, and conservatives were determined to enforce not only the inner dichotomy between the sexes but also their external manifestation. The New Woman was in fact a "cross-dresser" of sorts, and she was both mocked and slandered for daring to wear masculine garments. An article in the British medical journal *The Lancet* declared the wearing of trousers "detrimental to the health and morals" of women. New Women were accused at various times, by various commentators, of being sexually promiscuous, sexually neutered, or lesbians—accusations that were to reappear in the middle of the twentieth century, when second-wave feminists once again began challenging social norms of femininity.

The New Woman of the fin de siècle was often coupled in print with a similarly transgressive male figure—the dandy, or aesthete, epitomized by Oscar Wilde and other decadent artists and writers. Languorous men devoted to the "poetry of appearance," with an intense interest in fashion and interior decoration, dandies were not a new phenomenon, but in the context of late-nineteenth-century industrialization, they were newly disturbing. Wilde was gay, but many other dandies were heterosexual men, the forefathers of today's "metrosexual." With their attention to style and their embrace of elegance, extravagance, and artificiality, they expressed values coded "feminine" in the nineteenth century. In rejecting a focused professional life for an aesthetic dilettantism, the dandy expressed values once labeled aristocratic—but in the muscular new world of capitalist commerce, such languour appeared unacceptably feminine. The foppish masculinity of the dandies and decadents and their refusal to be "men," as that term was commonly understood, were just as much a threat to the established order as the steely femininity of the New Woman. This challenge to conventional sex roles went deeper than mere fashion, as conservatives understood very well. Fin de siècle sexual anarchy was the first modern Western assault on patriarchy, and its scouts were New Women, dandies, and "an avant-garde of male artists, sexual radicals and intellectuals who challenged its class structures and roles, its system of inheritance and primogeniture, its compulsory heterosexuality and marriage and its cultural authority," says Showalter.

Hirschfeld himself seems to inhabit a kind of borderline between traditional and modern views of masculinity and femininity. Asserting that "absolute" men or women who adhered perfectly in all respects to the traditional attributes of their sex as commonly defined were only "abstractions, invented extremes," Hirschfeld nonetheless appears to have shared the traditional view that women were by nature less suited to intellectual work than men, for example. Although he formed political alliances with feminists, he was far from being a feminist himself, as we would define the term today. Masculinity and femininity appear in

Hirschfeld's theory of intermediaries as something akin to Platonic ideals, rather than social roles; the masculine and feminine ideals and their varying expression are, in his view, firmly anchored in biology. "In each person there is a different mixture of manly and womanly substances, and as we cannot find two leaves alike on a tree, then it is highly unlikely that we will find two humans whose manly and womanly characteristics exactly match in kind and number," Hirschfeld writes.

This organic theory of gender variance led naturally for Hirschfeld to an acceptance of human sexual diversity, including a new tolerance for homosexuality, which was viewed then (as it still is in some quarters today) as the most extreme example of sexual "inversion." "In a radical departure from earlier medical practices, Hirschfeld developed a psychotherapeutic procedure that emphasized the client's ability to accept his own homosexuality, rather than to change it," writes neuroscientist and author Simon LeVay, who analyzed Hirschfeld's research in his book *Queer Science*. Hirschfeld and his colleagues at the institute focused on helping their clients develop "strategies for surviving in a world that was still hostile to homosexuals," writes LeVay. Hirschfeld's approach to cross-dressers was equally progressive. He provided letters to the Berlin police, asking that his patients be allowed to dress in the clothes they felt most appropriate, for medical reasons. In many cases, the request was granted.

And in 1920, Hirschfeld began referring patients for sex-reassignment surgery. Though a few surgeons had already carried out some incomplete sex-reassignment surgeries in Berlin and in the United Kingdom—removing the sexual organs of their patients without attempting to create new genitalia—the first complete surgeries, encompassing not only the removal of the male sex organs but the creation of a vagina and labia, were carried out by Hirschfeld's colleagues at the institute, Ludwig Levy-Lenz and Felix Abraham. Abraham published an article reporting the surgeries (with before-and-after photographs) in the journal *Zeitschrift fur Sexualwissenschaft* in 1931. One of the first to undergo the surgery was a longtime housekeeper at the institute, Dorchen (formerly Rudolf) Richter.

Even people who thought themselves sophisticated and open-minded sometimes found Hirschfeld's approach to "sexual intermediaries" disturbingly liberal. Christopher Isherwood, for example, provides an amusing and instructive account of his first encounter with the patients and staff at the Institute for Sexual Science. The young writer, who saw himself as a gay sexual adventurer, liberated from middle-class standards and sensibilities, found himself definitively "out-queered" by the institute's staff and guests. "I remember the shock with which Christopher first realized that one of the apparently female guests was a man. He had pictured transvestites as loud, screaming, willfully unnatural creatures. This one seemed as quietly natural as an animal and his disguise was accepted by everyone else as a matter of course. Christopher had been telling himself that he had rejected respectability and that he now regarded it with amused contempt. But the Hirschfeld kind of respectability disturbed his latent puritanism."

Another visitor to the Institute for Sexual Science also was disturbed by the sexual intermediaries she found there, though grateful for the support and healing she found within its walls. In the fictionalized biography *Man into Woman*, the author, Niels Hoyer, describes the torment that drove his friend "Andreas" (in real life the Danish painter Einar Wegener) to seek out Hirschfeld in Berlin in the spring of 1930. Wegener had been cross-dressing for years, and Lili, the female self, was growing stronger and more insistent in her demands for fulfillment. "Andreas" had visited doctor after doctor, searching fruitlessly for medical assistance, until he met the Dresden gynecologist who sent him to Hirschfeld. "Some of the doctors to whom he went thought him neurotic, some thought him homosexual; but he himself denied the truth of both these diagnoses," writes the British sexologist Norman Haire in the introduction to *Man into Woman*. The Dresden gynecologist "Kreutz," on the other hand,

agreed that Andreas [Einar] was probably an intermediate sexual type, furnished, by some sport of nature, with both male and female gonads. He explained that there were probably rudimentary ovaries in Andreas' abdomen, but that these were unable to develop properly because of the inhibiting influence of the testicles which Andreas also possessed. He proposed that Andreas should go to Berlin, where certain investigations were to be undertaken. If these investigations confirmed his suppositions he promised to remove Andreas' male organs and transplant into him ovaries from a young woman, which would, as the work of the Steinach school had shown, activate the rudimentary ovaries lying dormant in Andreas' abdomen.

Wegener traveled to Berlin to be diagnosed definitively by Hirschfeld. His first visit to the clinic was not auspicious. " 'Why have I been sent here?' he wondered. 'What do I have to do here?' He felt intensely uncomfortable. In this large room a group of abnormal persons seemed to be holding a meeting—women who appeared to be dressed up as men, and men of whom one could scarcely believe that they were men. The manner in which they were conversing disgusted him; their movements, their voices, the way in which they were attired, produced a feeling of nausea."

Wegener's meeting with Hirschfeld (called "Hardenfeld" in the book) was even more disturbing. "By means of a thousand penetrating questions, this man explored the patient's emotional life for hours. He had to submit to an inquisition of the most ruthless kind. The shame of shamelessness is something that actually exists, he thought, during those hours, and clung to this definition, which he had once found in some philosophical work, in an effort to banish the feeling he had of standing there as if in the pillory. His emotional life was undergoing an ordeal which resembled running the gantlet. And when this torture came at last to an end, the inquisitor dismissed him with the words: 'I shall expect you tomorrow morning at the same time.'"

With his status as a sexual intermediary validated by Hirschfeld, Wegener was castrated, his testicles removed—probably by Hirschfeld's colleague Felix Abraham (called "Dr. Arns" in the book). "The first operation, which only represents a beginning, has been successful beyond all expectations. Andreas had ceased to exist, they said. His germ glands—oh, mystic words—have been removed. What has still to happen will take place in Dresden under the hands of Professor Kreutz. The doctors talked about hormones; I behaved as if I knew what they meant. Now I have looked up this word in the dictionary and find that it refers to the secretions of internal organs which are important for vital processes. But I am no wiser than I was before. Must one equip oneself then, with wisdom and knowledge in order to understand a miracle?"

The "miracle" of sex reassignment continued in Dresden a few months later, when "Kreutz" removed Wegener's penis, opened his abdomen, and found the rudimentary ovaries that provided physical confirmation of the patient's intermediary status. In keeping with Steinach's theories, the doctor then implanted healthy ovarian tissue from a young woman into Wegener, tissue that was rejected, requiring further surgery. Nonetheless, Lili Elbe had successfully ousted Einar Wegener, a coup for which she apparently felt both relief and guilt. "I feel like a bridge-builder. But it is a strange bridge that I am building," Wegener (now Lili Elbe) writes. "I stand on one of the banks, which is the present day. There I have driven in the first pile. And I must build it clear across the other bank, which often I cannot see at all and sometimes only vaguely, and now and then in a dream. And then I often do not know whether the other bank is the past or the future. Frequently the question plagues me: Have I had only a past, or have I had no past at all? Or have I only a future without a past?" These were questions that would echo in the lives of later generations of transsexual people who crossed the bridge that Lili helped construct.

According to Hoyer, when Wegener's surgeon in Dresden opened his patient's abdomen he discovered "withered" ovaries. Einar/Lili was, in medical terms, a true hermaphrodite, possessing both testicular and ovarian tissue; this explained Wegener's feminine mannerisms, slight build, and small breasts, and also the genital "underdevelopment" noted by Norman Haire in the introduction to *Man into Woman*. After recovering from surgery, Wegener was issued a new passport by Danish authorities, in the name of Lili Elbe. The king of Denmark declared the marriage between Wegener and his artist wife, Gerda, "null and void." (The faithful Gerda, who had supported Wegener throughout the transformation, married a mutual friend shortly thereafter.) Another friend, called "Claude" in the book, who had known the secret of Einar/Lili for many years, then proposed marriage to Lili. She accepted, under the condition that he wait until she underwent one final surgery, one that would make her fully a woman in her own eyes.

A "womanly woman," Elbe wanted to become both a wife and a

mother. "All that I desire is nothing less than the last fulfilment of a real woman; to be protected from life by the sterner being, the husband," she wrote to a friend in August 1931. "You must sympathize with me in my desire for maternity, to have a child, for I want nothing more ardently than to demonstrate that Andreas has been completely obliterated in me—is dead. Through a child I should be able to convince myself in the most unequivocal manner that I have been a woman from the very beginning. Whether this wish can be fulfilled or not, the fact that I can openly acknowledge this desire from the fullness of a pure woman's heart is an infinite happiness for me. The fact that I may experience this happiness justifies everything that has happened to me here in Dresden."

However, medical science then (as now) had no means of fulfilling Elbe's wish to be a mother, though her physician apparently tried to do what he could. Elbe underwent a final surgery, most likely a vaginoplasty (surgical creation of a vagina). She speaks of "effecting a natural outlet from the womb" in her letters. This final surgery was "an abyss of suffering," Elbe writes. She was confined to bed for months afterward, without the recovery that had accompanied her previous surgeries. By early September, she intuited that she was dying. In a letter to her sister, she wrote, "Now I know that death is near." Lili Elbe died in Dresden on September 12, 1931, of an apparent heart attack. "Paralysis of the heart put an end to her short young woman's life which was so excruciating and yet so wonderful," writes Hoyer. She was buried in a cemetery on the grounds of the hospital. A medical pioneer, whose transformation was covered in the Danish and German press in 1931, Lili Elbe was largely forgotten as war swept over the continent.

Magnus Hirschfeld suffered a similar fate. As a homosexual, a Jew, and a spokesman for progressive causes, he found his position becoming increasingly difficult in Germany as fascist ideology claimed more adherents. His lectures were disrupted by hecklers, and stink bombs were thrown at the audience by agitators during some of his talks. He was threatened with bodily harm if he continued to give public lectures, but he ignored the threats and continued to speak. As early as

1920, he was assaulted and injured so severely after leaving a lecture that his death was reported in a number of newspapers, both in Germany and abroad. After it was revealed that he was not dead, merely injured, an editorial writer at a Dresden newspaper wrote: "Weeds never die. The well-known Dr. Magnus Hirschfeld has been hurt enough to be put on the death list. We hear now that he is in fact recovering from his wounds. We have no hesitation in saying that we regret that this shameless and horrible poisoner of our people has not found his well-deserved end." On October 31, 1928, the official paper of the Nazi party featured a headline denouncing "Homosexuals as Speakers in Boys' Schools. Magnus Hirschfeld, the fighter for the abolition of Paragraph 175, is allowed to speak in German high schools. The Destruction of Youth! German Mothers, Women Workers! Do You Want to Hand Your Children Over to Homosexuals?" *Der Sturmer,* another anti-Semitic paper, called Hirschfeld "an apostle of lewdness." Hirschfeld prudently decamped from Germany late in 1930, mere months after meeting Einar Wegener, to embark on an around-the-world lecture tour.

On May 3, 1933, a few months after Hitler assumed power in Germany, the Institute for Sexual Science, in Berlin, was vandalized and looted by a mob of Nazi "students." Three days later, the institute's archives—thousands of books, photographs, questionnaires, and other memorabilia accumulated by Hirschfeld during thirty years of research—were publicly burned in Berlin's Opera Square. Photographs of the book burning show the mob marching to the square with a bust of Hirschfeld held high. The bust was rescued from the flames by a friend, who sent it to Hirschfeld, then living in Paris, where he witnessed the destruction of his institute on a newsreel in a movie theater. Friends had managed to salvage a few mementos from the wreckage, but the Institute for Sexual Science was essentially obliterated. Some have argued that the institute's files contained sensitive personal information about members of the Nazi leadership, and while that might well have been true, it is also indisputable that the liberal acceptance of homosexuality and gender variance was anathema to social conservatives. The Institute for Sexual Science was an icon of Weimar culture—

and a symbol of all that the National Socialists and their silent allies in the German population found weak and decadent in that culture.

The fight waged by Hirschfeld and his allies produced greater tolerance for homosexuality and gender variance during the period of liberalism in Germany between the wars, but it also nourished a violent countermovement that viewed the liberal approach as morally bankrupt. The Nazis, like most social conservatives, insisted on firm boundaries between the sexes and compulsory heterosexuality. Hirschfeld's theory of sexual intermediaries and his advocacy of gay and gender-variant individuals were perceived as an assault on the natural order and a violation (akin to rape) of German society. For that reason, all memory of his work was erased. Sexology as Hirschfeld conceived it—as a science that would liberate rather than imprison desire and identity—had been dealt a blow from which it would take decades to recover. Hirschfeld himself died in exile in France in 1935.

Psychological explanations for homosexuality and gender variance prevailed after the Second World War and the Nazi persecution of homosexuals, when Hirschfeld's view that homosexuality and gender variance were biologically based "became very suspect," neuroscientist Simon LeVay told me in a 2001 interview. "The German academic community became totally absorbed in socialization theory. They rejected all biological explanations for human diversity. And the idea came about that Hirschfeld was somehow responsible for the Nazi persecution of gay people, that by portraying gay people as a natural kind, as being born that way, he put them in the same category as racial groups and opened the door to the idea of exterminating them. I've even read stuff saying that he actually collaborated in efforts to have gay people arrested. I don't think that any of that is true. But somehow the most positive thing you can read about him in the postwar German literature is that, yeah, he was trying to do something for gay people, but he did it in a very misguided way. And that he was wrong."

Among scientists, Magnus Hirschfeld's belief that homosexuality, cross-dressing, and all other forms of gender variance were "widespread and important phenomena" and "natural" variations, not perversions or pathologies, was largely abandoned. The postwar era was notable not only for its fertility, but also for its rigid reinforcement of sex roles. The theory of sexual intermediaries didn't resonate in an era devoted to reinforcing the distinctions between the sexes. Masculinity and femininity were no longer viewed as liquid entities, capable of being combined in varying proportions; instead they were once again solid and opaque. The middle ground between the sexes became as impenetrable a border as the wire-topped wall dividing the formerly liminal city of Berlin.

CONVERSATION WITH SUSAN STRYKER, PH.D.

Susan Stryker earned her Ph.D. in history at the University of California, Berkeley, in 1992 and held a postdoctoral research fellowship at Stanford University from 1998 to 2000. She has been executive director of the GLBT Historical Society in San Francisco since 1999 and is currently working on a documentary film about the transgender riot in San Francisco's Tenderloin District in 1966, and on a memoir for Oxford University Press. In 1992, Stryker cofounded Transgender Nation, an activist group. We spoke at her office at the San Francisco GLBT Historical Society.

Q: Who was the first transsexual?

That depends on what you mean by "transsexual." In all cultures, throughout all periods of history, there have been people who fall outside of what we think of as normal, heterosexual masculine male manhood and feminine female womanhood. The binary is really a historical construct; physical bodies are much more diverse than that. Gender systems historically are much more complex than that. When we say, Who was the first transsexual? do we mean who was the first person to use hormones and genital surgery to effect a legal change in their social status? I don't know who that was, because the medical techniques came together over time. Legal discourses came together over time.

It's really hard to say who the first person would be. When you start looking at transsexual history, it's like somebody had a hysterectomy, but they did it because they didn't like having a uterus because they thought of themselves psychologically as a man. Is that the first transsexual surgery? There was this person in New York in the early twentieth century named Earl Lenz who thought of himself/herself as a feminine soul trapped in a masculine body, and this person had their testicles removed, supposedly because they were having horrible problems with nocturnal emissions. And the doctors were like, "Oh, nocturnal emissions, bad news. Let's remove those testicles." Was that person a transsexual? He surgically modified his body so that his body more closely reflected his psychological sense of self. Was he a transsexual? I don't know.

Certainly by the early 1920s in Germany, at the Hirschfeld institute there were people that we could call at least proto-transsexuals. They were people who did what modern-day transsexuals do, which is to say, "If I do this thing to my body, if I change my genitals this way so that they more resemble the genitals of people who have a different social status than me, and if I take these hormones and redistribute my body fat and body hair, and present evidence of these medical procedures to civil authorities of some kind, then I can change my social designation as being a man or a woman, and I can then live in accordance with general social expectations of what a man or a woman is supposed to be." That was in place by the twenties or early thirties. The first well-documented case was in 1930 at the Hirschfeld institute. Felix Abraham, a young doctor at the Hirschfeld institute, published a paper on two transvestites who underwent genital surgery. That paper was written up in 1930 or '31. In the case of Lili Elbe, the book about her surgery was published in '33, though the events happened a couple of years earlier.

Q: It seems significant that these people transitioned in Germany. The research and treatment at the Hirschfeld Institute were so significant, both scientifically and socially, and yet most people, even many transgendered people, have never heard of him or the institute. Why not?

I think there are two reasons we haven't given Hirschfeld his due. One is that so much of his work was destroyed by the Nazis, and, secondly, he was also sort of a promiscuous publisher. He didn't care much about publishing in the most reputable journals. Then, too, some of his ideas about the endocrinological or somatic roots of sexual and gender diversity have really fallen out of favor—I think rightly so. However, even though he came out of a different conceptual or intellectual framework than is currently fashionable, or accurate—I mean I think he was wrong about a lot of things—I think his political approach to the topic was good. He did try to root cultural differences about sexuality and gender in the body and he did that as a way of attempting to naturalize these differences and say, "People can't help it. There are many different kinds of people, there aren't just two." He recognized that there are a whole lot of sexual intermediaries, and that more or less everybody is a sexual intermediary.

Hirschfeld taught that these are natural variations and that law and social customs should be brought into accord in a rational way with this naturally existing diversity of human kinds. I think that his motivations were really noble, and he did tremendous political work on gay rights, transvestite rights, abortion rights. He was a very conscientious, well-meaning, thoughtful man. And he was a modernist, a sexual modernist, who was bringing up these taboo topics, and who recognized that these things that were supposed to be so illicit are just a part of human life. His view was that we shouldn't act in an irrational, prejudicial, superstitious manner. "We're all men of science here."

Q: His unwillingness to pathologize sexual intermediaries was at odds with most of the other sexologists of the time, wasn't it?

In a sense I think that he did pathologize, in that he thought that gender and sexuality were appropriate targets for medical intervention. But do you want to call that pathological? What many transsexuals are looking for is a nonpathologized way to say, "I want to interact with medical service providers." So that treatment is offered much more on a service provider basis, which is of course part of a much broader shift in medicine.

Q: The history of interactions between transgendered people and the medical community is a very complex one, isn't it? In one sense, it was very consumer-driven, with transsexuals seeking out physicians and requesting that they provide certain services like hormone treatments and surgery. It seems that early on, the relationship was much friendlier between clients and service provider than it is today, though. Why do you think that is the case?

I think that there has always been a tension between people seeking services and people providing services. And as much as I firmly believe that people have autonomy over their own bodies and can choose best for themselves—that people have the capacity to give informed consent—I understand that service providers have concerns. If I as a surgeon am going to do something to a person's body, I need to be convinced that I'm doing the right thing, because of the Hippocratic oath, and its major principle, do no harm. I respect that and I understand that there's a need sometimes for transgendered people seeking medical services, to educate the service providers about why, even though this is something that you might not choose for yourself, this is the best thing for me.

However, you can't just talk about clients and service providers. You have to talk about the role of media as well, in publicizing the fact that certain options are available. At least in modern Western European culture, there are many people who feel like "my body isn't shaped right" and it's not an aesthetic question, really, so much as a question about how we internalize ideas about gender, historically and culturally. To develop a gender identity and feel like my body does not communicate my sense of self to my audience—and then to know that there are techniques for body manipulation that are available because I've read about them.

Even before Jorgensen, people who were looking for help would turn to science and medicine and say, "Look, I know you can do this, I'm reading about Eugen Steinach in Vienna, and he's doing these gonad transplant things and these hormone injection things; sign me up." And then they were perceived as crazy because they wanted to do that. So there's been an awareness on the part of people seeking services that some techniques were available, and they could see an application of that technique to their situation, and then they would have to persuade a service provider that it was a legitimate thing to do.

So there was always that tension, and there have been some service providers like Hirschfeld and Harry Benjamin who have been like, "Oh, okay, there's no reason we shouldn't do that." They get it, at some level, for whatever reason. And then there were many other people who were like, "No, get out of here."

Even with Jorgensen—though she certainly spoke well of her surgeons—there was more tension behind the scenes. She didn't know of any other way to get what she wanted. There really wasn't any other way at that point. So she volunteered to be an experiment. And her endocrinologist decided, "Yes, this is a rare thing, and this person is more female than male. This is the most advanced case of intersex we have ever seen—the most truly feminine balanced with the most obvious male." They wrote among themselves, evaluating. "Is this an effeminate homosexual? Is this a transvestite?" They knew those categories, but the prevailing belief at the time was there could be glandular imbalances, that she might have some female germ cells, and so the surgery was justified. It wasn't really that long ago either: this was in the fifties, in the lifetime of people who are alive and well and running marathons today. And when you look back and read the medical discourses around it, the belief in what endocrinology meant and how the gender system worked, it's so clear how ideologically constructed the relationship between gender and the body is.

That's not to say that there aren't real physical differences between bodies, but we have this cultural belief about the relationship between someone's sense of self and how they interact with other human subjects, and how that relates to their physical embodiment, and we materialize gender through the body in accordance with certain cultural assumptions. That's part of the radicalness about transgender politics in the later part of the twentieth century—that it just flies in the face of that construction. Part of why we (as transpeople) are so marginalized is that we offer this very radical critique of a very pervasive set of assumptions about gender.

Q: But isn't that critique somewhat paradoxical in that transsexuals do essentialize gender by saying that I need a certain kind of body in order to fully express my gender?

Admittedly my position is a minority position, but I see that whole "transsexuals are essentializing gender because they are so concerned with the body" as an artifact of Cartesian dualism, the mind/body split. You don't ever not have a body; your body is that through which you interact with other people. There is a language of the body. There is an appearance of the body. We're never disembodied people. My own sense of what I did is that I had this sense of self, whatever story you want tell about how that came about. There was that sense for me that it was more appropriate for me to answer to the pronoun "she" than "he"—it goes way back—and there was a perception growing up that "I'm in a situation that I can't control, and that I can't get out of," and there was affect around that. I was really sad about it. I would try to put it aside and go about my business in life, but it proved to be really intractable and unshakable, and when at some point I figured, "Oh, I can do these things," it was like a paradigm shift in my own head.

It's not that these procedures make me a different person. It's more like "if you cut on the dotted line, and I sign this piece of paper, I can legally be a different person. I can pay you these monies, and you'll stick a little electrified needle in my face, and I won't have hair there anymore. I'll take this pill and it will make my breasts grow." It's that recognition that the body is malleable, and that it is how we present to people. There's something very fundamental about being two bodies in communication with each other. Just the thought that I could use my body to communicate my sense of self to other people the way that everybody else does, instead of having to verbalize it or feel invisible. The idea that I could go to a beach, like I did yesterday, and lie around in the sun and drink beer and watch my kids play, and people would say "she" . . . Cool.

Q: What is gender? It seems clear that it is somehow neurobiological in origin.

I think our language is not really sufficient for talking about it. The words are too blunt. Gender means "kind" or "genre," it means "what kind of person are you?" But you can't divorce the question of gender from the larger question of how the human organism needs to live in culture. Humans are social animals. You can't take a baby human and throw it out in the wild and expect it to learn how to forage. We have to be in society. Unlike a kitten, human babies don't lick the gunk off and stand up on all twos and run about. They are born very young in a developmental sense. As soon as the lungs can work, the baby comes out. So the evolutionary pressure is for situations that provide care of the newborn. That, I really think, is the basis of culture, what we really physiologically need to reproduce the species—this familial economic social structure—and that has evolved with the human form, and the capacity for language has come along with that. We are creatures who live in language and we're creatures who have exploited the cultural sphere.

The exploitation of the cultural sphere, and the symbolic manipulation of the world, is the ecological niche that humans have developed; just like beavers cut down the trees to make their environment, we turn the world into language. That's what humans do, and I really think that gender is about how the cultural system interfaces with the organism. Part of how you are as a being, part of what we are evolved to be, part of our neurobiological capacity that evolved words is that capacity to self-reflexively place oneself in a cultural context.

For me, gender is both the cultural system through which you internalize as a subjective being, as an identification, how you situate yourself in language; and how other people situate you in language. And it's done through these very complex mechanisms that no one discipline in the sciences or the humanities is able to fully address. There needs to be an interdisciplinary gender studies. Because, so far, all of the theory and the research has come from a body of knowledge that has never had to be critical of its own foundational assumptions. And so it just becomes another vector for naturalizing particular kinds of ideological agendas. So I think that critically conscious transsexual or transgendered people, who can reveal the ideological constructions of the sex/gender systems, have this tremendous work in front of us. Unfortunately, it's really hard to get funding to do that work.

You know, in the orisha religion, there is a being whose name means "the destroyer of patterns through whom the shape of the cosmos is revealed." There is that sense of disruption that the trans figure brings, that rupture through the social construction of gender, and the revelation of the new, the different, the other. I once wrote a piece called "My Words to Victor Frankenstein above the Village of Chamonix." It's about speaking as a monster, and that sense of disruption that we transsexual people stage for other people. It's about trying to speak from this embodied place, that is technologically constructed—but is it human or is it not? There are many things about me that are very different from you. And I need to be able to speak the truth of my own process of embodiment.

Q: I am sure that there are many transgendered or transsexual people who would be very insulted to be viewed as monsters.

[*Laughing*] Yes, when I wrote it, people said, "That's not an effective tool for organizing." But I don't fear my monstrosity. The word "monster" comes from the Latin "monstrere" (just like the words "remonstrance," "demonstrate") and the noun means "to show something," and usually it was to show something about the supernatural. Angels and monsters are actually very closely linked, in that both show the providence of God and something about the nature of being. The word "monster" also has the subsidiary meaning of "assembled from incongruous parts." The classical monsters were the sphinx, the gryphon—the idea being these things combine elements that are not supposed to be together, but that their being together, being alive, demonstrates something supernatural, superhuman, and makes them beings that the gods speak through.

Q: What do you think about the assimilationist versus outsider argument that is so heated in the trans community today? Should transsexuals try to pass or should they stand out? Should they value and project their differences or should they strive to be just another person on the block?

I think of myself as a queer. Non-separatist, but anti-assimilationist. Saying that "I'm just like you" doesn't really get me where I want to go. In many ways, I am "just like you" but those aren't the parts that give me trouble. And so that insistence on my ability to be fully myself and not suffer violence or oppression because of that is what's important. You always fight your battles and draw your lines differently. When I first started transitioning, I didn't want to go to the corner store and say [*speaks heatedly and aggrievedly*], "All right, I'm here to buy a gallon of milk, and I can see that you perceive that I am a transgendered person, and it is my duty to educate you." I was just "keep your head down, buy the damn milk, go home, maybe they hate you, maybe they don't, but whatever." But I find a greater sense of comfort in being really open with people. I want people to see me as a woman. I want my deepest and most closely held sense of self to be visible and able to interact with other people. I don't feel like I have to hide my differences. Difference can be a real source of pleasure.

Q: In the past, transsexual people were advised to make a complete break with their pasts and to basically keep their gender transition a secret, even with intimate partners. Even today, it seems, many people feel safer revealing their status as a transsexual person to very few people. It seems as though that kind of invisibility would create tremendous psychic strain.

I've met people like that, certainly. I can't imagine it. I didn't want to do that at all. I just thought that felt very inauthentic. However, I understand that they do it because of other people's feeling about transsexuality. I don't know how many times in my own life people have met me on the street, or at a presentation, and it's "she, she, she" until I say, "I'm a transsexual," and suddenly it's "he, he, he, he." I'm like, "I'm sorry, you were having no problem with me fifteen minutes ago. What are you confused about? What changed, except your knowledge of my transsexual past?" It's that belief about gender and the body. Is change in the body shape a change in the essence of the soul? People trip up about that. And so I understand [the desire to keep quiet]. There's that paradox of visibility. I'm doing all of this so that people understand me the way that I understand myself. But if they know that I've done this, then they don't accept me as I understand myself. They see me as something different, and then all my hard work has been for naught. However, if I don't tell them, they will accuse me of being duplicitous. It's a catch-22.

For me, I think of how open I am about being transgendered or how I present at different times—it's kind of like the difference between using language for poetry and using language to communicate. If what you really want to do is communicate with someone "I need x, y or z," and you are using the language of gender for its communicative potential, and often that's what we want to do with gender, is communicate a sense of self with an other. But within certain contexts, within more closely held communities and other contexts, other kinds of communication for different uses are possible. Are you doing your gender like a funky bass riff, are you riffing on some gender improv? Are you using the way that you are doing your gender to test the boundaries of language? You can do gender more like an art practice or like a political practice. And at times those can be very effective things to do. They can be really fun.

Three

THE BOMBSHELL

I looked into a sea of faces, lined up along the ropes of the "quarantine walk" and held back by a sea of determined police, then heard a roar of voices shouting my name. I reeled under the impact. I thought for a moment that I had entered Dante's inferno, as flashbulbs exploded from all directions and newsreel cameras whirred. A crowd of three hundred shoving reporters, newsreel and still photographers had converged, all jockeying for position and camera angles. I learned later it was the largest assemblage of press representatives in the history of the airport.

CHRISTINE JORGENSEN, NEW YORK CITY, 1953

Christine Jorgensen was the first star of the dawning age of celebrity, the first American to become internationally known simply for being herself. Her fame was based not on her profession, her talents, her lineage, her looks, or her wit. None of these was particularly remarkable. Christine Jorgensen was famous simply for being Christine Jorgensen. She was a "reality" star decades before the concept was invented. A few other brave souls had undergone the same transformation before her, but Christine was the butterfly captured in the glare of klieg lights as she exited her cocoon. She was no more and no less than the man who had become a woman, and a pretty good-looking woman at that. "Ex-GI becomes Blonde Bombshell," the headlines screamed as the young American who traveled to Denmark in 1950 to seek help for a baffling medical problem returned home. She soon found that the world press treated her recovery from surgery both as a matter of profound international importance and as a sexual scandal.

Jorgensen was born on Memorial Day, May 30, 1926, the child of two first-generation Danish Americans, George and Florence Jorgensen. She was the second child born to the couple, and her parents named her George, Jr., after her father. Her sister, Dorothy (called Dolly), was three years older. Jorgensen's autobiography, published in 1967 and reissued in 2000, describes her childhood as a happy one. "Dolly and I were surrounded by a closely knit, affectionate family of the sort that gives a child a warm feeling of belonging. Happily we had the advantage of being in a family that enjoyed activities as a unit, and that still applies today," she writes. In her youth, Jorgensen was called "Brud," short for "brother." Brud was especially close to her grandma Jorgensen, "a person of grace and dignity," Jorgensen recalled years later. "Grandma was always my champion when others laughed at my 'sissified' ways."

From an early age, Brud was aware of the differences between him and the other boys in the neighborhood. "A little boy wore trousers and had his hair cut short. He had to learn to use his fists aggressively, participate in athletics, and most important of all, little boys didn't cry. Contrary to those accepted patterns, sometimes I did feel like crying and I must have felt that Grandma understood and didn't disapprove when I ran away from a fistfight or refused to play rough and tumble games." In her autobiography, Jorgensen describes George's crushing disappointment when instead of the "pretty doll with long golden hair" that he already knew enough not to request for a Christmas present at age five, he was given a "bright red railway train." She also describes a conversation that George had with his mother around the same time, asking why his sister, Dolly, was allowed to grow her blond hair long and wear dresses, things he envied and admired but was not permitted to have. "'Mom,' I asked, 'why didn't God make us alike?'" His mother explained that the world needed both men and women, and that there was no way of knowing before a baby was born whether it was a boy or a girl. "'You see, Brud,' she said. 'It's one of God's surprises.'"

"'Well,' I replied. 'I don't like the kind of surprise God made me!'"

Like many boys who fail to conform to society's views of masculine behavior, Brud was often ridiculed for his differences by both children and adults. In mid-century America, those differences were particularly jarring. The "sexual anarchy" of the fin de siècle had long since given way to a rigid sexual binary. Male and female were once more separate and distinct categories, with no discernable overlap. Home and family, not the office and factory, were defined as women's proper sphere, as Rosie the Riveter put on her apron and turned domestic goddess. Men were expected to be workers, husbands, and fathers. "After World War Two, there was the creation of this really rigid gender system in the West," historian Susan Stryker said in our 2001 conversation. "Like, the world is cut in two and you are on this side or this side. There are no anomalies. That construction of gender/sex/sexuality is I think as much an artifact of the Cold War as the Berlin Wall." Like the millions soon to be trapped behind the iron curtain of communism in the East, those who felt oppressed by the new gender regime in the West learned the virtues of silence, subterfuge, and secrecy. These were the skills they needed to survive. Not only gay and gender-variant people, but also those women growing more capable, independent, and self-reliant in the war years went underground rather than face the price of being "different" in an era that rigidly enforced sex-role conformity.

Jorgensen describes one particularly painful incident in the autobiography—the time a teacher called Mrs. Jorgensen to school after she had discovered a piece of needlepoint in Brud's desk. In front of Mrs. Jorgensen and the other students, the teacher asked Brud if it was his, and when he replied yes, she responded, "Mrs. Jorgensen, do you think that this is anything for a red-blooded boy to have in his desk as a keepsake? The next thing we know, George will be bringing his knitting to school." Both George and his mother were humiliated by this incident, though to Mrs. Jorgensen's credit, she didn't utter a word of reproach to her unhappy son.

Incidents like these increased Brud's feelings of loneliness and isolation, which became even more acute in adolescence. "Instead of assimilating into a group as most teenagers did, I felt like an outsider. I didn't like sports and I wasn't interested in dating girls, which had become the chief topic of conversation among the boys of my acquaintance," Jorgensen writes. "I tried to find some solace in books, and they became my closest companions." Jorgensen also developed an interest in photography and began to dream of a "time when I would have an important place behind the cameras of Hollywood, the gilded Wonderland of make-believe."

This new hobby led to a job as a stock librarian with the Pathé News Service in New York City, after George's high school graduation. "I wondered if my new associates would notice what I had long since known: that I was one who deviated, emotionally, from what had been termed 'normal,'" Jorgensen writes. "But I was determined to behave like a man, even if I didn't feel like one, and try to hide the pretense behind a brave exterior." It became even easier to "act like a man" the next year, when the nineteen-year-old George Jorgensen was drafted. Though he had already been rejected by the army twice during the war, owing to his thin build, this time he was accepted. "I wanted to be accepted by the army for two reasons. Foremost, was my great desire to belong, to be needed, and to join the stream of activities around me," Jorgensen writes. "Second, I wanted my parents to be proud of me and to be able to say, 'My son is in the service.' Although they never mentioned it, I was poignantly aware that Mom and Dad must have felt their child was 'different,' and hence unwanted."

Despite the triumph of passing the army physical, living with hundreds of other young men in close quarters during and after basic training provided yet more proof of George's "difference." As a clerical worker living in barracks and helping to manage the discharge of thousands of soldiers after VE day, George

couldn't help comparing myself with the boys in my group and I was aware that the differences were very great indeed, both mental and physical. My body was not only slight but it lacked other development as a male. I had no hair on my chest, arms or legs. My walk could scarcely be called a masculine stride, the gestures of my hands were quite effeminate and my voice had a feminine quality. The sex organs that determined my classification as male were underdeveloped. It was, of course, quite possible that some men having the same build would feel completely masculine, but my mental and emotional chemistry matched all the physical characteristics which in me seemed so feminine. "What is masculine and what is feminine?" I thought. The questions plagued me because I couldn't find a clearly established dividing line.

If George Jorgensen, Jr., wasn't able to find a dividing line between masculine and feminine, he was quite clear about another line, one that he was determined never to cross. "During the months in the service, I had seen a few practicing homosexuals, those whom the other men called 'queer.' I couldn't condemn them, but I also knew that I certainly couldn't become like them. It was a thing deeply alien to my religious attitudes and the highly magnified and moralistic views that I entertained at the time. Furthermore, I had seen enough to know that homosexuality brought with it a social segregation and ostracism that I couldn't add to my own deep-seated feeling of not belonging." This was true despite the strong emotions that were aroused in the young soldier by a childhood friend, Tom Chaney; and by Jim Frankfort, another man he met while attending the Progressive School of Photography in New Haven, Connecticut, after his discharge in 1948. Jorgensen describes the strong attraction that drew George to these two unambiguously heterosexual men, and his equally strong feelings of confusion and terror of the implications of that attraction. "I awaited a miracle to release me from the growing horror of myself."

In July of 2001, I posted a message on an Internet genealogy list, seeking family members of Jorgensen to confirm the information in the autobiography. I didn't hear from any Jorgensens but I was contacted by a few people who had known or encountered George or Christine Jorgensen at some point. One of the most poignant notes I received was from a woman named Peggy Stockton McClelland, whose parents, she said, had shared a house with Jorgensen in Connecticut.

Christine Jorgensen lived with my mother and father in Milford, Conn. My father, Richard Stockton, was attending Yale Photography School at the time and they shared the rent. Christine was known as George at that time. My mother loved him, as a friend, and he confided in her many feelings at that time in his life. My mother said he would babysit me for them and was the closest friend she had at that time. He loved to do more female type things, loved to be in the kitchen and take care of me. They lived in a beautiful stone home on the water in Woodmont, Conn., which is still there. Perhaps Christine was also attending school with my father? I never knew. I really do not know how my parents knew George, but eventually my parents returned to Muncie, Indiana, and they lost contact. My mother said they knew he was different, and she was not surprised by his decision.

While living with the Stocktons and other friends in the suburbs of New Haven, George Jorgensen continued to puzzle over his "difference" and to seek possible solutions. "The recurring questions of what to do about my effeminate appearance continued to plague me. Even if it were possible to adjust my mind and attitudes to a more male outlook, I wondered what could be done about a 'masculine' mind in a feminine body." In December 1948, while still living in New Haven, Jorgensen encountered a book that was to provide him with the answers he sought. The book, Paul de Kruif's *The Male Hormone,* a popular account of the science of endocrinology, was the catalyst that was to begin the process that transformed the anonymous George into the world-renowned Christine. "'Manhood is chemical, manhood is testosterone. Over and beyond testosterone, manhood seems to be partly a state of mind' . . . As I read on, my mind raced with this new knowledge, for throughout the narrative, there was woven a tiny thread of recognition pulled from my own private theories."

Reading Paul de Kruif's ode to the power of the male hormone, testosterone, today it is easy to understand the comfort that the tormented George Jorgensen, Jr., found within its pages—but more difficult to trace the intuitive leap that enabled him to conceive a novel solution to his problem. The book describes the "rescue of broken men," genital males who, like Jorgensen, seemed to lack key physical and psychological attributes of masculinity, or older men experiencing "the slow chemical castration" of aging. Early in the book, de Kruif describes a twenty-seven-year-old medical student, physically underdeveloped when he was first examined by physicians at Albany Medical College in 1937. "His hips were wide like a woman's; he had protruding breasts like a girl's; he had almost no Adam's apple; and his voice was high-pitched like a woman's. He had only a hint of hair under his arms and none on his chest or belly, and pitifully to kid himself that he was a man, he shaved about once in ten weeks," de Kruif writes. "There were large circles under his eyes, and his private parts were somewhat smaller in size than those of a four-year old boy. His penis, which the doctors measured, was one inch long and less than half an inch in diameter." The young man had also suffered throughout his life from severe migraines and the kinds of hot flashes that trouble menopausal women. As a result of these difficulties, he was socially withdrawn and often depressed. Curiously, he was engaged to be married—though he admitted to his doctors that he was unable to maintain an erection and had very limited sexual feelings. In medical terms, the young man was suffering from "hypogonadism," or testosterone deficiency.

James B. Hamilton, an anatomy professor at the college, was able to persuade the pharmaceutical company Ciba to send him "for purely scientific purposes—a supply of testosterone that was still worth more than its weight in gold," writes de Kruif. "For the first time into any American man, as far as published records go, anatomist Hamilton and the doctors sent shots of testosterone into the flabby muscles of this twenty-seven-year-old boy's arm and into those of his buttocks three times a week." The results impressed the scientists. Previously, the young man had "experienced only the feeblest and most fleeting sexual sensations," but within sixty hours of the first injection, he began to have erections. After a mere six days of injections, his erections "became more frequent and stronger; the size of his penis at rest became greater; and before the month of testosterone injections was completed, this man, impotent for life, was able to carry on sexual intercourse."

But the effects of the hormone did not end there. The doctors witnessed what appeared to be a complete physical and psychological transformation. "The boy's thyroid gland began to grow; his larynx became congested, and the doctors thought they could detect a lower pitch to his voice. The hot flashes that had bothered him for years disappeared completely. During that month he had only one attack of the migraine headache that had tortured him so long and so often. A curious new sap of self-confidence flowed through him, and energy, and he looked people in the face and was happy. Hair began to grow on his upper lip and his chest; and when he looked toward tomorrow, he no longer despaired."

Concerned that these effects might be caused by autosuggestion, the doctors replaced the testosterone in the syringe with inert oil, without telling their patient. "In five days he had four hot flashes and then an attack of migraine. The erections of his penis, signals of his new miraculous manhood, began to weaken. . . . With his new manhood ebbing, at the same time away went his new pride and confidence, and now he was tired all the time again, after doing nothing." When the doctors resumed the shots of testosterone (again, without informing the patient) "within a few days there was a startling upsurge in his total vitality and his march toward belated manhood."

The case of this young man—the first American to be treated with the newly synthesized hormone testosterone—proved what experiments with castrated rats, guinea pigs, and other animals had suggested decades earlier. Manhood was hormonal. Young men who had never been men could be virilized, and old men whose manhood was waning could be "rejuvenated" or restored to their previous virility, through injections of the male hormone. Paul de Kruif, the science writer whose book introduced this novel concept to George Jorgensen and thousands of other Americans, had begun to look into the testosterone cure as he felt his own "manhood" begin to slip away in his fifties. Not only were his sexual powers beginning to wane, but he felt his overall strength and enthusiasm for life and work—his vitality—begin to diminish. He looked to science for an explanation, and discovered the work of the "hormone hunters," as he termed the early endocrinologists whose experiments with animals and human beings had pointed to a link between virility and vitality.

Enthusiastically, de Kruif shared with his readers his quest for rejuvenation and the history of the science that had made rejuvenation possible. He narrated the tale of Arnold Adolf Berthold, professor of physiology at the University of Gottingen, who in 1849 removed the testicles from four roosters and watched two of them become "fat pacifists" while two others, in whom he had grafted new testicles, looked and acted like roosters once again. "They crowed. They battled. They chased hens enthusiastically. Their bright red combs and wattles kept growing." He soberly recounted the cautionary tale of Charles Edouard Brown-Sequard, the founder of the science of endocrinology, who at seventy-two made himself an object of public ridicule by injecting himself with a solution made from the testicles of dogs and guinea pigs and announcing that this "testicle soup" had restored his youthful sexual vigor, mental acuity, and intestinal functioning. The sensation created by Brown-Sequard's discovery quickly degenerated into ridicule as the elderly Frenchman's "rejuvenation" failed within a month.

However, other scientists investigating the structure and function of the "ductless glands" of the endocrine system established scientifically a fact that farmers had known for centuries: the sex of an animal was entirely dependent on the presence and proper functioning of its gonads—testicles in the male and ovaries in the female—and its overall strength and vigor seemed mysteriously bound up with the health of those organs. Moreover, animals could be "masculinized" or "feminized" by gonadal manipulation. No matter their sex at birth, animals surgically deprived of their gonads and later implanted with either testicles or ovaries exhibited the behaviors characteristic of animals born with those organs.

The Viennese endocrinologist Eugen Steinach had shown that young rats and guinea pigs castrated at around four weeks old remained sexually immature, but that as soon as a replacement set of gonads was implanted in their abdomens, "symptoms of underdevelopment or even retrogression passed away both in the male and in the female, even if they had been absent for some time." Steinach also found that the sex expressed by the surgically altered animals was entirely dependent on the type of gonad he implanted in their abdomens: "the female implanted with the male gland will always be a male with all of his characteristics; and the male implanted with a female generative gland will develop into a full-fledged female. By implanting a male and a female generative gland simultaneously . . . Steinach produced hybrids (hermaphrodites)."

Steinach's research had been followed closely by Magnus Hirsch-feld and his colleagues at the Institute for Sexual Science, in Berlin, as mentioned in the previous chapter. But it was Steinach's American disciple Harry Benjamin who was to build a clinical practice based on the professor's theories and to serve as the most fervent advocate of hormonal treatment for aging men and, later, transsexuals in the United States. By the time the future Christine Jorgensen read Paul de Kruif's popular account of the power of hormones on gender and sexual behavior in 1948, Benjamin had been working to promote Steinach's research in America for nearly twenty years. Steinach and, to a lesser extent, Magnus Hirschfeld were Benjamin's mentors, and through him a European-style sexology was imported to America.

Born in Berlin in 1885, Harry Benjamin left Germany in 1913, the year after receiving his medical degree, to carry out research on tuber-culosis in the United States. His return to Germany was prevented by the outbreak of World War I, and for a time he was interned as an enemy alien. "He came to America quite by happenstance, when a German doctor brought him to America to do TB research because he spoke a little English," Benjamin's friend and colleague Christine Wheeler told me in a 2002 interview. "He was on his way back to Ger-many when a British vessel seized the freighter and diverted it to Lon-don. He had very little money left, and he was essentially a POW because the war had broken out. But he was able to buy a one-way ticket back to the United States, and he hocked his watch to get back to New York because he had friends there."

Benjamin was released on the condition that he stay in the United States, and he began a medical practice in New York. "He started a small practice when he came to New York, living in the same room where he saw patients," says Wheeler, who recalls Benjamin saying that "he paid six dollars a week for the room." After the war, begin-ning in 1921, he returned to Germany each year to pursue his research interests and to renew his contacts with old friends and colleagues, including Magnus Hirschfeld (whom he had met in 1907). Because his major interest at the time was geriatrics, Benjamin was eager to meet Steinach, and the two men were introduced in 1921 in Vienna. "I was greatly impressed with his sex changes operations in rats and guinea

pigs by means of castration and transplantation of endocrine glands,"
Benjamin said in an interview a few years before his death in 1986.
"From then on, I visited him as his disciple almost regularly every summer well into the thirties. Thus, I became, as it were, a transatlantic
commuter, who tried to mediate between America and Europe."

Benjamin was quick to acknowledge his indebtedness to both
Hirschfeld and Steinach in later years. "Every year during the 1920s, I
went to Berlin and spent many hours at Hirschfeld's lectures at his institute, and more than once did I take part in the guided tours through
the institute and its unique museums," he said in an address given at
the Twelfth Annual Conference of the Society for the Scientific Study
of Sex, in November 1969. But significant as Hirschfeld and his institute were for Benjamin's development as a humanitarian and sexologist, it was Steinach who claimed his allegiance as mentor. "Benjamin
felt that Steinach was a genius," says Christine Wheeler, and the two
men carried on a forty-four-year correspondence, which is archived at
the New York Academy of Medicine. Steinach could be difficult to
deal with—Wheeler calls him "irascible"—but Benjamin remained
loyal to his mentor. Harry Benjamin "was a humanitarian, fiercely
loyal, very elegant, very old world," says Christine Wheeler. "They
used to call it breeding. So he protected Steinach."

Benjamin soon became the leading proponent of the "Steinach operation" in America. Steinach's researches with animals had convinced
him that vasoligation, or the severing of the vas deferens (spermatic
duct) in men—an operation that is today called vasectomy—resulted
in an almost miraculous "rejuvenation" of aging mammals. Steinach's
senile animal subjects grew glossy new coats of hair, gained weight
and muscle, and regained the strength and endurance characteristic of
much younger animals. Encouraged by these findings, other physicians began to perform vasoligation in humans, and the surgery was
soon being touted as a treatment not only for the lassitude of old age,
but also for age-related diseases such as cancer and atherosclerosis. It
appeared that the gonads were the seat not only of sexual identity and
virility, but also of overall health and vigor. "They were trying to find
sex hormones," says Christine Wheeler, "but they were also looking
for the fountain of youth."

Many men of the era, celebrated and unknown, underwent the Steinach operation, hoping to stave off the physical and psychological effects of old age. Indeed, when Harry Benjamin met Sigmund Freud (through a referral from Steinach), Freud admitted that he, too, had undergone the Steinach operation, and felt that "his general health and vitality had improved," and that "the malignant growth of his jaw had been favorably influenced. 'Don't talk about it as long as I am alive,' he said to me on parting. I told him I would not and I kept my promise," Benjamin said in 1969. Freud's unwillingness to publicize his surgery points to its somewhat unsavory reputation even in the days of his greatest success. Nonetheless, throughout the first decades of the twentieth century, Steinach's disciples and colleagues performed the procedure on their aging male patients and gathered data that appeared to confirm its efficacy.

Harry Benjamin, whose New York medical practice focused mainly on geriatrics, was the most enthusiastic proponent of the method in the United States. He contributed the introduction and a number of case studies to Paul Kammerer's 1923 study, *Rejuvenation and the Prolongation of Human Efficiency,* and arranged for a showing of the "Steinach Film," a silent documentary on Steinach's hormonal research, at the New York Academy of Medicine in 1923. "Broadly speaking, the Steinach Operation strengthens the endocrine system," Benjamin writes in the introduction to Kammerer's book. "On account of the inter-relationship of the different glands with an internal secretion and the influence these glands have over the nervous system, the strengthening of the glandular system will result in a re-energizing of the physical and mental capacities. Naturally such a strengthening should be resorted to if a glandular weakness or inferiority exists."

Benjamin's interest in the rejuvenation of aging patients was closely connected to interest in sexology, as both disciplines were at that time based in endocrinology. Soon after he started his gerontology practice, Benjamin began meeting with "a handful of physicians in New York, all of whom were deeply interested in aging," says Benjamin's colleague, Christine Wheeler. "They called themselves the Wednesday Night Group," and they discussed what was going on in the world of sexology. They called this interest "sex physiology." This study group, which began meeting in 1916, "explored the possible function and meaning of the ductless [glands], or endocrine glands, a full ten years before the *Journal of the American Medical Association* published its first article on the use of thyroid hormone," Benjamin's colleague Charles Ihlenfeld pointed out at a symposium on gender identity in 1975. A decade later, Benjamin, who worked as a consulting endocrinologist at the City College of New York in the thirties, "helped arrange financial support for Funk and Harrow who succeeded in the first isolation from human urine of a biologically active androgen," Ihlenfeld said.

According to Benjamin's protégée, Leah Cahan Schaefer, "Harry believed that the urine of young men might contain testosterone and he persuaded a professor friend at City College to collect the urine of his students. Subsequently, Casimir Funk developed the first sex hormones from the urine of young men. With the androsterone that Funk collected and produced, Harry Benjamin, once again at the forefront of scientific investigation, gave himself the first hormone injection. Funk almost fainted, but the only reaction on Harry was a terribly sore and bruised area where the injection had been made, due to the impurity of the new substance."

Like his mentors Hirschfeld and Steinach, Benjamin believed "that you couldn't separate the body from the mind," says Christine Wheeler. "He believed in the effects of hormones on behavior and motivation."

The effects of hormones were also very much on the mind of another New Yorker at that time. In 1948—the year that Harry Benjamin met his first transsexual patient—George Jorgensen, Jr., enrolled at the Manhattan Medical and Dental Assistants School, in New York City. Frustrated by his inability to understand the French and German medical treatises on "hermaphrodism" and "pseudo-hermaphrodism" he found in the library at the New York Academy of Medicine, Jorgensen stubbornly sought another route to self-understanding. "Still determined to find some cure or satisfactory compromise for what I considered an emotional and sexual disorder, I enrolled at the Manhattan Medical and Dental Assistants School," Christine Jorgensen wrote in 1967. At the school, Jorgensen learned to perform chemical analyses of blood and urine, and studied the principles of basal metabolism.

"However, it was the rare glandular disturbances which intrigued me more. Abnormal growth due to pituitary malfunction, steroids, enzymes, and sex hormones were all new areas of knowledge, but ones which I felt had some bearing on my own problem. Avidly, I discussed glands and glandular disturbances with the doctors who were my instructors," Jorgensen writes. "These studies occupied my every waking moment, and probably many of my sleeping ones to become an all-consuming drive."

Shortly after beginning studies at the school, Jorgensen received another in a series of propositions from gay men, in this case a Danish sailor, at a dance. Disturbed and confused by the desire he inspired in gay men, the student of medical technology turned for comfort to Paul de Kruif's book, *The Male Hormone,* which points out that the chemical difference between testosterone and estradiol is merely a matter of four atoms of hydrogen and one atom of carbon. "If Dr. de Kruif's chemical ratio was correct, it would seem then that the relationship was very close," Jorgensen writes in her autobiography. "That being so, I reasoned, there must be times when one could be so close to that physical dividing line that it would be difficult to determine on which side of the male-female dividing line one belonged." Jorgensen decided that she belonged on the female side, and a few days later she walked into a pharmacy "in an unfamiliar part of town" and requested a hundred tablets of high-potency estradiol. At first, the clerk was unwilling to hand over the hundred tablets of ethynyl estradiol without a prescription, but when Jorgensen claimed to be a medical technology student "working on the idea of growth stimulation in animals through the use of hormones," the clerk relented. "Once out of the store, I headed for the car and unwrapped the package," Jorgensen writes. "How strange it seemed to me that the whole answer might lie in the particular combination of atoms contained in those tiny, aspirin-like pills."

Although estrogen hadn't received quite the same star treatment as testosterone in the press, research on female hormones had been proceeding in tandem with testosterone research throughout the first decades of the century. In 1923 and 1924, the zoologist Edgar Allen and the biochemist Edward Doisy published papers describing the induction of sexual maturity in young female animals through injections of "the ovarian follicular hormone." They called the newly purified hormone "Theelin," a name that was dropped in favor of "oestrin" in 1926. In 1929, various researchers—including Allen and Doisy; Thayer and Veler in the United States; and Adolf Butenandt in Germany—succeeded in isolating oestrin in crystalline form. This pure crystalline oestrin was called "estrone." One year later, a researcher named Zondek discovered that the urine of pregnant mares was a rich source of the hormone. In 1932, at the International Conference on the Standardization of Sex Hormones, in London, the names "oestrone," "oestriol," and "oestradiol" were adopted, and in 1938, chemists working for the German pharmaceutical company Schering developed ethynyl estradiol, the first orally active estrogen. In 1939, diethylstilbestrol, a highly potent synthetic estrogen, was developed and marketed in Germany, and after review by the Food and Drug Administration, in the United States. By 1941, a pill made from conjugated estrogens collected from pregnant mares (Premarin) was being marketed in Canada, and a year later in the United States.

In tandem with these advances, scientists learned that women's urine contained the "male" hormone, testosterone, and the urine of men contained the "female" hormone, estrogen. Though the proportions were different, both sexes produced both male and female hormones. One researcher commented on the baffling discovery by noting that "the present wonder is not that intersexual conditions occur, but that the balance of endocrine factors usually comes down on one side or the other to produce a recognizable male or female—perhaps in these days, I should say, a more or less recognizable male or female."

Within two weeks of beginning daily doses of ethynyl estradiol in 1949, Jorgensen noticed physical effects ("sensitivity in my breast area and a noticeable development") and emotional ones. "The great feeling of listlessness and fatigue, which often seemed to be with me even after a full night's sleep, had disappeared. I was refreshed and alive and no longer felt the need to take little cat naps during the day." Encouraged by these results, Jorgensen speculated that "if the female hormones that I was taking without guidance could have such a pronounced effect on me, would it not be possible for an expert to administer them in proper proportions, so that my body's chemistry would be in complete and correct balance?"

Jorgensen craftily confessed her secret to a fellow student, Genevieve Angelo, whose husband was an M.D. The friend arranged an appointment with her husband, Dr. Joseph Angelo, and after weeks of discussion and research in medical journals, Dr. Angelo agreed to supervise the estrogen administration. "It was his plan to retreat and use strong doses of testosterone, thereby returning me to my original maleness, if the estrogen injections had proven unsatisfactory," Jorgensen writes. Around the same time, she received a letter from a Connecticut physician whom she had consulted a few years earlier, who pointed out "the course of treatment that you requested" (sex-change surgery) had been carried out in Sweden. Soon after finishing the course at the medical technician's school, in December 1949, Jorgensen decided to visit family and friends in Denmark, and to proceed from there to Stockholm, "where I hoped to find doctors who would be willing to handle my case."

Arriving in Denmark in May 1950, Jorgensen discovered that there was no need to go to Sweden. Instead, in July, she visited the Statens Seruminstitut, in Copenhagen, searching for Dr. Christian Hamburger, a prominent endocrinologist who had published a number of hormone studies. Learning that he was on vacation in the country, the impatient young American sought him out at home and, after pouring out "the whole story of my perplexing life," asked him point-blank "if he thought I was a homosexual." Hamburger replied negatively, and when pressed for an explanation, told Jorgensen that "the trouble is very deep-rooted in the cells of your body. Outwardly, you have many of the sex characteristics of a man. You were declared a boy at birth and you have grown up, so very unhappily, in the guise of a man. But inwardly, it is quite possible that you are a woman. Your body chemistry and all of your body cells, including your brain cells, may be female."

This theory, which had its roots in Steinach's guinea pig experiments and subsequent animal experimentation, remained untested in humans—even though, by 1950, rudimentary "sex change" surgeries had already been carried out in more than one European country, on both male-bodied and female-bodied individuals. But European views on these matters were not generally accepted, or well-advertised, in the United States. Meanwhile, in Denmark, Dr. Hamburger was looking for a human guinea pig, and he found one in the young American who had traveled to Europe to seek the knowledge and understanding that he hadn't been able to find at home. It was a fateful meeting. Jorgensen recalls Hamburger's proposal in her autobiography. "There are several questions about the interaction of the hormone which are not quite clear now and I am very much interested in having you help me clear up these complicated matters. They can only be accomplished by observing a person over long periods of time. Since they are based on urinalysis, it will be necessary to collect specimens carefully, for several months or even a year, each and every day. You must guarantee you will cooperate fully in this, and be very accurate." Anxious for help, the young American agreed to become Hamburger's research subject.

The first stage of the treatment involved discontinuing the oral doses of estradiol, and beginning a rigorous regimen of fluid collection. Hamburger's young patient was instructed to save every drop of urine excreted. "Thus began a period in my life when I was never to be without a two-quart bottle, discreetly concealed in a black bag," Jorgensen writes. "I began to refer to it jokingly as my *yor mor taske*, which means 'midwife's bag' in Danish."

After Hamburger had established baseline levels of male and female hormones in Jorgensen's body by running tests on the urine, he began injections of high-potency estrogen. "The first few injections brought my energy back up a startling rate," Jorgensen reports. The injections were then replaced by the administration of much higher oral doses of estrogen. "By these methods of hormone administration, the male complement of my system was being suppressed into a slumbering state. I was undergoing what medical experts called a 'chemical castration.'"

It was during this period that Jorgensen had her first plastic surgery—one that had nothing to do with sex but that corrected a condition that she had found a source of annoyance all of her life. She had her "prominent" ears, a source of lifelong teasing, pinned back.

Miraculously, the complex I'd had for years disappeared almost overnight. I regarded it as a small victory, as it was the first conquest of one
of the things I disliked about myself." At the same time, the high doses
of estrogen were "imparting added weight in the hips and some bust
development," without any adverse effect on the pituitary—one of the
doctor's concerns. Most important of all to Jorgensen, "when the male
chemistry was inert, I became alive and vigorous and felt fully capable
of meeting my responsibilities and problems with competence."

After five months, the doses of estrogen were halted so that the ex-
perimenters could assess their subject's reaction to the withdrawal.
"The hormone tablets were discontinued for several weeks and I was
upset physically and mentally as the male hormones, no longer suppressed, took over again. Almost at once the old fatigue and disturbing
emotions returned," Jorgensen reports. Around this time, Hamburger
sent his patient to see Dr. George Sturup, a psychiatrist. Sturup's job
was to find some psychological explanation for his patient's desire to
become a woman, some "childhood trauma or emotional aberrations
that would give me the cause." He never found one, and later told Jorgensen, "I felt you could not be cured, psychologically. After many
visits, it was finally clear to me." Jorgensen's physicians then applied
to the Ministry of Justice for permission to surgically castrate their
patient. Sturup applied to the Medico-Legal Council of the Ministry,
submitting his findings together with those of Hamburger and the
other physicians who had consulted on the case. Jorgensen too was
asked to submit a letter, stating why the surgery was being requested.
She closed the letter with a poignant plea, not only for herself but also
for the unknown others who shared the mysterious condition, which
her doctors were alternately calling "genuine transvestism" and "psychic hermaphroditism." "To return to my old way of life would destroy all my hopes and ambitions as well as my body. This operation
would not only be helping me, but perhaps open a whole new field of
investigation for similar cases. If you could really realize how desperately we, of my kind, need help."

The last hurdle to surgery was cleared when Helga Pederson, the
attorney general of Denmark, brushed aside the reservations expressed by the Ministry of Justice about performing a castration on

someone who was not even a citizen of Denmark. The operation was performed on September 24, 1951. Soon after the surgery, Jorgensen wrote to the Angelos, "As you can see by the enclosed photo, taken just before the operation, I have changed a great deal. . . . Half the time, people in shops call me 'Miss' or 'Mrs.' and it doesn't embarrass me because I'm not afraid of people anymore." As the months flew by and autumn turned to winter and then to spring, Jorgensen continued her daily visits to the Seruminstitut and her consultations with Dr. Hamburger. In May, she visited the American Embassy in Copenhagen for another momentous step—changing her sex on her passport. Presenting letters from her doctors and the Ministry of Justice, Jorgensen was greeted cordially by Mrs. Eugenie Anderson, the American ambassador to Denmark, who inquired what name Jorgensen wished to submit to Washington for the new passport. "I admit the question didn't take me by surprise, for I'd given it much thought in the previous year and to me the choice was a logical one. Dr. Hamburger was the man to whom I owed so much, above all others. I transposed his first name, Christian, into the feminine Christine, a name which I'd always thought attractive. Thus, my new name of Christine Jorgensen."

When the new passport arrived, Jorgensen "felt free at last to take my place in the outside world," and for the first time appeared in public in feminine attire. In June, she wrote "the most important letter of my life," to her parents, which a visiting aunt promised to hand-deliver. In the letter, Christine first tells her parents that she is "happier and healthier than ever before in my life," before offering a brief lesson in endocrinology. In a famous phrase, reprinted months later in hundreds of newspapers, she says, "Nature has made a mistake, which I have corrected, and I am now your daughter." The shocked but supportive Jorgensens responded with a telegram: "Letter and pictures received. We love you more than ever. Love, Mom and Dad."

In November 1952, Christine once again entered Rigshospital, in Copenhagen, for the second stage of her transformation, which she defined as "removal of the immature sex organs," or penis. Ten days after the surgery, as she lay recuperating in her bed, she was handed a telegram by a young woman who identified herself as a reporter for *Information,* a Danish newspaper. "Filled with a kind of unknown dread,

I reached out to take it from her hand, and read the message: BRONX GI BECOMES A WOMAN. DEAR MOM AND DAD SON WROTE, I HAVE NOW BE- COME YOUR DAUGHTER." A family friend, someone to whom her par- ents had confided their secret, had sold the story to the newspapers.

"To me that message was a symbol of a brutal and cruel betrayal," Jorgensen writes years later. "A lifetime of agonizing unhappiness, two years of medical treatment and two surgical operations had been telescoped into a couple of succinct lines on a telegraph form, and I knew without being told that it would go far beyond that hospital room." By the time the twenty-four-year-old photographer returned to the United States, in February 1953, after two life-transforming years abroad, she was arguably the most famous person in the world. More news stories were filed on Christine Jorgensen in 1953 than on any other single individual or event. A private decision, arrived at after much soul-searching and struggle, had become a public scandal.

One of the people who read about Jorgensen's surgery in the New York newspapers was Harry Benjamin, but unlike most Americans, Benjamin was not surprised. Beginning in the thirties, he had begun spending his summers in San Francisco, living at the Sir Francis Drake Hotel and seeing patients in the office building across the street. In 1945, he met the American sex researcher Alfred Kinsey, and like many other friends and colleagues, had his sex history taken by the Kinsey researchers. In 1948, while conducting interviews at the hotel, Kinsey met a young man who "wanted, as he said, to become a girl, and his mother supported him in this. Kinsey had never seen a case like this, and it was new even for me," Benjamin recalls in an interview years later. "It went well beyond the by then recognized transvestism. The concept of transsexualism did not yet exist. It only gradually took shape in my thinking, not least because of this first case."

Like Jorgensen, this patient (referred to as "Barry" in Benjamin's case studies) had from his earliest childhood felt that he was in fact a girl, and after reading about "operative procedures which feminized men" had "pressed his parents to find a surgeon who performed such operations." Unlike Jorgensen, however, Barry became emotionally disturbed when he was unable to fulfill this desire and had been institu- tionalized by the courts when his frustration erupted into violence.

Barry was taken by his parents to see Alfred Kinsey in 1948, when the famous sex researcher was taking case histories at the Sir Francis Drake Hotel. Kinsey, whose previous research had not prepared him for Barry, sent the boy to Benjamin, then seeing patients in the same hotel.

"Benjamin's first inclination was to send the boy to a psychiatrist, but he soon discovered that this was not a good idea," says Christine Wheeler. When asked whether or not castration and peotomy were indicated for the "very effeminate" boy, "the psychiatrists disagreed among themselves," Benjamin says. "Some were for it, others were against it." He started the boy on a course of hormones, which "had a calming effect," but was unable to find a urologist in the United States willing to perform surgery. He advised the boy (and his mother) to travel to Germany for the operation.

When the Jorgensen story broke, in 1953, Harry Benjamin was sixty-seven years old and looking forward to retirement. He had enjoyed a long and a productive career, and as his geriatric patients died, he stopped acquiring new ones. He recruited Virginia Allen, a doctor's wife whom he had met at a meeting a few years earlier, to help him slowly phase out his practice. "He invited me for drinks at the Sulgrave Hotel and told me he felt he had only a few years left and wanted to spend them quietly in a retirement practice," Allen recalled at the memorial that was held following Benjamin's death, in 1986. However, things didn't work out quite the way that Benjamin had planned.

At the memorial, Virginia Allen recalled the day that she stumbled upon a cache of patient folders that she found particularly puzzling. "While arranging files one day, I asked, 'What are these few records off by themselves? They seem so strange—the patients have male and female names.' H.B. sighed, 'They're transsexuals and transvestites, some referred by Kinsey. Not much is known about them.' 'Why don't we do something with them, since we have so much time,' I asked. He nodded and said, 'Yes, that may be very good. They are sad people and deserve help but they make everyone, even other doctors, so nervous and uncomfortable. Bring the records in here and we'll go over them.' And so it began."

Benjamin began seeing patients referred by Kinsey and others, including a husband and wife who had been married to each other twice—the second time, in reversed-gender roles. His remaining geriatric patients were not happy about the new crop of patients, and his long-awaited retirement had nearly materialized when Christine Jorgensen suddenly burst onto the scene, thoroughly upsetting his plans. In December 1952, Benjamin wrote to one of his transsexual patients, an artist named Doris, with whom he had carried on a long and animated correspondence: "The papers here are full of the Jorgensen case, the boy who went to Denmark to be operated on and is now coming back as a girl. I'll probably see the party when she returns home."

At the Benjamin memorial, in 1986, Christine Jorgensen described the circumstances under which the two pioneers had met. Returning home from Europe in 1953, she said, she "encountered a mountain of mail and I do mean a mountain—thousands and thousands of letters, many of which were from people who had problems that were similar to mine—in that mountain of mail was a letter from Harry Benjamin whom I had never heard of before and he asked me—told me that he was guiding people and so forth in the direction of transsexuality. And would I contact him which indeed I did."

Describing Benjamin as a "godsend," Jorgensen recalled that "I could recommend Harry to all these thousands of people who contacted me . . . because I didn't know where to recommend people to go, there were no gender identity clinics, there was no place for them to go. So suddenly the deluge fell onto poor Harry's shoulders." And a deluge it was. When he met Christine Jorgensen, and began monitoring her hormones and later sending her to see Los Angeles urologist Elmer Belt for the final stage of her surgery, Benjamin had treated fewer than a dozen transsexual patients. By the time he finally closed his practice, twenty-five years later, in 1978, he had seen more than 1,500 patients. It sometimes seems that every transsexual person in America in the sixties and seventies somehow found their way to Benjamin's office, even before the publication of *The Transsexual Phenomenon*, in 1966.

In *The Transsexual Phenomenon*, Benjamin seeks to dissipate some of the scientific and public ignorance shrouding the subject of gender variance. Early in the book he refers to Hirschfeld's research on transvestism at the Institute for Sexual Science, but he quickly distinguishes transvestism and transsexuality as clinical entities.

> The transsexual (TS) male or female is deeply unhappy as a member of the sex (or gender) to which he or she was assigned by the anatomical structure of the body, particularly the genitals. To avoid misunderstanding: this has nothing to do with hermaphroditism. The transsexual is physically normal (though occasionally underdeveloped). These persons can somewhat appease their unhappiness by dressing in the clothes of the opposite sex, that is to say, by crossdressing, and they are, therefore, transvestites too. But while "dressing" would satisfy the true transvestite (who is content with his morphological sex), it is only incidental and not more than a partial or a temporary help to the transsexual. True transsexuals feel that they *belong* to the other sex, not only to appear as such. For them, their sex organs, the primary (testes) as well as the secondary (penis and others), are disgusting deformities that must be changed by the surgeon's knife. This attitude appears to be the chief differential diagnostic point between the two syndromes (sets of symptoms)—that is, those of transvestism and transsexualism.

Benjamin created a chart, the Sex Orientation Scale, based on the Kinsey rating scale for homosexuality. In the Kinsey Scale, a completely heterosexual person is ranked zero, and a fully homosexual person six. A person who is equally attracted by either sex would be a three. In the Benjamin scale of transvestism/transsexuality, there are six "types," which together make up three "groups" of progressively gender-variant individuals. Group one includes the three types of transvestite ("pseudo," "fetishistic," and "true"), who cross-dress to varying degrees and for varying reasons. Only the final type, the "true" transvestite, expresses an interest in estrogen therapy or surgery, and this interest tends to be of an experimental nature.

Group two includes only one "type," the "nonsurgical transsexual," a person who "wavers between TV and TS," cross-dressing "as often as possible with insufficient relief of his gender discomfort." This non-surgical transsexual will be likely to request hormones for "comfort and emotional balance," Benjamin writes, but while he finds the idea of sex-reassignment surgery attractive, he will not pursue it with the intensity of the latter two types (group three), "true transsexuals" of moderate or high intensity. These individuals tend to feel "trapped in the wrong body," according to Benjamin, and will hope for and work for sex reassignment surgery. The major difference between these final two types is that the "true transsexual, high intensity" doesn't just dislike his genitals; he despises them and may attempt to mutilate his sex organs or commit suicide if unable to achieve his goals.

Like Hirschfeld, Benjamin focuses mainly on male-bodied persons in his book, even though he knew and treated female-bodied persons as well. He does include a final chapter on "the female transsexual," but as with Hirschfeld, his interest in these persons appears somewhat secondary. He notes that in his practice, the proportion of male-to-female transsexuals to female-to-male transsexuals is eight to one—though he defers to the three-to-one estimate of Christine Jorgensen's physician, Christian Hamburger, based on the letters from around the world that Hamburger received after the Jorgensen case was publicized. Hamburger received 465 letters from individuals desiring sex-change surgery in the months following the Jorgensen media blitz, with three times as many men as women requesting help. Benjamin notes the paradoxical fact that though Gallup polls report that "in our culture about twelve times more women would have liked to have been born as men than vice-versa," many fewer female-bodied persons requested sex-reassignment surgery.

Like male-bodied transsexuals, female-bodied transsexuals "resent" their sexual morphology—"especially the bulging breasts," says Benjamin, noting that his female patients "frequently bind them with adhesive tape until a plastic surgeon can be found who would reduce the breasts to a masculine proportion." Most of his female-to-male patients also requested a total hysterectomy, including removal of the ovaries, and treatment with androgens. The latter request was relatively easy to fulfill, though the former was more difficult, because of the unwillingness of most surgeons to remove healthy organs. Of the twenty female-to-male patients Benjamin reports on in his book, only nine underwent hysterectomy (at an average age of thirty-five). Five of those patients also underwent mastectomy. Another five patients underwent only mastectomy without hysterectomy. Sixteen of the patients were taking testosterone, which eventually produces "a physical state resembling pseudohermaphroditism (enlarged clitoris, body hair, etc.)," Benjamin reports.

In *The Transsexual Phenomenon*, Benjamin's compassion for his patients comes through clearly, although the distancing language of science and traces of paternalism can work to disguise this. As a result of his age and personal history, Benjamin was able to offer not only a clinical perspective on the subject, but also historical parallels to the resistance that he and other clinicians had encountered in their attempts to help transsexual patients. Near the end of the book he recalls his youth in Berlin and the fate of another pioneer. "Fifty years ago, when I was a medical student in Germany, plastic surgery began to shape noses and perform face-lifting operations for cosmetic purposes. I remember a surgeon in Berlin who specialized in nose operations. His name was Joseph and he was referred to as the 'Nasen Joseph' [Nose Joseph]. He was bitterly criticized for what he did. Surgeons such as he were refused membership in medical societies and were branded as quacks by some of their particularly orthodox colleagues. And then, sex was not even involved."

Though he doesn't say so explicitly, Benjamin must have been aware that criticisms of "Nasen Joseph" stemmed from discomfort with the manner in which rhinoplasty was perceived as facilitating another kind of "passing"—from Jewish to German. As a "foreign" physician, Benjamin understood exclusion. Although he was invited by friends to deliver presentations at the New York University School of Medicine in 1963, at the Albert Einstein College of Medicine in 1964, and at Stanford University in 1967, his academic affiliations were limited, and throughout most of his career his practice remained "isolated and unconnected," said Christine Wheeler. His insights and achievements seem all the more remarkable in light of these facts.

Benjamin "understood that you couldn't separate the body from the mind," Christine Wheeler says, and he looked forward to the day when an organic understanding of transsexualism was possible. "He always held out hope that the biological key would be found," she says, "but he also believed that we didn't have the tools to understand it" at the time he was working. Benjamin was "a product of his age," Wheeler says, and some of his views have been revised by later researchers and clinicians. His attitude about surgery is one of them. According to Benjamin, "you weren't a true transsexual if you didn't desire surgery," Wheeler says, whereas Wheeler, who has been in practice for thirty-three years, has many clients who "move in and out of transition . . . according to what feels safe at the time." She also sees about a dozen people who have lived in their birth sex their entire lives but who decided "in their sixties and seventies that they couldn't go to their graves" without talking with someone about their lifelong gender dysphoria. "They've never cross-dressed, they've never taken hormones," she says. Are they transsexuals? Not in Benjamin's view, but a new generation of clinicians and activists might argue differently.

Wheeler, along with her colleague Leah Schaefer, is the guardian of Benjamin's archives, the voluminous patient records, correspondence, and other products of a lifetime of writing and research on two continents. This archive will provide a rich trove of data for future historians and other scholars. Someday, a biography of Harry Benjamin—far more than the brief sketch of his work in this chapter—will illuminate the significance of his research not only for transgendered people seeking a solution to their personal difficulties, but toward a broader and more comprehensive scientific understanding of sex and gender in the twentieth century.

"Treating the gender dysphoric person was ultimately the sum total of all of Benjamin's previous interests and knowledge. One might say his work in the field was an accident for which he was totally prepared," Schaefer and Wheeler wrote in 1995. "The course and events of Benjamin's professional life were destined to crown a career that would unlock the door to an area of study that would have the most profound implications for our understanding of human nature and would change the lives of countless people forevermore." Transsexual people themselves often express a less adulatory, though still generally positive, view of Benjamin and his accomplishments. Susan Stryker calls him "a genial old paternalist, a really nice guy who cared about his clients and saw himself as doing what he could to help. Really going above and beyond the call of duty in trying to arrange surgery for people, really compassionate." Still, Benjamin could also be "very sexist and elitist and condescending to people," Stryker says. "He called [transwomen] his 'girls' and he would only work with, take under his wing, the ones he thought were really attractive."

Nonetheless, like his predecessor, Hirschfeld, "Benjamin did a lot of good progressive political work," Stryker says. His office was in San Francisco's Union Square, and many of his patients lived and worked in the Tenderloin, the city's notorious red-light district. She adds (though I have not been able to confirm this) that Benjamin also served as "clap doctor for some of the best whorehouses in town" and that he performed abortions for the city's elite Pacific Heights crowd. "If you look at some of these early sexologists, the people who are involved in doing transsexual/transgender work also tend to be involved in abortion rights and in prostitution rights," Stryker says. Benjamin and sexologist colleagues such as Kinsey were sexual pragmatists, Stryker says, whose attitudes can best be summarized as "people fuck, and they fuck in lots of ways—get over it. Some people dress in different ways—get over it."

Like Hirschfeld, Benjamin refrained from judging his patients/clients. He was aware that many dabbled in prostitution, for example, admitting in *The Transsexual Phenomenon* that "the unfortunate fact that a number of patients went into prostitutional activities right after their operations has turned some doctors against its acceptance as a legitimate therapy." He quotes a urologist who told him, "I don't want a respectable doctor's clinic to be turned into a whorehouse." Such a physician, Benjamin says, "may enjoy the feeling of being on the side of the angels but he scarcely has ethics or logic for support. Should a physician refuse to heal the injured right hand of a pickpocket because he may return to his profession and perhaps forge checks besides?" he asks. "Should a urologist—for argument's sake—decline to treat sexual impotence because a cure may induce the patient to start an illicit love affair, or, if married, lead him to adultery?"

Benjamin concludes that the responsibility of the physician is to heal, not to judge the morals or behavior of his patients. "A doctor could hardly be held responsible, and should not hold himself responsible, for what a patient will do with his regained health. That is none of his business. Such an attitude could lead to endless absurdities as the above examples show." This attitude was quite rare among physicians encountering transsexual and transgendered patients throughout the latter decades of the twentieth century, and remains rare today. Nearly every transgendered person I spoke with had experienced some painful interaction with a health care provider, most often a doctor, whose distaste for gender-variant people was hardly disguised. In *Trans Liberation: Beyond Pink or Blue,* the author and activist Leslie Feinberg describes a series of such encounters, one of which culminated in a physician shoving his hands down her pants and shouting, "You're a freak!" Whatever Harry Benjamin's flaws, he was at least cognizant of the fact that his Hippocratic oath applied to all his patients, not just the normatively gendered ones.

Benjamin died in August 1986, at the age of 101. His friend Christine Jorgensen, for whom he felt immense respect and gratitude, outlived him by only three years, dying of bladder cancer at the age of sixty-two. In the introduction to *The Transsexual Phenomenon,* Benjamin pays tribute to Jorgensen in words that echo the praise of his own friends and colleagues at his memorial service.

> Without her courage and determination, undoubtedly springing from a force deep inside her, transsexualism might still be largely unknown—certainly unknown by this term—and might still be considered to be something barely on the fringe of medical science. To the detriment if not to the desperation of the respective patients, the medical profession would most likely still be ignorant of the subject and still be ignoring its manifestations. Even at present, any attempts to treat these patients with some permissiveness in the direction of their wishes—that is to say, "change of sex"—is often met with raised medical eyebrows, and sometimes even with arrogant rejection and/or condemnation. And so, without Christine Jorgensen and the

unsought publicity of her "conversion," this book could hardly have been conceived.

In a 1953 letter to Benjamin, written soon after they met, Jorgensen explained why she had overcome her initial resistance and was beginning to speak to the media and accept offers to perform in nightclubs—in other words, to embrace her notoriety, rather than running from it. "As you know, I've been avoiding publicity, but this seems the wrong approach. Now I shall seek it so that 'Christine' will become such an average thing in the public mind that when the next 'Christine' comes along the sensationalism will be decreased. You know what I'm trying to do is not as great as the big medical discoverers in the past, but it will be a contribution. With God's help and those who believe *as you do,* I know this will be a step into the future understanding of the human race. I wonder where there are *more* who join us in this struggle."

CONVERSATION WITH ALESHIA BREVARD

Aleshia Brevard is an actress and writer. A graceful woman in her sixties, in 2001, Brevard published a memoir, The Woman I Was Not Born to Be, *in which she describes her childhood in Tennessee, her pre-transition years in San Francisco, performing as Lee Shaw at the famous drag club Finocchio's, and her post-transition life and career as an actress and a Playboy bunny in Hollywood. Brevard, who transitioned in 1962, is a member of the first generation of Americans who underwent sex-reassignment surgery, a group whose belief that one's identity as a trans-sexual is left behind in the surgical suite has been increasingly challenged by a later generation.*

Q: Do you have any childhood memories of the big media splash surrounding Christine Jorgensen's return to the United States after her surgery in Denmark? Was she an inspiration to you? Did you ever meet her?

I never met Ms. Jorgensen, nor can I even say that she was a true inspiration for me when contemplating my own surgery. The media frenzy that accompanied Christine's arrival at New York International Airport [*sic*], February 13, 1953, actually had a decidedly negative effect on me as a high school freshman. The hoopla surrounding the Jorgensen gender transformation focused an unflattering spotlight on me as an overly feminine teenager. "Buddy must have caught what Christine has," was my classmates' taunting chant for several weeks at Trousdale County High. I wasn't thrilled to have my carefully constructed male cover blown by Christine Jorgensen's high-powered publicity splash. I felt exposed. I felt very threatened. I was not yet aware that I was Christine's transgendered sister. I'd always believed I was meant to be a girl, but the jokes, horror, and general commotion that surrounded Christine Jorgensen's transition kept me from believing I might be a girl like America's first transsexual.

Q: One of the things I found so refreshing about your memoir was your honesty. Some of the earlier transsexual memoirists like Jorgensen were so circumspect, because of the times the authors were writing in. They really couldn't discuss their sex lives, for example. But you really don't pull any punches. You put it all out there.

I've heard that. And I'm flattered. That's what I wanted more than anything. If I'm taking this step, and coming forward at long last, I must be honest, and I can't sugarcoat anything.

Q: One of the things I've found interesting as I've been conducting my research is the conflicted relationship between homosexuality and transsexuality. Christine Jorgensen and many other early transsexuals were adamant about insisting that they were not homosexuals. One of the things I found unique about your book is that you admitted that you were a gay man . . .

Perceived to be a gay man. But I didn't think that was the case. Before I met Dr. Benjamin, well . . . You wear the badges that are available at the fair and that's what was available. I was not popular in the gay bars, and the men who were attracted to me were attracted because of the image I projected onstage. I was just too ultra for the gay community. If an interested potential partner thought that you believed it (that you were female), that's the difference. If it were bigger than life, drag, a parody of femininity, that's camp. Then, that was okay.

Q: Did you feel comfortable in the gay community before your transition?

No. I did not feel comfortable in the community. I do more so now, actually. Adore it, really. Because I've become an icon. I went to a book reading in San Francisco, and there was a very interesting young man who came by and said, "This book is so important to me because the movement in the gay community is now to exclude those of us who want to cherish our femininity." And I thought, yes . . . Because here he was in a lumber shirt and the whole thing. I view that as almost criminal. We just must learn to let people be as they are. The whole impersonation thing also [drag queens] . . . The community has turned on those representatives of the Stonewall era. They are ashamed of them now.

Q: You were a patient of Dr. Harry Benjamin. You met Dr. Benjamin when you were working at Finocchio's?
Yes. Started hormones, did all that. And of course with his rules and regulations, generally you have to dress in the clothing [of your preferred gender] for a time, but I didn't because I was working at Finocchio's.

Q: And he referred you to your surgeon, Dr. Elmer Belt?
Yes.

Q: Can you tell me a little about Dr. Benjamin, as you knew him?
He was doing extremely well in the early sixties. He had offices in Paris, New York, and San Francisco. As much as he did for me, and as much as I appreciate what he did for me . . . well, we were referred to as "his girls" and then there were RGs, "real girls." And it has only recently struck me that if we had our druthers, and in a perfect world, that distinction would not be there. And I question his putting it there. I was wondering what he really was thinking. He was very kind, very gentle, very embracing, but I'm not sure that he really got it, as I perceived it. But I don't think that we could have expected any more at the time.

Q: At the time you transitioned, there was no real "transgender community." You pretty much transitioned in isolation, didn't you?
Well, I did have friends. [*Laughs*]

Q: But you had no sense of being part of a movement?
Oh, good god, no. I would have run from that.

Q: Did Benjamin's clients, patients . . .
Children. [*Laughs*]

Q: Did you keep in touch with one another?

Pretty much so. For example, my friend Charlotte, whom I mention in the book. She was stepmother to three children. We ran around as couples, and of course neither husband knew.

Q: You were married three times and none of them knew about your surgery when you married?

I just didn't see the need to share that information. And actually still don't. It just seems to me that you are cutting out problems for yourself, if you say, "Before we go any further, I must share this with you." And then you have your first fight, and you think, "Had I not told him, would we have had this fight? What is he thinking? Is he judging me?" Now if you are secure enough in yourself, perhaps you don't go through that. I've never been that secure.

Q: So when do you tell?

If you wait until after the fact (and I have experience with this), that's worse. That can really be seen as betrayal. I don't have any answers with any of this. I would hate to be with a man and worry that he was with me because he couldn't quite accept homosexuality. And all those nagging ugly little thoughts. You buy your ticket and take your chances.

Q: Do you think things were easier when you transitioned?

No doubt about it. People did not know what to look for. There were so few of us, as I'm fond of saying, very few transsexual houses on the block. Forget community; there were few houses on the block. And the people that I knew were friends, for example, my friend Stormy that I write about in the book. She was a vivid character. But she also was very fortunate in that she was beautiful. And I don't mean to say that everyone must be. But passing, or blending, being able to survive in the world of your choice, is extremely important. I just don't see running up flags and banners to say, "We're different." Because that's what they are saying to me, "We're different than you are." And I don't feel different.

I went too far by denying my history. But . . . I have discovered that when I was teaching locally and the word went out [about my trans-sexuality] the principal said, "Why should I be upset? Come back next year." That is because I have done my job well. I have presented my-self respectfully, with some decorum. I would hate to be seated here with you and have a representative of the TG community come in and make a spectacle. It would make me feel embarrassed, but I would feel the same way if anyone came in and made a spectacle. It takes us back rather than pushing us forward.

Q: You haven't had the sense that you were discriminated against in your own life?

I was discriminated against when I was perceived to be a gay man. But after that, no. I mean, granted, there have been situations where a love of my life whom I had shared this information with said, "I can't stay." But he didn't hit me upside the head. This was his choice. And that could have been based on any number of things. So, no, I don't feel discriminated against.

Q: But others do feel discriminated against?

I understand that. When I first came here, I went to a support group, thinking that I could be a great deal of help. I was pretty much rejected by that group because what I was saying was, "My training is how to walk, how to sit, how to use makeup," and they were saying, "We are who we are, and society has to learn to accept us this way." And I don't think society has to do anything, nor does society owe us anything.

Q: Your view is a not a popular one in today's trans community. I'm sure that many don't want to hear it.

They don't. I'm not out there sharing this. But this is very impor-tant to me because I feel that what Dr. Benjamin labeled—I started to say "started," but we know that's not true—but he put a focus on something that he happened to call "transsexual," though it has little or nothing to do with sexuality. But his dream for us was that we should be able to fulfill our dream. That we go into society, that we blend and go on with our lives, and so it is an affront to me when I hear people say, "We want to shock. We want to," in my estimation, "be as offensive as possible."

There are not many of me around. They're dying off. And the others that are preaching the same gospel are not coming forward. They're comfortable in the life they've chosen. And I think I do probably tiptoe around that subject in the book. It disturbed me to see . . . well, we had no political agenda, and to see people getting mileage out of just being transgendered? This is something that you are. I personally see it as Benjamin saw it . . . something that happened during that hormonal bath and it's just something that we have to correct. Just like you have to get rid of your appendix, this is just something else we have to get rid of.

Over the years it seems to me—and I know that this sounds harsh—almost any troubled being thought they could put on a dress and say, "Here's a comfortable label." Because in the beginning we were medical problems, and there was a bit of understanding and sympathy, and I think that we attracted a lot of troubled people. That's not politically correct at all, but I've seen it. And I just say, these are not our brothers and sisters. And I have to say that is more true for our sisters. By and large, I don't think that I've ever met an FTM that I don't just adore.

Q: When did you first encounter the transgender movement?

I had not heard that term, "transgendered," until about two years ago. "Transsexual" I knew. I find it all very interesting. Sunday, I went to a group here called Mountain Women, predominantly lesbian-identified. One of the women wanted to hold hands and say, "We're not men, we're not women, we're just beings who are experiencing this day." And I thought, "Now I don't know how much alcohol it took her to get there, but isn't that a lovely philosophy." If we all felt that way, I think that maybe that's where we are moving as a species. It would be a great move for women, wouldn't it, to have that power?

But I'm disturbed that my brothers and sisters still need to label themselves, rather than just saying, "I am changing to the gender of my choice, and that's all there is to it." We do not need to unite, we do not need to do anything, or even ride in the Gay Pride Parade. What is this? I don't feel any more gay than the man in the moon. I just don't get it. But then I think perhaps I've been extremely lucky that I was allowed to be. I wasn't labeled. I could go on with my life.

Of course, coming from Dr. Benjamin's point of view and reference, the objective is to get this out of the way and go on to join the mainstream. So it disturbs me—not a major disturbance, but still—that there is a movement that's saying there's a third gender here. I think we're all on a continuum anyway, a mix of male and female. Just stop being so goddamn intellectually smug about this whole thing. At the same time, I don't want people in the transgender movement being slaughtered.

Q: When you first came out to California you began working at Finocchio's, the famous drag club in San Francisco.

Yes, Finocchio's was definitely a training ground. But as good as Finocchio's was for me, it was merely a stepping-stone. My life actually began in 1962, with surgery. It was a rebirth, truly. Everything prior to that was in preparation for a better life. I didn't know what that better life was going to be, or how I was going to get there, but I was very aware of not being comfortable in the life I was living. This was not me. I had that brief time span onstage at Finocchio's, when people applauded and said, "Ooh" and "Aah," but that was as close as I had ever gotten to what I wanted. But that was only on the stage, not off.

But going into television on *The Red Skelton Show*—that was really show business. I had worked prior to the show and had done a movie called *The Love God?* with Don Knotts. I got an agent, took acting lessons, then did a thing called *The Female Bunch,* with Russ Tamblyn, which is today a cult classic, but is so tacky, so terrible. I think I tell the story in the book, that because we didn't want to sleep with the grips, my girlfriend and I passed ourselves off as lesbians, and because of that . . . the dialogue was pretty much being invented as we went along, and the dialogue did take on a very lesbian overtone. [*Laughs*] And it was one of the first. Then I went to work at the Ambassador Hotel, and that led to the Skelton show. Usually you reverse that order, you do stage and then television and film, but I did film first and then television.

Then things really started to flower, with *The Red Skelton Show.* I started getting quite a bit of work. I did a lot of early television . . . in fact, recently I was auditioning and a young director looked at my résumé and said, "My god, you were there at the very beginning of television!" You start feeling hair sprout from your ears and a cane. [*Laughs*] But I was there doing all that variety show stuff. I did *The Andy Williams show,* and Leslie Uggams and Dean Martin. *The Partridge Family.* A skunk had gotten on the bus, and so Danny goes around to get costumes for the family with a cigarette girl or something in Vegas, and he's trying to get me out of my costume.

I also did *Night Gallery.* When Rod Serling interviewed me he said, "If I wanted a showgirl, I'd hire Kim Novak. If you pull any of that showgirl shit on me, I'm going to have you right out of there."

Q: So you had a reputation as a showgirl?

I did have that reputation . . . well, I didn't dare try anything else! So I was walking around on stilts and in miniskirts and very breathy. Smiling a lot. Not just in film, but in real life also.

Q: You were selling sexiness as a commodity?

I don't even know that it was sexy. It was a particular look. Do you remember *Little Annie Fannie,* the cartoon? Big eyes and the lips and the little perky nose and the long legs. That was the image. It was just another version of drag. The ultimate drag queen was Marlo Thomas. With the lashes and the hair. That whole image back then. I was very familiar with that. Once, when I was working at Finocchio's, I was going to work, and I saw Ann-Margret, standing on the corner in all of her glory. And it was the same act.

Q: Did you have the political consciousness to make the connection back then?

No, but I was shocked to discover that some of the people I considered to be the most beautiful women in the world were going through the same traumas that I was. We had the same goals; we were going about it the same way; we were going to private clubs in Beverly Hills, trying to be noticed, trying to be discovered, trying to find a sugar daddy. It was the same damn thing.

Q: The life of a starlet?

Exactly. And the "will somebody really love me for who I am?" This was not transsexual, it was being a woman.

Q: Did you enjoy your life as a starlet?

I loved everything that went with it. The restaurants, the parties. People treat you with great—they might be snickering behind their hands, but I don't think they were at that time. I don't think the word "bimbo" had been invented yet, but we were invited just to decorate the tables. And with some of the Syndicate, the attitude was "just zip it if you're not going to say something that's 'airhead.'" [*Affects a breathy, dithery voice*] "What's your name again, I just can't remember names for the life of me."

Q: Did you ever have a sense of "they don't know all of me"?

No. I don't know whether that is because I have this theatrical mentality, that I can believe whatever. I think I'm a really good actress, because the character becomes very real for me. So I was still being the reflection in the eyes of those that wanted me. So I saw myself as they saw me. And it was very comfortable for me.

Q: When did that start to change for you?

I think that I came into my own when I woke up one day in my late fifties and realized that—it seems like it was overnight—that men have stopped turning around on the street to look. So it gave me the freedom to really deal with me. To see myself. It's part of this whole gender thing, I think. Now at sixty-three (sixty-four in December), I get up in the middle of the night to go to the bathroom (and I never had to do that) and I'm stumbling down the hall, and as I pass a mirror and see myself, I think, "I'm really happy with this body—it's sagging, it's falling, it's all of that, but it's me." And it's the me that I wanted to be. So maybe the stomach is breaching and maybe the boobs are sagging, but it feels genuine.

Q: So your experience of aging is a woman's experience of aging?

Yes. You know, a female friend of mine from the early years, whom I had not talked to in over forty years, called after she read the book and said, "I know you're writing about a transsexual experience, but you've written my story." And that's very important to me. And I think that's also extremely telling. We can label it any way we want to, but the experiences are the same.

Q: One of the questions that I've asked everyone whom I've interviewed for the book is "What is gender?"

I don't even know what that means anymore, don't know that I ever knew what it meant. To me, how you are perceived dictates how you are treated, and I have been treated with the female experience. I've had some bad experiences. Part of that too is being raised in different times, not knowing that you have the option to make choices. My sisters, for example, were raised with the "don'ts." I didn't have any of those so I really made some serious mistakes. It took me a long time to realize that if the bar is closing and I'm in a really wonderful conversation that I want to continue, it does not mean that I can go to someone's apartment in the hope of continuing it. I'm a slow learner.

Q: What is it that made you aware from early on that you were female despite what your body was telling you?

For me . . . well, I've alluded earlier to this power structure, and that's how I explain it. I was very aware from a very early age that I did not want the responsibility that is inherent for the male. All of that: Going off and fighting our wars and being responsible for keeping peace, I suppose. Protecting those you love. I wanted to be protected. Now maybe that's just weak, but as life has progressed and I recall what I have experienced and survived, I don't consider that to have been weak at all. It was just another way of viewing your function and your place in the world. I wanted to nurture, but I don't think that is necessarily transsexual. I think there are a lot of men who are happy being men, who feel the same way. So I have no idea what the gender issue is about.

I thought for a long time that being male had to do with testosterone levels, and I still suspect that it does. But then we also have women who have higher testosterone levels, and I view them generally as expressing male energy. I don't think it's about genitalia at all. And that brings us back to those transgendered beings who say, "I don't want to mutilate my body." I thought it was being very clever when I said [in the book], "There was nothing wrong with my body, except that it had a penis attached to it." I like that, but I think there is a lot going on beneath that statement. It didn't work for me, but that would have been like wearing a green hair ribbon when everything else was blue. It clashed. I think that's true. But it's just another bit of baggage. Each one of these choices has its own baggage.

Four

MEN AND WOMEN, BOYS AND GIRLS

When I got to the carnival in Stroud, I walked around for a long while just looking at the exhibitions and trying to build up enough courage to ask someone for a job. Finally, I went to the freak sideshow and started a conversation with the barker. I told him that I was looking for a job and he said he'd see what he could do. He went inside the tent to talk with the show's owner and, after about five minutes, came out. "We've got a spot for a half-man, half-woman person," he said, with a laugh. "Do you think you can do it?"

HEDY JO STAR, *MY UNIQUE CHANGE*, BALTIMORE, 1958

Two years after Christine Jorgensen became an international celebrity, a Johns Hopkins psychologist named John Money began publishing a series of papers that were to have large consequences for intersexual and transsexual people, and for American society in general. Early in his career, Money's investigations into the psychology of intersexual patients convinced him that a person's deeply rooted sense of self as either male or female was largely formed not before but *after* birth, by a combination of factors, the primary one being "the sex of assignment and rearing"—the way that one is raised. "To use the Pygmalion allegory, one may begin with the same clay and fashion a god or a goddess . . . if certain conditions are met," he asserted. This theory was adopted not only by scientists and physicians, who used it to justify extensive surgical and hormonal manipulation of intersexual infants and children, but also by second-wave feminists who saw in Money's theory proof that women were socialized to be a "second sex," weaker, more dependent, more emotional. "Femininity" and "masculinity" were defined as roles adopted by essentially androgynous beings. Before we don the socially constructed personae of male and female, advocates of Money's theory asserted, we are all the same. However, Money himself was no proponent of androgyny—quite the contrary. In Money's view, psychological health was entirely dependent on the development of an unambiguous identity as either a man or a woman. Money's research thus combined radicalism (the theory of psychosexual neutrality at birth) with a profound conservatism (emphasis on sexual dimorphism). We are still grappling with the effects of this paradoxical theory, which so deeply penetrated our culture, today.

The research question that Money began to explore as a graduate student appeared simple, and unlikely to initiate sweeping social changes. What could or should be done to help those individuals born in bodies that defied traditional definitions of sex, such as the long-deceased and forgotten Herculine Barbin? Children born with genital anomalies presented a clinical riddle. To the eighteenth-century doctors who examined Barbin, the presence of undescended testicles was proof that the girl was *really* a boy. But by the middle of the twentieth century, the medical determination of sex had become decidedly more complex, no longer visible to the eye or the palpating hand of the physician.

In 1948, Murray Llewellyn Barr, a Canadian geneticist, made the discovery for which he would later be nominated for a Nobel Prize. While carrying out experiments on nervous system cells of various mammals, Barr and a graduate student named Ewart George Bertram noticed that some of the cells contained small dark masses. Attempting to identify the masses, Barr discovered that they were present only in the cells of female animals. Later investigators would discover that these "Barr bodies" were in fact inactivated X chromosomes, switched off to prevent an overload of genetic information in the cell. Initially, Barr bodies were identified in biopsies of skin tissue, but in 1956, scientists realized that simply scraping some cells from the mucosa of the mouth would produce accurate results. Sex chromatin typing gave rise to a new science, cytogenetics, and a new method to determine sex.

Intersexual and gender-variant persons were among the first to undergo genetic testing, and certain anomalies were revealed to be genetically caused. Others were found to have no apparent genetic basis.

"It was as a graduate student in the Harvard psychological clinic
that I first became directly acquainted with the phenomenon of human
hermaphroditism," Money writes in *Gendermaps,* published in 1995.
He describes the case of a seventeen-year-old boy born with two undescended testes and external genitalia that "resembled a vulva with
a clitoridean organ instead of a penis." The boy was suffering from a
condition then called testicular feminizing syndrome, but today known
as androgen insensitivity syndrome (AIS), in which cells throughout
the body of an XY child fail to respond to androgens. The child thus
develops a female body shape and genitals. Prior to the discovery of a
test to determine chromosomal sex, such children were usually raised
as girls, though as adults they were infertile. Money's first intersexual
patient "had been reared as a boy after a sex reannouncement from female to male early in infancy on the advice of a wrongly informed
physician who had promised surgical and hormonal treatment in the
teenage years so as to allow the boy to become a man."

No such treatment was available, but when doctors informed the
seventeen-year-old seeking the promised treatment that he could instead live as a woman, "it was an option too alien for him to contem-
plate," says Money. This first experience with an intersexual person
led Money to recognize the possibility that the sex of the mind could be
at odds with the visible sex of the body. "It pointed clearly toward the
principle of a discontinuity between the development of the body,
from prenatal life through puberty, as feminized, and the development
of the mental life as masculinized, despite the restrictions imposed on
genital masculinity by anatomical and hormonal femininity."

After completing his doctoral dissertation at Harvard, "Hermaphroditism: An Inquiry into the Nature of a Human Paradox," Money
joined the staff of the Pediatric Endocrinology Clinic at Johns Hopkins Hospital. A protégé of Lawson Wilkins—often called the father
of pediatric endocrinology—Money was recruited by Wilkins to work
at Johns Hopkins as a psychoendocrinologist, a clinician/researcher
whose primary goal was to develop an understanding of the mental

and behavioral changes caused by treatment with hormones. At Johns Hopkins, Money's caseload of intersexual patients expanded to sixty. His psychological evaluations of these sixty patients convinced him to "abandon the unitary definition of sex as male or female," based on the commonly accepted criteria of either chromosomal or gonadal sex. Instead, he identified "five prenatally determined variables of sex that hermaphroditic data had shown could be independent of one another"—chromosomal sex, gonadal sex, internal and external morphologic sex, and hormonal sex—and "a sixth postnatal determinant, the sex of assignment and rearing."

To these six variables, Money added a seventh, one that had previously been absent from scientific and medical discussions of sex: gender role. "The term 'gender role' is used to signify all those things that a person says or does to disclose himself or herself as having the status of boy or man, girl or woman, respectively. It includes, but is not restricted to, sexuality in the sense of eroticism," Money writes in his first published paper on the topic at Jophns Hopkins. The term "gender role" was conceived "after several burnings of the midnight oil," says Money, and was originally "conceptualized jointly as private in imagery and ideation, and public in manifestation and expression." In *Gendermaps,* Money confesses that in defining gender role he "had in mind the example of an actor whose greatness derives from his becoming the character whose role he plays on stage." In the same way, he says, gender role "belongs to the self, within, and concurrently manifests itself to others, without."

A few months after the publication of that first paper in the *Bulletin of the Johns Hopkins Hospital,* Money published an expanded definition of gender role in "An Examination of Some Basic Sexual Concepts: The Evidence of Human Hermaphroditism," cowritten with Joan and John Hampson. In this more fully articulated definition, gender role has expanded to include "general mannerisms, deportment and demeanor; play preferences and recreational interests; spontaneous topics of talk in unprompted conversation and casual comment; content of dreams, daydreams and fantasies; replies to oblique inquiries and projective tests; evidence of erotic practices, and finally, the person's own reply to direct inquiry." More significantly, in this paper Money and the Hampsons first attempt to establish which of the other six variables is *most* significant in establishing gender role in intersexual patients, and produce an answer that was not only to profoundly alter the medical treatment of intersexual children, but also to sever the link between biological sex (as manifested in chromosomes, gonads, and external anatomy) and the newly developed concept of gender role.

Money and the Hampsons based their findings on seventy-six intersexual patients treated at Johns Hopkins over a period of four years. They state early in the paper that the study's primary purpose is to explore the hypothesis first presented by Freud at the turn of the century—that human beings are innately bisexual, "that instinctive masculinity and instinctive femininity are present in all members of the human species, but in different proportions." Bisexuality in Freud's theory is a biological concept, not a description of a person's sexual orientation; it is an "innate and constitutional psychic bisexuality," the presence of both male and female elements in each person, irrespective of reproductive anatomy. Money and the Hampsons chose to study intersexual people in order to "ascertain if new and additional information relevant to the psychologic theory of sexuality might be obtained." From the very start they assumed that data obtained from intersexual people could be used to explain the process of gender differentiation in all people. A fatal assumption, some would later argue.

The 1955 paper describes patients with a variety of clinical conditions, from "true hermaphrodites" who possess both testicular and ovarian tissue to various forms of "simulant" males and females whose external genitalia are somehow at odds with either their chromosomal or their gonadal sex, or who have ambiguous genitals. In each case, the researchers compare the sex of rearing with the other six variables to determine the weight of each in determining the person's gender role. In each case, they find that the influence of the sex of assignment and rearing trumped the competing variable.

Of the twenty patients whose gonadal sex (ovaries or testicles) conflicted with their sex of assignment and rearing, only three rejected the sex they had been assigned at birth. Of the twenty-seven people whose hormonal functioning and secondary sexual body morphology (breasts, body hair, body shape) were at odds with their sex of assignment and rearing, only four displayed ambivalence or anxiety about their assigned gender role. Twenty-three of the seventy-six patients had lived for more than two-thirds of their lives with an obvious difference between the appearance of their genitals and their assigned sex (girls with penises; boys with vaginas). In all but one instance, according to Money and the Hampsons, they had accepted the gender role assigned to them at birth.

The life experiences of this last group appeared to make a great impression on the researchers, one that produced a marked difference in the language used to describe them. Money, the primary author of the paper, uses subjective emotional language to describe the travails of the subjects with ambiguous genitalia. He writes, "there was considerable evidence that visible genital anomalies occasioned much anguish and distress. Distress was greatest in those patients whose external genital morphology flagrantly contradicted, without hope of surgical correction, their gender role and orientation as boy or girl, man or woman. Distress was also quite marked in patients who had been left in perplexed conclusion about the sex to which they belonged, in consequence either of personal or medical indecision, or of insinuations from age-mates that they were half-boy, half-girl. Uniformly, the patients were psychologically benefited by corrective plastic surgery, when it was possible, to rehabilitate them in the sex of assignment and rearing."

Contained in this single paragraph are the seeds of the two most significant outcomes of Money's research: first, the promotion of corrective surgery for intersexual persons, to normalize their genitalia and to save them from that "perplexed conclusion about the sex to which they belonged"; second, the support of sex-reassignment surgery for people whose "external genital morphology flagrantly contradicted . . . their gender role and orientation as boy or girl, man or woman." Add to that the paper's conclusion—that "the sex of assignment and rearing was better than any other variable as a prognosticator of the gender role and orientation established by the patients in this group"—and one sees a virtual blueprint for Money's future career.

Throughout the next forty years, Money would continue to promote these themes in book after book, lecture after lecture. He insisted that "a person could not be an it"—neither male nor female, nor both male and female—and that psychosexual well-being was dependent on developing a core sense of oneself as either a man or a woman. He declared that an individual's sense of being either male or female was heavily influenced by the way that one was perceived and treated by parents and other close family members in the first two years of life, and that the behavior of parents was in turn heavily influenced by the external genitalia of their newborn. Any ambiguity in the appearance of the child's genitals creates doubt in the minds of the parents about their child's sex, Money said, which is then transmitted to the child like a virus, poisoning his or her life with uncertainty. He avowed that gender role "becomes not only established but also indelibly imprinted" by around eighteen months, and that by the age of two and a half years, gender role is "well-established and inviolable."

Using a metaphor that was to appear regularly in articles and books published throughout his career, in the 1955 paper Money compared the establishment of gender role "through encounters and transactions" with other people to the acquisition of one's native language. "Once imprinted, a person's native language may fall into disuse and be supplanted by another, but is never entirely eradicated. So also a gender role may be changed, or resembling native bilingualism, may be ambiguous, but it may also become so indelibly engraved that not even flagrant contradictions of body functioning and morphology may displace it."

By the time that Money and the Hampsons published their next paper, "Imprinting and the Establishment of Gender Role," in the prestigious *Archives of Neurology and Psychiatry*, they not only had established the crucial importance of the sex of assignment and rearing but also had begun to promote the recommendations that were to have such a profound impact on the lives of intersexual persons. A decision as to the sex of assignment and rearing of an intersexual infant must be made as soon as possible after birth, with "uncompromising adherence to the decision" throughout the child's life, they said. Moreover, the deciding factor in that crucial decision made in the first weeks of the child's life should be "the morphology of the external genitals and the ease with which these organs can be surgically reconstructed to be consistent with the assigned sex." No matter the gonadal or chromosomal sex of the child, the appearance of the child's genitals and their amenability to surgical manipulation become the key issue in determining sex. Finally, "the earlier the surgical reconstruction of the genitals is done, the better."

Surgery thus became the solution to the riddle of gender.

As the theories of John Money and his colleagues became increasingly influential, their views on the need for surgical intervention for intersexual children became standard practice. Those views are neatly summarized by Money himself in the second edition of his text *Sex Errors of the Body and Related Syndromes*: "Before contemporary medical interventions, many children born with a birth defect of the sex organs were condemned to grow up as they were born, stigmatized and traumatized. It simply does not make sense to talk of a third sex, or of a fourth or fifth, when the phylogenetic scheme of things is two sexes. Those who are genitally neither male nor female but incomplete are not a third sex. They are a mixed sex or an in-between sex. To advocate medical nonintervention is irresponsible. It runs counter to everything this book stands for, which is to enhance health and well-being to the greatest extent possible."

"Enhancing the health and well-being" of intersexual infants and children required a wide range of surgical and hormonal manipulations, all focused on transforming anomalous genitals into the standard model. Clitorises larger than the norm and penises smaller than one inch were amputated, so that the genitals could be shaped to look more like average male and female genitals. Testicles and ovaries were removed so that they would not secrete at puberty masculinizing or feminizing hormones at odds with the assigned sex. Adolescents were dispensed synthetic hormones (usually estrogen) to promote the development of a secondary sexual morphology to match their assigned sex. The bodies of intersexual children became a map, says historian Susan Stryker, on which was inscribed the cold war view of sex—you are on one side or the other. "I think that many other binaries were structured by that binary," says Stryker. "Material conditions do affect ideology, not in a strictly Marxian way, but they're not unrelated, however complexly related they are."

John Money's views on the need for surgical reconstruction for intersexual infants were to remain virtually unchallenged for decades. Though the goal of such surgery was ostensibly to maximize health and well-being, when intersexual people themselves began to speak out about the effects of these surgeries on their physical and emotional well-being, their testimony directly contradicted that of the psychologists and surgeons who had instituted the neonatal intersex protocol. In contrast with the "health and well-being" predicted by Money, intersexual patients suffered physical pain and scarring from repeated genital surgeries, and emotional torment as the secret of their births was withheld from them by parents trying desperately to adhere to the facade of normalcy. Very few genital anomalies were "fixed" by a single surgery in the weeks after birth; instead, intersexual children often endured repeated surgeries and doctor visits focused on their genitals throughout childhood—often without any explanation by their parents or the physician about the nature of their problem. The secrecy created a deeply rooted feeling of shame and isolation, akin to that suffered by victims of childhood sexual abuse. Like sexual abuse victims, intersexual children suffered from an excess of adult interest in their genitals, and their privacy and bodily integrity were violated systematically by various health care providers over the years of "treatment."

In 1993, Cheryl Chase founded the Intersex Society of North America (ISNA), a support and advocacy group, which began to break down the walls of "shame and secrecy" that had imprisoned intersexual people, ending their isolation. At the first weekend retreat of ISNA, participants spoke eloquently of their rage and pain, and their videotaped conversation was distributed by ISNA under the title *Hermaphrodites Speak!* On the tape, participants lash out at both physicians and parents who, attempting to follow the advice that they "uncompromisingly adhere" to the sex of assignment, had concealed from the patients their medical diagnoses and histories—even when surgeries and follow-up surgeries were performed in childhood, not infancy.

"I remember them removing my penis when I was five—oh, I'm sorry," one participant says mockingly, "reducing it to the size of a normal clitoris." The participant was diagnosed at birth as a "pseudo-hermaphrodite whose testes hadn't developed properly, giving me ambiguous genitalia," and the child's parents were told instead that their baby was a girl whose ovaries hadn't developed properly. "Basically, they [the doctors] lied to my parents, coercing them into letting the doctors perform plastic surgery, and giving me female hormones at puberty." Unlike many intersexual persons, this patient received counseling, which was, she says "more like brainwashing sessions in which they tried to convince me that I was a normal little girl."

Another participant says, "I was always led to believe that I was male. No one ever spoke to me at all about my state or condition," even though it was clear that his penis was not at all like those of other boys. "I did have genital surgery" in childhood, he says, "though it was not called that." Another participant recalled that his own surgery, for hypospadias (incompletely differentiated penis), was presented to him as a hernia operation. "For such a long time, I knew there wasn't something quite right, but it took me quite a while to figure out what it was," he says. Born with "a too small penis with a hole somewhere near the end and a femininized scrotal sac," he says, "I wish people would have just stopped 'helping' me. Why do they insist on 'fixing' things?"

"Hopkins is where all this comes from," says one participant bitterly.

In 2002, I sought out Dr. Paul McHugh, chair of the department of psychiatry at Johns Hopkins from 1975 to 2001—after John Money had repeatedly refused to speak with me, pleading old age and illness. McHugh frankly admitted that mistakes had been made. "We're now seeing plenty of people who are saying, 'Gee, why didn't you just let me alone,'" he says, adding that in his opinion, "the best thing to do at that time would have been to let these kids grow up and see, to decide themselves"—precisely the point made by intersex activists. He is nonetheless quick to point out that "Dr. Money didn't do this out of evil. He was trying to think about what would be the best [for the patients]. But we didn't know enough—even though by that time the organizing force of prenatal hormones on the brain and on sexual behavior was well known in the animal literature, well established. Therefore, in my opinion, we should have held back."

Dr. Ben Barres, the Stanford neurologist, proposed a different interpretation in our talk, one that acknowledges both the pioneering nature of Money's intersex research and its limitations. "Money had an idea, a real hypothesis. He studied these issues and asked questions about them, and that's the way that science gets done. You ask a good question, then you propose a good hypothesis, and then you test the hypothesis. Money did that. And that was pioneering on his part, and I think that he deserves an enormous amount of credit. Unfortunately, the problems begin in the way that he collected his data and designed his studies, and it ended up being an anecdotal report. I think the big moral of the story, as Simon LeVay has said, is that one should be careful about anecdotal evidence."

The distinction that Barres draws between anecdotal evidence and hard data is an important one in science and medicine. It's the difference between story and statistics, between my telling you that an herb has alleviated my depression and a clinical trial with 1,400 patients showing that a placebo is just as effective as the herb 90 percent of the time. Most scientists greatly mistrust anecdotal evidence. Until anecdotal evidence is rigorously challenged by laboratory experiment or in a large clinical trial, it remains closer to myth than to fact. The puzzling thing about the intersex research that John Money and the Hampsons conducted in the 1950s is that anecdotal evidence based on a relatively small sample was quickly accepted and assimilated by physicians despite the paucity of hard data supporting their sweeping assertions. As Ben Barres asks, "How could so many physicians, intelligent physicians, base so much treatment on one case study?"

By way of contrast, Paul McHugh points to research being conducted today by William G. Reiner, a pediatric urologist who advises a reexamination of the practice of sex reassignment of intersexual children. Reiner, says McHugh, is "a wonderful pediatric urologist and he's catching a lot of heat from people within the medical profession who have these very strong feelings about what should be done and why. But all he's trying to do is collect data, and that's what should have been done years and years ago." In a 1999 paper, Reiner indicates that his data show "that with time and age, children may well know what their gender is, regardless of any and all information and child-rearing to the contrary. They seem to be quite capable of telling us who they are, and we can observe how they act and function even before they tell us."

"This guy is terrific," says Ben Barres. "He's getting some papers in the journals. He feels very strongly, based on his research, that to operate on intersexual people before they can tell you is a tremendous mistake. And this is based on hard data." Regretting that research like Reiner's was not being conducted forty years ago, when the neonatal intersex protocol was being developed, Paul McHugh says that "maybe if all that kind of data had been collected, we would have known better. We would have our feet more firmly on the ground."

Scientific hindsight is, of course, not very comforting to intersexual people who have suffered a lifetime of physical and emotional pain as a result of the recommendations that began flowing from Johns Hopkins in the fifties. However, in one of those painful paradoxes that often characterize biomedical research, the same theory that created agony for the intersexual has helped make surgical and hormonal treatment for transsexual people more accessible. Although the surgical reconstruction of the anomalous genitals of intersexual children was becoming standard practice in 1965, the sex reassignment of genitally normal adults was still taboo. Christine Jorgensen was not the only American who sought what was then called "sex-change" surgery in the fifties and sixties—far from it. As previously noted, Harry Benjamin alone saw more than 1,500 patients from 1953 until his retirement in 1978; no doubt thousands more were unable to find the help they sought, or were inhibited by shame from seeking help at all. Well-informed, well-connected, affluent people were able to travel overseas for medical assistance, but many who sought counseling, hormones, or surgery in the United States were turned away or, worse, subject to various forms of "aversion therapy." *My Unique Change* by Hedy Jo Star, published in 1965, attests to the enormous difficulties and challenges faced by transsexual people in this era, and testifies to the great strength of will and determination that were necessary to pursue a "sex change."

Like Christine Jorgensen and Aleshia Brevard, Hedy Jo Star, born Carl Hammonds in 1920, felt like a girl from a young age—but in Star's case these feelings were reinforced by physical changes at puberty, including gynecomastia, or breast development. "Besides the rounding out of my hips and the slenderness of my legs (when I got into a gym uniform the boys would whistle and say, 'Ain't she sweet'), I noticed that my breasts were filling out. At first this didn't surprise me, because I assumed that this happened to everyone. But when I saw that this didn't happen to other boys, I was convinced that I was different from them physically as well as emotionally," Star writes.

The teenager's budding breasts were noticed by his mother, who took her child to a number of doctors, including a "brain specialist" who suggested "an exploratory operation to see if I had female sexual organs." Though Mrs. Hammonds refused to consent to the surgery for fear of complications, the response of the physicians "proved to my mother that beyond a doubt I was half-man and half-woman," Hedy Jo Star writes in her autobiography. "They proved her suspicions that my 'sissiness' was really inborn femininity." The doctor's prognosis was discouraging to Mrs. Hammonds, though she concealed this fact from her child. Years later, Mrs. Hammonds confessed to Star that "a couple of the doctors who examined me said that I would probably not live past thirty-five because of my dual sexual nature. One doctor told her that even if I did live a normal life span, I would probably go insane."

Instead, Carl Hammonds ran away at seventeen to join a carnival freak show. Dragged back home by his disgusted father, the unhappy teen ran away again and found work as an exotic dancer in carnivals. Living and working as a woman, Hammonds took the name Hedy Jo Star, and by age twenty-four she owned and performed in a traveling burlesque show called *The French Follies*. "The first couple of years on the road I worked harder than I had ever done before. I painted the scenery for the show, created the dances, trained the girls, made their costumes, and even was the show's barker," Star writes in her autobiography. "By the end of two years the show had earned enough money so that I owned my own tent, costumes, scenery, truck, car and a house trailer. I was proud of my achievement." Despite her business success, Star had one overwhelming problem. She might look like a woman and feel like a woman, but she was not a woman beneath her g-string. Despite her great legs, her rounded hips, and the small breasts that she enhanced with falsies onstage, Star had the genitals of a man—and those genitals were a source of torment to the dancer and to the men who fell in love with her. When it came time to reveal her secret to various lovers, Hedy Jo began the difficult conversation by telling them that she was a "morphidite"—a hermaphrodite or intersexual person—before revealing the truth: that she had a penis, but no vagina. Star's anatomy failed to intimidate her great love, a fellow carny named Red, and the two lived together for over six years. But eventually the relationship began to fall apart, and Hedy Jo placed the blame on her genitals. "Red was a normal man with a normal sexual desire, and I was a physically abnormal woman with emotionally normal wants. I had the sex organs of a man but the sexual feelings of a woman. I knew I could never be fulfilled the way I was, nor could I possibly fulfill a man sexually. If I was ever to be happy, I had to be a woman completely."

In 1956 Star traveled to New York to see a female endocrinologist, who performed physical and hormone tests that led the physician to conclude that despite her male genitalia, Hedy Jo Star was female—and to recommend sex-change surgery. The physician, whose name Star does not reveal in her autobiography, brought in a number of other specialists (also unnamed) to examine her unhappy patient. "My face was covered during the examination with a sheet. Then my doctor and her colleagues examined me. Later my doctor explained to me that what she was planning to do was illegal under New York law, which is the reason the other specialists she consulted wished to remain anonymous. It was all right, she said, for a doctor to straighten a cripple's twisted limbs, but not all right to straighten a sexual cripple."

Star's endocrinologist explained that "there wasn't a single hospital in New York who would take the case." Her disappointment was somewhat assuaged by the intermediate steps the doctor suggested—administration of estrogen and breast-enhancement surgery. "I was disappointed that I couldn't have the operation immediately but at least I knew I was heading in the right direction. I knew that eventually I would have the change and that was all that really mattered." But more disappointments were to follow for Star. Despite the feminizing effects of the hormones, and the testimony of twelve physicians in favor of sex-change surgery for her, the New York State Medical Society refused to grant permission for the surgery a year later. The decision of the society was based not on medical or scientific criteria, but on a fear of legal action. In New York State, as in almost every other civic jurisdiction in the United States, it was illegal to surgically remove a man's testicles.

These "mayhem" statutes, imported from English common law dating from the sixteenth century, forbade the amputation of any body part (fingers, toes, hands, or feet) that might prevent a male-bodied individual from being able to serve as a soldier. Although castration might not, strictly speaking, fall under the jurisdiction of the law, few American surgeons were willing to risk prosecution by becoming test cases. Christine Jorgensen circumvented the law by traveling to Denmark, where she had family and friends and knew the language. Hedy Jo Star had neither the money nor the connections to make such a trip possible. In the fifties and early sixties, mayhem statutes were the single greatest obstacle faced by every transsexual person in America unable to travel overseas for surgery or locate one of the few surgeons willing to flout the law by performing surgery in the United States.

On the advice of her endocrinologist, Star tried another route. In November 1958, she took a train to Baltimore and presented herself to the researchers at the Johns Hopkins Hospital who were becoming famous in medical circles for their work with intersexual children. Star was hopeful that they would be able to help her, too. "The hormone shots had done wonders. My testicles had all but disappeared. My penis had shrunk considerably. My physique was completely female. How could they refuse me?"

Star's efforts to convince the Hopkins researchers that she was intersexual, and thus a suitable candidate for corrective surgery, failed. After five days of examinations at the hospital, she was sent home to await a letter. The letter arrived, dated February 24, 1959. Its author (possibly Money, though the name is obscured in Star's autobiography) says that after he discussed Star's case with "Dr. Eugene Mayer, Dr. William Scott, Dr. Hampson, and Dr. Shaffer," the group's unanimous decision was to advise her "not to go ahead with the conversion type of surgery that you seek." The decision of the committee was based on both medical and legal considerations. "The studies that we have made would all indicate that your basic structure is anatomically male and that we would not be likely to find any evidence internally of ovaries or any female structures." The physicians feared that the narrowness of Star's pelvis would make the creation of a vagina difficult, and the possibility of postsurgical urinary difficulties might handicap her ability to make a living as a dancer.

"We do realize that you are psychologically more comfortable in your role as a female and perhaps it would be wise for you to continue as you have in the past," the letter continues sympathetically. "You deserve considerable credit for having been able to adjust as well as you have to some of the difficult situations that you have encountered in the past." Nonetheless the committee had decided that "there are numerous reasons from both your standpoint and from the standpoint of the surgeons involved that would suggest that the performance of this type of surgery might in actuality constitute mayhem and you must consider that possibility quite seriously before embarking on such a program."

Sympathetic or not, the letter was a heavy blow to Star, who objected to the physicians' paternalistic approach and their assumption that they knew better than she where her best interests lay. "I didn't feel any malice towards the doctors. After all, they were only doing what they considered best for me. But I was sure they were wrong. Not wrong as far as the possible medical consequences of the operation . . . rightly or wrongly, I felt their decision had been based more on 'moral,' psychological and legal reasons than medical reasons. Certainly there was a risk involved, but I felt that I should be the one to decide whether I wanted to take it or not. They were wrong to deny me this decision. But in denying it to me, they only increased my determination to do—somehow, somewhere—what I knew had to be done."

Star doggedly pursued her goal for the next four years, as her dancing career flourished and her romantic relationships continued to be sabotaged by the discrepancy between her gender and her anatomy. Eventually, she found her way to Harry Benjamin, who referred her to a "California surgeon" (most likely Elmer Belt) who could perform the surgery for about four thousand dollars. Estimating the costs of the surgery, hospital fees, travel expenses, and associated expenses at approximately six thousand dollars, Star began saving. Then, early in 1962, a friend referred her to a doctor in Chicago, who "examined me and told me immediately that he knew the man who could do the operation. Within a few minutes he had placed a call to a hospital in Memphis, Tennessee, and the appointment was made."

After this doctor and four of his colleagues examined her, the unnamed Memphis surgeon informed her that "the operation is extremely complex and, for that reason, dangerous. . . . If the operation is a success, it is possible that you might never dance again. It is also possible that you might never walk. Also, it is extremely doubtful that you will ever be able to have a sex life." As if that weren't enough, the surgeon added that Star might not survive the operation. Star's reply was simple. "Anything is better than living the misery I have lived my whole life. I realize it is a gamble, but the pot's too big not to take a crack at it."

The surgery was performed the next day. The initial operation took five hours. Nine days later, one of Star's doctors accidentally punctured her urinary tract during an examination, necessitating another two-hour operation to repair the damage. Forty-five days later she left the hospital, and entered her future as a woman. "Since the change and my adjustment to it, my life has flowered," she writes on the final pages of her autobiography. "Each day I discover something about my new self. Each day I gain even more confidence in myself, more interest in myself, and above all, more self-resect. Life has taken on a new look. It has become something to be enjoyed and lived, rather than a burden to make the best of."

Although Star was eventually able to locate a surgeon in the United States willing to perform sex-reassignment surgery despite the fear of mayhem laws, it is clear from her account of their meeting that her doctor was performing the surgery for the first time, and was far from confident about his ability to provide her with a functional vagina. Meanwhile, back in Baltimore, urologists and plastic surgeons at Johns Hopkins were perfecting their reconstructive techniques as they attempted to fulfill the evolving mandate to provide intersexual children and adults with "normal" genitals. John Money began to use his growing scientific reputation and the institutional power that it conferred to persuade his colleagues at Johns Hopkins that they ought to challenge the mayhem laws that prevented surgeons from "matching the body to the mind," as Harry Benjamin once wrote, and begin performing sex-reassignment surgery on adults.

By the early sixties, Money had met Benjamin and, as Money said at the latter's memorial in 1987, "he became my living link with early twentieth-century psychoendocrinology. He was my exemplar of the continuity of scholarly history—and of the dependence of my own scholarship on that of my professional forebears." Money shared yet another tie with Benjamin: like other pivotal figures in the mid-century study of gender variance, both were funded by a wealthy transsexual man named Reed Erickson. Like most early female-to-male transsexual persons, Erickson has remained largely invisible in popular accounts of transsexuality. Born Rita Alma Erickson in El Paso, Texas, in 1917, Erickson enjoyed a gregarious, colorful (some might say psychedelic) existence, marrying three times and fathering two children (by adoption). For the last twenty years of his life, he lived in Mazatlán, Mexico, at a house he called the Love Joy Palace, where he kept a pet leopard. Despite his hedonistic lifestyle, Erickson did more than almost any person other than Harry Benjamin to help create the medical model of transsexuality and to advance understanding of gender variance among the research community and the public.

Aaron Devor, professor of sociology at the University of Victoria and author of the book *FTM: Female-to-Male Transsexuals in Society,* has been researching Reed Erickson's life for several years. He became interested in Erickson as he worked on various books and research projects, and "the name of the Erickson Educational Foundation (EEF) came up from time to time," he says. "I'd hear from different people that the founder of EEF might be transsexual—sometimes I'd hear MTF, sometimes FTM." Characterizing these remarks as "gossip, rumor, enigmatic comments," Devor says that he didn't learn the truth until he was on sabbatical in California, in 1996, residing in a community for scholars doing LGBT research. "One of the fellows, who was also staying there at the time, Jim Kepner, lived down the hall, and Jim put out a little personal newsletter and in one of the newsletters he mentioned Reed Erickson of the EEF and he said that he was an FTM transsexual. At that time, I was aware that the EEF was important, though at that time I didn't know how important.

"I don't know all that much about Erickson's childhood," says Devor, aside from the fact that his mother was ethnically Jewish, but religiously a Christian Scientist, and that his father, Robert, owned a lead-smelting business. "In his early adulthood, Erickson lived as a lesbian, quite closeted as most were at that time. He was musical and played in his high school band. He—at that time she—had some secretarial training before studying engineering." By the time Robert B. Erickson died, in 1962, willing the lead-smelting business to his daughters, Rita Alma had graduated with a degree in mechanical engineering from Louisiana State University (the first woman to do so), worked as an engineer in Philadelphia, and founded a successful stadium bleacher–manufacturing company in Baton Rouge, Louisiana. The death of Robert B. Erickson made his children wealthy, Devor says, even more so when the company was sold to Arrow Electronics for millions of dollars a few years later. Reed Erickson eventually amassed a personal fortune estimated at over $40 million, and donated enormous sums of money to various causes over the years, through the Erickson Educational Foundation, which he established in 1964.

In 1963, Erickson began seeing Harry Benjamin, taking hormones under Benjamin's guidance, having already begun his life as a man. Benjamin was one of the first recipients of a grant from the EEF. This grant was to have far-reaching consequences, says Devor. "The EEF funded the Harry Benjamin Foundation from 1964 till 1968 for approximately $50,000 over those years. One of the activities that the money funded was bringing together a group of people working in the area to meet at Harry's offices in New York once a month—people like Richard Green and John Money. During the mid-sixties, there weren't a lot of people working on transsexuality; it was still a very hush-hush kind of subject. So bringing together this group of researchers produced a kind of synergy, and this synergy led to the founding of the Hopkins gender program. The thinking was, 'if we can do this kind of surgery for intersexual people, why not for transsexuals?'"

Reed Erickson himself did not experience tremendous difficulty transitioning, says Devor. Though he never underwent genital surgery, Erickson had a mastectomy in Mexico in the early sixties, and had some "touch-up work" on his chest in the United States, as well as a hysterectomy after becoming a patient of Harry Benjamin's. "There were doctors who would do this if you had the money, and Erickson had the money," Devor says. "Though it doesn't seem that Erickson had much trouble himself, I think he was very aware of the troubles that others were having. One of the first projects of the EEF was drawing up a list of helpful and sympathetic doctors and surgeons by city and region. EEF was started in '64 and this was one of their early projects. It was an ongoing project, and they were always adding new names to the list."

Erickson enjoyed a warm relationship with Money, whom he was also funding by that time. "They were quite close for a long time, enjoying lots of social interaction," says Devor. "They shared common interests. It was more than just a business relationship. . . . John Money was quite open and liberal and certainly not snobbish about socializing with transsexuals," he says. "I know they were friends, and of course Erickson was putting money into what Money was doing."

Erickson donated nearly $85,000 to the Johns Hopkins Gender Identity Clinic over ten years, says Devor. "It has become quite clear to me that the money from the EEF was essential to the start-up of the Johns Hopkins clinic. Media reports from the time said that the clinic was entirely funded by the EEF." The importance of Erickson's support, and Money's gratitude toward his benefactor, can perhaps be judged by the fact that Erickson was invited to contribute the preface to *Transsexualism and Sex Reassignment,* edited by Richard Green and

John Money and published by the Johns Hopkins University Press in 1969. In the preface to that volume, Erickson testifies to the difficulty that transsexual people had in finding physicians who understood their condition and surgeons both competent and willing to carry out the surgery. "Although here and there an occasional doctor or clinic performed sex-change operations—sometimes successfully, sometimes not—it was only after The Johns Hopkins Hospital provided its facilities and publicized its work that sex-conversion operations began to be undertaken openly by hospitals of high reputation."

By all accounts, the opening of the Gender Identity Clinic at Johns Hopkins Hospital in 1966, and the decision to begin performing sex-reassignment surgery there, was largely brought about by Money, who argued, cajoled, and arm-twisted reluctant colleagues into translating the expertise they had acquired treating intersexual people into treating transsexuals. In the introduction to *Transsexualism and Sex Reassignment,* Harry Benjamin writes, "Dr. John Money, psychologist at Johns Hopkins, widely-known and respected for his extensive studies on hermaphroditism and related endocrinopathies and sexual disorders, was probably more responsible than any other individual for the decision that such an august institution as The Johns Hopkins Hospital would take up this controversial subject and actually endorse sex-altering surgery in suitable subjects. This decision testifies to the high esteem in which Dr. Money is held by his medical co-workers."

Even those who do not hold Money in high esteem—quite the opposite—acknowledge his role in bringing SRS to Johns Hopkins. John Colapinto, a journalist whose book *As Nature Made Him* portrays Money as a diabolical figure, twisted by arrogance and ambition, describes Money's "campaign to establish Johns Hopkins as the first hospital in America to embrace transexual surgeries" in detail. Colapinto quotes Howard W. Jones, the gynecological surgeon who had developed the surgical techniques used in the neonatal intersex protocol, as saying that "for a number of months, maybe even years, John kept raising the question of whether we shouldn't get into the transsexual situation." Colapinto reports that Money brought in Harry Benjamin and some of his patients to help convince Jones and Milton Edgerton, the pediatric surgeon, "that this was something that maybe should be done."

Paul McHugh, who was to close the Gender Identity Clinic at Hopkins shortly after he assumed the directorship of the department of psychiatry in 1975, confirmed in a 2002 interview that Money worked hard to persuade his colleagues to perform adult sex-reassignment surgery, in the face of considerable resistance. McHugh, who is adamantly opposed to sex-reassignment surgery, says that Money was "a powerful and never-ending advocate for transgendering as a real disorder, as a real thing." His success in promoting SRS at Hopkins in the face of considerable institutional resistance was based on his scientific reputation and the institutional power it conferred. "Dr. Money is a very gifted scientist and psychologist who did superb work, pioneering work here before he became all taken up with sex," says McHugh. "He did wonderful work on, for example, language disorders and reading disabilities and the psychological states of these individuals that had a variety of chromosomal abnormalities and the like. He did pioneering work in those areas." As a result, says McHugh, his colleagues at Johns Hopkins "admired him" and were willing to follow him into the turbulent waters of adult sex reassignment.

McHugh, who is both scientifically and socially conservative, an avowed foe of psychiatric "fads" such as multiple personality disorder and repressed memory syndrome, calls Money "a victim of the sixties" whose views on the plasticity of gender were as much based in his politics as his science. "It was a very left-wing kind of view that we are fundamentally produced by our environment, almost Lysenkoist," McHugh says. He characterizes Money's decision to extrapolate the data and theories on gender fluidity that he had formulated working with intersexual people to all people as "a big mistake. It was a mistake driven in part, as I said before, by politics and being avant-garde at the time." Money's ideas were readily accepted by the public and fellow researchers for the same reasons, McHugh believes, because they meshed with the gestalt of the times, which encouraged a questioning of orthodoxies. "His science brought him so far, was bringing him so far, and then, like so many other people, the theme of 'overthrow the patriarchy, make change, it's the authority structures that are standing in our way'—I think that John bought that, hook, line, and sinker, and as a result, like so many others, came to suffer from it."

The press release announcing the opening of the Johns Hopkins Gender Identity Clinic came a year after the actual inauguration of the clinic, when news about the clinic's work had begun to leak out. Money says in *Gendermaps* that though the clinic had been "informally known as the sex change clinic," at "my instigation it had been formally named the Gender Identity Clinic, a name that should have broadened its scope beyond transexualism [*sic*] to the manifold issues of gender identity. The narrower meaning, however, would win the day. Gender identity disorder became inseparably linked with transexualism [*sic*]." The clinic was conceived as a research project, "a definitive study" of transsexualism. The press release quotes Dr. John Hoopes, chairman of the clinic's staff, saying, "This program, including the surgery, is investigational. The transexual [*sic*] has never previously been given adequate medical attention. The most important result of our efforts will be to determine precisely what constitutes a transexual [*sic*] and what makes him that way. Medicine needs a sound means of alleviating the problems of gender identification and of fostering public understanding of these unfortunate individuals. It is too early in the program to be either optimistic or pessimistic. We are still in the process of collecting accurate observations on the results of treatment." Hoopes also stated that the Erickson Educational Foundation "is the sole source of research support" for the clinic.

Conceived as a research project (and limited to interviewing two new patients a month), the clinic was viewed quite differently within the community of people seeking sex-reassignment surgery, and among physicians. The former viewed the clinic as a service provider and resented its parsimonious approach to patient care. Even before the opening of the clinic was formally announced, the staff had received more than a hundred letters requesting treatment. Many physicians, on the other hand, found even two "sex-change" patients a month too many. Paul McHugh, a young faculty member at New York Hospital at the time, says, "It looked like a fad to us, like following along with Jorgensen and all that." Nonetheless, the opening of the Gender Identity Clinic at Johns Hopkins was soon followed by the opening of similar research projects at other university hospitals, including Stanford and the University of Minnesota. Despite the generally positive media response to the hospital's decision to begin performing sex-reassignment surgery, many doctors and researchers continued to object to the practice—much to the sorrow of Harry Benjamin and the disdain of John Money. "The Johns Hopkins transsexual program was a source of immense satisfaction to Harry Benjamin, for it vindicated and authenticated his otherwise lonely advocacy of a group of patients generally despised and ridiculed by the medical establishment," Money said at Benjamin's memorial service in 1987. "Conversely the public repudiation of this program by medical moralists who were not members of the gender-identity team was to him a source of immense sorrow. I knew about that sorrow from my periodic phone calls and occasional visits with Harry Benjamin."

Paul McHugh, who has himself been attacked by Money for "medical moralism," maintains that resistance to the practice never really died down at Johns Hopkins. Soon after he became chair of the department of psychiatry there in 1975, he told me in 2003, he became aware of the discontent of the surgeons who performed the surgeries, he says. "The surgeons were saying to me, 'Imagine what it's like to get up in the morning and come in and hack away at perfectly normal organs because you psychiatrists don't know what to do with these people.'" Though he denies that he was recruited by Johns Hopkins for the express purpose of shutting down the unit, it is clear that he has no regrets about that decision. "When I came here and saw the incoherence of the unit, it became clear to me that it wasn't serving a good purpose," he says. "I felt that we'd try to find good evidence for it or against it. The evidence that I found was against it. People weren't being made better, all of it was anecdotal, there were real problems as to what the nature of this condition was, and even the surgeons were weary of doing it." McHugh formally based his decision to close the clinic on an outcome study produced by Dr. Jon Meyer, the head of the Gender Identity Clinic at the time. The Meyer study, which was immediately attacked for its poor methodology and which has been refuted by subsequent outcome studies, "was adequate for what it was intended to do," McHugh says, "which was to show, to find out, whether these people were over their psychological problems. And it turned out that they were no more psychologically stable—stable in their employment or relationships—than they were [before surgery]."

The Meyer study, cowritten with Donna Reter, noted the generally positive (good or satisfactory) outcomes reported by other researchers but reached a different conclusion. "Sex reassignment surgery confers no objective advantage in terms of social rehabilitation, although it remains subjectively satisfying to those who have rigorously pursued a trial period and who have undergone it." Meyer and Reter based this conclusion on a comparison of fifteen patients who underwent surgery at Hopkins compared with thirty-five who had not completed the Hopkins program but who, in some cases, continued to pursue sex reassignment and later underwent surgery elsewhere. "While not a rigorous control group, they provided the only available approximation to it," Meyer and Reter note of the latter group.

"Social rehabilitation" of the two groups was compared using a number of socioeconomic indicators, including job and educational levels, psychiatric and arrest history, frequency of change of residence, and cohabitation with "gender-appropriate" or "gender-inappropriate" partners. A numerical value was assigned to each of these categories in the Adjustment Scoring System. "Most of the scoring is self-evident," Meyer and Reter note, though "if the patient is male requesting reassignment as female, a gender appropriate cohabitation or marriage means that he lives with or marries a man as a female; a non-gender appropriate situation would be one in which the patient, while requesting sex reassignment, nonetheless cohabitated or married as a man." Male-to-female transsexuals who had female roommates, girlfriends, or wives were thus assigned negative scores, while marriage to a "gender-appropriate" partner was scored +2, a marker of successful adjustment on a par with a rise in socioeconomic status.

Critics have noted that "the most serious problem with this scale is its arbitrary character . . . it assigns the same score (−1) to someone who is arrested as someone who cohabits with a non-gender appropriate person. From this same set of cryptic values comes the assertion that being arrested and jailed (–2) is not as bad as being admitted to a psychiatric hospital (–3) or that having a job as a plumber (Hollingshead level 4) is as good (+2) as being married to a member of the gender-appropriate sex (+2). On what basis are these values assigned?" The same authors note that "there is confusion on the variable of cohabitation, particularly since Meyer never specifies whether this implies seuxal intimacy, interpersonal sharing or both. One can infer from the scoring assignment that a transsexual would be better living with no one (0) than with a person of the non-gender appropriate sex (–1) . . . Does Meyer mean to say that living in isolation is more adaptive than living with someone whatever his/her sex?"

Similarly, continued interaction with therapists and psychiatrists after surgery is viewed as a negative (psychiatric contact = –1, outpatient treatment = –2, and hospitalization = –3), as is failing to improve one's socioeconomic status (as measured by the Hollingshead job scale). Meyer and Reter's "objective" values of adjustment seem exceedingly value-laden in retrospect. Moreover, their failure to include any measure of personal satisfaction or happiness in the Adjustment Scale has been almost universally criticized, especially since "none of the operated patients voiced regrets at reassignment, the operative loss of reproductive organs, or substitution of opposite sex facsimiles (except one, previously noted)," as Meyer and Reter acknowledge. In other words, despite their unchanged socioeconomic status, continued tendency to change jobs and residences, and generally insecure and unsettled lives, those who underwent sex-reassignment surgery at the Johns Hopkins clinic appeared nearly universally happy with the results.

Ben Barres, the Stanford neurobiologist who transitioned in his early forties after a lifetime of gender dysphoria, confirms the importance of including affective data in any study attempting to assess the success of sex-reassignment surgery. "I've never met a transsexual who wasn't enormously psychically better [after the surgery]," Barres says. "And the studies I've read say that something like 95 percent are very happy that they did it. And in medicine, you don't usually find that kind of success rate. That's unheard of, to find a treatment that has a 95 percent success rate. So it seems to me that the actual facts are totally opposite to what this guy [Meyer] said."

The feelings of happiness and contentment expressed by postoperative transsexuals are irrelevant in the view of Paul McHugh, who closed the Johns Hopkins clinic after the Meyer study. "Maybe it matters to them, but it doesn't matter to us as psychiatrists. We're not happy doctors. We're not out there saying, 'What do you think would make you happy? Would you like a third arm?' That's not what we are," he says. "The best will in the world would be to say, 'These people have psychological problems that are dependent on the fact that they are fixed in the wrong body, and their psychological problems will melt away if we treat this. If we do this, it will make them better.' But we found that they were no better! So we thought, 'Maybe we're just masquerading here. We'd like to think that they are better and they aren't.'" McHugh dismisses sex-change surgery and the misery that drives it as "a craze" that started in the sixties and has been gathering steam ever since. "Crazes are crazes," he says. "They build up, and they build up in a particular kind of way. We've been sold a bill of goods, and vulnerable people are picking this up and running with it. And it will continue to be a craze for a while as they support one another and as our communication systems, for example the Internet, promote it."

McHugh's perspective is anathema to most transgendered people, and yet one can find support for certain elements of his critique in the literature of the community itself. In her memoir, *The Man-Made Doll*, for example, author Patricia Morgan tells a harrowing tale of prostitution, rape, and abuse—both before and after her surgery with Elmer Belt in the seventies—and of the way that sex-reassignment surgery became popular among the crowd of gay and transgendered prostitutes with whom she worked the streets. Morgan says that despite her struggles she was able to make the transition to "straight" life because she had a realistic view of what to expect. Others were not so fortunate, she claims. "There are far too many fags and TVs [transvestites] around today who think that sex-change surgery is the answer to all their problems," Morgan writes.

For most of them, it merely means trading one set of problems for another. They've lived so long in the underworld of fags and TVs, of pimps and prostitutes, that they're not equipped to cope with the everyday world. They have no idea of what "straight" society is like. To them, it's a fantasy land, like a child's conception of the grown-up world. Many of those who go through sex-change surgery think they'll wind up as sex symbols, love goddesses, movie stars. They think they'll be transformed overnight into dazzling creatures who'll sweep men off their feet and have millionaires clamoring to set them up in penthouses. It's quite a comedown for someone who has such illusions to find out she's just another broad—and not necessarily a very good-looking one—and that she still has to hustle to make a living.

Morgan also has sharp words for the underground surgeons who were beginning to offer sex-change surgery on demand. "A dozen years ago, when I had my operation, it was a rare thing. Now sex-change surgery has become as common as blue jeans, and many people are getting it who shouldn't," she charges. "For this I blame the doctors. Once I thought highly of doctors who did sex-change surgery. I regarded them as saviors of souls. Now I realize that they're rip-off artists just like everyone else. . . . Very few of them send their patients to psychiatric counseling to find out if they'll be able to function as women." Bluntly, she lists the challenges that confronted transwomen after reassignment in that era. "The girl who had sex-change surgery gets rejected by her family. She isn't able to hold a job. Most don't have experience or education. Some have legal problems, because their papers still list them as men. Others get fired when their bosses find out. She can't live the life of a normal woman. A man might fall for her, but when he finds out what she is, he says goodbye."

Patricia Morgan's assessment is couched in the tough talk of the streets, not the formal language of academia, but she reaches a conclusion similar to that of Jon Meyer's infamous study. Far from solving their problems, sex reassignment created a whole new set of problems for some troubled individuals, challenges that overwhelmed their fragile coping mechanisms. "Three of the sex-changes I've known are now dead—either from suicide or from overdoses of drugs," says Morgan. "And I've heard stories of about twenty others who've wound up the same way. . . . I might have wound up the same way myself, but as I said, I've been lucky." By the end of the book, Morgan has left prostitution and is living on an income generated by her purchase of real estate, funded by an older gentleman who loves and supports her.

The difficulty of distinguishing those individuals who might benefit from sex-reassignment surgery from those who would be crushed under the weight of postsurgical adjustment problems was a major preoccupation of the university researchers. They sought to define characteristics in prospective clients that might predict success in postsurgical life. For this reason, the university clinics have been lambasted by members of the trans community for creating a myth of the "classic" male-to-female transsexual. A classic transsexual was essentially a traditional woman who happened to have been born in a male body. She was attractive, with feminine mannerisms and a feminine outlook, and had felt like a girl all of her life. She was, above all, heterosexual and desired marriage and, when possible, children by adoption or stepparenting. "Back in those days, they used to say that you had to be hyper-feminine to transition, and I'd say, 'This isn't me. So maybe I'm not transsexual,'" says Dr. Dana Beyer, who transitioned in 2003 at the age of fifty-one. "If the only true transsexuals are Jayne Mansfield types, how the hell am I ever going to meet the criteria?"

Members of the trans community, with their sophisticated pre-Internet communications network, quickly sussed out the conservative criteria that the clinics were using to choose candidates for surgery. In a self-fulfilling prophecy that would be comic if it weren't so tragic, candidates for sex-reassignment thus began presenting themselves to researchers as demure heterosexuals who wanted nothing more than a good man and a stable home, with lots of delightful children running around. In fact, many MTFs were attracted to women both before and after sex reassignment, but were careful to keep this fact hidden, knowing that it would destroy their chances of being accepted for surgery.

The university researchers began to sense the deception and to probe deeper, eventually discovering that many of their patients weren't exactly the transsexual June Cleavers of their intake interviews. "They all claim that they are the same, but I don't believe that they are," Paul McHugh says today. "Most of them, the beginning ones, the ones that we were seeing here at Hopkins, were all men wanting to be women. And it was obvious that they weren't women. They were caricatures of women. They had ideas in their mind about what it meant to be a woman, and you brought a woman into the room to talk to them and the woman quickly got the idea, 'That's no woman!' Secondly, many of them would say, 'I am a woman in a man's body, but I'm a lesbian.' That's crazy," McHugh exclaims with some heat. "That's a long way around for a guy to get a girl. That's just nuts," he says.

Echoing the conservative view of gender roles and sexual orientation that guided the decisions of the Johns Hopkins Gender Identity Clinic, and eventually led to its closure, McHugh says, "Look, in this situation, the issue for the person who is making the claim is to prove to you that they really are a woman. When they start saying that they are lesbians, that should increase your level of doubt. Then they have no maternal feelings—none, zip! I think that maternal feelings are a common quality of women. Do you think that the only thing it takes to be a woman is genitalia? No. There is a psychology to womanhood. We've just touched on two elements of that psychology which many of these guys coming to be women don't have."

Admitting that some genetic women, socialized as women throughout their lives, also lack maternal feeling and also desire other women, McHugh nonetheless maintains that the population of transsexual women ought to reflect statistically the same prevalence of maternal feeling and heterosexuality as natal women. "It's our job as doctors to look at this issue closely when somebody says, 'I'm a woman in a man's body.' And when you look closely, these are the things that pop out immediately. These are not the subtle things about womanhood that women can pick out, but these are the things that anybody, common sense, would say 'This person says that he's a woman, but he's a lesbian.' Gee, you know, guys like women more than women like women. Secondly—geez, you know, where's the feeling for children, maternal feelings? It's zero here."

Operating with this set of assumptions, McHugh and the researchers who shared them began to view the transsexual people who presented themselves at the Johns Hopkins Gender Identity Clinic with distaste. Clearly, using their criteria, these individuals were not women. Many of them were, in Paul McHugh's view, "aging transvestites—the kind of people who had been going to Victoria's Secret since they were twelve years old. And Johns Hopkins is not a branch of Victoria's Secret!" McHugh characterizes Money's early advocacy of transsexuals as an ideology. "It's still an ideology," he says. " 'I believe in transsexuals, and I believe this is what they should be able to do.' It was an ideology. It was not psychiatry and it was not medicine and it was not science."

However, the research that might have made the study of gender variance something more substantial than an "ideology" came to an abrupt end when the Johns Hopkins clinic closed in 1979 and most of the other university clinics followed suit. "One of the things that I think was so tragic about SRS being forced off of medical school campuses is that it meant that almost all good research came to an abrupt end. That to me is a tragedy because there's just so much research crying out to be done," says Ben Barres of Stanford. At Johns Hopkins, research on gender variance took a conservative turn after the closing of the Gender Identity Clinic, one that denies the medical legitimacy of the condition that Harry Benjamin and John Money sought to define. "Our clinic is still looking at these patients; we still try to help them," Paul McHugh says. "We tell them that we're not going to do this surgery on them, because it's not right. We don't tell them to stop going to Victoria's Secret. It's up to them. But we tell them that they are not correct and that science doesn't bear them out and their psychology doesn't bear them out."

Transsexual people themselves rue the changes at Hopkins set in place by McHugh. "Hopkins's cachet with transsexual people desperately seeking services remained, so since 1979 those poor patients who didn't know any better were seen at Hopkins's Sexual Behaviors Consultation Unit (SBCU), which continued to do research on them but made them pay $150 per visit for that privilege," says Jessica Xavier, a local activist who in 2000 carried out a needs-assessment survey on transgender health care in the District of Columbia. "They also stopped referrals for sex-reassignment surgery, which McHugh was

quoted as calling 'psychosurgery' and hoped would go the way of pre-
frontal lobotomies. If seen at the SBCU, a transsexual patient would be
fortunate indeed to get referred for endocrinology."

According to Paul McHugh, the incorporation of the diagnosis of
transsexuality and later "gender identity disorder" in the *Diagnostic and Statistical Manual* has only "sustained the misdirection" put
in place by John Money and other researchers. "People were being
harmed, subjected to a ferocious surgery and being encouraged in an
overvalued idea that doesn't for most of them make sense," McHugh
maintains. "Fundamentally at the root of all this is an idea that is
shared by other people in the environment, that is, by other people like
Dr. Money, for example—the idea that sex is socially assigned and that
it could be changed. These individuals take that idea up and it becomes
a ruling passion for them. They don't think about anything else and it
becomes a part of what they call their identity. They have talked themselves into this just like other people have talked themselves into the
idea that they are not thin enough."

McHugh is nonetheless willing to concede that researchers may
someday find a biological explanation for at least some forms of gender variance. "If people are afflicted in fetal life by an abnormal hormonal thing, they can have all kinds of peculiar sexual attitudes when
they come out," he admits. But he is quick to distinguish between individuals who can prove that they were subject to "an abnormal hormonal thing" in prenatal life from those who, for whatever reason,
choose to dress and live as members of a sex other than that dictated by
their anatomy. And he remains adamantly opposed to any form of surgical intervention for the latter group. "This surgery is serious surgery
and it's a misuse of resources when I don't think that the problem lies
in the bodily structure."

Despite the controversy surrounding sex-change surgery and his
ongoing battle with adversaries within Johns Hopkins and without,
John Money was continuously funded by the National Institutes of
Health for more than thirty-five years, from the start of his career to its
ignominious end. In June 1997, Milton Diamond and Keith Sigmundson published an article in the *Archives of Pediatrics and Adolescent
Medicine* that cast doubt not only on Money's theories but also on his

credibility as a researcher. Sigmundson had for many years overseen the care of Money's most famous patient, a twin boy named David Reimer, who had been raised as a girl after his penis was accidentally severed during a circumcision. Money had long used this case (identi- fied as "John/Joan" in the Diamond article) as proof that the sex of as- signment and rearing trumped all other variables in the formation of gender identity in normatively sexed, as well as intersexual, children. Despite her XY genotype and male genital and endocrine profile at birth, "Joan" was a normal little girl, Money asserted in scientific articles, books, lectures, and interviews, who "preferred dresses to pants, enjoyed wearing her hair ribbons, bracelets and frilly blouses, and loved being her Daddy's little sweetheart." Sigmundson, who had witnessed firsthand the acute misery suffered by the child and his fam- ily as the boy's masculinity asserted itself in the face of repeated efforts to convince him that he was a girl, had been contacted by Diamond, who sought information about the child for many years.

As early as 1959, Diamond had challenged Money's view that the sex of assignment and rearing was the key to the formation of gender identity. Working in the laboratory of William C. Young at the Uni- versity of Kansas as a graduate student, Diamond had participated in animal experiments that showed the awesome power of hormones on developing fetuses. Female guinea pigs treated with massive doses of testosterone in utero were masculinized, not just in anatomy but in be- havior. "There was lots of older literature that clued us in so that this [data] wasn't coming out of the blue," Diamond told me in a 2003 in- terview, referring to the "chickens, the famous chickens" hormonally manipulated by Berthold in 1849. "But people weren't applying it to humans. Those were birds. This was the work that showed it could happen to mammals. That you could take a mammal, treat it in utero for a limited period of time, don't touch that animal until it's an adult, and then lo and behold it acts like a male." Subsequent experiments by the researcher Roger Gorski and colleagues showed the same effects in female rats. "With rats, the critical period for that sort of brain differ- entiation is postnatally," Diamond says. "So Gorski and others were able to give it after birth—a single injection! And that's so remarkable to me. You give one injection, a single day, and you forever influence that individual's life."

Over the next thirty years, Diamond's animal experiments and work with human intersexual patients convinced him that human beings are not psychosexually neutral at birth, as Money had attempted to prove, but are psychosexually biased at birth, although social factors play an important role in how that biological predisposition is expressed. "I think that any behavior, whether it be sexual behavior, eating behavior or religious behavior, starts off with some sort of biological predisposition," he says. "Some behaviors are more biologically oriented than others but they are always influenced by social and cultural factors." Diamond, who prefers the terms "androphilic" and "gynecophilic" to "homosexual," says that a gay person who lives in a society where homosexuality is brutally suppressed, for example, will probably not act on his feelings. "If you are a homosexual in Saudi Arabia," he says, "you keep that to yourself. So that's why I say that there is a biological predisposition, and society decides how it gets manifested." In the case of David Reimer, the child (known as Brenda throughout his childhood) "was socially constrained from acting as the male that he wanted to be by his parents, Money, and others who said 'oh no, you are a girl.'"

Despite his early and repeated championing of the view that humans are not psychosexual blank slates at birth, Diamond found it difficult to gain a hearing until he and Sigmundson published the article that revealed that David Reimer had threatened suicide at age fourteen if he were not allowed to live as a male. His parents then told him the truth about his history, and he immediately began living as a male. By the time Diamond located Reimer's former psychiatrist, Keith Sigmundson, Reimer was married and the adoptive father of three children. His life story became the basis of a best-selling book, *As Nature Made Him: The Boy Who Was Raised as a Girl*, a book that understandably is narrated from the point of view of David Reimer and his family. John Money is depicted as a monstrous figure, an unsavory amalgam of evil scientist and sexual pervert, a voyeur in a white lab coat. The undeniable harm that was done to David Reimer is foregrounded, and Money's theories are presented as bizarre fantasies shorn of social and scientific context. Though it is rather unpopular these days to defend John Money, some researchers are willing to say that the Colapinto book doesn't offer a balanced presentation of either the man or his research.

"The guy that wrote that book [Colapinto] is not a physican, and there are a lot of things in that book that are just wrong," says neuroscientist Ben Barres. "He never really understood Money's core idea—that our brains have, in the first couple of years, a critical period, a plasticity, a period where they are very susceptible to environmental stimuli, a critical period when our brains are affected in a permanent way, and after that period that's the way they are. Money said that in the first year or so, it's a critical period for gender, and that there could be plasticity during that period, but then afterwards [gender] would be fixed. And Colapinto never related it that way. For him, it was all one or the other, all biological or all social. And I think that a lot of times he wasn't really fair to Money or Money's ideas. Money was a pioneer in many ways, and I think that it's very easy in retrospect to kick him around."

Neuroscientist Simon LeVay agrees that the Colapinto book and the Reimer case in general do not provide a completely accurate picture of Money's theories. "The funny thing about Money is that in the context of the Colapinto book and that whole study with that kid, he sounds like a dyed-in-the-wool socialization theorist, but in other aspects of his work he was actually pioneering biological approaches to some of these things," LeVay told me in a 2001 interview. It is true that Money advocated replacing the traditional nature/nurture dichotomy with a more complex and nuanced "nature/critical period/nurture" paradigm that recognized the importance of biological and environmental triggers for sexual differentiation at key stages of development. In *Transsexualism and Sex Reassignment,* he even goes so far as to suggest that "it is possible that some as yet unknown fetal hormonal factor influences the fetal nervous system in such a way as to increase the chances that transsexualism will evolve, perhaps in association with or in response to some other developmental event, in the course of psychosexual differentiation." Milton Diamond thinks that this ambiguity in Money's thinking is due to the fact that Money recognized the influence of biology even as he promoted the primacy of socialization. "He waffled," Diamond told me in 2003. "He pays lip service to biology, but when push comes to shove he made his money, his reputation, on the idea that sex is socially constructed. You put them in the pink room and they are a girl; put them in the blue room and they are a boy. And I think that he didn't want to lose his reputation."

The theory of psychosexual neutrality offered liberation to some. Feminists in particular were quick to seize on the promise that biology was *not* destiny, and that females were socialized to be "women." "Especially when they homed in on John/Joan," says Diamond. " 'Oh, he took a little boy and made him a girl. Isn't that nice?' " he says sarcastically. "So *we feminists* know that gender differences are horseshit." Money's theory of gender plasticity not only offered scientific support for Simone de Beauvoir's famous assertion that "women are made, not born," but it also helped drive the second wave of feminism by convincing women that their supposed "differences" from men were, in fact, a social artifact, not a biological reality—a consequence of gender oppression, not a cause. In January 1973, *Time* magazine reported that Money's research, and the John/Joan case in particular, "casts doubt on the theory that major sexual differences, psychological as well as anatomical, are immutably set by the genes at conception." The magazine also noted that Money's research "provides strong support" for "women's liberationists." This is ironic, considering that Money himself grew to rue the "neutering of gender," "man-bashing," and the "demonification of lust" of much feminist theory. "In postmodern social constructionist theory, which includes feminist theory, gender is socially constructed to be a neutered version of sex, and lust is socially constructed so as to be, in women, a spiritualized version of sex, and in men a demonized version," he writes in *Gendermaps.*

By the time *Gendermaps* was published, in 1995, Money was aware that the Reimer experiment had failed, and was publicly reasserting the link between gender identity and biological sex that his earlier research had called into question. "We now know that he knew more than he admitted," says Paul McHugh, "in relationship to this boy." Though Money never went nearly so far as to admit that he had been wrong, his writing from this period places greater emphasis on biological determinants of gender identity and the interaction between "nature" and "nurture" than his previously published work. "I wrote to him telling him that the paper [about David Reimer] was coming out," says Milton Diamond, "and he threatened to sue me. He said, 'If you write that, I will sue you and I will sue the publishers.' And Richard Green was the editor of the journal at the time!" Green, Money's former student and coeditor on *Transsexualism and Sex Reassignment*, published the paper that revealed that Money had perpetrated a fraud by concealing the fact that the "John/Joan" experiment was a failure.

David Reimer committed suicide in May 2004, at the age of thirty-eight; in news reports, his mother said that she had never forgiven John Money for the harm he had inflicted on their family. (David's twin brother, Brian, had committed suicide in 2002.) After hearing of Reimer's death, Milton Diamond told the *Los Angeles Times*, "I hope people learn from it that you don't do something that dramatic to someone without their informed consent. You also have to deal with people with honesty. He was lied to by physicians and parents, the two groups you want to trust the most." Money refused to speak to reporters who contacted him after Reimer's suicide, maintaining his decade-long policy of silence on the case.

Many people have questioned why John Money hasn't admitted that he was wrong about the treatment he advocated for David Reimer—and more generally wrong in his view that the sex of assignment and rearing is the most significant variable in the development of gender identity. Milton Diamond believes that Money would "have gotten more credit, not less credit" by admitting his mistake. "It takes a lot to admit that you are wrong," he says, but ultimately "he would have gotten more credit for it." However, reluctance to report negative results, data that conflict with a pet theory, as Ben Barres of Stanford points out, is not confined to John Money: "Well, now we're talking about the psychopathology of science . . . and that's not something that's unique to him."

Today, the pendulum in gender research is slowly swinging back to biology. Hormones acting under the influence of genes are now thought to be the primary architects of gender identity, and the hypothesis proposed and vehemently defended by John Money—that gender is a mostly social construct—has been superseded by the biological school represented by Milton Diamond. However, the exact mechanisms by which a core gender identity (or sexual orientation) is developed remain unclear. Studies that seem to point to structural anomalies in the brains of gay men (like the studies carried out by Simon LeVay) or transsexuals (like those of Dick Swaab and other researchers) have produced tantalizing findings, but no definitive answers. Most of these brain studies have not been replicated. "People who look for things in the brain right now are shooting buckshot," says Milton Diamond. "They don't know where they are going to find the target and they look in a hundred places and they find one or two that are different and they say, 'This must be it!'" The truth is, Diamond says, "we don't know where to look. It might be in the biochemistry. It might be somewhere else." Diamond thinks that the seat of gender identity will eventually be located in the brain, "but it doesn't have to be something that's morphologically obvious," he says. "We'd like to see a little penis or a little vagina, so that we could say, 'That's it!' But I don't think we're gonna see that. What they're talking about now is bigger versus smaller, more cells versus fewer. Okay, so we may have to settle for that."

Of course, the very idea that the brain is sexed, that there are differences between male and female brains, makes some people suspicious. One doesn't need to be a radical feminist to fear the social implications of such a theory, the way that it could be used to justify regressive views about the "lesser" spatial and mathematical capabilities of women, and the "natural" violence of men. That may be one reason why John Money's theory of psychosexual neutrality at birth attracted so many people in the first place, because it seemed to offer a release from the limitations of biology and social norms. The work of John Money struck a chord with those who came of age in the sixties and seventies because, like the research of Magnus Hirschfeld half a century earlier, it provided scientific support for sweeping social changes then under way. "Like it or not, we are living in a sexual revolution and it is changing our lives," Money writes in *Sexual Signatures,* published in 1975. "We dare not depend on old answers, nor can we afford to cut off the pioneers who are exploring for new ways to meet these unprecendented challenges." The old order, which had imprisoned so many behind stone walls of racism, sexism, and homophobia, was crumbling. As they surged out into the streets to proclaim their liberation, their anger was exceeded only by their optimism. The revolution had arrived—and it would be televised, penetrating every home in America. The sexual anarchy of the fin de siècle had been a dress rehearsal; the sexual revolution of the sixties and seventies was the main event, one in which the boundary between performers and audience, like so many other boundaries, melted into a rainbow-colored pool of candle wax.

CONVERSATION WITH CHELSEA GOODWIN
AND RUSTY MAE MOORE, PH.D.

Chelsea Goodwin is an activist and was a founding member of Queer Nation. She worked at the Strand bookstore in New York City for many years and has also been a commercial sex worker. She currently works as a telemarketer. Rusty Mae Moore is a soft-spoken college professor and a parent of three children, with whom she remains close. Goodwin is an extrovert, who says that her childhood ambition was to be a Catskills comic. Moore is quiet and thoughtful. They have lived together for over a decade. Goodwin and Moore underwent genital surgery together in Belgium in 1995. Together they operate Transy House, a shelter for transgendered and transsexual people in Brooklyn, New York.

Q: You don't like the word "transgender"?

CHELSEA: What I don't like is that it's based on a false premise. There is a transsexual community. There is a cross-dresser community. There is a community of people like Jasmine here, or like Sylvia, or like Melissa, which pretty much involves that kind of underground, prostitution-based thing. Those are three different communities, with three different languages, three different sets of mores and values and folkways—all those groovy anthropology words they taught me to use in college. If I were an anthropologist from another planet coming to study trans earth people, I would say that those are three different tribes that are unrelated.

Q: So you don't see any value, political or social, in all those groups working together as a single entity?

CHELSEA: Frankly I don't, and I'll tell you why. One, cross-dressers insist that transsexuals are somehow just extremist cross-dressers. They don't understand. "You're a kumquat and we're avocados." We're not even in the same food group. You've got transsexuals. We're a pretty diverse bunch, but there's a commonality. A common language and culture which, yes, goes back to Benjamin and Christine Jorgensen and all that. And then you've got the street community, where there is a culture of trans street prostitute types. You've got the same thing in Brazil, in the Philippines, in Mexico. You've got it all over the world. It's a real phenomenon. But it's different than transsexuals like Rusty or me. I came out of the working class. Rusty came out of the middle class. But we're still transsexuals.

Q: I'm confused about the distinction between street queens and non-operative transsexuals. Isn't the distinction based purely on access to surgery?

CHELSEA: No, I think it's a different community. It's a different world. See *Paris Is Burning.* That is a different culture than you'll see with people who have had or are about to have surgery. That's a different track. A whole different world. And that's totally different from people who like to wear a dress on weekends and go to conventions with their wives. It's a whole different culture.

Q: Does age play a part in this? It seems like older folks tend to prefer to identify as transsexual, whereas younger folks prefer transgender.

RUSTY: I think that it's an age thing in part because some of those people who say transgender are going to evolve [into transsexuals] and some are not going to evolve.

CHELSEA: I think it's an age thing in that you have a generation— and some of them are still left, people like April Ashley and Christine Jorgensen, even Renée Richards—that pretty much came out of a pre-Stonewall mentality and they were the people who first went through the Benjamin Standards of Care.

Q: And they had a fairly hetero-normative view of gender?

RUSTY: Right.

CHELSEA: Right. And then you have a whole generation of trippies.

I'm a trippie. Trippies are people that are of the right age that we were hippies and yippies and freaks in the sixties and seventies.

Q: Testing all kinds of boundaries and gender was just one of those boundaries?

CHELSEA: Right. Transsexual is the least weird thing about me. I happen to be a transsexual. Aside from that, I'm way the fuck out there. So you've got that generation and then you've got the generation that Riki Wilchins represents, a generation that coincided in time, and then had a reaction to, that lesbian feminist crap from the seventies and eighties.

Q: What about the whole feminist attack on transwomen in the seventies? What was that all about?

CHELSEA: We met Janice Raymond. The short story is that Rusty came out to her minister in the Methodist Church. The minister said, "Take Chelsea out and shoot her. Just shoot her. She doesn't have the right to live." Then he said, "Read Janice Raymond's book." So I met this Janice Raymond. We were at this reading at some women's bookstore. The thing is that Janice Raymond was wearing a pair of alligator Texas boots, a pair of jeans with an armadillo belt buckle, a cowboy hat, like "Howdy, Tex." But she's anti-trans?

RUSTY: She was definitely gender variant in the way that she dressed.

CHELSEA: Why the hell did anybody publish that thing [Raymond's book, *The Transsexual Empire*]? Compare and contrast that book with *The Turner Diaries*, with the Unabomber's Manifesto. She's definitely out there with the rest of the crazies. Is it an exaggeration to compare Raymond's book to *Mein Kampf*?

RUSTY: But the problem is that book has been quoted again and again and again and used as the basis for legislation. It's like the role of Johns Hopkins. People have quoted to me over and over again this idea that "you must be wrong, because Johns Hopkins stopped doing transsexual operations." They were the first university hospital to do the surgeries and they got a lot of press. Their decision to stop doing that surgery had tremendous impact.

CHELSEA: But getting back to Janice Raymond. You look at the first wave of that lesbian feminist crap. Robin Morgan used to hang out and smoke pot with Abbie Hoffman and me. She was part of all that. But then she went on to that "the new left is sexist" stuff. Eventually they [lesbian feminists] started to write history like ground zero was 1974, which I believe was the year that they reached critical mass and their dogma was canonized. It was coming together before that, but that was when they had their version of the Nicene Council to do the official canon. This is where the basic tenets of the faith were agreed upon. So they took '74 as the cutoff point and if it happened before 1974 it didn't happen.

The second wave of feminism was happening at the same time as the Black Power movement. Certainly there was an extreme in the Black Power movement, and the Michigan Womyn's Music Festival and that whole mentality was the feminist version of the same thing.

You know what opened my eyes? I had finally figured out that I was transsexual. I had started taking hormones and started living as a woman. I figured out that I am bisexual too. Of course that's a problematic word because it implies that there are only two genders, but you know what I mean. I figured out a lot of things about myself. But one of the things it took me a long time to figure out, trying to find myself, was that a large percentage of the so-called lesbian feminists were political lesbians, lesbians for political reasons, but not because they were sexually attracted to other women.

There's a stereotype that I question that's been around since the fifties, that lesbians must hate men. In my experience lesbians tend not to want to sleep with men, but they tend not to hate men. After all, if you look at the traditional lesbian things—trucks and hot rod cars and guitars are cool. The lesbians weren't saying, "We hate men because they do those things"; they were saying, "We want to play with those toys too." A reasonable point of view.

Q: *That brings up a broader question, of course. What is gender anyway? Is there anything to gender?*

CHELSEA: Is there anything to race? You saw the movie *Bulworth?* Bill Bradley said the biggest problem in the United States, hands down, is race. I think that was true in 1776, 1876, 1976, and I think that it's true now. America is uniquely fucked up because of race. The peculiar institution of racially based slavery is essentially an American phenomenon. So, can you ignore race? Is there anything to race? Does race exist? Yes, obviously, some people have dark skin, some people have light skin, and social constructs have been built around that. Is the transgender movement basically all about bathrooms and who is going to piss where? Yes, but go back to Martin Luther King and before, what was the civil rights movement about? Getting rid of the whites-only and coloreds-only bathrooms, and everybody pisses in the same place.

So, as far as "is there anything to gender?" Let's say that originally there weren't very many Homo sapiens on this planet, and it was important that the reproduction rate be really high because of high infant mortality rates, medicine doesn't exist, people are being trampled to death, et cetera. It's that kind of world. I'm trying to make this funny, but I'm serious too. Now we're in a world that's overpopulated. There are too many people. Naturally, there's going to be more homosexuality.

Are we [transgendered people] more of a percentage of the population? I don't know. Are there more people with a propensity to gender variance? I don't know. Are more people manifesting it? Yes!

I belong to all kinds of e-mail groups, conspiracy theorists, UFO [abductees], whatever. I'm no better than the rest of the nuts, but at least I have a sense of humor. But I also belong to something called the climate concern group. I'm one of the few non-Ph.D.s on that group. It's a different thing from the UFOs and the "Lone Gunman" [theorists] and the other stuff, though that stuff is more fun. Anyway, actual scientific fact: there are more hermaphroditic polar bears than there used to be. There is a rise in hermaphroditism among arctic polar bears. I wasn't looking for transgender stuff but I just happened to run into it. The same is true of several species of fish in the Amazon River. There are all kinds of [transgendered and intersexual] animals. Maybe there are more transgender people because it was one of the unexpected results [of the scientific revolution]. Instead of the bombing of Hiroshima giving us Godzilla, it gave us me. Something is definitely happening. We can theorize about it, and I wish to hell that people would start theorizing about the scientific message, rather than [viewing transpeople as] signs of the end of the world foretold in the Bible.

I'm into science. I'm an avid science fiction fan. Something I've discovered . . . there's only one thing that the trans community agrees on. We all love *Star Trek*. It sounds like a joke, but it's true. Among MTFs anyway. I think that the two professions that have the most transsexuals in them, in no particular order, are prostitution and computer geeks. There are two basic groups of transsexuals, the prostitutes and the computer geeks. And most of us are people like me who have been both. If they wanted to make *Star Trek* more realistic, one of the captains would say, "Damn it, the computer system is on the fritz again. Where's the transsexual?" Am I right?

RUSTY: If they had really evolved, they wouldn't say, "Where's the transsexual?" They would've just had the transsexual come in and fix the computer. *Star Trek* is so popular with transpeople because they accept, without even thinking about it, all these weird-looking people. This total variation, no question asked.

Q: That's also true of certain kinds of rock and roll, isn't it? You can be anything you want to be onstage, and no one bats an eye.

CHELSEA: I want to say something about music, because it's something that gets ignored. Music helped me come out. Lou Reed's *Transformer* album, okay, helped immensely. [*Sings*] "Holly came from Miami FLA / Hitchhiked her way across the U.S.A. / Plucked her eyebrows on the way / shaved her legs and then he was a she." Later on, I actually met Holly Woodlawn, after I was out.

The New York Dolls helped me come out. David Bowie helped me come out. Iggy Pop helped me come out. I wrote Iggy Pop because a couple of albums ago he put his address on the back of the album and said, "Any fan wants to write me a letter, I'll answer it." So I sat down and I wrote a letter and said, "Ig, I'm a transsexual. I grew up in a conservative Christian home out in the boondocks and I would have had a much harder time figuring out who and what I am and what to do with my life if it hadn't been for you." He wrote me a beautiful reply—a beautiful, loving, supportive, un–Iggy Pop–like, loving answer—which I still have around here.

I know tons of transsexuals that were influenced by Jayne County, *Man Enough to Be a Woman*. Before *Hedwig*, before *Rocky Horror*, she was a transsexual that was playing with The Ramones at CBGB. Rocky Horror was one of the things that saved my life. That song, "Don't Dream It, Be It." Every time my transition got scary, every time I was physically assaulted, raped, everything that happened to me, that phrase from the *Rocky Horror Picture Show*, "Don't Dream It, Be It," kept me going.

Q: So you're saying that cultural influences affected your choices, or at least helped you deal with the choices that you've made?

I think that time and place have lot to do with it. I grew up in a very rigid, very conservative family. I'm the only person that's still alive in my family that's not a born-againer. I talk to my mother maybe once a year. What's to talk about? She's kind of gotten over it, but she used to attribute my being transgendered to demonic possession. So once a year, at Christmas, I'd send her a card and sign it "Chelsea, Princess of Darkness," and forget about her for the rest of the year. What are you going to do?

You've got to keep the books in balance. The gender thing was a bit more extreme. She thought that smoking pot and listening to the Grateful Dead were signs of demonic possession too. I used to be a Deadhead, and I was playing punk rock at CBGBs too.

Q: Let's talk a bit about Transy House. How did Transy House get started?

RUSTY: Transy House grew out of our thoughts on The Ramones. [*Laughter*] Actually, it just sort of evolved. The genesis of it was that Chelsea had been out for a long time. I was coming out around '91 or '92 and was basically heavy into transition then. And Chelsea told me that she was one of the last daughters of Sylvia Rivera, and Chelsea told me about STAR House [a refuge for homeless transgender youth], and that was sort of filed away in the back of my mind. We were living in Bellmore, Long Island, then, in an apartment, and after I came out definitively in '93 and was teaching as a woman at Hofstra, I wanted to buy a house rather than live in an apartment. Since my daughter and son were living in Brooklyn then, with their other parent, I wanted to be close to them. Chelsea and I walked the streets of Brooklyn looking for a cheap place and we found the house that we live in now, and I bought it. And another person, Julia Murray, was living with us and she went through transition about the same time I did. So Julia, Chelsea, and I moved in around August 1, 1994, and then gradually other people . . . it was sort of unique for trans people to own a house in New York, so other people started to say, "I need a place to live. Can I come and live with you?" I think that one of the first was Christiana, and there's been a dribble of people that have come and gone over the years.

Transy House just gradually evolved because it was a safe space for transpeople. A lot of transpeople who were fighting their way through their lives would come in and all of a sudden . . . Bingo! In this house transpeople are in the majority, and no longer is it "You're weird," but this is a normal environment for you. And people really appreciated that. They came during transition. A lot of lesbians also stopped by too, people who were just gender variant in any way.

Then also Chelsea and I were the mainstays of an organization called the Metropolitan Gender Network [MGN]. Because we had computers and telephones and fax machines and an office, we became sort of like an informational center for political activism. Definitely we were doing that from '96 on. And then, around 1997 Chelsea reconnected with Sylvia. And Sylvia at that time was living on the piers. She came and spoke at MGN, and that's when I met her. And she came over a lot to the house quite often and eventually she came there to live, in around '98 or late '97. When Sylvia came she was really bottoming out. She had a lot of drug problems and she had decided that she would concentrate on one drug, alcohol, and she drank like a fish. Honestly, Chelsea harassed her so much about drinking. I was putting pressure on, but I put less pressure on people. Chelsea had these knock-down, drag-out battles with her. I wrote this devastating story about her, sort of contrasting her power when she was sober with when she was drunk. So Sylvia finally decided about eighteen months ago to stop drinking. She went cold turkey and stopped drinking. So she came back into her power after she realized that she was destroying herself. [*Note:* Sylvia Rivera died in October 2002 of liver disease. This interview was conducted before her death.]

But when she came to live at the house, I used to say that Chelsea's and my role in life was to deliver Sylvia to her speeches. We would get her there sober, but she might not come away sober. So we would take her down to Washington or other places. I remember being in Washington at the AIDS parade with her, and someone said "You're Sylvia Rivera. I thought you were dead!"

Q: She is such a huge folk hero.

RUSTY: I would say that now that Sylvia has got it together again, she is definitely the most well-known transperson in the queer community, if you include gay and lesbian people.

CHELSEA: Sylvia was at Stonewall. She was doing stuff [organizing] with Lee Brewster; These people were doing stuff from '69 to '74. But then all this so-called lesbian feminist bullshit. Let me go on record about that. There's nothing wrong with being a nationalist. There's nothing wrong with being a socialist. But when you put the two words together and become a National Socialist, that's something else. There's nothing wrong with being a lesbian. That's a good thing. There's nothing wrong with being a feminist. This is a good thing. But for some reason when you string those two words together and make it lesbian feminist, the same thing happens as when you combined "nationalism" and "socialism." Why? I don't know, but it does.

So what happened is that in '74, they wanted to purge the drag queens out of the parades, out of the rallies. She apologized years later, but what happened is that one of the lesbian feminists, named Jean O'Leary, had Sylvia forcibly removed from the stage at the rally. So, basically, Sylvia went into a real funk, crawled into a whiskey bottle, and it was like '90-something before she crawled out.

The other thing that happened in '74, though, is that when the original gay rights bill was drafted in New York it included trans—it actually said "transvestites and transsexuals" in the parlance of the day.

In 1974, a bunch of people from the GAA [Gay Activists Alliance] cut a deal with the politicians, who said that if they took us out [drag queens and transsexuals], it would get the bill passed faster. That was '74. The bill didn't pass till '86 anyway, but we'll let that slide for now. So the point is that in '74 Sylvia just gave up; she wasn't going to do anything else.

But I thought what Sylvia was doing made sense, because I was hanging out with people like Abbie Hoffman. I was part of the New Left that's now called the *Old* Left. Anyway, my message has always been that this came out of the sexual revolution of the 1960s, and it started as something visible that could be seen in the press with Sylvia. Actually it started with Magnus Hirschfeld and what happened in Berlin in the '20's. But after that unpleasantness in the 1930s and '40s, all that got wiped out. And coming after the fifties cold war thing, the next visible figure was Sylvia.

Five

LIBERATING THE RAINBOW

We were led out of the bar and they cattled us all against the police vans. The cops pushed us up against the grates and the fences. People started throwing pennies, nickels, and quarters at the cops, and then the bottles started. And then we finally had the Morals Squad barricaded in the Stonewall building because they were actually afraid of us at that time. They didn't know we were going to react that way. We were not taking anymore of this shit.

SYLVIA RIVERA, IN *TRANS LIBERATION*,
BY LESLIE FEINBERG, NEW YORK CITY, 1969

Liberation. Revolution. In the summer of 1969, those were more than just words. As the song by Thunderclap Newman put it, "Call out the instigators / because there's something in the air / We've got to get together sooner or later / Because the revolution's here, and you know it's right." For gay men, lesbians, drag queens, and other gender outlaws, the revolution arrived on a hot night in June when, as so often happened, cops attempted to arrest the patrons of a gay bar—possibly because the owners were late in making their biweekly payoff to the Police Department. The Stonewall Inn, in Greenwich Village in New York City, was to become on that night, and the days that followed, ground zero for gay liberation, the rock thrown into the stagnant pond of social mores. The ripple effects of Stonewall are still being felt today as a steadily increasing number of cities and the states ban housing and employment discrimination based on sexual orientation; as gay men become the stars of a hit television show; as at least one state

permits gay couples to marry while another approves civil unions—
and as the medical diagnosis of homosexuality as mental illness fades
into history. This transformation in cultural attitudes was interrupted
by a backlash in 2004, with eleven states passsing ordinances banning
gay marriage, and gay rights itself becoming a major wedge issue in
the presidential campaign. Yet the backlash itself (like a similar backlash against feminism in the 1990s) points to the success of the movement, not its failure.

What happened on the night of June 23, 1969? Why have the Stonewall riots transcended history to become myth? For many people,
Stonewall crystallized the moment when homosexuals and gender-
variant people as a group stopped being ashamed, stopped being afraid,
and began to fight back—against police harassment, against bigotry,
against anyone who would deny them their human rights. Many point
to Stonewall as the day that pride was born—pride in being gay, pride
in being different. But like a couple whose future conflicts could be
predicted from their first date, Stonewall and its immediate aftermath
presaged difficulties and divisions that would haunt the gay, lesbian,
bisexual, and transgender (GLBT) movement to this day.

Numerous accounts of the Stonewall riots have been published, but
Martin Duberman's book *Stonewall* is probably the best-known and
the most respected. One of the activists whose story Duberman follows throughout the book is Sylvia Rivera, who was a nineteen-year-
old drag queen in 1969. Rivera had lived on the streets since age
eleven. Like Patricia Morgan, she had worked first as a boy prostitute
and later in drag. In most accounts, Sylvia Rivera and the other street
queens who hung around outside the bar played a crucial role in the
riots. Some say that Rivera or one of the other queens threw the first
rock at the cops who were attempting to hustle the Stonewall's patrons
into a paddy wagon, thus igniting the three days of intermittent rioting
that followed. Others deny this—and in the debate over that single fact,
thirty years of mistrust and suspicion are constellated. Who started
Stonewall, and by extension GLBT liberation? Was it the queens or
the gays? The gay men (and they were mostly men) being herded
into the paddy wagon, or the crowd of drag queens who began to
heckle the cops and eventually to pelt them with coins, stones, bottles,

high-heeled shoes—and later to overturn cars and pull up parking meters? "Hand out the arms and ammo / We're going to blast our way through here / We've got to get together sooner or later / Because the revolution's here, and you know it's right." In the end, it may not matter who cast the first stone, only that the stone was cast and that it led first to an uprising and then to a movement. For a time, gays (male and female), drag queens, transsexuals, and other gender-variant people did indeed "come together" to ignite the revolution.

Karla Jay's *Tales of the Lavender Menace* provides a vivid and compelling account of those early days, when everything seemed possible. Fueled by youth, idealism, and the sense that theirs was a righteous cause, the founders of the movement came together to plot the course of their revolution. Some came from the homophile movement, organizations such as the Daughters of Bilitis and the Mattachine Society, founded in the fifties to try to improve the status of gays. Others came from the Left (both New and Old)—Marxists, Communists, and student radicals who carried the weapons of ideology and intellectual dissent. "Hopeful (but not certain) that something was going to happen after the Stonewall riots had subsided, I went to my first GLF [Gay Liberation Front] meeting at the end of July, which was probably the group's second meeting," Jay writes. "I had seen an ad for it in the *East Village Other* or *RAT*. At first I didn't know what to make of this colorful, boisterous group. The chairs were pulled into a loose circle in which everything seemed to be spinning out of control. Everyone was shouting about what needed to be done without listening to what others had to say." Karla Jay points out that the bulk of these gay revolutionaries were "young, white and unemployed. Most were students or recent college graduates like myself. But some of the participants were simply what radicals referred to as 'street people'—generally lower- or lower-middle-class women and men without any prior political experiences, who came because they were incensed about the Stonewall riots or because they knew someone who had participated in them."

Jay writes that she became close to two of the "transvestites" (her word) she met at Gay Liberation Front (GLF) meetings in the heady days after Stonewall—Sylvia Rivera and Rivera's best friend, Marsha P. Johnson. "Sylvia Rivera, a Latina street queen, would hold forth at

GLF meetings, gesticulating wildly and puncturing her own comments with Dietrich's guttural laugh as she presented her views in
forceful, if ungrammatical, New Yorkese. Her friend Marsha (sometimes Marcia) P. Johnson was a sassy and funny Black transvestite.
Martin Duberman wrote in *Stonewall* that she once told a judge after
she had been busted that the *P* stood for 'Pay it no mind.' The laughing
judge demanded no bail." Rivera and Johnson occupy prominent positions in transgender history and lore. Together they founded STAR
(Street Transvestite Action Revolutionaries), in August 1969, providing shelter for homeless transgendered kids working as prostitutes.
Rivera and, to a lesser extent, Johnson organized and fought fero-
ciously for the rights of their sisters—a group that made fellow revolutionaries uncomfortable. "I had never met a real drag queen before,"
Karla Jay admits in *Tales of the Lavender Menace*. "Redstockings and
other feminist groups strongly believed that such men were an offensive parody of 'real' women—that is, those of us who were genetically
female and sentenced to a life of oppression because of our gender.
Such men could simply discard women's clothing and reclaim male
privilege. Feminists believed that transvestites caricatured the very
worst kind of femininity by donning pounds of makeup and by wearing the very kind of clothing we were fighting to free ourselves from,
especially short, tight, revealing skirts or dresses and stiletto heels."

In *Stonewall*, Duberman quotes Arthur Bell, a founder, in December 1969, of the Gender Activists Alliance, about the response to Sylvia
and other queens. "The general membership is frightened of Sylvia
and thinks she's a troublemaker. They're frightened of street people."
Duberman attributes the fear and occasional hostility aroused by
Rivera and the other street queens to their being on the "wrong side"
of a number of ideological markers: "Sylvia was from the wrong eth-
nic group, from the wrong side of the tracks, wearing the wrong
clothes—managing single-handedly and simultaneously to embody
several frightening, overlapping categories of otherness. By her mere
presence, she was likely to trespass against *some* encoded middle-class
white script, and could count on being constantly patronized when not
being summarily excluded."

Duberman's description of the primarily white middle-class gay response to Sylvia Rivera echoes the reaction of the aristocratic Christopher Isherwood to the cross-dressers in Magnus Hirschfeld's Institute for Sexual Science. Bell's GAA members and Isherwood may have been queer, but they weren't *that* queer. They may have dressed in drag on special occasions, but they didn't wear a full face of makeup on the street. They were radical, but they adhered to certain social niceties and conducted themselves in meetings according to middle-class codes of behavior. The members of the Gay Liberation Front, the first group formed in the wake of Stonewall, were (in the words of a local street figure) "a bunch of stoned-out faggots" who believed that their struggle must necessarily be joined to the struggle of blacks, women, antiwar protesters, and everyone else working for the Revolution. By contrast, the members of the Gay Activists Alliance (formed six months later) were dedicated solely to achieving civil rights for gays—and they were willing to work the system even as they "zapped" it. In *Out for Good: The Struggle to Build a Gay Rights Movement in America,* Dudley Clendenin and Adam Nagourney point out that the GAA, unlike the GLF, was far from a hippie enclave. "The more daring activists who had sprung forward in the months after Stonewall were joined by professional, middle-class homosexuals, people who understood government, business and the media, and who had connections throughout the establishment world. They found the Gay Activists Alliance as ideologically non-threatening as its founders had hoped."

In this context, a working-class Latina drag queen who wasn't afraid to bellow her opinions and agitate for her sisters on the street was a polarizing figure, tolerated and even respected by some members and loathed by others. Still, Sylvia Rivera was active in both the GAA and the GLF until 1973. "She would throw herself into every meeting, party, or action with such passion that those who insisted on remaining her detractors had to shift their vocabularies," says Martin Duberman. "She was no longer Sylvia, the flighty, unreliable queen, but rather Sylvia, the fierce harridan, ready to run any risk and run through any obstacle in order to achieve her frequently shrieked goal of *freedom*." As someone who had lived by the hustle since the age of eleven, Rivera knew the dangers of the life—the homelessness and drug addiction, random violence and police harassment. "Back then, we were beat up by the police, by everybody," Rivera recalls in Leslie Feinberg's *Trans Liberation*. "We expected nothing better than to be treated like a bunch of animals—and we were." When arrested "we were stuck in a bullpen like a bunch of freaks," she writes. "We were disrespected. A lot of us were beaten up and raped. When I ended up going to jail, to do 90 days, they tried to rape me. I very nicely bit the shit out of a man. I was an evil queen. I was strung out on dope."

Rivera knew the kids working the streets because she was one of them—though at nineteen, she was more like an elder sister than a peer. Her maternal instinct was strong and it led her to found STAR House, a refuge for homeless transgender youth. "Their first home was the back of a trailer truck seemingly abandoned in a Greenwich Village outdoor parking area; it was primitive, but a step up from sleeping in doorways," writes Martin Duberman. "The ground rule in the trailer was that nobody had to go out and hustle her body, but that when they did, they had to kick back a percentage to help keep STAR House going. Marsha and Sylvia took it upon themselves to hustle on a regular basis and to return to the truck each morning with breakfast food for everybody."

After the "abandoned" trailer was hauled away, the group rented a house from a Mafioso who owned a gay bar in the Village. The building was falling apart, but Sylvia and her supporters made it habitable. "Marsha and I had always sneaked people into our hotel rooms," Rivera says in *Trans Liberation*. "And you can sneak fifty people into two hotel rooms. Then we got a building at 213 East Second Avenue. Marsha and I just decided it was time to help each other and help our other kids. We fed people and clothed people. We kept the building going." Keeping the building going was tough, however, and Rivera and Johnson were not always able to make the rent. Duberman notes that when Rivera asked for help from the Gay Activists Alliance— rental of their stereo equipment to use during a benefit dance for STAR House—she was turned down. Later, when she was behind on the rent, she once again approached GAA for help and was once again turned down. Rivera and her "children" were eventually evicted and back out on the streets. "There was always food in the house and everyone had fun," Rivera says nostalgically in *Trans Liberation*. "It lasted for two or three years."

By then, the fragile post-Stonewall alliance between the street, the classroom, and the closet was beginning to fall apart. Most middle-class gays and lesbians didn't look or behave much differently from their heterosexual peers. They shared similar values; politically, some were quite conservative. In *Out for Good*, Clendenin and Nagourney quote a 1972 editorial in the gay paper *The Advocate*: "It is possible for all homosexuals to favor freedom and justice for homosexuals. But it is the wildest and most improbable jump to say that therefore they should all be against the Vietnam war, against capitalism, or in favor of destroying society."

Street people like Sylvia Rivera, on the other hand, were radicals in every sense of the word. Rivera herself had ties with the Black Panthers and the Young Lords and attended the People's Revolutionary Congress held in Philadelphia in 1970, where she met Huey Newton. "Huey decided that we were part of the revolution—that we were revolutionary people," she says proudly in *Trans Liberation*. One of the first occasions at which STAR marched as a group was a 1970 protest against police repression in Harlem. "I ended up meeting the Young Lords that day. I became one of them. Any time they needed any help, I was always there for the Young Lords. It was just the respect they gave us as human beings."

That respect was sorely lacking in other contexts. The lifestyle of a street queen was in many ways a flagrant challenge to traditional social mores. Surviving by prostitution and drug dealing, in and out of jail, the cross-dressing street queen was a figure of the underworld, viewed with distaste by many upscale gays who lived in an orderly, affluent world utterly inaccessible to people like Sylvia Rivera. "When attacked by a GAA man—who, in trying to liberate himself from traditional ridicule about being a surrogate woman, could be impatiently moralistic about cross-dressing 'stereotypes'—Rivera would attack back," says Martin Duberman. "She would remind him how tough you had to be to survive as a street queen, how you had to fight, cheat, and steal to get from one day to the next."

The tension between middle-class gays and lesbians and the street exploded at a June 1973 march and rally in commemoration of the Stonewall riots. The Gay Pride march, held annually, "was being seized by drag queens as their holiday, a chance to celebrate their role in the original uprising at the bar," report Clendenin and Nagourney in *Out for Good*. "They were demanding a prominent place in the line of march, and they wanted to be the centers of attention at the rally." The high visibility of the drag queens and the way that they drew the attention of the media rankled many gay men and lesbians who were increasingly convinced that these "extreme" members of the community were holding back the progress of the whole. Furthermore, many lesbians continued to be angry at what they viewed as the disrespectful parody of femaleness embodied by drag queens.

At the 1973 rally, when Sylvia Rivera took the stage and began to harangue the crowd about its lack of support for street queens, some of the lesbians had had enough. Jean O'Leary took the mike after Rivera and read a prepared statement denouncing transvestites as "men who impersonate women for entertainment and profit." O'Leary delivered a scathing attack on not only Rivera but any male-bodied person who wore makeup and women's clothes. Wearing dresses was not a revolutionary act, as some of the early (male) leaders of the gay liberation movement had asserted; it was instead an insult to women. O'Leary was challenged by Lee Brewster, who defended Rivera and reminded the crowd that "today you're celebrating what was the result of what the drag queens did at the Stonewall." But the damage had been done. Gay leaders were beginning to publicly dissociate themselves from cross-dressers, drag queens, and transsexuals. Some viewed this as pragmatism, others as selling out. Rivera, rejected by the movement she had helped found, "crawled into a whiskey bottle," says her friend and STAR daughter Chelsea Goodwin. It would take decades for her to reemerge as a public figure. When she did, the gay rights movement's betrayal of its transgender allies would be her major theme.

"We liberated them. They owe us," she shouted in June 2001, at a rally held in Sheridan Square, near the site of the original Stonewall bar. "I want to call on all the dykes and fags who think that transpeople are a separate community to come out in support of us. It's still open season on transpeople in New York City," she said, referring to the recent murder of twenty-five-year-old Amanda Milan in front of the Port Authority Bus Terminal. The rally itself was a call for justice for Milan and other transgendered victims of violence, and Rivera used the occasion to contrast the gay community's visible public support for Matthew Shepherd—killed in Laramie, Wyoming—and his family with the noticeable absence of such support in the case of transgender hate crime victims. "New York is the birthplace of so many battles for civil rights. Well, it's our turn. We stand here in the cradle of the gay rights movement, but trannies have been left behind. We're still in the back of the bus. We've been silent and invisible for too long."

At the rally, Rivera called for the passage of a trans-inclusive civil rights bill in New York City. "I've been working in this movement for thirty years and I'm still begging for what you've got," she shouted at pedestrians on Christopher Street, the heart of gay Greenwich Village. Rivera, like many transgendered and transsexual people, was infuriated by the passage of civil rights protections for gays that failed to include protections for people whose "real or perceived gender identity" made them targets of violence and discrimination. This strategy had been initiated in New York City in the seventies, when gay leaders, aware of the difficulties of passing any kind of legislation protecting the civil rights of gays and lesbians, had removed language from the bill that explicitly protected cross-dressers and transsexuals.

Continued gay resistance to the inclusion of gender-variant people in local and national civil rights legislation today is perhaps best exemplified by a syndicated article that appeared in GLBT newspapers after Rivera's death, in 2002. In "The Myth of a Transgender Stonewall," author Dale Carpenter objects to the "guilt-ridden commentary about how the gay civil rights movement has pushed aside 'the people that started it all,'" which followed in the wake of Rivera's death. "This commentary is wrong as a matter of history and unsupported as a matter of policy," says Carpenter, who adds that "historical disputes have no bearing—either way—on whether 'gender identity' ought to be included in gay civil rights legislation. Even if Stonewall was the casus belli of the gay struggle and even if transgenders were the only people there kicking shins and uprooting parking meters, so what?" Carpenter argues that "gay civil rights legislation would be stalled or effectively killed in many places if transgenders were included. The choice is often between a more inclusive bill that goes nowhere and a less inclusive bill that actually becomes law. These are hard realities. We should not feel guilty because we want to make progress, least of all because someone is telling us fairy tales about our past."

A law prohibiting discrimination on the basis of gender identity was finally passed in New York City on May 1, 2002. Hours before she died, Rivera met with a group from the Empire State Pride Agenda to negotiate trans inclusion in a civil rights bill then being debated in the New York State legislature (the bill was passed without a gender-identity clause). When National Public Radio's *All Things Considered* ran a program titled "Remembering Stonewall" in 2001, Sylvia Rivera sent the following update: "Since May, I've been the food director at the Metropolitan Community Church food pantry. My girlfriend, Julia, is my assistant and my computer person (because I still don't know a damn thing about these new modern contraptions of yours!). We have been rather busy with the resurrection of street Transgender Action Revolutionaries and are planning protests around the trial of Amanda Milan's assassins. So between the jobs and politics, you know how frantic it is. One of our main goals right now is to destroy the Human Rights Campaign, because I'm tired of sitting on the back of the bumper. It's not even the back of the bus anymore—it's the back of the bumper. The bitch on wheels is back."

She signed her note (dated July 4), "Revolutionary Love."

Sylvia Rivera remained proud of her participation in the Stonewall riots for all of her life. "I am proud of myself for being there that night. If I had lost that moment, I would have been kinda hurt because that's when I saw the world change for me and my people. Of course, we still got a long way ahead of us."

The lack of trust between gays, lesbians, and the various groups generally lumped together today under the adjective "transgendered" became a public rift in 1974 for reasons that were partly political and partly aesthetic. Overtly gender-variant people were viewed with suspicion and distaste by some politically savvy gay men focused on gaining civil rights. For people whose goal was integration, not revolution, men in dresses were a decided handicap to public acceptance. The former advocated a right to privacy in the bedroom and tended to oppose flamboyant public displays of "difference" as counterproductive. They also increasingly rejected the view that gay men were more feminine than the average straight man. Instead, they emphasized their masculinity, a trend that was to become even more pronounced as the androgynous seventies gave way to the muscular eighties. In the nineteenth century "there was this very strong association formed between gender nonconformity and homosexuality," says Simon LeVay, who sees an "overcorrection" of that association in the late-twentieth-century gay and lesbian communities, where "there's been an almost excessive denial between homosexuality and gender nonconformity." This attitude has been particularly acute among gay men, he says. "There's definitely a femmephobia in the gay male community, generally a dislike of men who seem feminine."

The political position of lesbians was complicated by their allegiance to feminism; neither gay men nor straight feminists fully understood or shared lesbians' concerns. But lesbians, too, were incubating a new kind of sexual chauvinism. Lesbian culture in the fifties had been just as wedded to the concept of gender dimorphism as the medical profession, dividing lesbian women into "butches" (masculine lesbians) and "femmes" (feminine lesbians). But a new aesthetic was forged in the late sixties and early seventies as young people of all sexual orientations began to reject the values and behaviors of their parents. "Gender issues stood at the forefront of the radical challenge. Antiwar activists rejected the masculine warrior ideal and feminists led a frontal assault on cultural injunctions that demanded feminine behavior among women," writes historian Joanne Meyerowitz in *How Sex Changed: A History of Transsexuality in the United States*. The sexual revolution was also a gender revolution, and the two aspects of the upheaval were inextricably entwined. For a brief period, fin de siècle sexual anarchy was reborn.

People began to play with gender, to "bend" gender, in ways that hadn't been seen before. The elegant female impersonators of Finocchio's, a San Francisco supper club popular in the fifties and early sixties, were a far cry from the Cockettes, a group of singing, dancing, gender-fuck hippies who began performing in San Francisco in 1969. The Cockettes were female impersonators on acid—a psychedelic mélange of beards, glitter, and colorful thrift-store robes and dresses—who spun about the stage like dervishes. Led by Hibiscus, a gay mystic who founded a commune of like-minded souls, the Cockettes ignored identity in favor of play and self-expression. Most of the Cockettes were gay men, but some were straight women and men who embraced the gender-fuck aesthetic. "They were people who brought together clashing styles," says historian Susan Stryker. "Full beards and pink tutus, silver glitter combat boots, fucking with gender, fucking up gender. A lot of glam rock came out of that sensibility, that sense of 'I'm not trying to pass as something.' It was a conscious way of manipulating the signifiers of gender to call attention to its constructedness, often in a playful, militant, and politicized way."

For a time androgyny, a blending of masculine and feminine, became the new ideal. "Many of us believed that the best way to eliminate the male/female divide was for all of us to look as much like one another as possible. Men were encouraged to wear their hair long and to sport jewelry such as beaded necklaces. Facial hair was discouraged," says Karla Jay. "In contrast, short hair was favored for women, and I was applauded when I finally cut my hair in 1972. . . . Most of the lesbians favored bell-bottom denims, boots, and flannel shirts with a T-shirt underneath. After all, we were dressing for the revolution, not *Vogue*." This new aesthetic posed some problems for those who were, quite literally, "androgynous"—drag queens, transsexuals, and other gender-variant people. On the outside many didn't appear revolutionary at all. Drag queens and transsexual women wanted to look like girls—and girls wore high heels, makeup, and short skirts or, in the hippie style espoused by folksinger Beth Elliott, granny dresses. Girls flaunted their womanliness. They didn't try to hide it under layers of flannel. Lesbian women and straight feminists were angry and appalled by what they perceived as the charade of femininity expressed by some drag queens and transsexual women. To them it exhibited a lack of respect, akin to the lack of respect shown African Americans by white actors in blackface. Drag was perceived as a kind of gender minstrel show.

Some lesbians and female-bodied transgendered persons were also having a difficult time adjusting to the new regime. If drag queens were too "feminine," butch lesbians were too "masculine" for evolving standards of gay gender presentation. In *Stone Butch Blues,* a novel that reflects hir experience coming of age as a young butch lesbian in Buffalo, New York, Leslie Feinberg poignantly documents the turmoil in hir community that followed Stonewall. The new androgyny affected not only the masculine lesbians who had previously found a measure of comfort and security in the tight-knit lesbian community in the face of society's hatred. Their femme partners, who were viewed by the new breed of lesbian as puppets of the patriarchy, were also attacked for acting out a kind of femininity that demeaned and oppressed women.

One day I came home from work and found Theresa stewing in anger at the kitchen table. Some of the lesbians from a newly formed group on campus had mocked her for being a femme. They told her she was brainwashed. "I'm so mad." Theresa thumped the table. "They told me that butches were male chauvinist pigs!"

I knew what male chauvinist meant, but I couldn't figure out what it had to do with us. "Don't they know we don't deal the shit, we get shit on?"

"They don't care, honey. They're not going to let us in."

"Should Jan and Grant and Edwin and I go to one of these meetings and try to explain?"

Theresa put her hand on my arm. "It won't help, honey. They're very angry at butches."

"Why?"

She thought about the question. "I think it's because they draw a line—women on one side and men on the other. So women they think look like men are the enemy. And women who look like me are sleeping with the enemy. We're too feminine for their taste."

"Wait a minute," I stopped her. "We're too masculine and you're too feminine? Whatdya have to do, put your index fingers in a meter and test in the middle?"

Rejected by the new breed of "woman-identified women" for being too butch, and shunned by society at large for being too androgynous, Feinberg's character Jess Goldberg, a "he-she," takes refuge in masculinity. Testosterone masculinizes hir body and deepens hir voice. Bearded and flat-chested after a mastectomy, Jess passes as a man without difficulty, but is consumed by loneliness and a sense of alienation. "As much as I loved my beard as part of my body, I felt trapped behind it," Feinberg writes. "What I saw reflected in the mirror was not a man, but I couldn't recognize the he-she. My face no longer revealed the contrasts of my gender. I could see my passing self, but even I could no longer see the more complicated me beneath my surface."

Jess Goldberg (like hir creator, Leslie Feinberg) chooses to embrace ambiguity and live in the undefined space between the poles of male and female—the space that would eventually be termed "transgender." The choice was not without peril. When sie was a butch lesbian, "strangers had raged at me for being a woman who crossed a forbidden boundary. Now they really didn't know what my sex was, and that was unimaginable, terrifying to them. Woman or man—the bedrock crumbled beneath their feet as I passed by." Goldberg relates the comment of a shopkeeper to a fellow customer—"how the hell should I know what it is? The pronoun echoed in my ears. I had gone back to being an *it*." As an it, the fictional Goldberg was beaten so badly that hir jaw was wired shut. As an it, the real Feinberg was denied medical treatment and nearly died from an untreated bacterial infection. Though *Stone Butch Blues* is a novel, the challenges faced by the book's protagonist remain all too real for visibly transgendered people.

Perhaps for that reason, many choose to disappear into more conventional gender presentations. This has been particularly true of female-to-male transsexual people (FTMs), who for the most part have far less difficulty "passing" in their chosen gender, as Jess Goldberg discovered. In contrast to the many memoirs and autobiographies published by male-to-female transsexual people (MTFs) in the sixties, the seventies, and beyond, the number of books by FTMs remains slim, reflecting the relative invisibility of transmen. Even today, there is no one FTM figure with the name recognition of a Christine Jorgensen, even though the first international "outing" of a female-to-male transsexual person occurred a few years after Jorgensen's media baptism. In May 1958, the *Sunday Express* of London revealed that a forty-two-year-old physician, Laurence Michael Dillon, heir presumptive to the baronetcy of Lismullen, had in fact been born Laura Maud Dillon. "The very day the *Express* story appeared it went round the world courtesy of the Reuters news agency," notes Dillon's biographer Liz Hodgkinson. Dillon, who had transitioned fifteen years previously under the supervision of the British surgeon Sir Harold Gillies, was devastated by his new notoriety, and promptly abandoned his career.

Like Dillon, many transmen avoid notoriety, and their stories remain largely untold. However, although fewer FTMs have written memoirs or spoken out about their feelings during the immediate post-Stonewall era, the ones who have acknowledge that they were just as uncomfortable with the new "androgyny" as the drag queens, stone butches, and MTFs. For one thing, most transmen adamantly maintain that they are *not* lesbians. They are men, period. In his autobiography, *Emergence*, published in 1977, Mario Martino clarifies the distinction between a "butch," or masculine lesbian, and a female-to-male transsexual.

"Proud of being a woman, she [the lesbian] responds to another woman who responds to her as a female. The lesbian's satisfaction is the woman-to-woman contact," writes Martino. "Unlike the lesbian, I did not want to be a woman and I felt I should never have been one, that I could be content only in the male gender. I have always wanted, will always want, only the male to female relationship." Martino's feelings are echoed in nearly every FTM memoir published to date, including *What Took You So Long? A Girl's Journey to Manhood*, by Raymond Thompson (1995); and *Dear Sir or Madam*, by Mark Rees (1996).

That said, it is also true that many FTMs today may have spent years and even decades in the lesbian community before transitioning. The decision to transition presents a terrible conundrum to many transmen, who feel loved and accepted in the lesbian community even if they never feel that the label "lesbian" really applies to them. "For me, some of the hardest people to come out to about being trans are some of my older lesbian friends. Some of them have been great about it, but some definitely had to struggle, feeling a sense of betrayal as butch lesbians," says Ali Cannon, a thirty-seven-year-old transman I interviewed in 2001. "A friend of mine has talked about the way that the lesbians from that generation, my generation and older, have become the parents that the younger lesbians who identify as trans have to come out to. Their feeling of loss, and 'you're not growing up to be what we wanted you to be' is very similar to that of straight parents first confronted with a child's homosexuality," he says. This is particularly true for those who came of age during the seventies, when lesbianism became almost synonymous with a deep and abiding mistrust of men and male power. "It was really hard," says Tom Kennard, a San Francisco computer programmer, about his decision to transition in the 1990s. "I'm fifty-one, so when I was coming up I was a big feminist, a white lesbian feminist and I was kind of a separatist. You know, there's all this stuff in feminism, like women are the highest of all, women are good. Women, good. Men, bad."

The woman, good/man, bad dichotomy that Kennard describes was forged in the feminist movement's rejection of patriarchy and its mandates for gender-coded behavior. Women as a group, gay or straight, revolted en masse against the limitations implicit in traditional definitions of womanhood. Few burned their bras, but many began to question why it was that a woman could not be a mechanic or a doctor, why women were expected to be demure and accommodating, why women were always expected to place their own needs and desires after those of men. Why were women raised to be second-class citizens? In this struggle for self-definition, men, both as a group and as individuals, became Man, the tyrant and oppressor. A collective howl of rage was heard across the land, as activist women in particular noticed that their male counterparts were no more progressive in their attitudes toward and treatment of women than the system they were attempting to overthrow. The New Woman was back, but this time she was loud, proud, and overtly political.

Robin Morgan—a feminist writer whose essay "Goodbye to All That" served notice to leftist men that their days of mouthing platitudes about liberation while expecting secretarial, sexual, and housekeeping services from leftist women was at an end—articulated the new ideology. Morgan encouraged women to claim the shadow side of femininity —to be "bitchy, catty, dykey, frustrated, crazy, Solanisque, nutty, frigid, ridiculous, bitter, embarrassing, man-hating, libelous, pure, unfair, envious, intuitive, low-down, stupid, petty, liberating." Like the Black Power movement that succeeded the more high-minded civil rights movement, women's liberation was about taking stereotypes and turning them on their heads. As Morgan noted in capital letters: WE ARE THE WOMEN THAT MEN HAVE WARNED US ABOUT.

Gay or straight, women began to name and resist male privilege and to reject a subservient role based on male definitions of femaleness. In *Out for Good,* Clendenin and Nagourney report on the bitter divorce of gay men and lesbians in the nascent gay liberation movement in the seventies, as lesbians became fed up with the tendency of gay men to focus exclusively on their own issues, ignoring or discounting the primary concerns of gay women. Del Martin, a longtime activist who had cofounded the Daughters of Bilitis and worked alongside gay men in the pre-Stonewall homophile movement, published a letter in *The Advocate* announcing her own revolution. "I will not be your 'nigger' any longer," she writes. "Nor was I ever your mother. Those were stultifying roles you laid on me, and I shall no longer concern myself with your toilet training."

In New York City, a group of lesbian women active in the Gay Liberation Front began meeting separately from the men within a year after Stonewall. Equally disgusted by the misogyny and arrogance of gay men and the homophobia of heterosexual feminists, this group wrote and distributed a passionate manifesto called "The Woman-Identified Woman" at the Second Congress to Unite Women, in May 1970. Calling themselves the Lavender Menace, a barbed response to Betty Friedan's characterization of lesbians as a "lavender menace" that would derail the blossoming feminist movement, the authors of "The Woman-Identified Woman" described lesbians as "the rage of all women condensed to the point of explosion." This ten-paragraph manifesto, Clendenin and Nagourney note, "called on feminists to cut their ties with men and the male culture, to redefine their own role in society by bonding with women—ideally lesbians, since they best understood the oppression women suffered in a male-dominated society." As Clendenin and Nagourney note, the document was "a road map to a separate political movement," lesbian separatism.

Karla Jay, one of the instigators of the Lavender Menace action and a founder of the Radicalesbians, a group formed in its wake, says that "for lesbians, the best thing that emerged from the Lavender Menace action was the group of protesters itself—the first post-Stonewall group to focus on lesbian issues. Only weeks earlier we had been a random group of women associated primarily with gay liberation and women's liberation. For the moment at least, we emerged a victorious organization with a sense of solidarity, common purpose and sisterhood. We knew we would no longer accept second-class status in the women's movement or the gay movement. We would be equal partners, or we would leave the straight women and gay men behind."

Nothing infuriated these "woman-identified women" more than biological males "masquerading" as women, particularly when these "women born men" claimed to be lesbian feminists themselves. At the West Coast Lesbian Conference held in Los Angeles in 1973 (three months before Jean O'Leary confronted Sylvia Rivera at the Pride rally in New York City), the keynote speaker, Robin Morgan, spoke for those who objected to Beth Elliott, a male-to-female transsexual folk singer performing at the meeting. Like Jean O'Leary and other lesbian feminists, Morgan characterized transvestites and transsexuals as men who flagrantly mocked and parodied women. "Man-hating," she proclaimed, "is an honorable and viable political act"—and in her view and in the view of many members of the lesbian-feminist community, male-to-female transsexuals remained men, despite their transformed genitalia.

The hostility of lesbian feminism toward transsexuals reached its peak in Janice Raymond's *The Transsexual Empire*, published in 1979. Charging that transsexual women were patriarchy's shock troops, medically constructed pseudo-females created to infiltrate the lesbian community and destroy it, Raymond characterizes sex-reassignment surgery as a new kind of rape. "All transsexuals rape women's bodies by reducing the real female form to an artifact, appropriating this body for themselves. However, the transsexually constructed lesbian feminist violates women's sexuality and spirit as well." Like Paul McHugh, the psychiatrist who closed the Gender Identity Clinic at Johns Hopkins Hospital, Janice Raymond rejects biological explanations for transsexuality and views it purely as a social phenomenon. Despite the extreme difference in their lifestyles and points of view (McHugh is a conservative Catholic and Raymond a radical lesbian feminist), Raymond and McHugh echo each other in characterizing transsexualism as "an ideology" and comparing sex-reassignment surgery to a lobotomy.

In *The Transsexual Empire* Raymond promotes a somewhat paradoxical view of sex and gender. On the one hand, she says that sex is determined by chromosomes; this assumption is the foundation of her belief that "it is biologically impossible to change chromosomal sex, and thus the transsexual is not really transsexed." On the other hand, Raymond denies that chromosomes and the cascade of physiological effects they initiate have any relevance in determining gender. Gender, in her view, is purely a matter of "sex role socialization." Although she attacks John Money and his research throughout the book, she says that the role of sex hormones in the development of gender identity "is clearly outweighed by environmental factors," a position that differs very little from Money's belief that the sex of assignment and rearing trumps all other variables in the formation of gender identity. Masculinity and femininity, Raymond asserts, "are social constructs and stereotypes of behavior that are culturally prescribed for male and female bodies respectively." Transsexuals, she says, are people who have been inadequately socialized into their culture's sanctioned gender roles. "The transsexual has not been adequately conditioned into the role/identity that accompanies his or her body."

These statements, with their underlying assumption that gender is a purely social construct, make it difficult to understand Raymond's vehement objection to sex reassignment. If gender differences are simply a matter of "sex role socialization" then men and women must be (in their pure, unsocialized state) psychologically identical. So why shouldn't they be free to express their "gender" in any way they please? Raymond's answer to the riddle of gender reflects the assumptions of the period in which she wrote *The Transsexual Empire*, and the community of which she was a part. Though it is clear that she recognizes significant differences in behavior between men and women, Raymond does not believe that these differences are biologically based. Instead, they are based on shared history and culture. In her view, "maleness" and "femaleness" are political categories above all, and the defining characteristic of womanhood is a shared subordination and victimization at the hands of men.

"We know that we are women who are born with female chromosomes and anatomy, and that whether or not we were socialized to be so-called normal women, patriarchy has treated and will treat us as women," she says. Transsexual women (or, to use the term that Raymond prefers, "male to constructed females") do not share this common history of victimization and subordination and so are not, and can never be, women. "No man can have the history of being born and located in this culture as a woman. He can have the history of *wishing* to be a woman and of *acting* like a woman, but this gender experience is that of a transsexual, not of a woman. Surgery may confer the artifacts of outward and inward female organs but it cannot confer the history of being born a woman in this society."

Discomfort with one's body, the sense of having been born in the "wrong" body—one that does not match one's view of one's self as a man or woman—is a manifestation of "sex role oppression," akin to racial oppression, Raymond says. Transsexual people suffer gender dysphoria because society has provided them with a stereotyped view of what it means to be a man or a woman, Raymond maintains. The fatal error of the transsexual is acceptance of the patriarchal gender system, swallowing patriarchy's claim that certain feelings and behaviors are reserved for certain bodies. Transsexuality is a political problem that demands political solutions, Raymond argues. By surgically and hormonally altering their bodies to achieve a better "fit" between gender identity and physical appearance, transsexual people play into the hands of the patriarchal enemy, men whose primary goal is to keep women powerless and subservient. "Transsexualism is thus the ultimate, and we might even say, the logical, conclusion of male possession of women, in a patriarchal society. Literally, men here possess women."

Transmen (female-to-male transsexuals) are, in Raymond's view, mere "tokens" whose role is to "save face for the transsexual empire." Female-to-male transsexual people adopt "stereotypes of masculinity," says Raymond, and "have been assimilated into the transsexual world, as women are assimilated into other male-defined worlds, institutions and roles, that is, on men's terms, and thus as tokens." Though Raymond seems to view all transsexual people as puppets or pawns of men and of the male power structure, she absolves transmen as victims (after all, they were born women), whereas transwomen (born men) are active collaborators with the real enemy—the doctors and researchers who have developed and maintain the transsexual empire. "The Transsexual Empire is ultimately a medical empire, based on a patriarchal medical model. This medical model has provided a 'sacred canopy' of legitimations for transsexual treatment and surgery." Sex reassignment is nothing more than behavioral modification, Raymond asserts, and its goal is social control through the creation of stereotypically female pseudo-women who will be used to keep biologically born females in their place as a second sex, prisoners of a male-defined "femininity."

Raymond's book, which despite its harsh rhetoric does in certain places provide a compelling critique of gender roles, deteriorates into outright paranoia near its close. "One hypothesis that is being tested in the transsexual 'laboratories' is whether or not it is possible for men to diminish the number of women and/or create a new 'breed' of females," she states darkly. "Scientists have already stated their 'scientific' interest in diminishing the number of women." She compares the relationship between transsexual people and the physicians and surgeons who treat them as "master/slave" and "sadist/masochist" pairings. Finally, and perhaps predictably, she drags in the Nazis, saying that "it is significant that the first physician on record to perform sex-change surgery was a German by the name of F. Z. Abraham, who reported the first case in 1931." Abraham, of course, was a colleague of Magnus Hirschfeld, whose institute was destroyed by the Nazis in 1933.

Janice Raymond's book was mentioned by nearly every transsexual person I interviewed. Until the publication of Joanne Meyerowitz's *How Sex Changed*, in 2002, *The Transsexual Empire* remained the best-known and most widely read and discussed book on transsexualism by an academician who is neither a physician nor a transsexual person. This is unfortunate, as Raymond's book provides an account of trans-sexualism that is far from balanced and is scientifically quite naïve. Though she accuses doctors and physicians of ideological bias, her book is itself anchored in ideology, the ideology of lesbian separatism. Reading the book today, one is struck not only by the vitriol of Ray-mond's argument, but also by its profound paranoia. One senses that under Raymond's rage lies a deep fear of men and an unwillingness to believe that any person born (and socialized) as a male can ever be "cured" of the desire to impose his will on women. As Tom Kennard notes, describing his years as a lesbian-feminist separatist, "Women, good. Men, bad."

A generation after the publication of *The Transsexual Empire,* that view seems comically simplistic, as does another of Raymond's core arguments—that transsexuals are, as a group, "more royal than the king" in adhering to stereotypical gender roles. Transgendered and transsexual people today (particularly young people) express a some-times bewildering range of gender identities and roles. For example, around the time I began working on this project a friend sent me an e-mail survey he had received from a Washington, D.C., area support group, which inquired:

> Do you identify as transgendered, transsexual, transvestite, cross-dresser, trangenderist, genderqueer, FTM/F2M, MTF, M2F, trans-man, transwoman, transperson, third-gendered, gendertrash, gender outlaw, gender warrior, trans, transfag, transdyke, tranny, passing woman/girl, drag king, drag queen, male lesbian, girl boy, boychick, boy girl, boy dyke, gender-bender, gender blender, transqueer, an-drogynous, transfolk, butch dyke, nelly fag, gender-different, gender subversive, man/boy with a vagina, chick with a dick, shape-shifter, he-she, she-male, transboy, transgirl, androgyne, gender variant, genderfucker, trannyfag, trannyqueer, trannydyke, Two Spirit, new man, new woman, she-bear, Tomboy, intersexual/female guy, tranz,

bearded female, herm, hermaphrodite, MTM/M2M, FTF/F2F, un-gendered, agendered, genderfree, bigendered, midgendered, polygen-dered, pangendered, omnigendered, crossgendered, byke, boi, pre-op, post-op, non-op, no-ho, epicene, othergendered, transkid, female im-personator, gender-atypical, ambigendered . . . or any other related term not on this list?

As this list illustrates, if gender-variant people agree about anything these days, it is about their right to express their identities and to label themselves (or not label themselves) in any way they choose. But even as Raymond was writing about the tendency of transsexual people to adopt highly conservative views of gender to placate their medical masters, individuals and groups were beginning to challenge that perspective. During the late sixties and early seventies, transsexual people, like almost everyone else, began questioning traditional gen-der norms—and were consequently liberated from the view that doc-tors and researchers were the primary authority on transsexuals and transsexualism. The Transsexual Action Organization—founded in Los Angeles in 1970 by Angela Douglas—for example, was a radical group that, like the Gay Liberation Front, stood shoulder to shoulder with other revolutionaries working to change American society and that viewed the system, and not the (transsexual or transgendered) in-dividual, as the problem. "I have a newspaper article in my files by An-gela Douglas from '70 or '71 that calls for 'transgender liberation now' and provides a whole political critique of the gender system," says Susan Stryker. "She was fairly self-aware in saying 'the things that are fucked up about me are the result of oppression, and I have a critique of the conditions that have produced me as I am.'"

Douglas was not the only transsexual or transgendered person con-necting her own oppression to a broader social critique, says Stryker. "There are some interesting connections between the antiwar move-ment and the transgender movement," she says. "I think it's not coin-cidental that these were the height of the war years, and that there is a relationship, particularly in what male-to-female transsexual people were able to accomplish, and a larger cultural imperative to fuck with masculinity, at least from the standpoint of the left. The way that you kept from being put in a green uniform and shipped home in a body bag was you became non-normatively masculine and therefore unfit for military service. The long hair, the love beads, the paisley shirt, the bell-bottoms—there was a way that the critique of gender became part of that larger critique, and it created a space for people who were coming from a more self-identified transgender place to work within the broader cultural synergy."

This new breed of transsexual activist rejected the attempts of doctors and researchers to define transsexuality as a form of control— well before Janice Raymond burst onto the scene. "By the mid-sixties, I think that transsexuals were using the scientific discourse as received for their own ends," says Stryker. "They were saying, 'Because I am a transsexual, I should be allowed to change my legal identification paperwork. Because I am a transsexual, I am going to work with the neighborhood legal defense fund, and we're going to wage this case and change employment law. Because I am a transsexual, I should have my medical needs met; therefore the city clinic should give me hormones.' So the classic transsexual medical discourse was being deployed for purposes of gaining civil and human rights. That started in '65 to '66 here in San Francisco."

Rather than applying to one of the university gender clinics, with their stringent criteria for acceptance, many transsexuals began to seek out private surgeons who were willing to perform surgery on demand. The most infamous of these, John Ronald Brown, "presented himself as the champion of transsexuals," says Joanne Meyerowitz in *How Sex Changed,* "but he also won a well-earned reputation as the back-alley butcher of transsexual surgery." But more reputable doctors and surgeons also began working with transsexual clients, and it became somewhat easier for people to access the services they required—if they had the money. Others traveled overseas for surgery, effectively subverting the medical model by contracting for services with health care providers who did not share American physicians' views of the need for an extended period of "real-life" experimentation prior to surgery. A number of transsexual memoirists have written of their surgeries with "Dr. B" in Casablanca, Morocco. Dr. Georges Borou was for many years the surgeon of choice for affluent transsexual people, such as British journalist Jan (née James) Morris. "He was exceedingly handsome," Morris writes in *Conundrum*. "He was small, dark, rather intense of feature, and was dressed as if for some kind of beach activity. He wore a dark blue open-necked shirt, sports trousers, and game shoes, and he was very bronzed. He welcomed me with a bemused smile, as though his mind were in Saint-Tropez."

Meanwhile, John Money's erstwhile benefactor, Reed Erickson, continued to fund research and public education on transsexualism through the Erickson Educational Foundation throughout the seventies. "What Erickson did on a small scale in Harry Benjamin's office in the sixties they did on a much larger scale later," says Aaron Devor. "The first three international conferences on transsexuality were all funded by the EEF." The first symposium was held in London, in 1969; the second in Denmark, in 1971; and the third in Yugoslavia, in 1973. A fourth conference, named the Harry Benjamin Fourth International Conference on Gender Identity, in honor of Benjamin's ninetieth birthday, was held in 1975. The EEF, says Devor, "chose the locations, invited the people, did the advertising. That synergy created a whole new field of research. He [Erickson] created a whole new discipline, as well as a support network for transsexuals themselves who would call the EEF to find out where they could find a doctor or a therapist."

The Erickson Educational Foundation also produced numerous publications for transsexual people and their families, brochures and pamphlets that explained in everyday language what transsexualism was and offered effective strategies for treatment. "In their day, these were the only educational material that transsexual people and their families could get their hands on. They were quality publications, and have been subsequently republished and are still in circulation," says Devor. "The EEF really created public awareness, public sympathy, even empathy for transsexuals. I give Erickson a tremendous amount of credit for bringing this issue to the attention of researchers and the public."

The EEF financed a steady stream of lectures at medical schools, at schools of social work and law, and to police officers in training.

"They sought out people in positions of power and influence over the lives of transsexuals and tried to educate them while they were being trained," says Devor. "The EEF made movies and then sent them around to medical schools. In collaboration with John Money, they produced definitions of transsexuality and transvestism, which they sent out to 105 dictionaries and encyclopaedias, so that when you looked for a definition [of those terms] you found the ones they had created. It was almost as though they asked themselves what they could do to make people aware of this issue on every front." The advice columnists Abigail van Buren and Ann Landers even referred people to the EEF in their columns. When the imminent closure of the EEF was announced at the Fifth International Gender Dysphoria Symposium, held in Norfolk, Virginia, in February 1977, the assembled group of researchers, under the direction of Paul Walker, M.D., discussed the creation of a new organization to carry on its work. The proposed organization, named for Harry Benjamin, was formally approved at the Sixth International Gender Dysphoria Symposium, held in San Diego, California, in February 1979.

In March 2003, I spoke to Jude Patton, a transman who was the first "consumer advocate" on the new Harry Benjamin International Gender Dysphoria Association (HBIGDA) Board of Trustees. Patton, a psychotherapist, was a graduate student when he became involved with HBIGDA through his doctor/patient relationship with Donald Laub, M.D., a surgeon at Stanford University's Gender Clinic and one of the first members of the board. "When the first HBIGDA conference was going to be held, I asked Don Laub, who was my surgeon, if I could attend, and I came as his guest. At that time I had also met Zelda Suplee [of the EEF] and Paul Walker through some of the early support groups that I had started," says Patton. At the meeting in San Diego in 1979, "there was a band of outspoken heterosexual TVs, consumer voices, who were very strident, saying, 'Why don't you include us?' and other things of that nature," says Patton. "So when they actually formed HBIGDA, Doctor Laub suggested that they include a consumer advocate, and he nominated me. The vote was fifteen to fifteen." Patton says that the votes against were not against him personally—as "nobody really knew me"—but against the idea of having a consumer voice on the board at all. "I remember that someone stood up and said, 'I will not serve on any committee that has a consumer on it,'" he recalls.

Laub cast the deciding vote in favor of Patton's membership, however, and Patton was elected. Patton served on the HBIGDA board from 1979 to 1981, and found the experience somewhat overwhelming. "I was very intimidated," he says. "I was still a grad student, and these people were big names in the field." Still, he says, "they were polite and they listened to me." But after his two-year term expired, the board did not appoint another consumer advocate until 1997, when Patton was once again asked to serve, together with Sheila Kirk, M.D., an MTF surgeon. "It was my understanding that the position [of consumer advocate] would always be there," he says. "But it didn't happen again until 1997, when Sheila Kirk and I were contacted by the board. They knew our work and trusted us. I give Richard Green, who was president at the time, credit. He said, 'It's time.'" Patton believes that he was recruited to serve on the board again because of "the personal relationships I had developed over the years" with board members, and also because he is "an educator. I'm not a rabble-rouser," he says.

The first order of business for the new Harry Benjamin International Gender Dysphoria Association was the development of a treatment protocol, or "Standards of Care," for transsexual people, one that would both protect them from unscrupulous practitioners and also continue to exert some measure of medical control over the process of sex reassignment. "HBIGDA recognized the rise of private practitioners and tried to guide their professional behavior," writes Joanne Meyerowitz in *How Sex Changed*. "Under its original Standards of Care, private endocrinologists and surgeons could not offer treatment on demand. Psychologists and psychiatrists . . . were to recommend medical treatment, and they were to have seen their clients for several months before making such recommendations. MTFs were to live as women and FTMs were to live as men for at least a year before they could undergo surgery. If they adhered to these guidelines, private practitioners could protect their professional standing and distinguish themselves from 'chop shop' doctors like John Brown."

The Benjamin Standards of Care were put into place by researchers associated with the Erickson Foundation, and carried over many of the practices (for example, the "real-life" test and the role of psychotherapists as gatekeepers) that had first evolved in the university clinics. "The first version of the Standards of Care was very similar to the guidelines that came out of the EEF-based research of Benjamin and the Hopkins clinic," says Aaron Devor, who is working on a biography of Erickson. "I have to infer that Erickson was comfortable with the model as it was developing," says Devor. "In the context in which the model was created and the opposing view—that anyone contemplating taking these steps was out of their mind—this is understandable."

Nonetheless, the Standards of Care and the medical model of transsexuality that they represented stood in direct contrast to the activist approach born in the seventies. Many transsexual people did not want to be "medicalized" and they did not want to be "pathologized." They wanted access to surgery and/or hormones on demand without having to jump through a series of Standards of Care hoops. Their most radical claim, and the one that was to create a nearly unbridgeable chasm between proponents of the Benjamin model and an increasingly vocal and active transgender movement in the early nineties, was that American society, not transgender or transsexual people, had a "gender problem."

CONVERSATION WITH TOM KENNARD

Kennard and his partner, Marianne, have been together for four years. Kennard was fifty-one at the time of this interview and spent many years in the lesbian community prior to his transition. Marianne is forty-three; she identifies as bisexual and has had relationships with both men and women. Soon after Kennard completed transition, Marianne discovered that she was losing her sight. On the morning I visited them in their home in San Francisco, Marianne was out with her mentor in a local support group, learning how to navigate the city alone. After her return, we went out for breakfast. I was impressed by the great tenderness Kennard displayed toward Marianne and by the way that they were working together to ease Marianne's transition into a challenging new world.

Q: Tom, could you speak about your experience crossing over from the lesbian-feminist community to living as a transman?

It was really hard. I was big feminist, a white lesbian feminist, and I was kind of a separatist. I didn't like men, I didn't like the patriarchy, and I never wanted to grow up to be a straight white guy. I fought it for a long time.

Growing up, I didn't identify as anything, really. When you are little . . . I knew I was kind of different but I don't really know how I knew that. I knew that there was a difference between boys and girls, because in school everything is segregated by gender, so I would have to get in the girls' line, but I was like, "Why am I in the girls' line?" [*Laughs*] What is it about me that makes me a girl? So it's all kind of murky. I know this is the stereotype, but I always wanted to do what the boys wanted to do. When I reached puberty I liked girls, and I told somebody in Girl Scouts that I really liked this woman and if I was a boy I would marry her. And all through high school we had to wear dresses all the time, and that was incredibly horrible for me. I felt like I was cross-dressed all the time.

But then I went away to college and started reading books and I found out that "Well, okay, you can be a lesbian." So I did that for a long time, but I always felt like a spy. In the bathroom especially, in gym, I always felt like a spy. "I'm not supposed to be in here." So it wasn't until I was forty-seven that I started taking hormones. There's an FTM support group here [in San Francisco]. I went there in 1990, and there was this whole roomful of men. Oh my God! I didn't go back for six years. It freaked me out so much. I'm like, "There's a bunch of men in there. I don't like men. Men are the patriarchy. Men are bad." But finally, I just got really angry. I'd go to the store or something and give people my driver's license to write a check and they'd read the female name and call me "ma'am." And I would feel really angry because I'm not that person. Don't call me "ma'am." And I was a butch lesbian, so people would a lot of time call me "sir" but then when I would talk, because I had a female voice, they'd say, "Oh, I'm sorry," and maybe they would be nice to me or maybe they wouldn't.

Q: Did people mostly read you as female at that time?

Here in San Francisco, because there are so many lesbians, and a butch lesbian is identifiable, people would identify me as a butch. So then of course there was all the homophobia.

Q: In San Francisco? [interviewer feigns shock]

Yes. And gay men don't like women very well either, so you go down to the Castro, and gay men weren't really happy to see you. I went in to get my hair cut one time, and they just left me sitting there for an hour. I kept waiting and waiting.

Q: Sounds like you couldn't really find a home in any community—in the lesbian community or the larger gay community. When did you begin to think that you might be transgendered?

I always wore men's clothes. I got rid of women's clothes sometime in the early seventies. I remember taking them all to the dump. You know those big Dumpsters? I left them all draped over it. So I always wore men's clothes. And I always felt like transgendered people were my family, but I didn't really know why. I always kind of gravitated toward drag queens, people who were on the edge of gender somehow. Those were always the people I liked. In queer bars these people were often on the outside of things. So one night I'm at the lesbian bar, and I see a man dressed to the nines, and he's a transvestite, and he's with his wife who is a transvestite the other way. So we become friends, and I start hanging out with them. She tells me about a television show that wants to talk to female-to-male transvestites. It's not a category that anybody talks about. Women can wear men's clothes, and nobody looks at them. So that's when I go, "Oh, there's a transgender community." I was about thirty-five at the time.

So I sat with that for a while. I was a cross-dresser for a while. As I met more and more people in my community, and I heard FTM transsexuals talk, I'm like, "Gee, that sounds really familiar." I spent a long time going, "Well, we're kind of the same, but I go up to this line but I don't go over, and they do." Finally, I decided to go to that meeting in 1990 when I was about forty. And I got so freaked out. I was like, "No, I don't want to be a straight white guy." But by '96 or '97, I said to myself, "This isn't working out at all." And I thought, "Who can you live your life for but you? I'm in my forties." So I started hormones in October of '97. And I met Marianne right before I started hormones. So she's seen me as a girl, and now I'm a boy. [*Laughs*] She's seen the whole physical thing happen, and it's a really intensive personal time, so she's had to live through all my adolescent male stuff. All I talked about was transition for years. I'm just now getting out of it.

Q: How would you define where you are now?

I fully recognize that I am not born male. I did not have that experience. I never will. I am transgendered. I am a transman. I live in the world as male, and that's fine. But I still feel sort of like a spy. I'm not like everybody else.

Q: Because you've lived in both worlds, lived as both a woman and a man?

Yeah, and I'm still struggling with a lot of things that come with being male. Like being perceived as a threat. I can't talk to kids, and women are like this. [*Holds his hands far apart*] I'm really sad about the whole distance between women and me. I understand why that's there, but I would never hurt a woman.

Q: What are some of the other liabilities of being a man?

Back hair. [*Laughs*] I'm not really sure I'm happy about that.

But I love Halloween and there's a whole bunch of children in the neighborhood. And I just love it when the kids come, but now when they come I have to take Marianne to the door with me. Because the parents are like, "Ooh, this middle-aged white guy standing there with his candy." It's really upsetting to me. And I have to learn how to use my voice. My voice has gotten really deep, and I need to sort of sound like [*softens it*] so I don't sound threatening. I'm not a tall person, but I'm kind of a big guy. Which brings up a whole other area. If you are a big woman . . . people used to yell at me stuff like "fat bitch, fat dyke." Big is bad if you are female; big is good if you are male. Now I just go to the Big 'n' Tall, and they're like, "Big Tom is coming!" [*Laughs*]

It's a lot to negotiate. It's a lot to try to have these hormonal changes and the body changes and then try to figure out, "Now how do I be a man?"

Q: How important is it to you to have a penis?

It's really important to me, but I'm never going to have enough money to have that operation [phalloplasty]. I don't really want to mess with my body like that. It doesn't really go well; it doesn't work. They can't do those hydraulics. I would rather keep what function I have. I'm sort of half and half now. My body is . . . I'm a different kind of a thing, a new thing, and that's okay. A lot of guys find it incredibly important [to undergo phalloplasty] and I honor that. If they need to do that, I think they should do it. But I'm never going to have that much money and . . .

Q: And for you it doesn't seem to define your manhood?

No, it doesn't define my manhood. If they could just snap their fingers and give me one that works, I'd say okay. I don't want to diminish the importance of it. . . . I just don't feel like it right now. Now, I know some guys change their minds; you can change your mind sometimes as you go through this process. Some guy asked me about it one time, and I'm like, "Okay, all of the men in the room, let's just get up there and line it up by how big it is. Come on, you guys, let's go." I mean, it's ridiculous.

Q: Do women relate differently to you as a man?

Yes, yes. It really surprised me. Women will touch me, and I'm like, "I can't believe they're doing that. Wow. They're being nice." They talk to me, play around with me. I love women. I really do. We were just having a discussion about that last night. That is really one of the wonderful things, that I can really enjoy women in a way that I never could before. Because I'm not like them. My body is not like that. Before it was really sexually difficult. Because I didn't want people to see me naked. It was just really hard.

Q: In your experience, is there a difference between male and female sexuality?

It's really hard to make generalizations, but testosterone is incredible stuff, incredibly powerful. I'm so much more visual now. I understand why there's *Playboy* and porno. I never got that. I always liked women, I liked the way they looked, but I never . . . it's not like I wanted to watch [pornographic] movies or anything. Now, the thing that's really distressing to me is how much women's bodies are used to sell things. I knew it intellectually. I was a feminist. But now I know it at this visceral level, and I am just appalled. It's like there are these receptors in your body, there are estrogen receptors and there are testosterone receptors. Your testosterone receptors just aren't working right now. You have them, but they are just not working. But mine all got activated. I remember about three years ago—I remember this so clearly—I was walking downtown, and this woman had like a dark gray sort of tank top on, and she was walking down the street and her breasts were just kind of jiggling. And I'm like, "Oh my god!" If I had a penis, I would have had an erection. So I have that now, I have those physical reactions. Like, I'm watching the *Soul Train Awards,* and those women have, like, no clothes on, and I think I must be old or something because I'm thinking, "These children should not be going around like that." I think that women must have a clue, because women have used this to control us for a long time, and mostly I'm really happy about it. I mean, Marianne can control me with that. I'm happy, okay, honey.

Q: Perhaps that's the reason that women lose power as they get older, while men gain power.

Yes, and you don't even have to be an attractive man! You just need to be an old man, just an ugly old guy. It's the whole thing about not having to worry about your appearance. For women, falling in love, and attraction, is about your mind and your heart. But I picked Marianne because . . . I probably wouldn't have talked to her if I hadn't been physically attracted to her. We're all like that, but men sort of take it to an art. I buy her a lot of things I want to see her wearing, and she lets me do it.

Q: Did you not do that kind of thing in your old life?

I kind of did, but it's not the same as it is now. I mean, I liked feminine women always . . . but it's a different thing now. It's like I'm watching movies now that I never really watched before.

Q: Like action adventure, or shoot-'em-ups?

Oh, yeah! Actually, that's really interesting, because the action adventure movies get to me now in a different way they didn't before. It's like, "Oh yeah, great, blow something else up." It's not like I want to see people killed; it's not like that. It's like, "Blow that up, make that car really fast." It's crazy.

Q: So do you still keep in touch with friends from your old life? How do they feel about this change?

It depends on how old they are. If they're my age, they think I've gone over to the enemy. I'm dead. They don't talk to me.

MARIANNE: Or like that woman on your soccer team who could sort of relate to it, but she was afraid. She actually felt a lot of the same things, but felt like the penalty of making that change would be the loss of a community that had been home for so long.

KENNARD: That was painful. And a lot of the guys who were lesbians really feel that. And a lot of times they tried not to transition, or to hold on to it as long as they can. It's really hard. Like I'm completely invisible as a queer person now. I'm queer. I think of myself as queer. I can see queer people. We have queer radar, we do. But they don't see me at all. Really, the place I'm most comfortable is with gay men. I love gay men. One of my best friends is a gay man, who taught me how to shave, took me to men's bars, showing me what it was like to be a man. I mean he's a gay man, but he's a man. I can touch him— straight men are so touch-phobic. I can feel what his beard is like. He got naked in front of me. I'm like, "Okay, this is how men are made." So I love gay men and I like to be with him. And when I'm with gay men, I'm part of this great community. I'm not invisible. They think I'm queer; I mean they think I'm gay, but that's okay. If I'm with Marianne, I'm invisible, and people want to know why we're there.

Q: And this is San Francisco, the home of the LGBT community?

KENNARD: It's still a binary gender system. They don't even think about it.

MARIANNE: And so much of life is organized around it that whatever else may be up for reevaluation, by God, not the M and the F. So many things are constructed on that, it's sort of like if you change that, talk about changing your center of gravity, it really confuses everything.

KENNARD: And a lot people won't allow you to change. Some people—it doesn't matter what I tell them, I'm not a man [in their eyes]. I never tell people what my name used to be, for example, because that is like the kiss of death. If I tell someone that I'm transgendered, I'm all of a sudden "she." They never get over it.

MARIANNE: And they never would have thought that, when they're meeting him. They're like, "Oh, I would never have known." But I think that the other thing that can get oversimplified in the queer community is that straight people have complicated gender identities too. There are some men born in male bodies who have spent their whole lives as males who are also trying to figure out what it means to be a man. And trying to negotiate not wanting to automatically fall into certain roles.

Q: We all need to negotiate gender every day of our lives.

MARIANNE: Yes. And if you are a woman and you want to be with women, that's perceived as a gender-transgression thing. That's the point that we're trying to make. That's why we're all in this community. That's why LGBT and intersexed people should be in this community together. It's a gender thing; it's not just sexual orientation. The first thing that people want to know about you: "Who do you sleep with?" Once they get "Oh, he's a transman," it's "Who do you sleep with?" And then "What bathroom do you use?"

KENNARD: Yeah, that's my favorite question, when they ask me what bathroom I use. Sometimes I get a little short. If a woman asks, [*feigns concern*] "Do you want me to go in the women's bathroom with you?" I'm like, "Come on. Are you crazy? What do you mean 'what bathroom do I use?'"

MARIANNE: But I actually do understand that question, because it's so core. Those details of daily life. If you get so far as to say, "Okay let's just pretend that I get to be this guy, where would I go to the bathroom?" Especially when things are organized on that binary gender line . . . you are transgressing a big rule.

Q: Maybe we should just have unisex bathrooms.

KENNARD: But that was one of the things that shot down the ERA, don't you remember? People get really weirded out about the issue of bathrooms!

When I finally decided to go through this transition, the thing that really got it for me was that I worked for this bank and had a membership for a health club. So I always wore shirts and ties to work, and then I go to the health club and you have to tell them your name. Okay, I had this female name. Okay, I have to go into the women's locker room. It sent me right back to high school. It was one of the most traumatic things that ever happened to me. There were these nude women in there, and I was like this. [*Mimes shielding his eyes and slinking by*] I was not looking. The staff person was like, "And here we have the sauna," and I'm like, "Okay, all right." I just felt like I can't go and be in women's locker rooms anymore. And it was right after that I said, "Okay, I'm taking hormones" and transitioned. So now I have the other problem. I can't go into the men's locker room and get naked.

MARIANNE: There is a certain amount of privilege in walking around the world in a body that fits who you feel like you are. Not just with gender, but with all kinds of things. Not having that privilege makes negotiating the things that are usually much harder.

KENNARD: Another problem for us is health care. I had gone through menopause at about thirty-seven. And I went to the doctor, and I said, "I think I'm going through menopause," and he said, "No, you're too young," and I said, "No, I don't think so." So he does the hormone test, and says, "You are." And he wants me to take estrogen! Then, when I started on testosterone, I had really bad problems with cramps. So when I started having the cramps, I went to the doctor and he's like, "You don't have cramps. It's colitis." And I'm like, "No, I've finally figured out where my uterus is, and it hurts."

Then came the saga of trying to find a gynecologist as a male. I'd call up and say, "I'd like to make an appointment," and the receptionist would say, "This is gynecology." And I'd say, "I know that." And she'd say, "Do you know what we do in gynecology?" And I'd say, "I know what you do in gynecology. Could you just make an appointment with the doctor, please?" So I went to this guy, who did a hysterectomy and he'd never seen an FTM and he'd never heard of it, and he wasn't very cool at first, but he kind of got okay.

One day before the surgery, the doctor said, "Do you want to be in a men's room or a woman's room?" And I'm like, "You know, here's the thing. I'm Thomas. If you put me in the woman's room, she's going to be like, 'What is that man doing here?' And if you put me in a man's room, I'll be really uncomfortable with that because I'm having a hysterectomy." So he said, "I think I'll get you a private room." And that's what we did.

The last appointment, when we went back there so that he could make sure everything was okay, the receptionist came out into the waiting room and she says, "Miss Thomas Kennard." So now I have to stand up. The [receptionist] looks at me, she looks at Marianne. We go back to the room and [she] starts talking to Marianne, saying "When was your last period?" Marianne says, "I'm not the patient." The [receptionist] just kept it up. Marianne said, "I'm not the patient. He's the patient. He had the hysterectomy. He needs to see the doctor." The woman just went white.

MARIANNE: She was an older lady. She was really just afraid. She was freaked out.

KENNARD: I was really uncomfortable. I said, "You know, I have to go to the men's room. I can't even do this." I said, "Where's the men's room?" And she's like this. [*Frozen*]

MARIANNE: She couldn't even speak. She was afraid.

KENNARD: So I went out, and when I came back she was gone. Marianne had gotten rid of her. What did you say?

MARIANNE: I said, "What are you afraid of?" I don't even remember now exactly what I said. She was terrified.

Q: I've heard a lot about gynecologic problems among transmen.

KENNARD: We all seem to get this problem with the cramps, because of the testosterone. But other than that, I only had menopause early. You'd have to pull teeth to get me to a gynecologist. Going to a gynecologist is like acknowledging that you are really female somehow, and we're not having any of that. Like, I didn't know where my uterus was. They made me get a sonogram before my surgery, and they didn't tell the woman [technician] anything, I guess. And she's running it over my abdomen, looking over at the monitor, looking at me. She asks me, "Can I ask you a really personal question? Do you have ambiguous genitals?" So I said, "No, I'm just a regular transsexual."

Q: And what was her response?

KENNARD: "Oh, okay." She was really nice. But then this gynecologist wrote me a note and said that I had to have a mammogram. And I called for the appointment and I went there for it, and they helped every woman in the room. Finally: "Can I help you, sir?" I said, "I have an appointment at two." And she said, "Well, you don't have one here, but I'll find out where it is." And then she's like, "Oh, you *do* have one here." And we go back, and I said, "Marianne has to go in the room with me." And I think this woman was a lesbian and she was my age, and she was not happy with the situation.

MARIANNE: She really wasn't.

KENNARD: She said, "No, nobody can go in." I said, "Marianne has to go in. We have to figure out a way for this to happen." So I got her in there. But she didn't give me a thing to cover up. I'm already sensitive, because I'm really hairy. I felt like a freak.

MARIANNE: And I remember saying, because he was so freaked out, "Maybe we should say something to her, like 'I'm really uncomfortable with this situation,'" because then the person will usually, even if they are not real keen on it, [it's] at least an opening for them to maybe become a bit nicer. But you did that, and it didn't help. She was still very short.

KENNARD: If you appeal to people's humanity, especially women, they're usually okay. I just said, "It's really hard for me. I feel like a freak. I don't want to be here." But it didn't work with her. It was like I had gone over to the enemy or something. It's like I was saying before: younger people are much better about it than lesbian women my age.

Q: Would you mind if we talked a little about your relationship and how you got together and the challenges of being in a relationship with a person who is transitioning?

MARIANNE: One thing that was helpful was that Tom wasn't the first trans person that I knew. I was friends with other transpeople and their partners. Some of my friends have been in a situation where they came to know their partner as one gender, as one identity, and then in the context of their relationship that changed, and so they had to make that transition, to give up that identity that they had shared as a couple and transition into a new one. And that is a journey that I really respect. But Tom was already transitioning, and that definitely was an advantage for us as a couple.

I think that part of transition, no matter what kind of transition, is that it is a selfish process. Speaking as a person who was a sighted person and now I'm losing it and having to learn to be in the world in a whole different way, to me that's a selfish process. It's pretty much all I can do sometimes to deal with that. And it's hard to have something so absorbing in your life, and be a couple. And at the time that Tom was having his transition about gender, I was having a transition about becoming a middle-aged woman, losing my vision, and my children growing up and leaving home. And then Tom had lived in a relationship but in his own space, alone, for a long time. So then there was another transition as we started spending a lot of time mostly here. He had this whole apartment to himself. So some of those things are unique to a couple that has a transgender person in it, and definitely there is a part of this process that I can't enter. It's a personal process. I can be feeling fine about his body, that I like his body, even as it changes, but he could be having different feelings at different times about his body. And that's not about me, but it has an effect on me.

Q: Have you noticed any significant changes in Tom after transition?

I wasn't in a relationship with Tom before, so I don't know what his communication style was. But we have a really different style of communication, in that mine tended to include more words than his does. And compounded by the problem of losing my vision, I need more words, and talking in a way more than some people might. I also think there is also the whole thing of what Tom refers to as a kind of adolescence. And a lot of guys talk about it that way. It's very confusing to be in a relationship with someone who is on the one hand six or seven years older than you are, and has gray temples, but also has another adolescent part, trying to figure out things like how to be a man. It is this process you have to go through. Then there's this whole phenomenon that Tom mentioned of having to talk about it [transition], in a lot of detail. I think it's really interesting. So there is a way that I really like talking about it, but I also like that more time has passed and he's had more experience, that if we go into a social situation, there is a range of topics, not just that one.

I think that's a struggle that I've heard from other partners, friends, and allies close to people in transition. It's really key that you maintain a boundary, and that you continue to put energy into yourself. You have to hold your own place, and that seems especially important and also difficult to get that balance. And then the other thing is when Tom was really early in transition, we didn't have the kind of ease that we have now. Because his body had changed, and so the perception on the street of him—how he looks on the outside, how he feels, and who he feels himself to be . . . there's no incongruity—they take him as a male. And so when I first started going out with him, those changes weren't as dramatic yet. If we had been somewhere more rural, not the Castro, not San Francisco, I think that even at that point most people would have taken him as a male. But because of the consciousness here that a woman can look a lot of different ways and a man can look a lot of different ways, there were people who did spot him and see him as female still. And I know that was really hard for him. You have a kind of protectiveness in that you don't want the person you love to be hurt, and there's nothing you can do about that.

Six

CHILDHOOD, INTERRUPTED

I wonder what my parents imagined would happen to me in a mental hospital. They wanted the doctors to tame me but they didn't ask, and the doctors didn't say, exactly what this process entailed. It was the doctors who came up with the idea that I was "an inappropriate female"—that my mouthy ways were a sign of a deep unease in my female nature and that if I learned tips about eyeliner and foundation, I'd be a lot better off. Who would have told my parents this? Not me. Once I was locked up, I lost interest in holding a meaningful conversation with my parents.

DAPHNE SCHOLINSKI,
THE LAST TIME I WORE A DRESS, CHICAGO, 1981

In 1974 millions of Americans were suddenly cured of mental illness when homosexuality was deleted from the *Diagnostic and Statistical Manual of Mental Disorders* (DSM), often referred to as the "bible" of psychiatry. This reference book, which today runs to nearly nine hundred pages, defines and classifies more than three hundred mental disorders. The DSM is used not only by psychiatrists, but also by courts, schools, and social service agencies in making decisions about matters as varied as child custody, criminal liability, placement in special education classes, and receipt of Social Security benefits. The DSM also profoundly affects the way that we as a society think about mental health and disease. "Defining a mental disorder involves specifying the features of human experience that demarcate where normality shades into abnormality," write sociologists Herb Kutchins and Stuart Kirk in *Making Us Crazy*, a study of the rhetoric of science in the practice of psychiatry. This boundary shifted dramatically for gay people in the late seventies, after activists inside and outside the psychiatric profession called into question the scientific merit of the diagnosis of homosexuality as a pathology.

As early as 1956, the psychologist Evelyn Hooker showed that gay men did not exhibit signs of psychopathology in their performance on a series of three testing instruments often used to provide evidence of mental health. After the Stonewall riots, in 1968, gay activists began to picket and disrupt the annual convention of the American Psychiatric Association (APA) and other professional meetings, demanding to be heard. From 1970 to 1974, activists within the psychiatric profession and without forced the profession to examine its basic assumptions about human sexuality and the way that it defined pathology. Ultimately, a majority of APA members conceded that their views on homosexuality were based on moral considerations rather than scientific ones. In 1974, when ballots were mailed to the members of the association asking them to vote on a decision of the board of trustees to delete the homosexuality entry from DSM, 58 percent of the ten thousand psychiatrists who replied voted in favor of the deletion. For a few years, an alternative diagnosis of "ego-dystonic homosexuality" (individuals unhappy with their own homosexuality) was retained, but then this, too, was dropped in the 1987 revision of the DSM.

The deletion of homosexuality from the manual was viewed as a major victory for gay rights groups, who knew that their revolution would not advance very far as long as homosexuality was certified as a pathology in the DSM, as Kutchins and Kirk note in a chapter chronicling the review process that led to the decision. However, in medicine as in law, the transgendered were left behind when gays and lesbians entered the mainstream. Homosexuality may have been deleted from the DSM, but "gender identity disorder" has taken its place as the diagnosis most frequently assigned to children and adults who fail to conform to socially accepted norms of male and female identity and behavior. "When the DSM-III came out, the first edition without homosexuality, the gay community was so happy and so empowered that by the time the DSM-IV came out, nobody was watching anymore," activist Dylan (née Daphne) Scholinski told me in 2004. "Since then the category has just grown broader, mostly because they've combined all the old categories."

The DSM serves as a kind of dictionary of psychopathologies. It is used both as a diagnostic tool and as a justification for insurance coverage. Without a DSM diagnosis, insurance companies will not reimburse mental health treatment, either inpatient or outpatient. "DSM is the psychotherapist's password for insurance coverage," note Kutchins and Kirk. "All mental health professionals must list a psychiatric diagnosic label, accompanied by appropriate code number, on their claims for insurance reimbursement." Since its inception in 1952, the DSM has been revised five times, though the 1980 publication of DSM-III is viewed as the most significant for a number of reasons. First, it is much more comprehensive than previous editions, with many more diagnoses. "The DSM-III Task Force was predisposed to include many new diagnostic categories," say Kutchins and Kirk. The reason for this was twofold: The practice of psychiatry was moving out of the hospital and into outpatient settings, and practitioners were seeing a much broader range of problems. At the same time, third-party (insurance) coverage was becoming more common, and coverage required a diagnosis. These two factors working together account for the sudden increase in diagnostic categories in the DSM-III—suddenly many more people were susceptible to a DSM diagnosis (and thus eligible for insurance reimbursement for treatment) than previously.

Kutchins and Kirk's analysis provides a clue to understanding why homosexuality was stricken from the DSM, while, first, transsexuality, and, later, gender identity disorder became part of the nosology, or system of classification. One of the many profound effects of the gay liberation movement was the sudden shift in the way that gay men and lesbians thought about themselves and their sexual orientation. After Stonewall and the activism that followed in its wake, many people who might once have sought out psychiatrists and therapists hoping to be "cured" of their desires achieved a level of self-acceptance they had previously lacked. They no longer needed the services of psychiatrists because they no longer perceived themselves as ill. Transsexual people faced a far more complicated situation, however. Even if they didn't consider themselves "sick" per se, they still needed to secure the services of health care providers. They needed endocrinologists and surgeons but, according to the Benjamin Standards of Care, they first needed to spend up to a year in therapy in order to secure the all-important "letter" from their therapist recommending hormones or surgery. They remain locked into the health care system in a way that gays and lesbians are not.

Dr. Ben Barres of Stanford described this painful conundrum very succinctly in our conversation in 2001. "I have very mixed feelings about this. I think if gay people weren't victims of societal ignorance and maltreatment, most would be very happy and well-adjusted, whereas I'm not sure that is true for transsexuals, at least most transsexuals that I've met who grow up feeling that they are the wrong gender. So there's a certain amount of pathology. Nevertheless, I don't think that transgendered people need to be in the DSM any more than gays do. It's unfair, just as unfair as it was for homosexuals."

In DSM-III, published in 1980, "transsexualism" first appeared as a diagnostic category distinct from transvestic fetishism (cross-dressing for purposes of sexual excitement). The diagnosis was limited to "gender dysphoric individuals who demonstrated at least two years of continuous interest in removing their sexual anatomy and transforming their bodies and social roles." The concept of gender dysphoria was developed by researchers at Stanford who realized that many of the adult patients presenting for treatment did not fit the profile of "classic" transsexualism. Dr. Norman Fisk, clinical instructor of psychiatry at Stanford School of Medicine and codeveloper of the Stanford Gender Identity Clinic, recalls that when the Stanford program was initiated, "due to inexperience and naïveté we went about seeking so-called ideal candidates and a great emphasis was placed upon attempting to exclusively treat only classical or textbook cases of transsexualism." The classical criteria included a lifelong sense or feeling of being a member of "the other sex," early and persistent cross-dressing without any associated sexual excitement, and a "dislike or repugnance for homosexual behavior," says Fisk. "We avidly searched for those patients who, if admitting to homosexual behavior at all, insisted that they always adopted a passive role and avoided the stimulation of their own genitals by their partner," says Fisk.

As noted previously, researchers eventually realized that prospective candidates for sex reassignment were altering their life histories in order to meet the clinical criteria for "classic" transsexualism, to increase their chances of treatment. Rather than rejecting nonclassic patients outright or acceding to surgery on demand, the Stanford researchers conceived a novel solution. They created a "grooming clinic" for prospective patients, which became a kind of support group, "a group therapy situation in which individuals met on a once-per-month basis to exchange information, opinions, experiences and to mutually share feelings, successes, and failures." The charm school/support group also enabled the Stanford researchers to develop long-term relationships with attendees and to gain "both time and increasing experience." As a result of this ongoing follow-up, the staff at the clinic abandoned their previous "rigid and truly unrealistic diagnostic criteria" for transsexualism and developed an alternative diagnosis, "gender dysphoria syndrome." Gender-dysphoric individuals were described as individuals who were "intensely and abidingly uncomfortable in their anatomic and genetic sex and their assigned gender" and who "functioned far more effectively and comfortably in their gender of choice, as clearly demonstrated by obvious and objective criteria."

Following evolving psychiatric opinion, DSM-III TR (Text Revision), released in 1987, includes a third, more expansive, category: "Gender Identity Disorder of Adolescence or Adulthood, Non-Transsexual Type (GIDAANT)." The DSM-III TR authors write that GIDAANT "differs from Transvestic Fetishism in that the cross-dressing is not for the purpose of sexual excitement; it differs from Transsexualism in that there is no persistent preoccupation (for at least two years) with getting rid of one's primary and secondary sex characteristics and acquiring the sex characteristics of the other sex."

In 1994, the diagnosis of transsexualism was deleted from DSM-IV by combining its diagnostic criteria with those of GIDAANT and absorbing GID of childhood into the category. In "Gender Identity Disorder of Childhood, Adolescence or Adulthood," the expressed desire for surgery now becomes only one of a number of criteria to be taken into consideration when making a diagnosis. The key elements of the diagnosis in both adults and children are "a strong and persistent cross-gender identification" and "a persistent discomfort with his or her sex and sense of appropriateness in the gender role of that sex." The disturbance must also be sufficiently obvious or intense to cause "clinically significant distress or impairment in social, occupational, or other important areas of functioning." Clearly, a far greater number of people meet these criteria than meet the more limited criteria for transsexualism. In shifting the focus from an expressed desire to change sex to cross-gender identification, distress, and impairment in functioning, the new diagnosis encompasses not only the relatively few individuals who desire sex reassignment, but also the far greater number who are perceived by themselves or *by others* to express some form of gender variance. However, in the absence of a strong desire for body modification, are the "distress and impairment" experienced by such individuals due to the disorder itself, or are they a consequence of the harassment and social ostracism gender-variant people endure?

Activists argue that the decision to delete homosexuality as a mental disorder from the seventh printing of the second edition of DSM-III and the subsequent creation of the diagnosis of gender identity disorder was a kind of psychiatric sleight of hand. Although the focus of the diagnosis has changed from deviant desire to subversive identity, the core of the diagnosis remains the same: the individual is not a "normal" male or female, and his or her deviance from the norm is conceived as illness or pathology. The diagnosis of gender identity disorder becomes a particularly troubling matter, activists say, when applied to children and adolescents. Four of the following behaviors must be present to justify a clinical diagnosis of gender identity disorder in children: (a) a repeatedly stated desire to be, or insistence that he or she is, the other sex; (b) in boys, a preference for cross-dressing or simulating female attire, and in girls, an insistence on wearing only stereotypical masculine clothing; (c) a strong and persistent preference for cross-sex roles in make-believe play or persistent fantasies of being the other sex; (d) an intense desire to participate in the stereotypical games and pastimes of the other sex; (e) a strong preference for playmates of the other sex.

A little boy who enjoys playing with dolls, avoids sports and other rough activities, prefers the company of girls, and says that he wants to take care of babies when he grows up is likely to be diagnosed with gender identity disorder—even though such behavior is perfectly acceptable in girls. "Behaviors that would be ordinary or even exemplary for gender conforming boys and girls are presented as symptomatic of mental disorder for gender nonconforming children," says Katharine Wilson, Ph.D., an advocate for GID reform. "For boys, these include playing with Barbie dolls, homemaking and nurturing role play, and aversion to cars, trucks, competitive sports and 'rough and tumble' play. For girls, pathology is implied by playing Batman or Superman, competitive contact sports, 'rough and tumble' play, and aversion to dolls or [to] wearing dresses. It is unclear whether the intent of the DSM is to reflect such dated, narrow and sexist gender stereotypes or to enforce them."

The diagnostic criteria for GID have been steadily broadened in successive revisions of the DSM, critics of the diagnosis point out, and the broadening of the criteria points to its essentially subjective (and disciplinary) character. "Recent revisions of the DSM have made these diagnostic categories increasingly ambiguous, conflicted and overinclusive," says Katherine Wilson. "The result is that a widening segment of gender non-conforming youth and adults are potentially subject to diagnosis of psychosexual disorder, stigma and loss of civil liberty." Wilson and other activists fighting to have GID redefined or removed from the DSM point out that even children who do not express discomfort with their gender identity are now subject to the diagnosis, if significant adults in their life (parents, teachers) feel that their behavior is inappropriate for their gender. "GID of Children is clearly not limited to ego-dystonic subjects. High functioning children may be presumed to meet criteria A and B on the basis of cultural nonconformity alone," Wilson argues. "A child may be diagnosed with gender identity disorder without ever having stated any desire to be the other sex." She points out that "overbroad diagnosis contributes to the stigma and undeserved shame that gender nonconforming youth must endure," and that parents who accept their children's gender nonconformity "live in fear of persecution by courts, school officials, and government agencies who infer a broad interpretation of GID of Children and seek punitive treatment remedies."

Critics of the diagnosis have also pointed out the paradoxical fact that while homosexuality is no longer included in the DSM as a psychopathology, research shows that boys diagnosed with GID in childhood are far more likely as adults to identify as gay men than as transsexuals or cross-dressers. They argue that the GID diagnosis is thus being used by parents and clinicians to target children (mostly boys) suspected of being "pre-homosexual." Although "there are simply no formal empirical studies demonstrating that therapeutic intervention in childhood alters the developmental path toward either transsexualism or homosexuality," according to experts, gender-variant children and adolescents are subject to a range of interventions focused on changing their behavior and self-concept. In a paper titled "The Disparate Classification of Gender and Sexual Orientation in American Psychiatry," Wilson notes that "American psychiatric perceptions of etiology, distress, and treatment goals for transgendered people are remarkably parallel to those for gay and lesbian people before the declassification of homosexuality as a mental disorder in 1973."

There is also a clear parallel between the treatment of intersexual children and transgendered children, many allege. Just as the bodies of intersexual children are surgically manipulated to conform to anatomical sexual dimorphism, transgendered children are subjected to psychiatric interventions focused on having them conform to socially sanctioned standards of gendered behavior and appearance.

Transgender youth face formidable challenges. Along with all the other conflicts and confusions associated with adolescence, they must come to terms with a gender identity that all of society tells them is "wrong" or "bad" or "sick." "No single group has gone more unnoticed by society, or abused and maltreated by institutional powers, than youth with transgender needs and feelings," say Gianna E. Israel and Donald E. Tarver II, M.D., in their book *Transgender Care*. "The overwhelming message from family, adult society, and youth peers says that gender nonconformity is a sick, mentally unstable condition to be feared, hated, and ridiculed." All adolescents struggle to understand

and accept their gender and sexuality, but for transgendered kids this is a perilous pursuit, fraught with risk and uncertainty. The pressure to conform to societal expectations of "normal" behavior and appearance comes from all sides—parents, school authorities, the media, and (most daunting for an adolescent) peers. Though there are no Robert's Rules of gender posted at home, in schools, and in churches, the rules exist and are often harshly enforced by peers, parents, and school authorities.

People who have never known a lesbian, gay, or transgendered child often assume the child knows exactly who he or she is. Nothing could be farther from the truth. The process of self-realization and self-understanding is often a slow and painful one. People surrounding the child may take note of the child's gender variance long before the child articulates a sense of being different. In a healthy, accepting environment, the child's process of self-discovery is facilitated by the emotional support provided by a loving family—even when the family knows little about gender variance per se. Family members simply love the child and respect his or her individuality, without requiring that he or she conform to certain codes of dress and behavior. "If there is any cure for children or youth with gender-identity issues, it can be found in the key words *acceptance, androgyny, compromise,* and *communication.* It is important for parents to recognize that all children need to be accepted for what they are, not for what others believe they should be," say Israel and Tarver.

But such understanding remains all too rare. "Parents with resources large or small will spend their last penny trying to help their young son or daughter conform to their concept of what is 'normal,'" according to these researchers. When a family is coping with other stressors, such as alcoholism, separation and divorce, or financial problems, the gender-variant child is very often scapegoated as the source of the family's difficulties. The same thing happens in families devoted to maintaining the appearance of perfection. "Because gender-identity conflicts are still perceived as a mental health disorder by uninformed care providers, today's transgender youth still are at risk of being treated in the same manner gays and lesbians encountered years ago. Sadly, these treatment approaches are little more than abuse, professional victimization, and profiteering under the guise of support for parents' goals."

When the parents' goal of having a "normal" child conflicts with the child's goal of self-understanding and self-realization, the child may wind up either in a coercive therapeutic relationship focused on transforming him or her into a socially acceptable boy or girl, or, when the child refuses to conform, out on the streets. Even when parents are supportive, other adults and peers can be vicious. "Children with gender issues frequently are regarded as unruly or disruptive in the classroom and more often than not are punished, expelled or otherwise made an example by school administrators," note Israel and Tarver. Official disapproval, combined with the teasing, harassment, and general ostracism that many gender-variant children and adolescents suffer at the hands of peers, can make school such a hostile environment that many transgendered kids drop out. The mother of Gwen (born Eddie) Araujo—the seventeen-year-old murdered in Newark, California, in October 2002—told reporters that her child had dropped out of high school because of unending harassment. "People were really mean to him at school. He really tried, but no one accepted him," said Sylvia Guerrero.

In March 2003, I spoke to Alyn Liebeman, an eighteen-year-old self-described trannyboy activist, who comes from an Orthodox/ Conservative Jewish family in Los Angeles. Liebeman's background—Jewish, upper-middle class—could not be more different from that of Gwen Araujo's, and yet he suffered many of the same indignities perpetrated on Araujo. At the time that I spoke to Liebeman, he was waiting to hear from the Ivy League schools to which he had applied for college admission—Harvard, Brown, Princeton, and others. Liebeman is highly gifted and has been enrolled in programs for gifted students since the second grade. He has always been one of the brightest kids in his class. Yet from the start of his school career, Liebeman says, he was harassed, isolated, and singled out for punishment not only by his peers, but also by school administrators, who often blamed him for the abuse other kids heaped upon him. "I had no friends," he says simply. "I was a loner. I didn't fit in." When he was verbally and sometimes physically assaulted by other students, "I was blamed by administrators for being different. They would tell me that if I would just conform, this wouldn't happen."

On one occasion, when he was in sixth grade, "I got beaten up by two eighth-graders while doing pull-ups at the pull-up bar in the gym. They chased me, pummeled me. I went to the security guard, who said, 'What did you do to start this?'" The principal at the school to whom Liebeman and his mother appealed after the incident occurred said, "If you had long hair and wore nail polish, this wouldn't have happened." After this incident, the principal suspended Liebeman, not the perpetrators. Liebeman and his parents considered filing a lawsuit against the school, but, Liebeman says, his mother didn't want to "put me in the limelight" and make him any more of a target than he already was. So the harassment continued. In eighth grade, "eight kids surrounded me and beat me up. We filed a police report on all eight, but nothing happened."

Even worse than the physical abuse, Liebeman says, was the constant harassment. "I was called 'Pat' a lot in middle school," he says, referring to the ambiguously gendered character on *Saturday Night Live*. "I've been called butch, dyke, queer, homo, fag, and she-he-it (shit)." Students who knew him from middle school spread the word about Liebeman on the first day of high school, thus ensuring that he would be isolated and harassed there as well. "I had no friends," he said. "No one would talk to me. I got really depressed. Normally I'm an outgoing person, but I got very withdrawn." When he did find a friend in the high school gifted program, a boy who thought that he himself might be gay or bisexual, the two of them were together targeted by other students. "We wrote notes back and forth, and the kids I knew from middle school wrote stuff from the notes on the board." Liebeman describes himself as "suicidal" during ninth grade.

His family became concerned when his report card came back with five Ds and an F, Liebeman says. At that point, he came out as a lesbian to his family and "built some allies" in the high school administration. He eventually founded a gay/straight alliance at his school. "We had five members in our first year," he recalls, "and we literally met in a closet—ironic!" As a result of his leadership in the school group, Liebeman attended a queer student conference in Los Angeles. The conference proved to be a turning point for him. "It was the first time I ever met a transgendered person," he says. "I already knew that I was trans, but I was confused and afraid to admit it. I talked to this guy at the meeting and went to a session called 'Trans 101.' On the way home, my mom asked me what sessions I attended, and when I told her about that one, she pulled the car over on the side of the road and basically freaked out." After overcoming her denial, Liebeman's mother and other family members, including his uncle and grandparents, eventually came around and supported him. "The only ones who don't know about me now" are his ultra-Orthodox relatives in Israel, he says. This family support helped Liebeman get through the last years of high school. "In eleventh grade, socially it got better, though the emotional and verbal abuse was still pretty bad," he says. On one occasion, the school's gay/straight alliance created a display case during Pride Week. The case was vandalized, with swastikas scratched into the glass. Liebeman and other members of the alliance received intimidating notes from students and teachers. "Some of the right-wing born-again teachers actually signed their notes," he marvels. "We got a lot of negative feedback from the faculty, but the administration was somewhat supportive. Their attitude is 'We're allowing you to be here, but we're not going to do anything to protect you,'" he says.

A survey conducted by the Gay, Lesbian and Straight Education Network, a national organization that works to end harassment of LGBT kids in schools, found that 69 percent of LGBT youth (ages twelve to nineteen) reported having been victims of harassment or violence in their schools. Half of them said that they were subject to some form of harassment every day. Constant harassment and rejection put transgendered kids, like gay and lesbian youth, at high risk for depression, substance abuse, and other self-destructive activities. "Because isolation and ostracism are key components of transgender youth experience, it would be irresponsible to overlook the associated mental health concerns of substance abuse, self-abuse, depression, and suicide

or suicidal ideation," say Israel and Tarver. They note that "the difficulty these individuals face is evident when we consider that approximately 50 percent to 88 percent have seriously considered or attempted
suicide."

One of the most devastating accounts of the brutal challenges of
a transgender adolescence was published by Daphne (now Dylan)
Scholinksi in 1997. In *The Last Time I Wore a Dress*, Scholinski describes a lonely, fearful childhood that spiraled into an angry, rebel-
lious adolescence. She skipped school, stole, hung out with gang
members, and experimented with drugs and alcohol. Scholinski was
fourteen years old when she was incarcerated in the first of the three
psychiatric facilities where she would spend her adolescence. When, at
her second psychiatric facility, she was given a list of feelings and
asked to circle the ones that applied to her, she "skipped over hope, joy,
love and anything else positive. The ones I circled were: *lonely, angry,
unloved, puzzled, disgusted, defeated, rejected*—I wrote in *hopeless* since
it wasn't on the list."

Throughout her childhood, Scholinski had been tagged a tomboy.
She "wore Toughskin jeans with double-thick knees so I could wrestle
with Jean [her sister] and the neighborhood boys. My mother cut my
hair short so my father wouldn't brush my long-hair snarls with No
More Tangles spray. I took off my shirt in the summer when the heat in
Illinois smothered me in the yard and I got on my bike and glided
down the hill no-handed. The wind on my chest felt like freedom until
three boys from my neighborhood saw me and said, 'Daphne, let me
see your titties,' which was ridiculous since my chest was as flat as
theirs but they held me on the ground. My ride was ruined and I put on
a shirt but not before I punched one of them hard in the stomach and
they all backed off." When she was in seventh grade three of her female friends held her down and painted her face with makeup. "Linda
opened her purse which was a wreck inside, torn-up Kleenex and lint
in the crack of her lipstick case. She handled Michelle a compact of
turquoise eye shadow, which Michelle applied with a heavy hand to my
eyelids. From another compact she rubbed on blush across my cheeks
thick as dust. Red lipstick she dabbed on fiercely. 'Look at Daphne
in makeup.' All of them ha-haing like crazy." Staring at herself in a

mirror after escaping from her torturers, "I kept waiting to feel a pull, there you are, glamorous, older, prettier. Nothing."

Slightly older, Scholinski waits with "sick dread" at a roller-skating rink when the lights dim and the couples' skate is announced. Girls, thinking that she is a boy, ask her to skate. Sometimes she says no and sometimes she says yes, and for a brief moment enjoys the fun of being young and carefree, skating with pretty girls "with their long hair flowing behind them." In either case, she is found out and accused of trying to pass herself off as a boy. She shoves and taunts the boys who challenge her, and they back off. "They got to be afraid of me. All you have to do is look a little bit like a boy and they think you're a crazy girl who's going to rip their heads off and spit down their necks."

Never does Scholinski say that she felt like a boy trapped in the body of a girl, or that she yearned for a boy's body. She was just "being a girl in the only way I knew how." But like many gender-variant children and adolescents, she was a target for abuse in both her home and her community. Her father beat her, but not her younger sister. Her mother at one point took her sister back to live with her, leaving Scholinski with her father. Both boys and girls mocked and humiliated her for being different. And a few adults took advantage of her youth and vulnerability to molest her.

"Genderqueer kids present an ideal profile for sexual predators," writes activist Riki Wilchins, director of the lobby group Gender Public Advocacy Coalition (Gender PAC). "We are often emotionally transparent, hungry for adult attention and approval, out of touch with our own bodies, socially isolated, lacking in any sense of boundaries, confused about what is 'normal' and used to keeping secrets about our bodies. If there are sharks in the water, the social thrashing of genderqueer kids is bound to attract them." Scholinksi's "social thrashing" attracted numerous sharks. Even before entering psychiatric facilities, Scholinski was molested by an adolescent babysitter named Gloria; a burly neighbor of her mother's named Frank, "who took me out for dinner and gave me money and Ziploc baggies of green marijuana"; and a married couple who invited her to hang out in their apartment to listen to music and drink beer. "The second time I was over, the man kept his hand on my shoulder a long time. His wife started rubbing my back and my mind emptied out and I was a shell being rubbed. The wife spoke in a quiet voice and said she and her husband liked my body because it was so boyish. Their hands went further and further and my mouth couldn't speak any words." While incarcerated, Scholinski was raped on two occasions by fellow patients, boys whom she knew and trusted, and groped by another while in restraints.

In an informal survey taken at Camp Trans, a protest held outside the Michigan Womyn's Music Festival after organizers of the festival decreed that only "women born women" could attend, the activist Riki Wilchins discovered that of twelve "mostly white, mostly middle and working class" transgendered participants at the protest, 100 percent of them (twelve of twelve) had been physically abused or beaten as children and 75 percent (nine of twelve) had been sexually abused, with 40 percent of those (five of twelve) victims of incest. Fifty percent (six of twelve) had been raped at some point in their lives. This is, as Wilchins admits, a very small and unscientific sample; however, on the basis of the stories I've heard since beginning research on this book, I don't believe that a more formal testing instrument would find those numbers hugely inflated. Gender-variant kids are often brutally mistreated. Riki Wilchins says that such abuse "appears not as an anomaly but as a cultural norm: the means by which gender-queer kids are instructed in the limits and consequences of gender difference."

One of my sources, a transman who requested a pseudonym ("Brad") because his daughter and in-laws don't know about his past, said that his father beat him regularly throughout his childhood. "I was being physically abused at home all the time. . . . Whether I was being sexually abused, I don't know, because everything is blacked out. I have like a minute here, a minute there. Years and years of nothing. But I know that I was physically abused. My whole family knows, and it all came out finally when my dad died and they were all like, 'We're really sorry, we should have stepped in.' But they didn't."

Brad's father was "a military guy, Navy for twenty-three years," and "a white-knuckle alcoholic, a non-drinking alcoholic," enraged by his "daughter's" masculinity. "I think that my dad's biggest problem was that I looked like him and I acted like him. He didn't perceive me as male but he saw me doing male things all the time, and that went against the grain. He would stay stuff like, 'If you're gonna be a girl you need to wear dresses and you need to wear this and that.' I would refuse to wear dresses. I always wore jeans." When Brad's father became angry at his three children for various infractions, he would "line us up and scream at us and then beat the shit out of me. Or he'd start beating all of us, and I would say that I did it 'cause I couldn't deal with my sister and brother crying. And I was like, 'Go ahead, beat the crap out of me. I can deal with your shit.' Because I was so mad at him," Brad says.

Daphne Scholinski describes a similar dynamic with her father. Touchy and violent, he would become angry at minor infractions, and he and Daphne would get into shoving matches. "I'd walk up to him close enough so that his angry face was all I could see of the world, and he'd push me away, so I'd push back, and we were off. . . . He poked me on the chest, thud, thud, until I cried. *Go ahead, hit me. I know you want to,* I taunted. This was thrilling. If he hit me, I'd won— I'd cracked him open and reached his center." Beaten with a belt regularly, Scholinski intervenes on the one occasion when her father threatens to beat her usually compliant younger sister. Like Brad, she assumed the role of protector of her sibling and absorbed the impact of her father's rage.

Scholinski notes that when the patients at the Michael Reese Hospital, her first psychiatric facility, were bored, they would ask the nurses for a copy of DSM-III and look up various diagnoses, including their own. "Someone would ask, 'What are you in for?' We looked up anorexic for Julie and Lisa. Manic depression? Borderline personality? Obsessive compulsive? I didn't tell anyone about my gender thing. I said I was in for Conduct Disorder." Even in a psychiatric facility, surrounded by profoundly troubled adolescents and adults, being "a gender screw-up" is a shameful thing, something to keep hidden. When she was admitted to Michael Reese, her psychiatrist told her that "due to the complexity of my situation" she had a multiple diagnosis— conduct disorder, mixed substance abuse, and gender identity disorder. The fourteen-year-old Scholinski was horrified. "I didn't mind being called a delinquent, a truant, a hard kid who smoked and drank and ran around with a knife in her sock. But I didn't want to be called something I wasn't. Gender screw-up or whatever wasn't cool," Scholinski writes. "He [her psychiatrist] was calling me a freak, not normal. . . . He was saying that every mean thing that had happened to me was my fault because I had this gender thing."

At Michael Reese, Scholinski learned that she was first diagnosed with gender identity disorder in third grade, when she was sent to a school counselor by a teacher who had noticed her depression. "We played games together," says Scholinski, and one of the games was "The Career Game." "She held up cards with a picture of a policeman, a farmer, a construction worker, a secretary and a nurse, and I said which ones I'd like to be: police officer and construction worker. She looked at me with a curious face like a mother robin. She was the first one who said I had a problem with my gender. I didn't know what that meant, but later I found out that she thought I wanted to be a boy."

At each of the three psychiatric facilities where she was incarcerated, the staff took careful note of Scholinski's appearance and mannerisms. "Daphne presents a tomboyish appearance with jeans, T-shirt and a manner of relating which is not entirely feminine," wrote the staff at Michael Reese in Chicago, where her psychiatrist asked, "Why don't you put on a dress instead of those crummy jeans?" At Forest Hospital in Des Plaines, Illinois, she at first pretended to be a drug addict because it provided some sort of explanation for her family's difficulties. "Drug addiction offered itself to me like a blanket of forgiveness. *It's a disease. It's not my fault.* My parents too would be absolved of blame. We'd have something to tell ourselves and the world that seemed a lot more understandable than *my daughter won't wear a dress, my mother doesn't want me around, my father beats me, she's plain out of control, I don't know why I stole the money.*" But one day she confided a secret to her journal ("p.s. I think I like girls"), which was read by the staff and led to her being transferred out of rehab and subject to a new treatment plan focused on "identity issues and sexual confusion." This included spending time with a female peer each day, combing and curling her hair, experimenting with makeup, and "working on hygiene and appearance." After being made up by her roommate, she looked in the mirror. "I sneaked a glance, and it was a jolt. My beige face gave me a creepy dead look. The blue eye shadow, the blush—I looked like a stranger." With a staff member eavesdropping outside the door, "I told myself that I didn't care if I looked like a dead stranger." To pacify the staff and gain "points" that could be traded for a few precious moments outside alone, she said out loud, "I love my eyeliner. I like my blue eye shadow."

Persevering in order to gain more points, Scholinski strove to become a more pleasing "girly-girl dead stranger." She let her roommate, Donna, make her up each morning, curl her hair, and paint her fingernails. She wore Donna's blouses instead of T-shirts and a pair of new jeans, and hugged male staff members. Donna, trying to be helpful, pointed out that Scholinski's walk, an athlete's walk, "a strong walk with my weight in my feet," was not very feminine. "Donna wanted me to walk skittery, like a bird. Like the pigeons in the park near my mother's apartment, strutting, with their chests sticking out, their tail feathers wagging. She said, Try this. She came up behind me and placed her hands on my hips. She knew I was in deep about the femininity stuff, she was trying to help, so I tried too. I took a step with my right foot. She moved my hips to the right. Left foot, left swing of my hips. Step, swing, step. I thought, *Forget this.*"

Fed up with the "femininity discussions," she told her psychiatrist that she really was a drug addict. "I'd rather be a drug addict than walk around with this crap on my face." But before the staff could alter her treatment plan again, she was transferred to the Wilson Center in Minnesota. At Wilson, the goal of treatment was "for Daphne to come to terms with herself as a sexual female human being." By the time she was released from Wilson, a few weeks after her eighteenth birthday, Daphne Scholinski had spent three years in psychiatric facilities, from September 1981 to August 1984. Just before her discharge, her final psychiatrist said that all of her problems were "in remission except for my gender thing." Looking back on those three years a decade later, she says, "I still wonder why I wasn't treated for my depression, why no one noticed I'd been sexually abused, why the doctors didn't seem to believe that I came from a home with physical violence. Why the thing they cared about most was whether I acted the part of a feminine young lady. The shame is that the effects of depression, sexual abuse, violence: all treatable. But where I stood on the feminine/masculine scale: unchangeable. It's who I am."

In their critical analysis of the DSM and the way it is used to create psychiatric diagnoses for "everyday behaviors," Kutchins and Kirk point out how difficult it can sometimes be to distinguish an internal mental disorder from a patient's reaction to external environmental stressors. DSM's role as a coding tool for insurance companies generally resolves this difficulty, they say. "The limited evidence suggests that individuals are given DSM diagnoses when family, marital and social relationships are clearly the problem; that treatments are shaped to adhere to what is reimbursable, rather than what may be needed; and that troubled individuals are getting more severe and serious diagnoses than may be warranted." These diagnostic distortions are not the fault of the DSM, Kirk and Kutchins say, but a symptom of the way in which we try to craft medical solutions to social problems. Critics of the DSM diagnosis of gender identity disorder make the same argument. "No specific definition of distress or impairment is given in the GID diagnosis," says Katharine Wilson. "The supporting text in the DSM-IV Text Revision (TR) lists relationship difficulties and impaired function at work or school as examples of distress or disability, with no reference to the role of societal prejudice as the cause. Prostitution, HIV risk, suicide attempts, and substance abuse are described as associated features of GID, when they are in truth consequences of discrimination and undeserved shame."

Dylan Scholinski spoke eloquently about the lifelong effects of shame when I spoke to him in 2004. "The stigma attached [to the GID diagnosis] is devastating" for a child or adolescent, he said, as we sat in an outdoor café below the Washington, D.C., row house where he keeps a second-floor art studio. The most emotionally devastating aspect of being institutionalized for gender identity disorder was the message that "there was something so wrong with me that I couldn't be out in the world," he said, "that all these different types of people are out there walking around the streets, but I couldn't do that, I was so dangerous. I felt lethal," he says now, looking back on Daphne's adolescence. "Like I was the bomb always waiting to go off in people's lives."

Scholinski points out that though his primary diagnosis in the various institutions where he spent his adolescence was gender identity disorder, the psychiatrists and therapists who met with his parents told them "they were working on my depression. Well, I was depressed because the world was treating me poorly, but their plan was to get me to act more feminine so that the world wouldn't treat me so badly—instead of realizing that if you try to make me be something I'm not, I'm going to be even more depressed. I never felt worse than on the days when I forced myself to wear makeup and had people telling me, 'Wow, you look really pretty today,'" he says with feeling.

In its Standards of Care for the Treatment of Gender Identity Disorder (SOC) in both adults and children, the Harry Benjamin International Gender Dysphoria Association notes that "the designation of Gender Identity Disorders as mental disorders is not a license for stigmatization or for the deprivation of gender patients' civil rights. The use of a formal diagnosis is an important step in offering relief, providing health insurance coverage, and generating research to provide more effective future treatments." However, it must be asked whether the present classification of gender identity disorder as a psychopathology meets these goals.

First, the designation of GID as a mental health problem does provide, and has provided, a license for stigmatization, and has undoubtedly contributed to the difficulty that gender-variant people have encountered in passing legislation protecting their civil rights. It is disingenuous to pretend that the deletion of the entry on homosexuality from the DSM has not greatly improved the status of gays and lesbians, or that the continued inclusion of gender-variant people in the DSM has not retarded their efforts to be recognized as healthy, functional members of society. Indeed, Dylan Scholinski says that since writing *The Last Time I Wore a Dress* and becoming an activist, he finds that "some of the toughest people to convince" that kids are still being institutionalized for gender identity disorder are gays and lesbians. "It's like it brings up people's worst fears," he says. "People don't want to believe that these kinds of things can happen now, they think that we're beyond that. I tell them, 'Well, maybe it didn't happen to you, but it did happen to me.'"

Second, the diagnosis of gender identity disorder does not facilitate insurance coverage of medical or surgical procedures for people desiring hormonal or surgical treatment; it does not guarantee coverage of anything other than mental health treatment by a psychiatrist or a psychologist. "DSM is a red herring. It barely covers anybody," says Dr. Dana Beyer, a retired surgeon who underwent sex-reassignment surgery in 2003. "Why we feel the need for this crutch is beyond me. This DSM crutch. But it's the only recognition that it's medical—it just happens to be in the psychiatric field, which causes more problems than it's worth. So why can't we just shift it from the psychiatric problem to congenital or genetic or developmental or whatever? That should be easy. But again it becomes a turf war. The psychiatrists don't want to give it up. You'd think they'd want to get rid of us. But no, they don't want to do that. As far as insurance goes, that's a crock; it doesn't cover anybody."

Finally, rather than "generating research" or research funding, the classification of GID as a mental disorder seems instead to have limited the research done on physiological mechanisms for gender variance, or on the intriguing connections between GID and prenatal exposure to DES and other exogenous estrogens and androgens. Christine Johnson, an engineer who is using systems theory to analyze the connections between environmental estrogens and gender variance, says that available data simply do not support the theory that GID is a psychiatric disorder. "There's all this empirical data, exceptional data, data that doesn't fit their [psychiatric] theory. The U.S. military, for example, has generated a whole set of body measurements that include about thirty different things that they've characterized over a large population, and they have curves that describe what the distributions look like for height, for proportion, for all these various body measurements. For 90 percent of them I'm right on the female mean. Now, I've yet to see any psychologist explain how it is that I managed to change my skeleton if this [transsexualism] is in fact due to some sort of a mental pathology. The fact is that I'm an exception, an anecdote, and they are not willing to explain it. They are treating me as an exception, and that's fine, but it still doesn't support their theory. If there's unexplainable data, that's something they need to address."

High rates of polycystic ovary syndrome (PCOS) in female-bodied persons diagnosed with GID are another anomaly that cannot be explained using the psychopathology paradigm. PCOS is an endocrine disorder affecting women of reproductive age and has been associated with excess production of androgens by the ovary. Researchers currently view PCOS as a developmental disorder in which fetal or prepubertal overproduction of androgen causes "hypoandrogenism" in adulthood. Though most women with PCOS are not gender-variant, the fact that many female-bodied persons diagnosed with GID have a history of PCOS would seem to indicate that the two conditions are related and may have a common etiology. Such suggestive connections and potential avenues for research are masked by the common view that GID is a psychopathology, however. The same is true of the overlap between various intersex conditions and GID; I know of at least two transmen who were diagnosed with congenital adrenal hyperplasia (CAH) in childhood, for example. In CAH, excess androgens create ambiguous genitalia in XX babies, who are born with an enlarged clitoris and a fused labia. However, the literature provided to parents of CAH babies fails even to mention the possibility that prenatal exposure to excess androgens may affect gender identity.

The DSM has nothing at all to say about the etiology, or causes, of the various psychopathologies it describes; it is a purely descriptive nosology. Moreover, its overall validity and reliability are questioned by people who are not particularly supportive of transgender activists' agenda. Just because something is in the DSM, that doesn't make it a real disease, they say. "Listen, there are things in the DSM that are false. The DSM is only a nomenclature," says Dr. Paul McHugh, retired chief of psychiatry at Johns Hopkins Hospital. "This is a dictionary in which various experts have been given the license by the American Psychiatric Association to say 'what are the criteria by which they choose to call this' and they get the names up. If we still believed in witches, witches would be in DSM-IV! Because these are operational criteria. That's the whole point. You can put anything in, if you can get enough guys to agree that it exists without any other proof than that you think it exists in the way that you claim."

For all of the reasons noted above, many people argue that the GID diagnosis should be either revised or retired. "I think that it [gender identity disorder] should not be in the DSM any more than homosexuality should be in the DSM," says Dr. Ben Barres, of Stanford. "I think that it's offensive. I don't think I need a DSM diagnosis. I think that I'm perfectly healthy. I did need some medical help to deal with my transition, but there are lots of things requiring medical help where you don't need to be in a book of mental pathologies."

"To the extent that it is in the DSM, I don't think that it should be applied to everybody," said a male-to-female attorney I interviewed in New York City in 2001. "Though it hasn't been my experience, I think that there are people who perhaps experience it as a disorder, for whom it makes life uncomfortable and miserable, just as there are probably certain gay and lesbian people for whom homosexuality is ego-dystonic, as the psychiatrists term it. But I think that there are many, many people for whom this is not a disorder; it does not disorder their lives."

The great majority of the people whom I encountered while doing the research for this book did not appear to suffer from any kind of mental pathology or derangement. They were competent and productive people with homes, families, and jobs they enjoyed. This is particularly true of those who had completed the process of transition or who were post-transition. Those who are still working through transition, on the other hand, often suffer enormous stress as they attempt to renegotiate relationships with family and significant others, with co-workers, and with their own sense of self. This is a years-long process, which does eventually end. But there is no "exit clause" in the DSM, as Katharine Wilson and others have pointed out, by which someone who experiences a high degree of discomfort and distress prior to transition is considered cured afterward.

Indeed many people, including those who chose not to undergo surgery and/or take hormones at all, experience relief after admitting to themselves and others that they are transgendered. Accepting and integrating this new identity and seeking out a community of people who love and accept them despite their "difference," some find their gender dysphoria transformed to gender "euphoria," as they are released from the bonds of shame and secrecy. "Brad" described his first visit to the Tom Waddell Center, in San Francisco, to me as a kind of homecoming. "It was a wonderful situation, because it was through the city health plan and it was free and they totally understood me and supported me. Even though when I first went there, I was sitting in a hallway with all of these really ugly women, I mean really ugly, some of the freakiest fucking scary women you've ever seen in your life and some really strange-looking men. But I was at home. They accepted me for who I was even though I still had not transitioned yet."

Many people who argue that GID should be removed from the DSM support a reclassification as a medical diagnosis. "Louis Gooren, one of the major Dutch researchers on transsexuality, was finally asked just in the last year to contribute a chapter to one of the major endocrinology textbooks about transsexuality, which is I think the proper place for it," says Ben Barres. This perspective was shared by most of the trans physicians and scientists whom I interviewed for the book. "It's not as if there is no data," says Dr. Dana Beyer, who, like Dr. Barres, was exposed to a synthetic hormone in utero.

Many of my transsexual sources were extremely reluctant to support the deletion of GID from the DSM, however, until a formal medical reclassification had taken place—possibly in the ICD (International Statistical Classification of Diseases) produced by the World Health Organization. The ICD is used internationally to track morbidity and mortality of diseases, and unlike DSM it is updated yearly. All of the diagnostic codes in the DSM-IV (published in 1994) and the DSM-IV TR (published in 2000) were selected to match valid ICD-9 codes. However, as the ICD is updated yearly and the DSM-V will not be published until 2010, there will be discrepancies. A reclassification of gender identity disorder from a psychiatric to an endocrinological condition in the ICD would have a major impact—but as that reclassification has not yet occurred, some argue that it is important to retain the DSM diagnosis for both medical and political reasons despite its flaws. The DSM diagnosis affirms the legitimacy of gender variance and at the same time pathologizes it—making gender variance something more than the perverse lifestyle choice that fundamentalist Christian and other critics believe it to be. More important, this diagnosis legitimizes the range of hormonal and surgical interventions developed over the years that have provided relief for thousands of transsexual and transgendered people. Activists who argue that the "medical model" of gender variance "pathologizes human diversity" tend to miss this point. Without some sort of diagnosis, sex reassignment becomes nothing more than a kind of extreme cosmetic surgery/ body enhancement, or in the view of critics like Paul McHugh, a fad, a fashion, a "craze."

"If you talk to post-op transpeople, most are what you would call conservative on this question," says Chelsea Goodwin of Transy House. "I'm conservative in the sense that I accept the medical model but I believe that anybody who needs to see a doctor should, and anyone who needs surgery should be able to have it reimbursed. I'm a pragmatist really. In the 1970s and 1980s the argument was that the transsexual community looked down on cross-dressers because transsexuals got legitimacy from the Benjamin medical model. Well, that legitimacy made it possible for us to exist. Nobody likes to look at the fact that Christine Jorgensen managed to do this [sex reassignment] at the height of the McCarthy era. There was still this incredible respect for scientists among the public back then. If a doctor at a time when medicine was the most respected profession in America said that this was okay, then the public believed it. That was the only way that this revolutionary act of sex change could be done at the time. To throw that legitimacy away now is crazy."

Therapists and other professionals who work with gender-variant clients express many of the same reservations. Christine Wheeler says, "My fear is that it [the GID diagnosis] will get thrown out of the DSM because of some of the strident views coupled with malpractice issues that continue to frighten physicians. I'm afraid that we will see a time when people won't be able to get the help they need." Wheeler, who is on the APA task force for DSM-IV and is one of the drafters of the HBIGDA Standards of Care, says that both committees are "looking at standardizing the child and adolescent GID definitions and reexamining the protocol for intersex conditions around the world, as well as the protocols for intervention in GID." She admits that there are problems with current definitions. "Sometimes the language is archaic, and I apologize for that," she says. However, the essential point to remember when discussing the value or lack of value of the diagnosis, she says, is that "something has to be wrong in medicine in order [for it] to be fixed."

Dylan Scholinski articulates this conundrum from the perspective of the trans activist, admitting that whereas "initially most people were advocating the straight-out removal of GID from the DSM," a more nuanced position is now developing because "you don't want to fuck with people's access to health care, not till there's something else in place. You can't just leave the community with nothing."

Not only does the GID diagnosis ensure continued access to surgery and hormones for those who require them (even if they are not covered by insurance), but it is also used as a legal tool. Those states that permit transsexual people to change their sex of record on birth certificates, driver's licenses, and other legal documents often require letters from psychotherapists and other health care providers attesting to the medical validity of the claim. Some require proof of genital surgery; others do not. The broad definition of GID ensures that even those who have not undergone genital surgery (as most FTMs do not) qualify for such legal remedies. Attorneys Collin Vause, Shannon Minter, and Karen Doering relied heavily on the medical model in the case of *Kantaras v. Kantaras,* a child custody lawsuit argued in the state of Florida in 2002. In this groundbreaking case, Florida Circuit Court judge Gerard O'Brien ruled in February 2003 that Michael Kantaras, a transman, was legally male, and that his marriage to Linda Kantaras was legally valid. The court awarded custody of the two children that Michael and Linda had raised together during their marriage to Michael, who is the biological uncle of the youngest child, who was conceived through artificial insemination of Linda with sperm donated by Michael's brother. The elder child was three months old when Linda and Michael married in 1989, and Michael adopted the child shortly afterward. Linda was aware of Michael's history when the couple married, but neither child knew about Michael's past until Linda revealed the details after the couple's separation.

In the trial, which was shown in its entirety on Court TV, Linda and her attorneys argued that Michael should be considered legally female, that their ten-year marriage should be deemed void, and that Michael should be stripped of his parental rights and prevented from seeing the children. Judge O'Brien ruled otherwise, partly on the basis of extensive medical evidence presented by Walter Bockting, Ph.D., a clinical psychologist and former president of the Harry Benjamin International Gender Dysphoria Association; Ted Huang, M.D., a surgeon; and Collier Cole, Ph.D., a professor in the Department of Psychiatry and Behavioral Sciences at the University of Texas, Galveston. One of the major issues disputed in the case was Michael Kantaras's decision not to undergo phalloplasty (surgical construction of a penis). Linda Kantaras's attorneys argued that Michael's lack of a penis indicated that he was not a man, and that the marriage was therefore invalid. The medical experts testified that gender identity disorder was a legitimate medical condition and that Michael Kantaras had followed the Standards of Care of the Harry Benjamin International Gender Dysphoria Association for the treatment of gender identity disorder. Kantaras actually relocated to Galveston for two years in order to carry out his transition under the care of the Gender Identity Clinic there. (He met Linda shortly after his return to Florida.) The doctors pointed out that most female-to-male transsexual people do not opt for phalloplasty, because of its great expense and uncertain outcome, and that Michael Kantaras's decision was therefore congruent with prevailing treatment norms. They also testified that most married transmen enjoyed satisfying marital relations with their wives irrespective of their genital status, and that they did so as men, in the male role.

Most observers agree that the medical testimony was crucial in establishing an outcome favorable to Michael Kantaras. Previous court cases in which the legality of marriages contracted by a transsexual person were at issue did not rely as heavily on the testimony of expert medical witnesses. In two of the four U.S. cases (*Gardiner*, *Littleton v. Prange*), the marriages were ruled invalid. "To our knowledge this is the first transgender marriage case in the U.S. in which extensive medical evidence was presented, including testimony from three of the foremost experts on transsexualism in the country," attorney Shannon Minter said in a statement when the Kantaras ruling was announced. "As the court has recognized, the medical evidence overwhelmingly favors recognizing that the law should accommodate transgender people so they can be productive, functioning members of society. This includes permitting transgender people to marry and have children."

Under the circumstances, many transsexual and transgendered people and their allies are understandably wary of any attempt to eliminate the GID classification without replacing it with a medical diagnosis. The solution to the GID issue, and to many of the other medical and legal challenges that confront the transgender community, they argue, is research. "Basically, we know squat about our community," says Julie Maverick, a university professor in the physical sciences who heads the research subcommittee of the National Transgender Advocacy Coalition (NTAC). (Like many cross-dressers, Maverick is closeted and has requested anonymity.) In 2002, Maverick and colleagues at NTAC requested that Congress allocate funds to the National Institutes of Health for new and expanded efforts in the collection of medical and demographic information on transgendered and gender-variant people. "The transgendered community, including transsexuals, cross-dressers, and the intersexual, is believed to represent as much as 2 percent of the American populace and has specific needs regarding mental and physical health," Maverick and NTAC point out in their request for research funding. "They have the highest suicide rate for any demographic group, a very high incidence of depression and other mental health problems and a very high incidence of substance abuse. They have unique medical needs associated with hormonal therapy (breast cancer in genetic males, for example), sexual reassignment surgery and misdiagnosis of ailments (like ovarian cancer in female to male transsexuals)." Transgendered sex workers are also a "critical vector" for the transmission of HIV, as the request notes. Surveys carried out in Washington, D.C., San Francisco, Los Angeles, New York, and Philadelphia found high rates of HIV infection among trans sex workers in those cities.

Despite the serious health problems confronted by transgendered people, they remain a largely invisible and untreated population for a number of reasons. Some fear exposure, many lack health insurance, and more than a few have encountered hostility, ridicule, and rejection from health care providers when they have sought treatment. "Transgendered people commonly receive substandard or inadequate medical treatment due to discrimination, ignorance, confusion and loss of health insurance due to job loss," the NTAC request for funding notes. To a certain extent, the difficulties that transgendered people encounter are shared by other members of the LGBT community. "Most physicians get no training at all" with respect to treating transgendered patients, says Dr. Ben Barres, but "this is related to an even bigger problem, because let's face it, transgendered people are very rare, but homosexuals are very common, a couple percent of the population, and there's no training in medical school about that. For example, most physicians are very insensitive to that issue when they do a history and physical. They'll ask a person if they use birth control before they've even ascertained whether they are gay or not."

Speakers at the American Medical Students Association's 2001 conference concluded that "LGBT patients face many barriers to adequate health care. These problems range from poor physician access to a lack of awareness in the medical community about the health concerns of LGBT patients, not to mention the failure to address these health issues in most medical school curricula." The failure of medical schools to train future physicians to treat LGBT patients is yet another consequence of the lack of research on the specific health care needs of these populations. Research on LGBT issues typically begins and ends with AIDS research. AIDS remains a significant problem, to be sure—rates of HIV infection among male-to-female transsexuals in cities remain shockingly high. But the circumstances that drive those high rates of infection—needle-sharing among users of black-market hormones, sex work, substance abuse, and possibly depression—remain understudied, and therefore largely invisible. This lack of research has very large consequences for the transgender community, even beyond the basic but somewhat esoteric question of the etiology (cause) of gender variance.

"In this culture, and in most of the civilized world today, research data is used to determine public policy, to determine legislation, making cases in court, is used in determining protocols in medicine and psychiatry. Virtually every place you touch, people are coming up against this system where research data would be helpful," says Kit Rachlin, a psychotherapist with a doctorate in applied research who has worked with transgendered clients since 1990. "Everything from the quality of the medical care I get to whether I can get custody or adopt children, or have my license changed to reflect my gender—all of the services people want to be there for them, they don't realize that for it to be there for them in a consistent way, in a supportive way, you need to have research data, and the data has to be of a certain quality. And it will have to come from outside the community, if the community hasn't yet grown its own researchers."

In her plenary lecture at the 2001 True Spirit Conference, Rachlin focused on the mistrust many transpeople feel toward scientists and physicians, and the need to overcome that suspicion and participate in research studies. She noted that the two questions transgender people heard most often were "'how many of you are there' and 'why would you do this?'" With regard to prevalence, Rachlin says, "we're never going to get good numbers," owing to the nature of the condition. Most cross-dressers, for example, remain deeply closeted. "So it's the 'why would you do this' question that's the most important." If gender variance were proved to be "unchangeable and physical," she says, it would have a very big impact, not only on public perceptions but also on the availability of insurance benefits for those who require surgical and hormonal intervention, and legal decisions regarding marriage, child custody, and discrimination on the basis of gender identity.

"What you need when you go to court is persuasive data showing that this is a sane thing to do, it's a necessary thing to do, there's nothing antisocial about it, that it doesn't make you an unstable person," Rachlin says. "We saw recently with the Kanteras trial, all those accusations and how hard they are to refute. And then you need to be able—especially men—to justify physical choices, which Michael Kanteras had to do at the trial when they asked him, 'Why didn't you have genital surgery?'" Solid data would give Michael Kanteras and all the men like him the opportunity to say, "I am a man and I should be given all the rights and privileges of men no matter what my genital status is," she says.

Rachlin also sees a great need for outcome studies, particularly those comparing outcomes for people who do not follow the Standards of Care drafted by the Harry Benjamin International Gender Dysphoria Association, which are considered the gold standard. "I think that anyone who is doing anything medically should know the outcome," Rachlin says. "The Standards evolved at a time when people were going from one gender to another. They were following a sequence, fairly structured; and using that system, they had incredibly low levels of regret. We don't know why, because there are no controlled studies. All that we know is that using the SOC, people had low levels of regret. We don't know whether the SOC contributed to that; we don't know what the relationship is. Maybe the SOC didn't have anything to do with it, maybe it was just a small piece of the SOC, maybe it was just that they got the medical care they needed. And someone else might say that the SOC had nothing to do with it, but my reply is that all the data was gathered from people who were treated using the SOC. What we need now is research that looks at people using medical and social interventions to suit their own unique gender identity or unique ways of expressing their gender identity, which shows that their way of using medical interventions produces just as good results as the traditional model."

Such research might help alleviate one of the major problems encountered by transgendered people, the lack of insurance coverage for medical and surgical interventions. Rachlin points out that the failure of most insurance companies to provide benefits covering SRS or hormone therapy is due to the lack of research establishing that this is a legitimate medical problem with treatments that have been proved effective. "If somebody approached an insurance company with a large current sample done well it should be taken seriously. But people think that insurance companies are discriminating against transgendered people because they are transgendered, and they get very angry about it. But we don't have the same research that every other thing has that gets funded by insurance companies. We're just not meeting the usual criteria." As a consequence, some people buy hormones on the black market because they are cheaper, and they self-administer them, while those who can afford to do so see physicians and absorb the cost of all medical (and surgical) treatment themselves.

Like many people I interviewed, Rachlin is not convinced that all transgendered people suffer from gender dysphoria. She makes a distinction between body dysmorphia—"discomfort with parts of your body or all of your body"—and gender dysphoria. "For me, gender identity and body dysphoria are related but not the same thing, and people have made an assumption that if you are transsexual or transgender, you are unhappy with parts of your body, and that's not really the case all the time. And it's certainly not true all of the time, with all of your body, and all of the parts of your body. Some men can live with the genitals that they have; they like them and relate well to them. Others can't at all. And when you see enough men who are having these feelings you realize that it has nothing to do with gender identity. Body dysmorphia is something else, though it's related."

These kinds of distinctions are confusing to those wedded to the classic paradigm of a transsexual as a "man trapped in a woman's body" or vice versa. But the distinctions are borne out by a largely invisible population of gender-variant people who choose not to alter their bodies in any way, though they live in the social role of the "opposite" gender. "As a therapist in private practice, I see people who refuse, for one reason or another, to meet other transsexuals or enter the community because they are so mainstream-identified, they are more likely to feel that they need a body that physically matches [their gender identity]," Rachlin says. "I also know people who think 'maybe I'm not transsexual because I don't mind my penis. It works and I like it. But I'm a woman and I've always thought I was a woman, so what's the matter with me?' I say that there's nothing the matter with you and I think they are lucky if they can live with what they have and enjoy it. You have such an advantage over people who need the surgery."

The lack of research on gender variance makes it impossible to understand or predict why some people are comfortable with their anatomy even though it does not match their gender identity, and others attempt to remove the offending organs themselves if denied surgery. Why is this important, some might ask? If for no other reason than that increasing numbers of young people are identifying as gender-variant, and are transitioning at far younger ages. The True Spirit Conference, for example, is a very young meeting. Most participants appear to be in their twenties and have already begun hormone treatments and had (or are considering having) "top surgery" (mastectomy). A 1991 article published in the online journal *Salon* quoted staffers at the Callen-Lord Community Health Center, in New York City, who said that in the previous year, the number of transgender people under twenty-two in the gender-reassignment program had tripled. This increase in the number of trans-identified young people has been noted by members of the community as well. "I'm online a lot and I see these eighteen- and nineteen-year-old kids coming on and saying, 'I want to transition,'" says Brad. "And I think, 'How can you do that?' But then I think, 'Wait a minute, when you were five, you knew.'"

Like many older people in the trans community, Brad feels a certain degree of envy and resentment of these young people, who transition at eighteen or twenty or twenty-five, thus avoiding the lifelong misery and struggle that older transsexual men and women like him experienced. "There are a few of them that piss me off," says Brad. "They come online and say stuff like 'Oh, I'm twenty-three and I sure am glad to see some young guys here, instead of all these old guys.' Fuck you, you little brat. If it wasn't for us old guys, you wouldn't be here. I thank all the guys who went before me—and the women that have gone before me to set the pace, that have paved the way."

However, as Kit Rachlin points out, there is no outcome research proving that these young people will not at some point regret their decision. Transitioning at forty-five, after a lifetime of pain, one can be reasonably sure that the individual has thoroughly considered the positive and negative effects of the decision. But what about someone who transitions at twenty or even younger? "A typical case would be somebody very young, queer-identified, going through top surgery, and the parents saying to me, 'What does the research say? Is my fifteen-year-old capable of making this decision?'" says Kit Rachlin. "'Are people happy after doing this?' And I have to say, 'I don't know.' There's no good research data on queer-boy identified butch fifteen-year-olds making this decision. And so we need more therapists and doctors documenting what's happening right now in terms of medical care."

The lack of data creates conflicts for health care providers working with trans youth. According to the Benjamin Standards of Care, kids under eighteen are not candidates for hormone treatment or surgery, despite the fact that puberty tends to be a nightmarish experience for some transgendered kids, whose bodies grow daily more estranged from the kids' gender identities. Some find a way around the rules by taking hormones they purchase on the street, without medical supervision. Others may find a health care provider willing to prescribe hormone blockers, which don't create permanent changes, but slow or postpone the morphological changes of puberty. Some providers who do adhere to the Benjamin Standards of Care will prescribe hormone treatment for adolescents if they seem emotionally and intellectually mature enough to make the decision. Medically and ethically, the decision is a tough call, as Maria Russo, author of the *Salon* article, discovered in her interviews with health care providers. "As more young transsexuals push to begin transitioning at a younger age, the social workers and medical providers who work with them are confronting a new frontier in gender ethics. What's the best way to help kids who say they want to switch sexes? Should we make them wait as long as possible, to be sure their decisions are not simply adolescent rebellion? Or should we take them at their word and let them begin hormones during puberty?"

As even this brief treatment of the issue shows, questions far outnumber answers in the realm of transgender health care and research. In no area is this more true than in the biggest and most controversial question of all—what causes gender variance and why do there seem to be so many more gender-variant people in the world today than there were fifty years ago?

CONVERSATION WITH DANA BEYER, M.D.

Dr. Beyer was trained as an opthalmologic surgeon, though she no longer practices in that field. She currently serves as co-moderator of the DES Sons Network, founded by Scott Kerlin. I interviewed Dr. Beyer on two separate occasions; during our first meeting we addressed general issues and in the second, personal history. When I met Dr. Beyer early in the summer of 2002, she was still living as a man, though actively planning her transition. When we met for the second time, she had become markedly more feminine in her appearance, owing to estrogen therapy and electrolysis, and was preparing for facial feminization surgery in January 2003 and genital surgery in June. At the time we spoke, Dr. Beyer was living with her second wife and two teenage sons. The couple later separated. What follows is a portion of the transcript of our second conversation.

Q: So what has changed since the last time I saw you?

I'm out with my wife and kids. I haven't been doing anything differently since I last saw you, but she just finally came out of denial, even though I had transitioned and de-transitioned once before, nine years ago. But I didn't have the strength to do it then. And it's interesting now as I come out more and more, it's such a relief. No matter how difficult this is, it is such a relief just to be myself. All of what you've been trying to project, express, what society demands of you, the role that you're expected to play, the way you're supposed to look and dress and behave. It's complicated but it all comes down to denying your identity. And I would say that I've expended at least 50 percent of my life's energy fighting this one way or another. All that energy needed to be a man in this society, when you're not. You can't imagine. I guess it's like what it might have been like for some Jews to pretend to be Christian in order to survive. You're constantly on guard, constantly aware that you are who you know you are but you can't let it slip. Because when you are a child, if you let your feminine gestures slip, you're spanked or slapped.

Q: Can you give me some examples of what sort of feminine mannerisms or expression of femininity you would have to hide or repress?

Many things. The trivial are usually the best example. I used to be pretty active with my hands, with hand gestures. Women do this all the time.

Q: Maybe you just need to be Italian? Italian men are pretty expressive.

Maybe, but I wasn't. My family is Lithuanian and Ukrainian Jewish. We didn't do that. And I remember my mother saying, "No no no, sit on your hands. Don't do that." It's a trivial thing, really. What difference does it make? Now that I don't care anymore, now that I'm coming out and I gesture naturally, it's a relief. Or "don't cry," if you feel like crying. Or you have to go out for a sport, or "go out and play with the boys," even if you don't want to play with boys. "Go out and play with your friends." Well, they're not really your friends, and you know that they're not your friends. And you know that they know that you're different. And you keep trying to be more of what you know they expect you to be so that you can fit in and have friends.

Q: Some of the things that you've mentioned other XY individuals who feel comfortable being male might also wish to do or not to do—not playing sports, for example. So what's the difference?

There are some people—and since I do DES work, I'm involved with the intersex community, and you know that I consider transsexuality to be a form of intersex—there are some intersex activists who believe that if we could reform society and destroy the gender binary, there wouldn't be any need for transsexes. There are some very reasonable, caring, loving, intersex people who feel that is the case—because they don't fit into either category, they don't want to be in either category. One thing that I've come to realize . . . my wife says,

"What kind of woman do you think you're going to be?" and I say, "I don't know." And my son says, "Okay, you're doing this. Are you going to be sort of froufrou and frilly and have dinner on time every day?" and I'm thinking that this is interesting, that this is what he imagines that women do—and this is 2002?

Q: And he has had a working mother?

Several working mothers! His grandmother barely did that! And yet this is what he imagines. And I said, "No, I'm going to be me." And it made me realize that I have male parts in me. I have a male history. I can't forget that. I wasn't "pinked," as the feminists say, and of course the Janice Raymond crowd says, "If you haven't been pinked, you can't really be a woman." But I am doing something they have never been asked to do. I am renouncing male privilege. It just hit me about a month ago, just how intense that is. I was lying in bed one night and I go, "You know, I really am giving this up."

Q: Can we talk about how this all began for you?

My mother was a New York City master teacher. She taught for twenty-five years, math. She took DES in 1951 because her gynecologist told her to. She'd had one miscarriage. I had an older brother who didn't make it. But it's kind of strange now, as a physician, to think after one miscarriage they would do this. I mean, one out of every three pregnancies ends in miscarriage.

Q: Well, they put DES in pregnancy vitamins . . .

I know. That's one of the issues we have to deal with now, when we ask people, "Did your mother take DES?" and they ask their mothers and they say, "No, they just gave me lots of vitamins." But that's what they called them; that's how they marketed them to women. "Oh, these are just vitamins." Some of them were more honest in saying, "This is to prevent miscarriage." But some women were given DES who hadn't even miscarried, in vitamins and so forth.

I was born and, supposedly . . . my father hates talking about this, but when I blasted them for the DES thing years ago he just sat stone-faced, no response, while my mother broke down and cried and wailed. But about twenty-five years ago—I was twenty-five at the time—he made a comment that during my circumcision, during my bris, they had noticed that there was something different with me.

Q: No more details than that?

No. And they may not have had any more details because it is still the common procedure of pediatric urologists, which is the group that usually deals with this, to hush this up and to oftentimes not even speak to the parents and to make whatever corrections need to be made.

Q: But your parents were not aware that you had any surgery or procedure after birth?

No. But I have scars, and have had urogenital problems my whole life. DES causes a host of problems, so I don't know what they saw. And you're talking about a bunch of older Jewish guys looking at a penis, so what do they know? They don't look closely, they're not doing an exam, so I don't know. And there are many like me who just don't know. There are scars, there are whispers, and that's all you have. There are no records. They still don't keep very good records. In some cases, they've burned the records. So, there's a real problem.

My first physical problems manifested when I was twelve, in 1964. When I began bleeding on urination, and the hematuria [bleeding from the penis] progressed. It started off microscopically—obviously I didn't know that—but it became a gross hematuria. I urinated blood.

Q: All the time, not periodically?

All the time. And eventually, I got caught and my parents had to deal with it.

Q: You must have been scared to death?

I thought I was menstruating, actually.

Q: Because by that point you were already aware of the gender issue?

Yes, and I was twelve, and that's what girls start doing. So I thought, in my confused mind, that I was menstruating. It turns out it probably was because I have a partial uterus, so it is biologically

reasonable to think that at times I cramped and bloated and menstru-
ated. Talk about bizarre—but this is intersexuality, so who knows? But
a lot of this was during urination, and how many times do you urinate
a day? Four or five times? You can imagine the fear. There was the
anxiety and anticipation of pain that was worse than the pain.

Q: So this was also a painful urination?

Extremely painful. It turned out, the diagnosis was urethral meatal
stenosis, which means that the opening of the tip of the urethra was
scarred down, closed down. It could have been scarred because of surgery that had been performed much earlier or it could have been some
sort of overgrowth of tissue in that area due to DES. This has been
recorded [in the data]. And I let this go on because I was scared to
death about it. I had started cross-dressing when I was about eleven or
so. I first felt like a girl, or like I should have been a girl, when I was
about seven, but when I was eleven I started praying that my breasts
would start growing and wearing my mother's clothes, which finally fit
me. I was her height, five-six or -seven, and I was just getting to the
height where I could wear her clothes. And I would do that, and then
forget to put them back exactly the same way, intentionally so that
someone would notice. And they finally noticed and said, "You never
do that again, or we'll have you institutionalized at Creedmor."

*Q: So your parents' response wasn't "What's going on with you? Why are
you doing this?" It was "We're going to put you in a mental institution"?*

Yeah. "We don't want to deal with this." And then I started
menstruating—this painful urination and hematuria—and I tried to
hide it from them because I knew what their response was to this sexual thing, and stuff that comes out of the penis is sexual, and what the-
hell do I know? I'm in a fever talking about God, and fearing God.
Iwas preparing for bar mitzvah. And I remember one day I painted
my nails, and my father freaked out. I wasn't as bad as many, okay? I
wasn't one of those hypermasculine overcompensators or anything.
I just learned to blend into the woodwork, just do my work at school
and manage.

So this is going on, and I started bleeding even between urinations, and I had to try to wash out my underwear, and it's so hard to get blood out, and I'm stealing money from my mother's pocketbook to buy more underwear so she doesn't see it. Eventually, I couldn't keep it up. I was only twelve. What could I do? And they caught on. And they took me to a urologist, an Austrian fellow with a very heavy German accent, and he made some sort of diagnosis. The only thing that's come down to me is the urethral meatal stenosis. No questions about DES, so far as I know. This was '64, and I go to this urologist and he decides to treat me with this bizarre treatment that I have never in all my years as a physician been able to elucidate any better than I'm going to tell you right now. When I describe this to urologists today, they say, "What the hell was he doing? What was that?"

He had me lying down on a table, strapped down, with what I now know to be a fifty-cc syringe with a long cannula on it, filled with some sort of viscous black material. Viscous gook that he would then insert into my penis. And then he would just stand there, this big German guy—and remember, I'm only twelve; I haven't had my growth spurts or anything, and he's standing there injecting this into me. This was the most painful thing imaginable. And there was no sympathy, no nurse there, no feminine energy in the room. No explanation. Nothing. I went through this for four months. My parents have since pointed out that this was an attempt to expand my urethra. But they were never in the room; they were always outside. And there was no sympathy. None whatsoever. They never talked about it. "How do you feel? Can we get you some ice cream?" Typical stuff that kids would get if they were getting their tonsils out, but never anything. And I went through that for four months. And it didn't work.

I've blocked most of this stuff out. It was just awful. I don't want to think about it. And the German accent didn't help. I was learning about the Holocaust at the time, and even though he was Jewish, that didn't help. And of course, there were all those sexual associations that I was making, and that I guess everybody else was making, but no one talked about it. And I'm praying to develop breasts and I'm menstruating, and here they're doing this to my penis. And finally they decided that they had to operate. So I was taken to surgery and operated on. I don't know what was done, but I have a scar the length of my penis, along the dorsum of my penis. I think I was basically filleted open. I developed septic shock during that procedure. Of course I didn't know it at the time, but my mother said, "We came back to see you after the surgery and you were missing and then we tracked you down and you were in the ICU and you had a fever of 106 and we thought you weren't going to make it." They freaked out. Of course, I don't remember anything because I was in shock. I was in the hospital for three weeks, on IV antibiotics and eating lousy hospital food. It was the only time in my life that I ever developed an aversion to water. Forcing fluids. "You've got to drink the water." I remember hating it, becoming nauseated by water.

And again, nobody ever talked about this. My penis was bandaged up. I had a Foley [catheter] in for the longest time. It was just unspoken. It's very reminiscent of the way women were treated if they had breast cancer. This was a big secret. In the Jewish community it's called a "shanda," a shame. You don't talk about it. You go hide. You take care of it but you don't talk about it. My grandmother died of breast cancer. She was so ashamed that she did nothing about it. It actually infiltrated her skin. I had to go to Africa to see the disease's natural history like this! This happened in the United States of America fifty years ago. And it's like that kind of silence . . . "This is sexual and so we're not going to talk about it." And nobody talked to me about it. I didn't even have psychiatric consultations. Nobody. It was ignored.

Q: Did you in some way connect your feelings about being a girl and think that it was somehow related to this physical problem, like it was a punishment?

Well, it was more of a religious thing. I thought this was a punishment from God for my feelings. I remember my parents bringing me my homework and I had half-Hebrew and religious studies and half-secular studies, and I'd work even harder to try to get it better. There's a phrase in the early-morning prayers that the Orthodox still say: "Blessed art Thou, Lord our God, King of the Universe, for not making me a woman." Somebody said once, I don't remember who, that having to repeat that on a daily basis was like swallowing crushed glass. And here I am, top of my class, and I know all the rituals and routines, and I'm being forced to say this but I know that I'm living a lie. But I couldn't talk to anyone about it. They would have totally freaked out. You just didn't discuss these things.

But those three weeks in the hospital were hellacious. I felt like I was bad and that there was something very wrong with me. Luckily, my way of coping was just to work harder. I never did drugs, I never did alcohol. And I grew up in that era [the sixties]! I was a control freak; that's how I dealt with it. I was scared to death at letting myself go because I saw what was happening with my friends, and they looked happy and carefree and so on but they would say things when they were stoned that they would regret later, and I couldn't let anybody find out about this. I couldn't let anybody know. So I became sort of like Newt Gingrich—very uptight, very serious. I grew a mustache and, after a couple of years at Cornell, in the early seventies, I let my hair grow. But for the most part I've been in deep cover, protective coloration, all of my life. I couldn't let on. I've never smoked grass, can you believe it? I smoked opium once, in Thailand, and it did nothing for me. I had to do something because my wife was provoking me. I was too straight.

But get this, the surgery didn't work. A month later, I was bleeding again. I got out of the hospital in June. I finished the year at school. I was thirteen. I had my bar mitzvah. I was actually bleeding during my bar mitzvah. I came out, and because of my illness my parents hadn't made any plans for the summer. I had been going to day camp, which was very common in Queens in those days, and they had to hustle to get me in, and because it was late there were no slots in my age group, so I was in a group of fifteen-year-olds instead of thirteen-year-olds. Boy, you talk about somebody who just went through this profound surgical/medical experience relating to sexuality and getting thrust in with kids two years older! The girls . . . I lusted to be like them, but I couldn't. I was just this little nerd, you know, who was getting picked on by the guys all the time because I wasn't with it, and I had a small penis, and everything like this.

Q: They teased you about your penis?

Oh yes, because we had to undress; we went to public swimming pools and we had to get undressed.

Q: So after everything you'd just been through, you had these older boys mocking you?

And I wanted to be with the girls, and I couldn't. Because if you're a boy, you don't go with the girls. And I had to go to the boys' locker room to change. We had to go three times a week, and I wanted to die every time. I remember they had a high board, and I used to be a pretty good diver, and I'd think, "I just want to do this wrong just so I don't have to do this again." It was awful. I remember standing with my body turned so that nobody could see me. Because I had my scars and stuff too. It looked bad. And I think it [the penis] was relatively small anyway, but I was post-op. And then I had to go back to that schmuck and get that treatment again! And I guess it worked that time, because it [the bleeding] stopped by the end of the summer. It was the most hellacious summer . . . year of my life.

But I coped. I had to cope. And I became a control freak and I became an academic superstar and a topflight surgeon and everything, and I kept on till I was thirty-eight, and then I crashed.

But at that time, I came out of it and I went to junior high and then high school. The whole time I felt like "I don't belong. This isn't me." I had girlfriends. Back in those days, we used to pass each other notes, and if a girl signed it L-O-V-E, it meant it was time for sex, and if she signed it L-U-V, that meant "you're a good friend." And I had lots of LUVs. And I liked it, but I knew that I was supposed to be doing better than that, and I couldn't.

I remember an incident when I was fourteen. This was when I first knew that I was transsexual. My religious school, the yeshiva, had an annual trip to Washington, and they take a photo of the entire group on the Capitol steps. I still have it somewhere in the basement. So I had a girl "friend." She was a friend because we were the two tallest kids in the class and we always sat in the back, and we were friends for six years. And it was sort of understood that, well, we're getting sexual, people, it's time to take this friendship to the next step. So I would try to hold her hand, and she might hold my hand, but there was no chemistry. And we sat together on the trip, because you paired off, and I figured, "Well, I need to kiss her." People are looking at me, they're expecting this of me. The boys and the girls, and it didn't work. I kissed her, but she pushed me away, and it didn't work. And I was devastated that I was a failure.

At one point I didn't want to leave the bus. We were touring the city and the class got off and went wherever they were going, and I stayed on the bus and just hung around, and I remember crying. Well, I'm one of those people that's such an avid reader that I can't sit still without a newspaper; I just have to be reading something. And I picked up a teen magazine—I forgot the name—and I was just leafing through it. Nothing that really interested me because I was more interested in *Scientific American* at the time, but there was an article titled "Sixteen— and I Had to Change My Sex." It was like a sledgehammer. I devoured that in an Evelyn Wood–like speed-reading experience. I was like, "That's me!" My God! I had been hiding it. I didn't want anybody to know. And then all of a sudden, it was this kind of combination of exhilaration and fear. Sort of like the way I feel now. The possibilities. The knowing. Of course it wasn't a medical article and the term "transsexual" wasn't used in it. It was a like a lot of cross-dressing fiction, where there's an element of coercion because you can't admit that this is what you want, so this article was like "these girls caught me in panty raid and these girls forced me into it." I don't think it was quite that pornographic. But it was the name that captured me: "Sixteen—and I Had to Change My Sex."

But something happened to me because right after that, my classmates got back on the bus and I'm sitting there, I'm sweating. I had made this discovery that I couldn't share with anyone. But something had changed for me. This other girl named Phyllis came and sat down next to me, and by the end of the trip we were making out! And about a year later Money made the news in *Newsweek* and *Time* about the Gender Identity Clinic at Hopkins and that they were doing sex-change surgery. I came out to my parents, and they mentioned Creedmor. It was not a pleasant place. It was where the bogeyman lived when I was growing up.

But I was liberated. Yet I could only go so far. After school ended I worked at a camp as a junior counselor, and I used to bike down to be with her [my girlfriend] and I remember thinking, "I don't want to do this. I want to *be* her." She wanted me to take off her bra, and I'm thinking, "I want to wear it." I just couldn't do it. I was mortified and ashamed and didn't know what to do. So it ended. She thought I was weird, I guess. Guys are supposed to want it. But I didn't.

In high school, I didn't have any sex or any girlfriends till the end of my junior year, when I met my first wife. And we hit it off. We were both traumatized kids and we helped each other, we provided succor to one another. Sex was hard for both of us. Her mother was an extreme narcissist who used to play around with her friends' fathers and had a bad reputation and so forth. So she had a tough upbringing.

But when I was eighteen we spent the summer right after high school in Israel, my first trip to Israel and her first trip back home, and in our apartment in Jerusalem in this Orthodox Jewish neighborhood, when my three best male friends were out, she and I were in bed together and with my heart racing at around 180 beats per minute and the sweat pouring off my body, I came out to her. And she accepted me. She told me subsequently that she thought it was weird and she didn't know what to make of it, but she was going to try to help me, try to fix me.

Q: Did you want to be fixed at that point?

Sure, what do I know? What was I going to do, come out and have surgery? That scared the hell out of me. I knew I was transsexual, but I kept thinking, maybe I'm just a cross-dresser.

Q: And you were aware of the distinction?

Well, it wasn't quite the academic distinction but I thought, "Maybe this will be enough." And she went through the stage of "Maybe, if I'm more feminine, you won't feel like you have to be." So we went through that phase. But she had no sense that this was a perversion that she needed to run away from, which is interesting. But it made her feel less of a woman. She felt inadequate. I felt like I was perverted. Here I am, a high school student, a pretty bright one, at one of the best public high schools in the country, and I would go to libraries and search out all the literature I could find, and there would be nothing there. I didn't find any of Harry Benjamin's early stuff. I didn't even discover the trans community. This is post-Stonewall already, this is New York! And I'm a New Yorker, I'm leaving from Port Authority [bus terminal] to go to Cornell . . .

Finally—I think it was my sophomore year of college—I had some time to kill and I get off at Port Authority at Forty-second Street and I'm just walking around and I come across Lee Brewster's Mardi Gras Boutique. Of course, I didn't know what an important person this was at the time but I was like, "My god, there are other people like me." But I was scared to death that I would be seen. That's where I was introduced to the pornography, which was exciting and degrading simultaneously, as pornography is. But there was no alternative, nothing to say to me, "This is a medical condition." Because it was considered a psychiatric condition. It still is now; we're still fighting this fight. I thought I might be gay, and you know, the gays are still saying, "Why don't you just admit that you want to have sex with a guy? Come on!" And then, after that, every time I came home, I'd make a side trip there.

Q: Did you talk to anyone?

No, because I couldn't be found out. Then you start thinking, "I did that. That's me." How do you think that makes you feel? On the one hand, you're going to this good school, and you're going to go to medical school and become a doctor, and on the other hand, you're skulking around town. You get no positive reinforcement. It's all totally negative and shame-based. Now I didn't know that term in those days, but that's exactly how I felt. I was living in a pool of shame. And I would run away from it. I would tell my first wife, "I can stop," and I would count the days down but I could never stop thinking about it. I could stop wearing women's clothes for years at a time, but I realize now that it wasn't the clothes that was the issue, it was the *being*. But that was the only way to express it in those days. I couldn't stop thinking about it. What does it mean? Who am I?

Unbeknownst to anybody, I remembered the article about Hopkins, and I wrote to them and set up an appointment. I have a love/hate relationship with Hopkins. The love is that I do recognize that they did this. They were at the forefront in America. Harry Benjamin started it, and they picked it up academically. That's how things work in medical culture. And they performed a service. Now, granted, it was completely twisted the way they went about it at the time. But they performed a service. Before you had to go where? To Casablanca? Thailand today is a mecca, compared to what Casablanca was like. So I appreciate that. John Money was part of it. He did the work when being a sexologist was not an easy thing to do. I can appreciate too how difficult it was for the surgeons to want to do this. The book on the history of transsexuality [*How Sex Changed*] makes that point. The terms didn't really exist. There's this one little group of Jewish doctors in Weimar Germany that were beginning to do this, for the first time ever in the history of civilization. And it's not easy to go from that, through Nazism and the Holocaust, and then come to America and keep going with it. There's so much shame in this country; we're so puritanical. So the people who did it were pioneers, and I'm grateful to them.

But anyway I went down there [to Baltimore]. I left school early and I went down there and I thought, "Let's do this." I got an intake form and stuff like that and I filled it out, but I got cold feet. I didn't feel comfortable. I didn't feel welcome. I felt dirty. I felt like they were making me feel like a pervert.

Q: How old were you?

I was twenty. I called ahead and made an appointment. I suppose my records are still there somewhere. But I just freaked out. I couldn't do it. I did not feel welcome. It's amazing how today, when I go to my electrolysis, my hair stylist, my surgeon, these people bend over backward to make you feel like a human being. And in those days, they did not. No matter how much they felt they were trying, it was so damn paternalistic. I'll give them the benefit of the doubt, but they made you feel like a real freak. I couldn't do it. So I went back to searching the stacks at school libraries, but all I could find were textbooks with the relevant pages ripped out or aversion therapy, putting electrodes on your penis. And I was thinking, "No way!"

But there was no place else to go. I wasn't going to a shrink. Nobody was out there saying, "We welcome gender-variant patients."

Q: You never heard of Harry Benjamin?

No, there was only Creedmor. To me, psychiatry was Creedmor. I didn't know any different. I wasn't in medical school at the time. Even when I went to medical school, I found nothing. Nobody talked about sex at all. I took a one-week externship in urology. DES was never mentioned. Of course, I didn't know about the DES at that point. I didn't know that till the end of my medical career. I first came across the book *First, Do No Harm* [*sic*] in the eighties. It was only when I saw that, that I thought, "Oh, could this be?" And I asked my mother, and she just came right out and said, "Yes." I was born in New York in 1952, there were certainly thousands of other Jewish kids exposed. I'm not the only one.

Q: You and your mother must have a very complex relationship as a result of the DES exposure.

She still blames herself. I told her that I've gotten over that. I don't blame her anymore. She's responsible for it, yes, but I can understand how it happened in the social context of the time. I don't blame her.

Seven

FEAR OF A PINK PLANET

Developments in the last decade have highlighted the reproductive, behavioral, and anatomical effects of endocrine disrupters on animals exposed to these chemicals. Effects due to endocrine disrupting chemicals are observed at concentrations as low as parts per trillion for animals in the laboratory, indicating that the fetal endocrine system is more sensitive to disruption than any other known body system. These results of toxicology are significantly related to the field of gender identity and indicate a causal relationship between exposure to these chemicals and anomalies in the expression of gender identity and other disorders such as reproductive failure.

CHRISTINE JOHNSON,
"ENDOCRINE DISRUPTING CHEMICALS
AND TRANSSEXUALISM," SEATTLE, 2001

Christine Johnson is a petite, blond transwoman, thirty-eight years old. She is an engineer, with bachelor's and master's degrees from Drexel University, in Philadelphia, currently living in Seattle. Her major research interest is systems theory. I sought her out online after she posted "Endocrine Disrupting Chemicals and Transsexualism" on the discussion list of the National Transgender Advocacy Coalition (NTAC). The list members, most of whom are activists focused on civil rights for transgendered people and the passing of anti-discrimination legislation, didn't seem interested in Johnson's article, but it hit me with the force of a depth charge.

In 1995, I had been asked to be a coauthor an article for an environmental magazine called *Garbage* on the potential effects of endocrine-disrupting chemicals (EDCs). The editors of *Garbage* (known for tipping the sacred cows of environmentalism) had wondered if the spate of panicky articles then appearing in the popular press—articles that ominously detailed falling human sperm counts, Florida alligators with micro-penises, hermaphroditic birds and fish in the Great Lakes region—were scientifically credible. Soon after my coauthor—a friend who was then a professor in the Department of Environmental Health Sciences at the Johns Hopkins School of Public Health—and I signed the contract to write the article, the magazine went under, but by then I had downloaded two years of articles on the topic. I found the information in the newspaper and magazine articles disturbing, but as a feminist I was also deeply suspicious of the subtext, neatly summarized by the title of a BBC documentary on the topic: *Assault on the Male*. The media coverage of the "environmental estrogen" hypothesis seemed to me a transparent expression of male anxiety about the growing political, economic, and social power of women. All this talk of males being "feminized" and emasculated by exposure to estrogen seemed so clearly an expression of the antifeminist backlash that I was determined to call my article "Fear of a Pink Planet" (a riff on the music industry satire *Fear of a Black Planet*). However, *Garbage* sank, and as I wasn't very far into the project, I abandoned it when the magazine ceased publication.

When I encountered Christine Johnson's article sketching out a hypothesis between endocrine disrupters and transsexuality, I was two years into the research for this book. I had spoken to literally hundreds of transgendered and transsexual people at meetings and online. By then, it was abundantly clear to me that the people I was meeting were not mentally ill. Like the friend whose decision to transition had caused me to embark on writing this book, they seemed like regular people who had been dealt a tough hand by life, and were dealing with it as best they could. I also rejected the popular notion that gender was entirely "performative"—the newest twist of the social construction theory, most cleverly articulated in the work of the Berkeley scholar Judith Butler. Certainly, I thought, people "perform" gender in various ways, learned from their parents, community, and culture. However, most people also seem to feel comfortable basing their performance on the gender that is consistent with their anatomy. Most do not feel a dis-connection between their anatomy and their "most deeply held sense of self," as Susan Stryker phrased it, and as most of my sources de-scribe it. So if gender-variant people weren't mentally ill anarchists bent on bringing down the binary gender system through subversive performance, what was the source of gender variance? I searched the scientific literature and was frustrated by the paucity of hard scien-tific research on transsexuality, transgenderism, and gender variance. Searches on Medline (an online search engine) and PubMed (the Na-tional Library of Medicine's search service) using those keywords brought up very few articles, and most of those were the work of researchers with whom I was already familiar. Then I encountered Christine Johnson and discovered that there was, in fact, a substantial scientific literature on anomalous sexual differentiation, but that I wouldn't find it in journals of endocrinology or psychiatry. I would find the hard science in the last places I would have thought to look: toxicology and environmental health, the disciplines in which I had been trained as a science writer.

I e-mailed Johnson in November 2001, introduced myself, and shared with her my questions and concerns about the environmental endocrine hypothesis and its possible relationship to our fin de siècle anxiety about masculinity threatened by female power. She responded, "Yes, there seems to be a great deal of discomfort in the media and in our society generally about gender roles and identity. But apart from the media response to these findings, in my opinion, this problem is much more serious than people are generally aware. So while the media may have reacted strongly because of existing social mores, it essentially acted correctly in raising red flags about the relationship between chemicals and sexual developmental anomalies."

I told Johnson that I had been asking the transgendered and trans-sexual people whom I was interviewing whether or not there were more gender-variant people in the world today, or whether they were simply becoming more visible as society becomes more tolerant and accepting. She answered bluntly, "I don't think that asking transgen-dered people is the proper way to ask this question. This is equivalent to asking cancer patients if the rate of cancer is increasing. How can one know this? What is required is epidemiological studies, period. The fact that there is not a registry is suspicious in my view. Keeping track of the number of sexual developmental anomalies is important in gaining an understanding of the impact."

Johnson also rejected the notion that the growing visibility of transgender and transsexual people was due to greater social tolerance of gender diversity. "Ts find increased acceptance inside the T community, and to a lesser extent within the larger GLBT community, but to extend that acceptance to the general population is a bit disingenuous. Where is the evidence that society is more accepting of Ts? It seems to be that most people claim increased social benevolence, but in general are unable to identify in what tangible ways this benevolence is manifested. We have not achieved many basic civil rights, and if you ask the average (non-TG) person to name a single TG, they would be hard pressed to name anyone, because we are, in essence, the invisible ones. Also to be noted is the fact that Ts are excluded in most cases for insurance reimbursement—this is decidedly not benevolent. So while I see relatively large increases in the number of teen Ts, I see no significant increase in benevolence, at least in the U.S., towards transpeople."

Regarding the environmental endocrine hypothesis itself and its relationship to transsexuality, Johnson points out that the scientific literature "makes it abundantly clear that it is possible to feminize males and masculinize females by application of exogenous hormones. This is reproduced reliably in the lab on animals, so there should be little argument over the potential of hormonal compounds to alter the 'normal' path of development. For the last 40 years, gender researchers have been saying that hormonal variations can indeed cause altered development of the anatomy of the genitals and the brain. And so now we find endocrine disrupters all over the place, and yet we still take the incredibly naive view that somehow we develop independently from our hormonal environment? I find this view totally inconsistent with my understanding of how natural systems work."

We agreed to meet in the spring, to discuss these issues in more detail. In the meantime, I learned that colleagues at the Johns Hopkins

Bloomberg School of Public Health were holding a workshop on endocrine disrupters in February 2002. The workshop would bring together scientists from industry, academia, and regulatory agencies from the United States and abroad to discuss progress in identifying and testing hormonally active substances, and ways to implement those goals that would not require a massive animal testing program. I was particularly interested to see that one of the speakers at the meeting was Dr. John McLachlan, the Tulane University researcher considered one of the primary architects of the environmental estrogen hypothesis. McLachlan has been studying the effects of endocrine-disrupting chemicals for over thirty years. I approached him after his presentation at the February 2002 meeting and asked him, with some trepidation, if it was possible for endocrine-disrupting chemicals to affect human gender identity and sexual orientation, and to increase the prevalence of intersex conditions.

"Absolutely," he replied, pointing out an already documented increase in the incidence of hypospadias (incompletely differentiated penis) in baby boys. Having studied the effects of endocrine-disrupting chemicals on one-celled organisms, fish, reptiles, and mammals for more than two decades, McLachlan said that he can predict with some certainty what effects endocrine-disrupting chemicals will produce when administered in sufficient doses to animals at critical stages in fetal development. But he also said that no one has yet linked these effects, which have been confirmed in laboratory animals and wildlife, to the development of gender identity or sexual orientation in humans. "You should have a look at the DES literature," he said. Soon after the meeting, I did so. What I discovered astonished me.

DES was first synthesized in 1938, in the laboratory of Sir Charles Dodds, a professor of biochemistry at the Middlesex Hospital Medical School at the University of London. Researchers working independently in England and Germany had succeeded in isolating natural estrogens for the first time in 1929, but natural estrogens were very expensive and difficult to produce. Further, the supply of natural estrogens could not meet the demand; Dodds's discovery of a synthetic estrogen that could be easily and cheaply produced was hailed as a great boon. Dodds and his colleagues tested the effects of this new synthetic estrogen on female rats that had first undergone ovariectomy (removal of the ovaries). The ovariectomized rats responded to DES as though it were an endogenous estrogen produced by their own bodies—even though DES, manufactured from coal tar products, is not at all chemically similar in structure to natural estrogens. Indeed, DES appeared to be even more potent than natural estrogen, mimicking its biological effects when ingested in much smaller doses.

Within a year, DES was being manufactured and marketed in mass quantities by drug companies in Europe and North America. Never patented, the drug was sold under more than 400 different brand names by 257 pharmaceutical companies in the United States alone. DES was used as "hormone replacement therapy" for women, and was approved by the U.S. Food and Drug Administration for that purpose (among others) in 1941. DES was also initially prescribed to suppress lactation in the growing number of women who did not wish to breast-feed their infants, to treat amenorrhea (failure to menstruate) and vaginitis, and (surreptitiously) to prevent miscarriage, though it was not approved for the last purpose in the United States until 1947.

The use of DES to prevent miscarriage was strongly advocated by a husband-and-wife team of researchers from the Harvard Medical School: George Smith, an obstetrician-gynecologist, and Olive Watkins Smith, a biochemist. In 1945, Smith and Smith asked 119 obstetricians in the United States and Europe to participate in a clinical trial on the use of DES in high-risk pregnancies. Seven published papers subsequently reported that DES not only reduced miscarriage but also produced bigger babies in high-risk pregnancies. It was later noted that three of the seven studies that reported the efficacy of DES to prevent miscarriage had used no controls at all, and none of the control participants was treated with the experimental cohort or by the same physician. A larger, controlled study at the University of Chicago in 1953 showed that DES had no beneficial effect whatsoever on the prevention of miscarriage; this finding was reinforced by six other controlled studies done in the fifties. Nonetheless, more than three million pregnant women in the United States alone were prescribed DES between 1941 and 1971. Many more mothers and fetuses were exposed to the drug in pregnancy vitamins in which DES was the active ingredient. Ads that appeared in medical journals and women's magazines promised "a healthy pregnancy" through the use of DES. "DES became a routine part of the quality care that private practitioners gave their predominantly middle-class patients, including their own wives," write Drs. Roberta J. Apfel and Susan M. Fisher in their 1984 history of DES, *To Do No Harm: DES and the Dilemmas of Modern Medicine.* "DES was considered the best possible pregnancy enhancer and it was even included in vitamin tablets for pregnant mothers."

Beginning in the early forties, DES was also used in commercial agriculture, added to the feed given to livestock and chickens in pellets—a practice given added impetus when, in 1947, researchers at the Purdue University Agricultural Station discovered that DES was a potent growth stimulant in cattle. In 1959, high levels of DES in meat were discovered to produce "disturbing symptoms" in agricultural workers and consumers, including sterility, impotence, and gynecomastia (breast growth) in men. As a result, the FDA banned the use of DES pellets in chicken and lamb feed in 1959. However, the use of DES in cattle feed was not prohibited by the USDA until 1979, after nearly a decade of wrangling between cattle breeders and regulatory agencies.

The number of people exposed to DES through meat consumption from 1941 to 1979 is incalculable. The effects of this secondary exposure are unknown, though recent data on the epigenetic effects of maternal diet on fetal development make the subject well worth investigating. Epigenetics is a relatively new science that investigates how environmental factors such as diet, stress, and maternal nutrition can change gene function without altering DNA by inducing mutations. Genes can be activated or inactivated by a process called methylation, in which a group of four atoms (methyl group) attaches itself to a gene at a specific point and relaxes or tightens the coiled strands of DNA, regulating gene expression. Methylation is critically important during prenatal and postnatal development, silencing some genes and activating others—one of the two X chromosomes in female cells, for example, is "turned off" by methylation. The mixture of genetic traits inherited from one's parents is controlled by this process, and the process is highly vulnerable to environmental influences. "Fleeting exposure to anything that influences methylation patterns during development can change the animal or person for a lifetime," the science writer Sandra Blakeslee reports in an article describing the impact of maternal diet on fetal development published in the *New York Times* in October 2003. "Methyl groups are entirely derived from the foods people eat. . . . Maternal diet during pregnancy is consequently very important, but in ways that are not yet fully understood."

DES had one other major use—it was used to treat prostate cancer in men by suppressing the production of testosterone, which stimulates tumor growth in the prostate. "DES also feminizes these patients," Apfel and Fisher note. A fact sheet on DES produced by the National Toxicology Program notes transsexualism as one of many effects of DES, and the *Dictionary of Organic Compounds,* a standard reference book for organic chemists, notes that DES "causes male impotence and transsexual changes particularly in offspring exposed in utero." Far more potent than natural estrogen, DES was sometimes prescribed to induce feminization in male-to-female transsexuals. This superpotency has ominous implications for those exposed in utero. In recent decades, researchers have learned that "fetal tissues are even more sensitive to DES than to natural estrogens because the fetus has to use other biochemical pathways to deactivate the synthetic substance," say Drs. Apfel and Fisher in *To Do No Harm.*

The chemical structure of DES is very different from the chemical structure of natural estrogens, and metabolizing DES thus forces fetal tissue to perform a task for which it is not naturally primed. Even more important, researchers have discovered that "the fetus probably becomes sensitized to all estrogens by DES exposure, a sensitization that may become important later in life." In other words, DES exposure in utero causes the fetus (whether male or female) to become more than usually responsive to the effects of later estrogen or estrogen-mimicking substances. Prenatal exposure to DES primes an individual to be supersensitive to estrogens, whether endogenous (produced within the body) or exogenous (outside the body) for the remainder of his or her life. This sensitivity has major implications for DES mothers and daughters, who are exposed to their own (endogenous) estrogens throughout most of their lives and who may also be exposed to exogenous estrogens through the use of birth control pills and hormone replacement therapy in menopause.

To understand how DES produces this range of effects requires a brief lesson in embryology and endocrinology. The human embryo, like that of other mammals, has the potential to become either male or female. Each embryo develops two paired sets of germinal ducts—the mullerian duct and the wolffian duct. Without the influence of the Y chromosome and its chemical messengers, the wolffian ducts will begin to regress in the sixth week of pregnancy, and the primitive gonad will differentiate into an estrogen-producing ovary. Under the influence of the Y chromosome (and the androgen receptor gene on the male fetus's X chromosome), the mullerian ducts will atrophy, and the gonads differentiate into androgen-producing testicles. The sexual differentiation of a fetus is an exquisitely choreographed ballet, and the Balanchine directing this intricate dance is the endocrine system. Testis-determining factor is released on day fifty-six of human gestation. As researcher Lindsey Berkson notes in her book *Hormone Deception,* "If the timed sequence of hormone signals is disrupted, development of the male reproductive organs can be skewed, resulting in undescended testicles or other problems."

It is often said that the "default" sex in mammals is female, because even in the absence of ovaries, the fetus will develop a female reproductive anatomy unless exposed to sufficient levels of circulating testosterone. Many women object to this way of phrasing the biological reality that females are the basic model and males the frill. "The term *default sex* has such a passive ring to it, suggesting that girls just happen, that making them is as easy as unrolling a carpet downhill; you don't even have to kick it to get it going," science journalist Natalie Angier writes in *Woman: An Intimate Geography.* "A number of women in biology have objected to the terminology and the reasoning behind it. . . . Just because hormones don't appear to be responsible for female sex determination doesn't mean that *nothing* is responsible; other signaling systems exist and participate in fetal growth, though they're harder to find and study than a sharp and unmistakable burst of androgens." Despite dislike of the bias implicit in the notion of a "default sex," no one seriously questions the fact that without that "sharp and unmistakable burst of androgens" in development, fetuses develop in the female direction. All the evidence from animal, in vitro, and clinical studies points to the critical importance of circulating testosterone in establishing a male reproductive anatomy and brain structure.

Doctors often prescribed massive doses of DES to prevent miscarriage in the first trimester of pregnancy—but as researcher Lindsey Berkson discovered, even a single shot of DES in the first trimester could have devastating results. The protocol recommended by Smith and Smith "began during weeks 5 and 6 of fetal life and the dosage increased until the 36th week of pregnancy." Thus, precisely at the crossroads when the developing embryo begins to differentiate sexually, the children of DES mothers were subjected to a barrage of synthetic estrogen. "Most of the first trimester, when embryonic development is most active and differentiation of structures is rapid, was blanketed by DES," say Apfel and Fisher. "The dosage schedules used in other studies varied somewhat but all included significant doses during the first trimester and increasing doses until at least mid-pregnancy." DES was administered in pills, injections, vaginal suppositories, and vitamins. The DES Cancer Network estimates that approximately ten million mothers and unborn children were exposed to DES from 1941 to 1971. A great many of these individuals, both mothers and children, have no idea that they were unwitting participants in the DES experiment. "Many of these people are not aware that they were exposed," the National Cancer Institute admits on its website. Lindsey Berkson says that the estimate of ten million Americans exposed to DES either during pregnancy or in utero "probably underestimates the number of *in utero* exposures of DES since many private physicians administered the drug and hospitals often did not keep records of 'enhancement' treatments. Even if they did not receive direct injections of DES, many of our mothers ate contaminated food before and during their pregnancies."

In April 1971, a paper published in the *New England Journal of Medicine* noted the appearance of a rare form of vaginal cancer among very young women. Though the first case of clear cell adenocarcinoma (CCA) had been diagnosed in 1961, doctors at Massachusetts General Hospital stumbled on a cluster—eight women under the age of twenty—with a disease that normally manifested itself only in much older women, and then quite rarely. One of the mothers wondered if her daughter's cancer could be related to the DES she took during her pregnancy. It was a smart guess; a search of medical records revealed that seven of the eight young women treated at Mass General had been exposed to DES in utero. Those seven cases were followed by others. By November 1971, twenty-one cases had been reported. The snowballing cases led to an FDA bulletin to all physicians in the United States, warning them that the use of DES was "contraindicated in pregnancy."

Because the first victims were young women, and because the health effect that was first identified was a rare carcinoma, DES very quickly became a story about mothers, daughters, and cancer. The DES narrative shaped by the media (and by women's health advocates) was in many respects a product of the 1970s and two of that decade's major preoccupations—the plight of women under patriarchy and the carcinogenic potential of chemicals. First (and most explicitly) DES illustrated the evils of medical paternalism. The first visible victims were very young women, whose sexuality, fertility, and very lives were threatened by an awful, disfiguring disease. The CCA daughters and their heartbroken mothers were an appealing patient group whose plight would move the hardest of hearts. DES was viewed as a textbook example of the male medical establishment's abuse of women, its lack of concern for women's health, and its tendency to pathologize female bodies and view natural functions and women's life passages such as pregnancy and menopause as illnesses requiring treatment.

The ability of DES to cause cancer was also discovered at a time when carcinogenicity was a primary focus of toxicological testing. The Delaney Amendment to the Food, Drugs and Cosmetic Act, passed by the U.S. Congress in 1958, required manufacturers to furnish data establishing the carcinogenic potential of a product prior to its marketing. From the fifties through the eighties, carcinogenicity was a primary concern of regulatory agencies worldwide. DES was a known cancer promoter, as were natural estrogens. As early as 1938, studies showed that mice and rats exposed to DES developed mammary tumors. However, DES was approved by the FDA seventeen years before the passage of the Delaney Amendment. In 1941, all but four of the fifty-four academic experts who had reviewed the data submitted by twelve pharmaceutical companies wishing to market the drug approved DES as a "safe" drug. This despite the existence of a 1939 editorial in the *Journal of the American Medical Association*, titled "Estrogen Therapy: A Warning," cautioning against the "long continued and indiscriminate therapeutic use of estrogens. . . . The possibility of carcinoma induced by estrogens cannot be ignored," the author of the editorial writes. This Cassandra-like prophecy was ignored. However, by 1971, when DES was proved to be the cause of vaginal cancer in young women who had been exposed to DES in utero, the carcinogenic potential of xenobiotics had become the primary concern of toxicologists and regulatory agencies. DES thus fit perfectly into the "cancer" paradigm of the toxicologists as well as the "evils of medical patriarchy" paradigm of women's health advocates.

An advocacy group, DES Action, was formed in 1975 by a DES mother, Pat Cody, and in 1982 the DES Cancer Network, "an international, non-profit, consumer organization that addresses the special needs of women who have had clear cell adenocarcinoma of the vagina or cervix," was founded. These advocates worked hard to spread the news about DES and lobbied for research funding to study its effects. "DES was one of the prime movers behind the nascent women's health movement back in the seventies. *Our Bodies, Ourselves,* that kind of thing," says Dana Beyer. "DES Action was formed as the political clout of women was beginning to change, in the seventies, so they focused on women's health. It was conceived as a mother-daughter thing because of the cancer—vaginal cancer, which is not common. That's what was weird and caused people to make the connection. If it had been a slight increase in uterine cancer, it would have gone unnoticed. So that was lucky, I guess. So they formed this organization and they've worked very hard, lobbying Congress and drafting female representatives who support them, getting House appropriations to get the National Cancer Institute to fund this [DES research]. That's where the activism has been."

The bulk of the educational efforts were directed at mothers and daughters, and focused on cancer risk. Women who knew that they had been exposed to DES were told to inform their health care providers, particularly gynecologists, about their exposure, and obstetricians and family practitioners who had administered DES to pregnant women were asked to inform their patients that they and their children had been exposed. Many failed to do so. Apfel and Fisher attribute the "subdued, even paralyzed responses of practicing physicians" to the "fear of facing their own mistakes, of failing in the eyes of peers and younger colleagues, of being criticized, regulated and even sued." They conclude that "most doctors go out of their way to avoid concluding that a patient's problem has been iatrogenically induced." In the case of DES, that resistance to assuming responsibility has been shared by the pharmaceutical companies that produced the drug, and by the research establishment as a whole, which continues to resist a full investigation of the tragedy. Half of the fetuses exposed to DES in utero were male, subjected to a barrage of synthetic estrogen during the period of sexual differentiation, chemically primed to be exquisitely sensitive to estrogen and estrogen-mimicking chemicals for the remainder of their lives. Their stories remain untold, and no one—not DES Action, not the Centers for Disease Control, not the National Cancer Institute, not the drug companies that manufactured DES— wants to hear them.

"For a very long time, we've been battling with the forces that would try to keep the DES radar screen narrowly focused on cancer and, in particular, on vaginal and cervical cancer alone," says social scientist Scott Kerlin. A DES son, Kerlin founded DES Sons Network in 1999, an online support and advocacy group for the XY children exposed to DES in utero. For years, Kerlin has been fighting the perception that DES is a women's health issue. "Compared with research on DES daughters, there is a paucity of published research studies and public awareness focusing directly on the health effects of DES sons. The reasons for this remain at question, although evidence points in part to a history of inadequate commitment to male reproductive and sexual health issues by the DES-exposed victims advocacy groups which first called for public investigation about the effects of DES in the 1970s. It is also quite possible that the level of public awareness and U.S. governmental funding for further DES research was kept deliberately narrow (i.e., focusing on "known" effects such as vaginal cancer), and other areas of potential health effects were simply not addressed by public health funding agencies."

Kerlin says that the latest round of research and educational materials produced by the U.S. Centers for Disease Control will not change the perception that DES is primarily a women's health concern. "I've gotten advance looks at the CDC materials and it goes without saying, sons' issues are really being neglected. It seems that this is the biggest obstacle we are facing; DES is not just about increased cancer risk or infertility, but our 'advocates' would never want you to know that." Kerlin himself suffers from hypogonadism, or testosterone deficiency. Hypogonadism is one of the "unproven" effects of DES in exposed males, though animal research has shown that DES exposure causes imbalances in fetal hormone levels and impairment of normal functioning in hormone receptors. Other structural effects of exposure to DES and other estrogenic chemicals in males include epididymal (testicular) cysts; hypoplastic (small) testicles; undescended testicles, or cryptorchidism; microphallus (abnormally small penis); and testicular varicoceles (irregularly swollen veins on the testicle). These enlarged veins produce a higher-than-normal temperature in the testicles and can, over years, lower sperm count, resulting in sub-fertility. Hypospadias, a condition in which the opening of the penis is located on the underside rather than at the tip; and urethral meatal stenosis, a narrowing of the opening of the penis, have also been noted in DES sons. Gynecomastia, enlargement of the male breast, has been noted not only in DES sons but also in adult male agricultural workers exposed to the chemical.

Scott Kerlin stumbled onto another potential outcome of DES exposure in sons when his DES Information Network was a few months old. Kerlin had created the online discussion group to fill the need for "greater interconnectedness" and communication among DES sons. Mothers and daughters had being doing so for years, online and at meetings. DES sons, by contrast, were a mostly silent, mostly invisible group. By creating a forum for the men to discuss their concerns, Kerlin hoped to prod the DES advocacy groups and government funding agencies to recognize the wide range of health effects experienced by sons and the lack of attention to their needs. "The DES Sons Online Network was also formed to expand awareness about the range of existing research about DES and males' health and to explore other issues affecting the physical, mental, sexual, and psychosexual health of DES sons—particularly issues which had been suggested in previous existing research studies about DES and males but which need further investigation," Kerlin says. For that reason, he asked all new subscribers to the online group to submit a brief overview of their health concerns and past health issues as well as a confirmation of DES exposure. Over a quarter of the first forty members of the list noted concerns about issues relating to sexuality and reproductive health.

Men are notoriously tight-lipped about health problems, and Kerlin was congratulating himself on having managed to create a safe, trusting environment in which list members felt comfortable discussing such personal concerns. Then, a new list member raised an issue that initiated a flood of responses, saying that he had, from his earliest youth, felt like a girl, and that he was, in fact, transsexual. Once the issue had been raised, it did not go away. Other list members began to speak about their own gender-identity issues, and "over subsequent months, these issues became more substantial in list discussions, at times becoming the dominant themes raised by members," Beyer and Kerlin note in a 2002 paper. Some list members objected to the turn that the discussions were taking. They may have had reproductive health problems, but they were heterosexual men, and they were uncomfortable with the new focus on gender identity. Eventually, Kerlin and Beyer (who had become co-moderator of the group in 2001) set up a separate list (DES Trans) for list members who identified as transgender, transsexual, or intersexual.

"About 50 percent of our two hundred people in the DES Sons Network exhibit some form of gender variance. Most of them joined us when we didn't talk about gender variance at all," says Beyer. "I would say about half of the people on our list came unknowing that

DES was connected with gender." In July 2004, on the fifth anniversary of the DES Sons Network, Kerlin reviewed his data and concluded that of the approximately six hundred individuals who had contacted the list for information or support in the previous five years, two-thirds of those who joined the list did not mention gender issues or concerns during their introductions, health histories, or subsequent postings. However, ninety-three individuals with confirmed prenatal DES exposure had indicated that they were either transsexual, transgendered, gender dysphoric, or intersexed. Another sixty-five individuals who "strongly suspect" DES exposure identified themselves using one of those four categories.

Kerlin and Beyer are convinced that the DES Sons Network has broken the seal on the conspiracy of silence about the effects of DES exposure on sons, particularly its association with gender identity disorder in males. Not a single DES cohort study has explored this question. "It seems that the entire focus of any ongoing 'cohort' tracking for sons is to look for signs of cancer risk. Other health issues just don't seem to be included," Scott Kerlin told me during a series of e-mail and telephone conversations in 2002 and 2003. All current DES research is based on the DES Combined Cohort Studies (DCCS)—approximately five thousand women exposed to DES during pregnancy; four thousand unexposed (control) mothers; five thousand exposed and twenty-five hundred unexposed daughters; and two thousand exposed and two thousand unexposed sons. According to the U.S. Centers for Disease Control, "the goal of the DCCS is to determine whether the health risk of cancer among DES-exposed individuals is increased as a result of exposure to DES. Other health outcomes, such as infertility and pregnancy outcomes, are also being investigated through the DCCS." It goes without saying, Kerlin and Beyer note, that there is no mention of gender variance in these studies. "Those studies are just not looking at the question of gender variance or anything remotely connected to it."

Kerlin has located a few articles raising the issue of prenatal DES exposure and feminization in males dating as far back as 1973, when researchers at Stanford found not only increased incidence of hypospadias but also "lower ratings on variables related to general masculinity, assertiveness and athletic ability" in twenty six-year-old boys whose mothers had taken DES, compared with a control group. A study published in 1992 by researchers at the Kinsey Institute shows significant differences in spatial ability between DES-exposed males and their brothers. The sample sizes in both studies were small (ten in the Kinsey group and forty in the Stanford study). However, when one considers that seven cases of clear cell adenocarcinoma in 1970 led to an investigation of the relationship between DES exposure and cancer in exposed females, one wonders why the investigation of the effects of DES on male psychosexual development and reproductive anomalies has been so muted. Even if the sample sizes have been small, "it's not like the topic has never been examined," says Scott Kerlin. "I'm beginning to think that sample size isn't necessarily the most critical factor to consider when examining the published 'findings' of DES research."

Pat Cody, founder of DES Action, has responded to Kerlin's persistent questioning about the lack of attention to these issues by that organization by noting that "this subject, as I don't need to tell you, is one that no one wants to look at and therefore we do not have any good research with a large number of random subjects and equal number of controls." Kerlin, who admits the limitations of existing studies, remains frustrated by the unwillingness of DES lobby groups and funding agencies to investigate further the concerns of DES sons. "Since we cannot create fresh studies of DES in humans and trace its effects from birth, we are pretty much forced to look at the existing adult populations. But it would be almost impossible to gather such a population in one place physically in order to verify who they are and whether they were, in fact, DES exposed. That is, unfortunately, one of the reasons that the control/cohort studies like the Dieckman cohort from the University of Chicago have continued to be used in CDC and other DES sons and other DES sons' longitudinal tracking studies," he says.

Because those studies have not posed any questions about subjects' gender identity or sexual orientation, they provide no support for the contention that DES affects the psychosexual development of males exposed in utero. Even the evidence linking other reproductive effects in males (such as cryptorchidism, hypogonadism, and epididymal cysts) is considered inconclusive. Yet funding for further research on sons' issues has been sparse. "Of course there are a handful of people saying, 'Yes, we need more on sons.' But when push comes to shove, sons' issues, even the ones that are least threatening, are being ignored," Kerlin notes. "Oh, maybe they'll discuss the possibility of increased risk of testicular cancer later this year, when the CDC holds its teleconference on DES sons' health, but I doubt much else is going to be addressed. It seems like this is an issue where the National Cancer Institute has been just so influential that other groups have been ignored."

The difficulties of researching the effects of DES on sons is acknowledged by the sexologist Milton Diamond, who told me that "the problem with DES is that there is no test that we can give today to determine if an individual has been exposed to DES. There are many individuals who say, 'Well, my mother took DES,' and you say, 'How do you know?' and they say that their mother told them or an aunt told them. Could have been, but there's no proof." In the larger population, there may well be DES children with gender issues, but "not only will the guys themselves be in the closet, but so will the physicians and parents." "This is what we get from DES Action: 'There's no proof,'" adds Dana Beyer. "You know, there was no 'proof' that DES caused vaginal carcinoma either. There were seven cases. There was a cluster. But it scared the hell out of people that all these young women had cancer, so all of a sudden they accepted the fact that there was a correlation. But there's never been any large randomized double-blind study. Nobody has yet found DES molecules in the cancerous cells. The technology just wasn't there yet. But it's accepted, so why not us?"

Another body of research is beginning to provide support to DES sons who believe that their gender and/or reproductive anomalies may have been caused by prenatal exposure to an endogenous estrogen. In 2001, researcher Niels Skakkebaek and colleagues published an article in the journal *Human Reproduction* providing evidence of the link between exposure to estrogenic chemicals ubiquitous in the environment and a condition that the researchers have termed "testicular dysgenesis syndrome." Epidemiologic evidence from around the world has shown a rise in testicular cancer, low and declining sperm quality, reproductive tract abnormalities, and abnormal sexual differentiation in humans—a collection of effects that the authors attribute to prenatal exposure to chemicals that disrupt endocrine signaling. Such chemicals (collectively termed "endocrine disrupters" or EDCs) have become the target of major research programs in Europe and the United States. DDT, a potent endocrine disrupter, was banned in the United States following publication, in 1962, of Rachel Carson's book *Silent Spring*, but many other chemicals in heavy use today also bind to hormone receptors, producing well-documented reproductive and other abnormalities in wildlife and laboratory animals. The publication of the book *Our Stolen Future* sounded the alarm in 1996 with its argument that some man-made chemicals disrupted chemical signaling in the body, creating myriad negative health effects. Subsequent studies have reinforced the environmental endocrine hypothesis advanced by the book's authors: Theo Colborn, Dianne Dumanoski, and John Peterson Myers. Evidence has been steadily accumulating that the effects of endocrine-disrupting chemicals are not confined to wildlife. In fact, as the Skakkebaek article makes clear, many of the same effects are increasingly being observed in humans.

In April 2002, the U.S. National Institute of Environmental Health Sciences and the World Health Organization released a joint document that concluded that "the biological plausibility of possible damage to certain human functions (particularly reproductive and developing systems) from exposure to EDCs seems strong when viewed against the background of known influences of endogenous and exogenous hormones on many of these processes. Furthermore, the evidence of adverse outcomes in wildlife and laboratory animals exposed to EDCs substantiates human concerns. The changes in human health trends in some areas (for some outcomes) are also sufficient to warrant concern and make this area a high research priority."

The environmental endocrine hypothesis was germinated in 1979, when researcher John McLachlan, at that time working in the Laboratory of Reproductive and Developmental Toxicology at the National Institute of Environmental Health Sciences, in Research Triangle

Park, North Carolina, organized the first symposium on the effects of estrogenic chemicals in the environment. McLachlan had been studying DES since 1971 and he was using DES as a model for investigating the effects of DDT, on the basis of similarities in their chemical structure. At the 1979 meeting on "Endocrines in the Environment," McLachlan and Retha R. Newbold presented data showing the effects of DES on the genital tract development of a mouse model. McLachlan and Newbold linked the effects of DES to those of industrial chemicals including bisphenol A, widely used in the production of plastics, and other environmental chemicals that exhibited estrogenic effects— essentially "tricking" the body into responding to them as estrogens. Bisphenol A (BPA) was developed in the laboratory of none other than Sir Charles Dodds, the man who developed DES. "It is somewhat ironic that two synthetic chemicals, the potent estrogen DES and the weak-acting estrogen BPA, which have been so important to our understanding of environmental estrogens, can be traced to one laboratory, that of Sir Charles Dodds," McLachlan writes in a 2001 paper.

In the early years of his research on the effects of environmental estrogens, McLachlan found it difficult to publish in mainstream scientific journals. "Reviewers considered the work metaphysical, pointing out that these compounds weren't really hormones. According to McLachlan, his detractors claimed that he was stretching the limits of endocrinology and that his work was more like toxicology. He himself characterized his research as crossing the boundaries of endocrinology, developmental biology, and toxicology without fitting neatly into any of the disciplines," Professor Sheldon Krimsky writes in *Hormonal Chaos,* a study of the scientific and social origins of the environmental endocrine hypothesis, published in 2000. "He and his colleagues were creating their own branch of science and it would take some years before it became accepted."

Part of the problem in gaining scientific acceptance for the environmental endocrine hypothesis was that it challenged the prevailing paradigm in toxicology, which linked potency to dose. The foundational assumption of toxicology, unchanged since its inception, was "it's the dose that makes the poison." The focus of testing was to determine at which dose a particular chemical would cause death (acute toxicity) or produce various types of morphologically apparent damage to experimental animals, especially carcinoma. Upping the dose of a toxin was expected to produce increasingly pernicious (and quickly observable) effects. "The higher the dose, the greater is the expected effect. However, in dealing with hormones and hormone mimics, small quantities might yield an effect, whereas large quantities of the same compound might shut the system off entirely, producing no effect," says Krimsky. Professor Milton Diamond, whose early experiments with guinea pigs showed the gender-bending effects of androgens on female fetuses, told me that when the research team attempted to feminize males with similarly large doses of estrogens, "we couldn't do it. We got 100 percent abortions."

Another difficulty encountered by the early exponents of the environmental endocrine hypothesis was that effects manifested themselves not in adult animals exposed to the chemicals, but in their offspring, and in many cases the effects were delayed. The authors of a 2000 paper published in the *Quarterly Review of Biology* contrasted the traditional toxicological approach based on carcinogenesis and acute toxicity, with the endocrine-disrupter approach, which "relies on a developmental model and delayed dysfunction." A fetus exposed to an endocrine disrupter might not show any effect at all until puberty— like the first cases of cancer in DES daughters. The delayed effects of DES, DDT, and other estrogenic compounds allowed potential problems to escape detection for many years. Not until the mid-eighties did scientists begin to link the kinds of reproductive anomalies that had been observed for years in wildlife with possible human health effects. In 1990, pharmacist-turned-zoologist Theo Colborn published the results of an extensive literature search on the Great Lakes ecosystem, which revealed signs of reproductive anomalies in eleven of the fourteen species previously identified to be declining in population. Colborn found that though adult animals seemed unharmed by pollutants, "some of their offspring were not surviving, and those that did were afflicted with a variety of abnormalities of reproduction, metabolism, thyroid function, and sexual development."

Around the same time, a reproductive physiologist named Frederick vom Saal published studies on what he called "the positioning effect," showing that male mice positioned in the womb between two female fetuses receive extra doses of estrogen, and female fetuses positioned between two males receive extra doses of testosterone just prior to delivery, as the hormone circulates in the amniotic fluid. "The differences in hormone exposure caused by the positioning effect of the mice in the uterus were quite small, yet the behavioral and physiological effects were nonetheless significant," writes Krimsky in *Hormonal Chaos*. "Some animals that experienced the positioning effect become more aggressive and territorial—the result of one-time exposures to additional estrogen (or testosterone) that seemed to have made imprints in their brains. These experiments revealed that even minute changes in the hormone exposure of the developing fetus during certain sensitive stages could result in measurable effects."

Colborn, vom Saal, and other researchers began sharing data, "a unique cross-fertilization of scientific disciplines," says Krimsky, which soon produced provocative results. Toxicologists were forced to rethink the dose-response paradigm and to consider the possibility that barely detectable doses of estrogenic chemicals could disrupt the functioning of the exquisitely sensitive, self-regulating endocrine system—a system that engages in "cross talk" with every other system in the body, including the nervous system. In July 1991, researchers from a number of different disciplines met at a seminal scientific meeting to discuss "Chemically Induced Alterations in Functional Development: The Wildlife/Human Connection" at the Wingspread Conference Center in Racine, Wisconsin. The consensus statement signed by twenty-one scientists at the meeting laid the groundwork for future research and marked the start of public debate on the subject of environmental estrogens.

This debate was given added impetus by Danish researcher Niels Skakkebaek and British researcher Richard Sharpe, who, working independently, had both identified spiking rates of male reproductive problems. Together, the two wrote a paper, published in the British medical journal *The Lancet* in 1993, linking fetal exposure to estrogens or estrogen mimics to declining sperm counts, sperm quality, and motility. The threads of the environmental estrogen hypothesis began coming together in the mid-nineties, as scientists in various disciplines who had been working separately began meeting and pooling their data. Funding agencies, too, began taking notice, and as more money became available to study the problem, generating more data, the environmental endocrine hypothesis achieved a greater degree of scientific legitimacy. "Additional research funds to study different components of the environmental endocrine hypothesis soon became available. Scientists in a variety of subfields of molecular and cellular biology, toxicology, and enviromental sciences, taking notice of the new funding opportunities, began to reorient their model systems to compete for a share of the newly available grant money," writes Krimsky. "Once it enters America's network of biomedical and environmental funding streams and is incorporated within program requests for proposals, a scientific hypothesis gains new constituencies."

As a result of this focused research program over the past decade, scientific understanding of the mechanisms by which estrogenic chemicals exert their effects has grown dramatically. Studies have shown that environmental estrogens may alter production of normal hormones, disrupt the transport of hormones, affect the metabolism of hormones, interfere with hormone signaling at the receptor level, or modify hormone-regulated gene transcription. Adverse effects include reproductive failure, developmental effects, immune system dysfunction, and cognitive and behavioral pathologies of various types. The types of chemicals that may produce these effects include pesticides, organocholorines, plasticizers, heavy metals, and plant estrogens. In *Our Stolen Future,* Theo Colborn and her coauthors list eighty-five chemicals known to be estrogen disrupters, many of them ubiquitous in the environment. We are living, scientists now say, "in a sea of estrogens." Does this have any relevance to the issues discussed earlier in this book? Some people say that it does.

"Is it a coincidence that since the introduction of the chlorinated pesticides around 1935–1940 the rate of transsexualism has been climbing steadily? The first generation born after the introduction of pesticides was also the first generation to have significant numbers of transsexuals. The condition is virtually absent from the U.S. historical record prior to 1952, when Christine Jorgensen made headlines,"

Christine Johnson writes in a brief posted on the TransAdvocate website. "Every generation since then has had higher and higher rates. Clearly researchers knew that sexual developmental changes were observed with DDT in animals as early as 1950, yet this information was ignored, deliberately or not. Fifty years later, large numbers and quantities of EDCs are being distributed around the globe without adequate consideration of the consequences."

I met with Christine Johnson in May 2002, in Philadelphia. As I soon discovered, Johnson is passionate about this subject. She speaks eloquently about the damage that she believes has been inflicted on transsexual people who have been told for years that their gender variance is a mental health problem, when the scientific literature shows quite clearly in animals that in utero exposure to exogenous hormones and hormone mimics affects the brain and behavior. "When I saw the words 'endocrine disrupter' a lightbulb went off in my head. Because for years and years I had been reading what all these shrinks have been telling us—that in theory transsexuality *could* be due to hormonal problems, but they don't measure any natural hormonal variations [in adults]. That's been commonly reported throughout the literature. Diamond showed in '57 in guinea pigs that when exposed to opposite sex hormones [they] would develop in the opposite gendered way," she says, describing her realization that rising rates of transsexualism might be linked to EDCs. "So I knew that hormonally active chemicals, anything that modifies the function or behavior of the endocrine system, is going to have this kind of effect, whether it's a natural hormone or a hormone mimic—the body can't tell. As far as the body is concerned, it's all information."

In 2002, Johnson submitted the results of her research on endocrine-disrupting chemicals and transsexualism to the peer-reviewed *International Journal of Transgenderism*, published online. The journal rejected it in a somewhat cavalier fashion, Johnson says. She believes that the psychiatric profession in general and the HBIGDA "establishment" in particular don't want to promote discussion of the endocrine-disruption hypothesis because it poses a direct challenge to their power and authority as gatekeepers of services for trans people. "They are arguing from their paradigm against our paradigm, but the paradigm is what is in question," she says. "So they can't use their paradigm to argue against the endocrine-disruption paradigm. Their attitude is 'we're not going to talk about this.' That is in violation of the scientific tradition." In her view, the scientific community and the trans community are so blinded by traditional ways of viewing gender variance that they are failing to see the obvious. "If you look at the evidence that Benjamin presented, he acknowledged that 45 percent of his patients had hypogonadism. That's another thing they don't explain."

Scott Kerlin recently uncovered a provocative lead suggesting that Benjamin was aware of a possible correlation between prenatal DES exposure and transsexuality. A new member of the DES Trans online discussion list, completing her transition from male to female in 2004, told Kerlin that in 1971 she and her mother had actually seen Benjamin and discussed the mother's belief that DES was implicated in her child's gender dysphoria. According to the list member, Benjamin had indicated that he too suspected that prenatal DES exposure was a likely culprit.

Kerlin then searched Benjamin's publications, and although he was unable to find a direct reference to DES, he did find this intriguing statement in a 1971 *American Journal of Psychotherapy* article titled "Should Surgery Be Performed on Transsexuals?": "A discussion of the etiology of this syndrome is not my subject here, but I do not want to ignore it entirely. Let me state, therefore, that my clinical impressions suggest to me more and more a prenatal neuroendocrine anomaly as perhaps the foremost causative factor for a majority of cases."

Two years later, in an article published in the *American Journal of Nursing*, Benjamin stated more firmly that "in many respects, transsexualism in the anatomic male might be regarded as an incomplete expression of testicular feminization syndrome (AIS, CAIS or PAIS) with the defect affecting only sex-specific areas of the hypothalamus. . . . Recent research indicates that in the genetic male the hypothalamus is masculinized by fetal androgen at a specific period somewhat after the masculinization of the genitourinary tract. The genetic female, with her XX chromosome complement, lacks fetal androgen and therefore develops along typically female patterns. The important principle here is that effective androgen is necessary for masculinization. Without androgen, masculinization will not occur. Thus, the prenatal hormonal environment is critically important for all future development."

Over the past three years, as I've researched this book, I've been struck by the fact that most of my sources trace their feelings of gender dysphoria to their earliest childhood. Sometimes their intuition of the disjunction between their bodies and their sense of themselves as boys or girls is their very first memory. They can recount exactly where they were and what they were doing when they first admitted to themselves that they were not the children that others assumed them to be—usually before the age of five. Many transgendered people believe that these feelings (which in the case of transsexuals are so overwhelming that those who experience them eventually seek surgical and hormonal sex reassignment) are the result of "hormone surges" in prenatal life that somehow alter the link between their physical sex and their gender identity. More than one person I interviewed compared transsexuality to a cleft palate—characterizing both as "birth defects" that require surgical intervention. A few mentioned the increased incidence of reproductive deformities and "transsexualism" (feminized males, masculinized females) in wildlife and wondered if there might not be some connection to their own situation. But few are willing to state as bluntly as Christine Johnson that their lives and gender identities may have been turned inside out by an environmental toxin.

In March 2002, I asked the subscribers of the National Trans Advocacy Coalition's online discussion list what they thought of the environmental endocrine hypothesis as a possible explanation for their gender variance. I received some interesting replies. Rozlyn Manley, a Vietnam veteran who worked as a claims adjuster prior to her transition, posted the following response.

My former career was in the insurance industry, where I handled high-exposure claims on behalf of the international insurance market. Among those claims were pollution, environmental, and product liability claims. In addition to managing the defense and negotiation of existing litigation, I was also in constant contact with the Fortune 500 companies regarding potential litigation they were concerned with. This is because they self-insure the first five or ten million of coverage and have a duty to keep the excess insurers fully informed of what was in the pipeline. Before I left, I began hearing from the pharmaceutical and petro-chemical companies about "gender bender" claims. Each have waste by-products that they dispose of in settling ponds, mostly in Puerto Rico, Germany and our Gulf Coast. They were becoming aware of animals displaying homosexual behavior and transsexual changes. For example, female birds in the Gulf Coast were nesting with each other and non-mating with the male birds. Marine and land animals were displaying distinct transsexual changes in their external genitalia and internal organs. We, of course, are all aware that human male sperm count has been rapidly declining during the last few decades. There are claims being filed against these companies, and they are concerned. At least when I left, they had a working hypothesis but no specific proof of what was going on. None of this says that our trans condition is solely the result of someone's negligence, but it may indicate that something occured that may have trigged our propensity.

Another example might be my hometown of Huntingdon Beach, California. When I graduated in 1964, the population was about 10,000 and there were 2,000 students in the high school which served the surrounding counties. I can now identify 18 post-op transsexuals that graduated between 1964 and 1975. Clearly, this rate is far beyond the generally expected incidence of transsexuality. Is this simply an example of the rule of large numbers, or could it be that Huntingdon Beach had its own aquifer, and it is severely polluted from oil drilling and is no longer used for drinking? I won't begin to state that one led to the other. I simply do not know. I do believe, however, that by sharing these occasional tidbits, some biochemist or geneticist just might have their "idea bell" ring. What follows will be for the next generation to benefit from.

Vanessa Edwards Foster, the chair of the NTAC Board, responded:

Wonderful! For years, I lived just ½ mile from a lot of those settling ponds and 1 block from petroleum gathering tanks next to the ship

channel in Corpus. My dad used to bring the family when he'd go fish-
ing . . . along the ship channel! And a lot of those places around the
Tule Basin, and back in the Tuloso area, and in the back side of Nue-
ces Bay all had settling pools of whatever variety (besides eight oil re-
fineries, we also had a PPG chemical plant as well). While my dad
fished, we had to entertain ourselves—usually playing next to or
around those pools, and on a rare occasion, stepping or falling partially in them. Other than stinking a bit, and being a little messy, I
really don't think they did anything though. It never affected my
brother. . . . Truthfully, though, I really don't give a crap about litigation or suing anyone over it. We're resourceful and resilient, and
don't look for handouts or anything. If the worst health issue I ever
have from living around this chemical soup all my life (San Diego,
L.A., Corpus, and now chemical and smog-laden Houston) is gender
dysphoria, then I came out of it all right, from a health aspect. My
only request would be that general society—from political to religious
to corporate—would just simply understand what happened and just
allow us to live, to work and to enjoy our lives to the fullest without
having to be further penalized (by systemic discrimination, ostraciza-
tion, ridicule, violence and persecution) for something that may have
had no bearing on any free will on our part, save for choosing not to
repress what innately compels us to be ourselves.

Julie Maverick, the university professor who chairs the National
Transgender Advocacy Coalition's research committee, told me that
there are valid scientific hypotheses that link transsexual behavior and
physiology in many animals to endocrine-disrupting chemicals and
hormones in the environment. "These include fish, frogs, and alligators," says Maverick. "Endocrine-disrupting chemicals have also
been linked to malformation and malfunction of sexual organs in these
animals and there is some evidence, though not much and mostly anecdotal, to suggest a higher incidence of transsexualism in humans
due to elevated exposure to various organic chemicals, particularly
DES." However, Maverick said that at present it would be rash to as-
sert a causal relationship between these chemicals and transsexuality,

cross-dressing, or any other form of anomalous gender identity or expression. "To claim any causal link is decidedly premature. Rather, it [existing data] should foster research in this area."

The science of endocrine disruption is still in its infancy, so it is not surprising that no one has investigated possible links between human gender variance and exposure to EDCs. In some ways, "the concept is ahead of the science," says my friend Jim Yager, senior associate dean for academic affairs at the Bloomberg School of Public Health at Johns Hopkins University. Yager, a toxicologist, has been studying the relationship between estrogens and breast cancer for more than two decades, and even in that well-studied endeavor there have been no definitive data establishing causality between exposure to EDCs and rising rates of breast cancer. Yager says that one of the challenges researchers have encountered in EDC research is that "we're seeing [biological] effects at concentrations that we couldn't even detect ten years ago." Much of the laboratory research thus far has been carried out in vitro, and while it is clear that there are measurable biological effects on cells exposed to various EDCs, and on gene expression within those cells, "you can see an effect, but is it a biologically meaningful effect?"

Then, too, "estrogens are considered reversible cellular signals," as John McLachlan writes in a 2002 review titled "Environmental Signaling and Endocrine Disruption," meaning that when the estrogen is withdrawn, the effects of the estrogen fade—as any trans person who has gone on and off hormones could testify. "On the other hand, when estrogens are given to newborn mice, at least one gene under estrogen control is expressed persistently, even in the absence of estrogen," McLachlan notes in the paper. "This leads to the question, how does a reversible signal became irreversible in the absence of a detectable gene mutation?" McLachlan says that "the actual mechanism underlying the molecular feminization of genes by estrogen still has not been elucidated." Nonetheless, studies have shown that estrogen can "imprint" genes in such a way that "when a gene programmed to respond to estradiol at puberty is misprogrammed or reimprinted by developmental exposure to a hormonally active chemical, it will respond abnormally to the secondary cue, resulting in a functional cellular abnormality." This process has been elucidated most clearly in chicken and frogs. But it does lead one to wonder what might be the effects on human fetuses whose gene expression may have been chemically altered by exposure to estrogens in the womb and who are then re-exposed again and again to estrogenic chemicals in the environment?

It's a long way from cells in a dish to a complex human trait such as gender identity, but the path from cell to animal to human in biomedical research is a well-traveled one. The neurological basis of psychiatric conditions once considered the result of inadequate parenting (schizophrenia) or insufficient willpower (alcoholism and other addictions) is now recognized, even if the mechanisms that produce the condition remain incompletely understood. McLachlan points to one interesting example of a behavioral disorder gradually revealed to be a signaling problem in "Environmental Signaling and Endocrine Disruption." The condition, once called "St. Anthony's fire," is today called ergotism and is recognized as a consequence of "the human body's misreading of a fungal signal." In the Middle Ages, individuals exhibiting the bizarre symptoms of St. Anthony's fire were thought to be possessed by the devil. "This level of knowledge was consistent with the unpleasant consequences usually visited on such individuals," McLachlan notes dryly. In later centuries, they were incarcerated in mental institutions. Eventually, the disorder was shown to result from eating moldy rye bread, and an understanding of the biochemical etiology of the condition led to a public health solution—"prevent mold from developing in rye flour or, if it does, don't make bread from it."

No one believes that an understanding of the manner in which gender identity develops will be so simple—nor do many believe that gender variance itself is a problem requiring a solution. Milton Diamond, for example, objects to the characterization of the different forms of gender variance as "anomalies" and prefers to term them simple variations. Still, science liberated the victims of St. Anthony's fire from the stigma of mental illness, just as I am certain it will eventually reveal the actual biological mechanisms that produce the wide range of anatomical and neurological intersex conditions. Many of the anatomical conditions, of course, have already been elucidated. The "natural" genetic and/or biochemical mechanisms that produce Klinefelter's syndrome,

CAH, Turner's syndrome, AIS, and various enzyme deficiencies that produce anomalously sexed bodies were identified decades ago. Yet there is still resistance in some quarters to accepting that many individuals born with these conditions are fine as they are—that they don't need to be "fixed" to conform to some rigid aesthetic or medical concept of what "normal" genitals or "normal" human beings look like.

"More people are coming around," says Milton Diamond. "They have to. The data is accumulating. I gave a talk at the American Academy of Pediatrics in '98 and I really thought they would throw stones at me. I was telling them that, first, I thought that what they were doing [intersex surgery on infants and children] was wrong; number two, that they have to do the research to discover the effects of what they were doing; and number three, they have to be honest. Well, they didn't want to hear any of that. Now I have to give them credit. They did listen. In 2000, they changed the standard procedure. I gave a similar talk in England in 2000 and in 2001 they changed their procedure." The current guidelines, he points out, "basically say, 'think twice'" before correcting anomalous genitals. Diamond and legions of intersex activists would like physicians to wait permanently—or at least until the child expresses a gender preference. In many cases, the children might opt to stay exactly as they are.

The challenges faced by transgendered and transsexual people in their dealings with scientists and physicians are even more daunting. Like the general public, most hear the word "transsexual" and immediately visualize an episode of the *Jerry Springer Show*. They don't conceive of gender variance as a medical condition, nor do they view it as a legitimate focus of research. Not many people are well acquainted with the kind of professional transpeople whom I interviewed for this book or with the data that point to a biological etiology for gender variance. In many ways, the scientific and medical professions mirror the prejudices of society at large with respect to trans people. No wonder so many trans people show little interest in participating in research and avoid seeking medical care. The history of interactions between trans people and health care providers has been a complicated one, as this book indicates. Arrogance, paternalism, dishonesty, manipulativeness—the accusations fly back and forth while the civil status and health status of transgendered people hang in the balance. Many in the trans community recognize that their efforts to achieve civil protections are somehow bound up with scientific and medical perceptions of their condition, while others heatedly deny that science and medicine will make any contribution at all to their efforts to gain job protections, to marry, to retain custody of their children, and to achieve the degree of social acceptance that has thus far eluded them.

Dr. Dana Beyer believes that further research combined with activism is essential. "People need to understand why this happens; they need to understand about DES and the effects of EDCs, and that this isn't going away. This is personal for me. I live with this twenty-four–seven. But as a society we've got a real problem. Fish changing sex? Hermaphroditic frogs? But they don't make the connection. And then when a story comes out, local sperm counts down 20 percent, they just sort of ignore it."

The only way that the scientific community will accept the possibility that exposure to DES and other endocrine-disrupting chemicals is driving a silent epidemic of gender variance is if (a) epidemiologic studies show a clear correlation between an exposed population and a statistically significant increase in manifestations of gender variance; or (b) laboratory studies illuminate the mechanisms by which exposure to estrogenic chemicals might produce changes in sex-dimorphic brain structures and consequently in gender-specific behavior. Of course, this latter point raises another provocative question—what is gender-specific behavior and how might it be affected by exposure to EDCs?

In 2003, Simon Baron-Cohen, a professor of psychology and psychiatry at Cambridge University in the United Kingdom, published a book that attempts to anchor readily observed differences in male and female behavior in the brain. In *The Essential Difference: The Truth about the Male and Female Brain*, Baron-Cohen admits that "the subject of essential sex differences in the mind is clearly very delicate" and that his theory could "provide grist for those reactionaries who might wish to defend existing inequalities in opportunities for men and women." Nonetheless, Baron-Cohen believes that compelling data exist to show that the brains of the average man and woman are skewed to perceive and respond to the world differently. On average, he says, females spontaneously empathize (identify and respond to another's emotions and thoughts and respond to them with an appropriate emotion) to a far greater degree than males. The average male, on the other hand, spontaneously systematizes (analyzes, explores, and constructs systems) to a greater degree than the average woman. Baron-Cohen is quick to point out that neither of these modes of interacting with the world is better or worse than the other—they are just different.

> Systematizing and empathizing are wholly different kinds of processes. You use one process—empathizing—for making sense of an individual's behavior, and you use the other—systematizing—for predicting almost everything else. To systematize you need detachment in order to monitor information and track which factors cause information to vary. To empathize you need some degree of attachment in order to recognize that you are interacting with a person, not an object, but a person with feelings, and whose feelings affect your own. Ultimately, systematizing and empathizing depend on independent sets of regions in the human brain. They are not mystical processes but are grounded in our neurophysiology.

Calling the two types of brains *E* for empathizing and *S* for systematizing, Baron-Cohen stresses that not all women have the E type and not all men have the S type. The evidence does suggest that more women are E and more men are S, however, and Baron-Cohen marshals much behavioral data to support his claim. When it comes time to explain the neurobiological mechanisms that might create this difference, he cites some of the same evidence that I have presented in this book, including the effects of hormones on the sexual differentiation of the brain. Indeed, he points to studies of DES sons that found the youngsters "likely to show more female-typical behaviors—enacting social themes in their play as toddlers, for example, or caring for dolls." Studies of male-to-female transsexuals show "a reduction in 'direct' forms of aggression (the physical assaults that are more common in males)," Baron-Cohen points out, and "an increase in indirect or 'relational' aggression (the style of aggression that is more common in females). This is strong evidence that testosterone affects the form the aggression takes," he concludes. He also explores evidence for an anatomic and/or genetic basis for the E/S distinction.

Most provocatively, Baron-Cohen characterizes autism, a relatively rare condition in which a person shows abnormalities in social development and communication and displays obsessional interests, and Asperger's syndrome, a more common and less disabling version of autism, as extreme cases of the male (systematizing) brain. Autism is diagnosed ten times more often in males than in females. Indeed, Hans Asperger, an early researcher on autism, suggested in 1944 that "the autistic personality is an extreme variant of male intelligence." This "monumental" idea, Baron-Cohen says, went unnoticed for nearly fifty years, and it wasn't until 1997 that researchers began exploring this "controversial hypothesis." Diagnoses of autism, like those for gender identity disorder, have been rising steadily over the past few decades, and though Baron-Cohen does not suggest any linkage between environmental factors and autism, one does wonder what might explain the sudden upsurge in cases of autism and Asperger's syndrome.

Baron-Cohen's research and his book, which was the subject of a cover story in *Time* magazine, provide another indication that the theory of psychosexual neutrality in particular and social constructionist views in general are steadily being eroded in both scientific and popular accounts of gender. A few months after Baron-Cohen's research was highlighted in *Time,* a cover story in the *New York Times Magazine* inquired, "Why Don't More Women Get to the Top?" The answer: "They Choose Not To." Author Lisa Belkin concluded that "as women look up at the 'top,' they are increasingly deciding that they don't want to do what it takes to get there," namely neglect their families and their own emotional well-being. One of her sources says: "I think some of us are swinging to a place where we enjoy, and can admit we enjoy, the stereotypical role of female/mother/caregiver. . . . I think we were born with those feelings." Belkin notes that "when these women blame biology, they do so apologetically, and I find this tone as interesting as the words. . . . We accept that humans are born with certain traits, and we accept that other species have innate differences between the sexes. What we are loath to do is to extend that acceptance to humans. Partly that's because absolute scientific evidence one way or another is impossible to collect. But mostly it's because so much of recent history (the civil rights movement, the women's movement) is an attempt to prove that biology is not destiny."

Like it or not, we seem to be reaching the point (again) at which we are willing to entertain the possibility that there may in fact be "essential" differences between the average man and the average woman, differences grounded in biology, not culture. In our attempts to sort out what those differences might be, and how they are formed, and how vulnerable the human reproductive anatomy is to environmental assault, intersexual, transgendered, and transsexual people are a hugely important and almost completely ignored source of information. Not everyone will want to participate in research studies or discuss personal struggles with strangers, of course, but in the three years that I spent researching this book, I found among many transgendered people a real hunger to be heard and understood. There is some fear, however, that if a cause for gender variance is found, the search for a "cure" will inevitably begin. "Once the source is found, the drive to cure or eradicate our particular form of biological variation is probable, based on current medical mentalities. Isn't it better not to address this issue at all?" says one of the trans friends I asked to review this chapter. Dylan Scholinski also voiced this concern. "I have a real problem with this being conceptualized as a birth defect," he said. "I am not 'defective.'"

Many gay people express the same reservations about the search for a gay "gene," or organic etiology for homosexuality. Neuroscientist Simon LeVay acknowledges that studies like his, which identified structural difference in the brains of gay and straight men, are perceived by some as an attempt to "re-pathologize homosexuality and take us back to a time when it was considered some sort of disease. In all my writings and lectures I don't present it that way. I'm gay myself. I'm happy to be gay. I think the world would be a better place if gay people were more accepted. But of course you can never know how other people will use material like this. There could always be some-body to say, 'This shows that there are cells missing in the brain. Let's go and put some in.' If gene tests become available to test babies or fe-tuses, I'm sure there will be some people who would want to abort or have their baby genetically altered. I think myself what we should strive for is to create a world where that won't happen. I think that's a kind of urgent task to accomplish, and I think that's not only in the area of sexual orientation but basically across the board. There's so much human diversity that is controversial in terms of 'is this good, is this acceptable, is this something that we don't want?' People are really going to have to debate these issues and decide what is acceptable and not acceptable, what is within the parents' right to decide."

LeVay also points out that studies have shown that people who be-lieve that homosexuality is an inborn trait, as opposed to a freely cho-sen lifestyle, tend to have more positive views about gay people in general. "There have been studies where the researchers get a whole bunch of college students together and give them some reading mate-rial. One group of students will read material suggesting that sexual orientation is an inborn trait, referring to papers like my own kind of studies; another group of students read material suggesting a lack of biological differences. There was nothing in what they read that was a value judgment—they are just summaries of research. Then afterward they gave these kids a test—the homophobia index or something like that—and they found that the kids who read the 'born that way' kind of material were more favorable than the kids who read the other stuff. So to some extent it looks like there is a connection between beliefs about causation and attitudes about how gay people should be treated. In that sense, it [research on etiology] is not merely a scientific enter-prise—though I think that it is a perfectly worthy scientific enterprise to understand basic aspects of human nature like sexual orientation and gender identity—but it really is embedded in this kind of social controversy about gay rights."

Thirty-five years after Stonewall, and ninety years after Magnus Hirschfeld's advocacy of gay and gender-variant people in Weimar Germany, transgendered people remain, in Christine Johnson's phrase, "the invisible ones." For some, that invisibility seems a kind of protective cloak, but for others it is a dark closet that prevents them from being known and accepted as they are. The community itself is riven with conflict about the pros and cons of assimilation, and the value of difference. Many young trans people especially question why they should be forced to choose a "box"—male or female—given that making such a choice feels like self-betrayal. "In a world that separates gender, I have found the ability to balance the blending of supposed opposites. In a world that demonizes non-conformity, I have found the purest spiritual expression in celebrating my otherness. In a world that exterminates the heretic, I have embraced the danger inherent in holding a belief not shared by the majority of people in my society," writes Alexander John Goodrum, an African-American transman, in an essay published in the program for the True Spirit Conference in 2002.

Goodrum, who served as director of TGNet Arizona, a transgender advocacy and education organization, committed suicide in 2002 while being treated for depression. He was a gentle soul, who conceived of his transgenderness as "a spiritual act, an offering of the highest kind. It is a sacrifice of the pre-defined self created by societal doctrine. It is the act of laying that pre-defined self upon the altar, ready to be sacrified in a supreme act of faith. And it is that act of faith, to whomever or whatever one perceives as god, in which lies the ability to express the infinite."

Some might call Alexander Goodrum a victim—of society's prejudices or of his own conflicted nature. I prefer to think of him as a prophet. If the stories contained in this book teach us anything it is that gender variance is neither a fad nor a revolution. It is a biological fact. Our continuing failure to acknowledge this fact virtually ensures that there will be more Alexanders and Tacys and Gwens, individuals whose pain cannot be assuaged by a syringe or a scalpel and who die violent and premature deaths. Whether dying by their own hands or at the hands of uncomprehending others, these individuals have been sacrificed to an illusion, the belief that the spectrum of gender contains only two colors, black and white, and nothing in between.

CONVERSATION WITH JOANNA CLARK

Joanna Clark served in the United States Navy for seventeen years, rising to the rank of chief petty officer. She was discharged early in her transition but later served for eighteen months as sergeant first class in the army, after informing her recruiter and superiors about her sex reassignment. When the army later charged that she had fraudulently enlisted, she fought the charges and was eventually granted an honorable discharge. After becoming an activist, she lobbied for the California law that permitted replacement birth certificates and wrote two books on transsexualism and the law. She helped establish the Transsexual Rights Committee of the Southern California American Civil Liberties Union and, after taking vows as an Episcopal nun (a move at first sanctioned but later repudiated by church officials), founded the first and largest AIDS and online HIV information service, AEGIS (AIDS Education Global Information System). I spoke to Clark in the mobile home she shares with her elderly father and the bank of computers required to run AEGIS.

Q: Can we talk a little about your military service?

The navy discharged me in '74 and I had my surgery in '75. Then in the last part of '75 an army recruiter came through the building and wanted to put posters up, and I said, "Sure you can put 'em up," and he says, "Why don't you join the Reserves?" And I said, "I'd love to but I don't think I'm eligible." He said, "What do you mean?" And I said, "I was a chief petty officer in the navy, and the navy discharged me because of what I was going through." He said, "What was that?" and I said, "I had sex reassignment." And he says, "Well, it [sex reassignment] wouldn't keep you from doing your job, would it?" and I said,

"No," and he said, "Why don't you send me your D2-14 and your ré-sumé, and I'll see what I can find out?" So I sent it. Well, Congress had gotten my records changed to show that I had served in the navy as a female (at my request) through the late Senator Phil Hart, who was chair of the Armed Services Committee and who my dad knew from when he was a city councilman. We were told later that when Senator Hart went to the navy and said, "I want the records changed and it's been done in the past," the navy's argument was "Well, it's never been done for a chief petty officer who had a long career of seventeen years in the military." It had been done for people who had been in the service for three to four years.

Q: And why would that make a difference?

Status, I guess, and embarrassment for the navy that they allowed someone in the navy for that long. So Hart says that he wanted the records changed, and the navy said no. Hart, who was chair of the Senate Armed Forces Committee, said, "Well, you have an appropriations bill here for a new aircraft carrier. I'll schedule hearings when you change the records." Well, whether that's true or not, or whether the person in his office just told my dad that to make him feel good, I don't know. It made a good story.

Anyway, they changed my records, so when the army got my stuff, they said, "Fine, we can take you as long as you can pass the physical." So I went out and took the physical and the army gynecologist did a pelvic on me and passed me. So I served in the Army Reserves for about six or seven months, and they liked my work and said, "How would you like to work full-time for us as an army technician, civil service?" I said, "I'd love to." So I filled out the paperwork and I was hired as a GS-7 and went to Psychological Operations as staff training assistant. Later, they wanted to promote me to warrant officer. So then I had to have security clearance, and that created a problem because, of course, fingerprints don't change, and I'd had top secret before, so I had a full file with the FBI. So anyway, I get a call: "We got your fingerprint card back and it has written across it in red ink 'Michael Clark.' What is that?" I said, "Very simple. That's what my name used to be. It's all on the card. I went through sex reassignment."

The colonel said, "I didn't know about it." And I said, "Well, the commanding general of the Sixth Army knows about it." "How could he?" I said, "Because I had lunch with him three weeks ago! Because everyone wanted to meet me. The general asked me, 'Are you happier?' and I said, 'Yes, I am.'" Nobody cared, because I was doing a great job. But when Washington found out about it, when the paperwork went through and they began to put two and two together and realized what had happened, then they started asking questions coming down the line, or in the proverbial military terms, it became CYA time: "cover your ass." They wouldn't admit to the fact that they knew. So all of a sudden my commander calls me in and says, "Someone is out to get you." I said, "What do you mean?" and he says, "Well, the Inspector General is coming down, and you're being charged with subversive activities, prohibited access to classified documents, immoral sexual activity, and fraudulent enlistment." They had about fourteen charges, and that was the saving grace because they had gone so overboard. . . . They wanted to discredit me so badly that if it got into the press, the press would simply write me off as a bad apple. But when the press started looking at the record, they said, "Something's wrong here. No person could be this bad and get this far in their career without being discovered and discharged years ago."

I met Christine Jorgensen around this time. Long story, but my friend Jude Patton invited me to come with him, and I was in uniform at the time, and when we got into her living room she turned around and looked at me and said, "Do they know?" And I said, "Yeah, the ones that count locally know. I was open with them." She said, "Your day will come." So when the colonel announced that I was being charged with all these things, I called Christine and . . . it was ten o'clock in the morning . . . and she said, "Do you know what time it is?" I said, "Yeah, it's ten o'clock," and she says, "I don't get up till two in the afternoon. I'm a night person." Click. So I called back about three and apologized for waking her up and said, "This is Sergeant Clark. Do you remember me?" and she said, "Oh yeah." I said, "Do you remember what you said to me? 'Your day will come.' Well, it has." She says, "Come on down." So I drove down and brought all my paperwork. And she looked it over and said, "This is great stuff. Do you mind if I call a friend of mine at the *Times?*" and I said, "Not at all." The reporter for the *Times* came down and looked at everything and she looked over at me and said, "This is what we call a 'gee whiz' story." So she interviewed people all the way up the line. Basically, they had me walking on water without getting my feet wet, is what she told me. So I took her article and a TV interview and I mailed it all to President Carter and said, "I need help." Well, Christmas Eve of '77 I get a letter from the White House, three pages long, clearing me of all allegations but saying, "Don't call us, we won't call you. Transgendered are deemed to be psychologically unstable, therefore unfit for military service." I only had nine months left to go before retirement, but they wouldn't let me finish my service. Nine and a half months and I would have retired with a pension that included my service in Vietnam.

Q: When were you in Vietnam?

Sixty-eight during the Tet Offensive. I wasn't on the ground. I was in naval aviation flying out of Camh Ran Bay, Ton Son Nhut. We were stationed out of Okinawa and we would fly down the coast looking for shipping two or three times a month.

Q: Have you met any other Vietnam vets who have transitioned?

Yeah, sure. Including one SEAL.

Q: That's one of the most unexpected things I've discovered during my research, the number of transgendered veterans. Nobody outside the community knows about that.

Yes, well there is a tendency, I think, within the transgender community to go into the military or very macho roles that will help you conform. I liked scuba diving and I wanted to become a navy diver, but I liked to fly also, so I wound up in aviation. I was very happy to get out [of the service] and I didn't think that I would miss it, but I did. To this day, I still miss it.

Q: What did you do when you got out of the army?

When the army discharged me, I went back to college and I enrolled in a class in career development to find out where my interests lay, and my counselor said, "You're not going to believe this. Numbers one and two on the list are Catholic nun social worker and Catholic nun teacher." And I said, "Well, you're not going to believe this, but that was my dream as a child. I wanted to be a nun." We were Protestants but we lived in an all-Catholic neighborhood and we lived across the street from the convent. And all throughout my childhood I would go across the street and sit on the steps and talk to the nuns. I loved them.

So then I spent the next ten years looking for a community that would accept me. Because of all the notoriety [from the military case] I would always be up-front with them and say, "This is my past, but I feel called," and I always got nice letters back saying, "Thank you, but don't call us and we're not going to call you." So, finally, I was down at Saint Clements, and a very dear friend of mine said, "Have you ever considered the Franciscans?" In the meantime I had a spiritual director and I told him that I had written to them, and he said, "Well, they probably won't write back," but I got a letter back that said, "Why don't you come visit?" So I drove up and spent a week with them, and I got some interesting lessons when I was there. The first morning, I was walking down the hallway with the mother superior. She came about up to here on me and she was Scottish and about seventy years old—and I referred to her as a nun and she did an about-face and looked up at me and said, "The cloistered are nuns and we are sisters, and don't you ever forget that." I said, "Oops." Then she explained the difference to me.

Then I came back here and talked to my spiritual counselor, and he said, "What do you want to do?" I told him I wanted to close up my business and join the Franciscans. They invited me to come up and spend another week, and I did, but in the end they couldn't do it [accept her into the community]. It was a small community, and they felt that because of my notoriety, the press would probably come down on us like a ton of bricks.

I told my spiritual director that I had been turned down, and he said, "You don't need those old ladies anyway. What God is calling you to do is start a new social order for social justice. Write to the Episcopal nuns here and get their instructions on how to start a rule." So they sent me the book, and I started writing the rule, and soon I had two other women join me and we wrote the rule together. All of a sudden the doors started opening up and we got support, even from the hierarchy. I got a letter from the bishop congratulating me and saying he wanted to come down to the service. Then the press got hold of it, through a woman that I worked with, and the next day it was all over. The bishop renounced me in an article in the *L.A. Times.* So I made my vows, but it was a fiasco. The Episcopal Church jumped ship. They didn't bother to put the lifeboats down; they just bailed. They had a Spanish Inquisition at Saint Clements, and so I finally left Saint Clements.

Q: Obviously, you've had some horrific experiences with the press but you've also had some good experiences—the articles that have run in the Los Angeles Times *about AEGIS, for example. This ties into some questions I wanted to ask you about Christine Jorgensen because I know that you were friends with her in the last years of her life. How does one not just come to terms with that media attention but also learn to use it for your own purposes, as she did?*

She certainly didn't want it. What happened was that she wrote a letter to her parents, and somebody saw the letter and picked it up and sold it to the papers for two hundred dollars. She went into hiding for about six months, then thought that since there was nothing she could do about it, she might as well capitalize on it. She did a very good job of capitalizing on it. But also in the capitalization process, she went on with her career, working at movie studios, where she was a film editor. As a result, she got to know all the big stars. I'll never forget, one night I was taking care of her dog while she was gone and all of a sudden, at two o'clock in the morning, her phone rang and I rolled over, half awake, and this voice says, "Christine?" I said, "No, Christine's not here. This is Joanna," and he says, "This is Uncle Milty. Tell her I called."

She was an absolutely wonderful human being. I think that there was a part of her that was very lonely because of things that she had gone through. She realized that she had very good friends in the world, but a lot were just her "friends" because of who she was. For the first four or five years she worked very hard trying to answer letters that came to her, people saying, "I'm like you," and so forth. Then she came to the realization that there were a lot of crazy people out there, and she would help who she could help. She of course knew Harry Benjamin really well, Paul Walker, some of the folks at Hopkins, John Money.

She loved to party. She would have her "Christmas in July" party every year. She put up a fully decorated Christmas tree that would stay up till after Christmas, then come down. At least twice a month she'd have a big party at her house. When I got involved with her she made me part of her circle, and I would go to her parties. Of course there was a lot of drinking, and I don't drink. At two o'clock in the morning she'd go into her bedroom and pass out and go to sleep. I'd go home and get up in the morning and go over and clean the house for her.

Q: Do you think she enjoyed her life?

I think she did. Even though there was a lot of pain in her life. I think she overall led a good life and had her good times and her bad times. The best of times and the worst of times. She chose to remember her good times. She wasted very little time on her bad times. She went to the colleges and universities and did her lectures. So did I, but I made a mistake because she got paid and Jude [Patton] and I went and did them for free. Eventually Jude stopped and I stopped. I still do one though, because I really like the professor. It's at the Southern California Christian College, and he really prepares his class. They are all fundamentalist Christians, so it's an opportunity to really go in and open minds. That's probably the only reason I continue to do it.

Q: That leads to another thing I wanted to talk with you about: faith background and whether religion and spirituality are a source of nurturing or otherwise for transgendered people.

I think spirituality is a very key component to success. Of course, there is a big difference between spirituality and religion. At the program where I work as a consultant, one of the questions I ask people is, "What is your relationship with God?" But most take offense to it and they are like, "I don't need God." They were raised in a very fundamentalist environment, and it was shoved down their throat that what they were doing was sin, and they just don't want to deal with it. My response is, "I don't care what your religion is. I'm concerned about how you've dealt with it. If you've decided that you're not going to deal with it, rest assured that it will come back and haunt you."

The real issue is that if the person going through the transition has a good spiritual relationship with the Creator, and realizes that the Creator loves them and isn't condemning them to hell because of their feelings, they have the support they need to get through the difficult times. But to just close it out and say, "I don't need this," because of the bad experiences they've had, they don't have closure. This is where you are going to see the problems, because it will keep resurfacing. In terms of finding a church where you can be accepted, it's the same as the gay issue. As long as they don't know about you, they are fine. If they find out, you'll have problems.

Q: Which denominations are most accepting?

I think Unitarians have been very accepting. But in reality it doesn't matter what denomination it is. Every denomination is going to have a community that is really a community of God, that loves, that is not going to judge, that is going to accept you as a child of God, as you are. They are going to say, "Are you happier now than you were before? Yes? That's all that matters." And they'll be supportive.

Q: Have you ever considered your transgenderness to be a spiritual gift?

No, but I do look at myself as being blessed. There were times when I didn't look on it as a blessing, prior to surgery and the misery that I inflicted on my ex. She never knew what was going on in my head, why I was standoffish. And yet, society forces us into roles that we weren't meant for with no consideration that, by doing this, instead of hurting just one person, you're going to wind up hurting lots of people. It's tragic, and small wonder that so many suicides have occurred.

I was also blessed that when the time came that I had to finally acknowledge who I was and go for help, I had supportive parents. Dad told me that at first they didn't understand so they went to see a psychiatrist, who told them, "I don't know very much about the subject but I will tell you this: if your son is a transsexual, then get used to the idea that you are going to have a daughter, because she's always been your daughter but has just worked overtime to hide it from you." So Dad took the position that this wasn't my fault, this wasn't my choice, and he was very supportive. Mom had more difficulty than Dad but I think it was because of her family. My mother's side was military and Republican and very straitlaced, and so it was hard for them. My grandmother was about eighty-two when I started transition and wanted nothing to do with me.

But she was a paraplegic and she would spend two weeks with Mom and Dad and two weeks with my aunt and uncle. I came home from the hospital the day she was to come back for her two weeks here. I had taken a shower and I was lying on the bed, changing my dressings, and she rolled into the room, saw me, was shocked and apologized, but she had this look on her face. She was curious as all get-out. And I said, "All right, Grandma. If you want to look, come over." And my mother came in and said, "Oh, I'll get Grandma out of here," and I said, "No, it's okay. Grandma wanted to see." And I could see that mother wanted to see also. And so they came over to the edge of the bed, and Grandma leaned forward and she looked at me and she said to my mother, "She looks just like us."

That was the first time she had ever used "she," and from that moment on I was Joanna. And she never once slipped. And if anyone else slipped she corrected them.

ANSWERING THE RIDDLE

The various answers to the riddle of gender that have been proposed by scientists are no less culturally influenced than the answers proposed by religion or law. Scientific attempts to solve the riddle are determined not only by cultural beliefs about the different roles of men and women but also by the state of science itself—the kinds of questions that scientists are able to ask and answer in any given era. Milton Diamond repeated to me the old joke about the man who had lost his most valuable possession and was searching for it under a lamp on a street far removed from the place where he had lost the object. "Why are you looking here?" a passerby asks. "Because the light is better here," the man responds. Scientists have searched for the solution to the riddle of gender in the place where the "light" of scientific inquiry has shone brightest in various eras—endocrinology, psychiatry, embryology, and neuroscience. Yet those searches have produced no definitive answer to the riddle, only more tantalizing questions.

Scientific responses to the riddle of gender have been used to police gendered behavior, but have also at times been helpful in liberating us from limiting beliefs about the nature of the differences we observe between males and females. It's surely no accident that the birth of endocrinology coincided with the first wave of feminism, nor that the social construction hypothesis was generated by, and helped fuel, the second wave. It cannot be mere coincidence that gender-variant people became highly visible during those periods of "sexual anarchy," when the scientific and social markers of gender suddenly became less fixed and less immutable. Gender, as distinct from sex, was defined during an era when many people hoped that biology was *not* destiny, an era in which women acquired reproductive freedom and were liberated from menarche-to-menopause childbearing. The biological basis of gender is being reasserted during an era of resurgent social conservatism, when many people are feeling disenchanted with the excesses of feminist rhetoric, and seeking a way to be both pro-woman and pro-family.

The belief that gender is a social construct enables us to diminish the limitations assigned to the female sex in most cultures, but it also penalizes women in subtle ways. Like it or not, women remain the bearers of children and their primary caretakers. Any theory of gender that ignores this elementary fact, and the economic and social impact of childbearing and child rearing on women, is bound to fail because it ignores not only social reality but biological reality. Yet not all women choose to bear children these days, and even many who do, do not not wish to be perceived primarily as mothers. In this realm, as in so many others, a middle-ground perspective that acknowledges women's unique biological responsibilities and yet does not seek to define women solely in terms of biology seems most appealing.

And who can speak more authoritatively of what it is like to inhabit the middle ground between biology and culture than gender-variant people? An individual who has inhabited the social roles of both man and woman, with all the cultural baggage that accrues to both states—or to neither—acquires a kind of gender gnosis: a secret knowledge denied the rest of us who live in our assigned boxes, M or F, without really probing the boundaries. Yet rather than letting these individuals be themselves, or even soliciting their insights, society in general continues to try to force gender-variant people (whether transgendered, transsexual, or intersexual) into one of the two socially acceptable boxes. This seems not only cruel but also foolish. In certain cultures, transgendered or "two spirit" people were considered wise counselors, shamans in fact. There are traces of this belief in our cultural tradition. Tiresias, the ancient Greek sage—who transformed into a woman after seeing two snakes mating, and then back into a man many years later—was wise because of, not in spite of, his metamorphoses. The religions of the world are replete with androgynous deities, or deities able to transgender themselves at will. Even Christianity and Judaism, together with Islam, the most androcentric of religions, retain traces of an ambigendered deity. Shekinah is the feminine face of God in Judaism, just as Wisdom in Christianity is gendered female. Neither Shekinah nor Wisdom is a separate being; both are a part of God, who is perhaps just as omnigendered as the embryo, and as potent with possibility.

These philosophical and theological musings are, of course, of little interest or value to many gender-variant people, who are focused on the battle to achieve civil rights as they remain the most vulnerable minority group in our culture, and the target of the most virulent discrimination. What can one say about the case of Peter Oiler, the truck driver who was fired by the Winn-Dixie supermarket chain after twenty years of exemplary employment when his supervisor discovered that he occasionally dressed in women's clothing? Oiler was not wearing dresses to work, nor was he negligent in his duties in any way. However, he did make the mistake of being honest when his supervisor called him into his office to discuss rumors that Oiler was gay. The married Oiler said that he wasn't gay but that he cross-dressed occasionally and had attended support group meetings, dined in restaurants, gone shopping, and occasionally attended church services while dressed in women's clothing. He was asked to resign shortly thereafter, and when he refused to do so, was fired, with his health care coverage and other benefits terminated.

Oiler, backed by a number of trans advocacy groups and the American Civil Liberties Union, appealed to the courts of the state of Louisiana, which denied his claim of discrimination and request for damages. Cross-dressers, transsexuals, and other gender-variant people are not covered by existing federal civil rights legislation, so people like Peter Oiler have little legal recourse when they are fired from their jobs or refused an apartment or a loan or harassed in the workplace or in a restaurant or store. Another book could be, and I hope will be, written about the legal travails of gender-variant people and the manner in which they are consistently denied the most basic liberties that most Americans take for granted.

At the fifth annual symposium sponsored by the *Georgetown Journal of Gender and the Law,* held on February 27, 2002, trans attorney and activist Phyllis Randolph Frye delivered a keynote address that laid out some of the challenges that have confronted transgendered people and their allies as they have sought protection under the law. Like Sylvia Rivera, Frye continually reminds audiences that despite their crucial role in the Stonewall riots and in the early days of gay liberation, transgendered and gender-variant people have been consistently excluded from proposed legislation by gay leaders who feel that various bills would not pass if they included transgenders.

"In 1989, I became aware that even though transgenders began the Stonewall Riots in 1969, we were not welcome in the struggle for lesbian and gay rights. And as the other speakers here today know, beginning in 1989, we of the transgender community began a decade-plus-long fight for that reincorporation. . . . Today, we are an almost completely reincorporated LGBT community. Unfortunately, transgenders plus gender-variant lesbians and gays and bisexuals remain excluded from the Employment Non-Discrimination Act (ENDA) before the U.S. Congress." ENDA, first introduced in Congress in 1994 and resubmitted each year since then, would provide federal protection for gays and lesbians—but as Frye notes, "each year since then, ENDA has been introduced with sometimes different language, but always with a deliberate and intentional exclusion of transgenders and gender variants." At the 2001 Gender and the Law Conference, Professor Chai R. Feldblum of Georgetown University, one of the original drafters of ENDA, said that she had since come to believe that it was crucial to include protection for gender-variant people in any proposed legislation. Many of the legislators who support ENDA maintain that the act cannot be passed with such a clause, however, even though a number of cities and towns have passed laws protecting the civil rights of transgendered Americans over the past two years.

At the Georgetown conference, Phyllis Frye noted that much progress had been achieved in recent years, notably that "more and more transgenders are coming out of their closets" and that "although rampant employment discrimination still exists . . . more and more companies, some that used to fire transitioning transgenders in upper management, . . . are now giving transgenders a try." Still, challenges remain, legal and other, she said. One of the most important of these is a matter of language, which reflects outdated perceptions. "A very important change that has yet to be made is the time we transgenders are no longer called "sex changes.' After all, consider this: we are NOT CHANGING anything! Indeed, we are merely CORRECTING pronouns, names, manner of dress, hormones and flesh to MATCH what has always been in our brains. . . . The law must learn to assimilate the advances of medical science in a quicker manner and not remain legally stuck in the medical thinking of thirty years ago."

Frye is right about the tendency of the law to lag behind science, and yet science and medicine, too, are inherently conservative endeavors that tend to cleave to old paradigms until forced to do otherwise. Harry Benjamin acknowledged this fact in the introduction to *The Transsexual Phenomenon.* "Conservatism and caution are most commendable traits in governing the progress of science in general and of medicine in particular. Only when conservatism becomes unchanging and rigid and when caution deteriorates into mere self-interest do they become negative forces, retarding, blocking and preventing progress, neither to the benefit of science nor to that of the patient. More power, therefore, to those brave and true scientists, surgeons, and doctors who let the patient's interest and their own conscience be their sole guides."

In researching this book, I have been greatly impressed by the courage exhibited not only by the "true scientists, surgeons, and doctors" who sought to help their gender-variant patients find greater happiness and fulfillment, but also by the incredible bravery of gender-variant people themselves. Presented with a seeming dilemma, they have struggled to create a solution in the face of nearly universal incomprehension and condemnation. "I made a decision a long time ago that when I successfully pushed through a door, metaphorically speaking, that I would never let the door swing shut to block the way of other people, but that I would instead remove the door from its hinges," Phyllis Frye said at the Georgetown Law School. The same might be said of Christine Jorgensen, Reed Erickson, Sylvia Rivera, and the many other activists, scholars, and citizens who have labored to find an answer to their own personal "riddle of gender," and in doing so, have

opened the door to greater freedom and authenticity for all. In an era
in which scientists are being cautioned not to use hot-button words and
phrases such as "gay," "men who sleep with men," or "transgender" in
AIDS grant applications, that may seem a naive conclusion. However,
as the history cataloged in this book illustrates, the pendulum of policy
may swing from left to right, but it always swings back to the other
side eventually, and each time it does, the arc of understanding widens.
Will we ever find a definitive solution to the riddle of gender? Maybe
not—but as this history indicates, the questions we ask about gender
tend to be more liberating than the answers. I would prefer to live in a
society that gave me the freedom to ask those questions, rather than
one that enforced autocratic conclusions.

As I neared the end of the research for this book, the friend whose
journey inspired it asked me if my own gender identity or sexual orientation had changed at all as a result of the things I had learned and
the people I had met over the past few years. My answer was no. I am
hardwired as a heterosexual woman, and I am comfortable with that
identity; it feels authentic. However, I no longer view my sexual orientation and gender identity as "normal," generic, or "regular." Instead,
I see that my particular expression of gender and sexuality are unique
to me. Straight people, like gay or transgendered people, have complex and multifaceted gender identities. My sense of what it is to be a
woman, for example, is quite different from that of Laura Bush or
Venus Williams or Condoleezza Rice, or the other women on my
block. All of us are natal women, but our sense of ourselves as women,
and the way we express our gender, varies from person to person.
There are similarities, it's true, but the range of gender expression
within the categories "man" and "woman" seems to vary nearly as
much as it does between them. Prior to writing this book, I did not see
that variation. Now I do, and I am grateful to those who enabled me to
see the world of gender through their eyes, and consequently expanded my range of vision.

With that new perspective, I have come to view gender less as a
riddle that should be solved and more as a collage, which we each assemble in our own fashion. Nature provides the canvas, and on that

canvas we assemble scraps of meaning from family, religion, science, friends, and the media—a kind of surrealist montage that, like children's art, is a natural expression of being, so natural that we forget that it is art. Rather than insisting on the primacy of either nature or culture as the source of gender differences, perhaps we now need to recognize that both play a role and that neither explanation makes sense without the other. Nature may provide the architecture of gender, but culture does the decorating. If gender identity is, as seems increasingly certain, hardwired into the brain at birth, and if the way we choose to express our sense of ourselves as gendered beings is dependent on cultural norms, shouldn't culture follow nature's lead and celebrate variety? Difference can be, as Susan Stryker points out, "a real source of pleasure," if only we can overcome our ancient suspicion of diversity. In an era in which Americans are fighting and dying purportedly to free other people, perhaps we might take this one small step toward freeing ourselves by finally outlawing discrimination based on gender expression. What is freedom, after all, if it is not the freedom to be one's self?

ACKNOWLEDGMENTS

Many individuals and organizations have contributed to my education on the topics discussed in this book. My informal conversations with people at various conferences attended during the course of my research, as well as my participation (and lurking) on various online discussion lists has helped me to understand that members of the trans community (or more properly speaking, *communities*) are quite diverse in their backgrounds, beliefs, and goals. I regret that I have been unable to cover many of the topics that various individuals encouraged me to explore: for example, the challenges faced by trans elders and veterans; the impact of race and socioeconomics on access to health care and other services; the problems encountered by homeless, disabled, and incarcerated trans people; and the role of faith and family in the lives of trans people. Each of these subjects is important and worthy of discussion but, unfortunately, falls outside the scope of this book. My apologies to those who generously contributed their time and expertise on these matters, only to find that I have not covered their issues. My deepest thanks go to those individuals who shared with me sometimes very painful and private information, and permitted me to use their names and stories—and also to those whose personal or professional responsibilities required that they assume the cloak of anonymity. I am profoundly grateful to all my sources, both named and anonymous, whose candor helped me to understand their lives and struggles.

There are a few individuals and organizations I would like to thank by name, as I doubt I would have been able to undertake the research for this book without their assistance. First, I would like to thank Aiden Faust, Jaina Hirai, and Chris Griffey, friends who introduced me to the trans community and helped me take my first fumbling steps on the road to understanding. I am grateful to the members of the National Trans Advocacy Coalition, particularly Yosenio Lewis and Rozlyn Manley, for providing introductions to many of the individuals profiled here, and to Naomi Goring, for sharing with me her collection of difficult-to-locate autobiographies and memoirs. Thank you also to those who discussed these issues with me at length, by phone, in person, and via e-mail as my questions multiplied over the course of my writing this book, in particular Drs. Ben Barres, Dana Beyer, Scott Kerlin, and Julie Maverick. Special thanks to Dr. Aaron Devor for sharing the results of his yet unpublished research on Reed Erickson.

My agent, Flip Brophy, provided guidance and support throughout, and I feel blessed to have such a smart advocate and great friend standing beside me as I write. Marty Asher, my editor, gave me the greatest gift an editor can give a writer—the freedom to pursue the story in my own way and in my own time. I am grateful for his support and wise advice. My friend and colleague Ann Finkbeiner, director of the science writing program at Johns Hopkins University, not only read and commented on successive drafts of the manuscript but also was a constant source of support, encouragement, and empathy. Her probing questions have made this a better book.

I could not have written this book without the support of my colleagues and employers at the Center for Talented Youth—Pat Wallace, Ben Reynolds, and Sylvia Kielsznia—who were willing to offer me time off and a flexible work schedule to write. The friends who wined and dined me during the course of the writing, providing much needed relaxation, also deserve acknowledgment—Nancy, Claudette, Paula, Liz, Kathy, Mark, and those other friends (you know who you are) who took me out and lifted me up when I was feeling overwhelmed. Finally, I'd like to thank my family—my children, Amelia, Jake, and Sofia, and their father, Rafael; my mother, Jean, and brother Jeff; and my nieces Jessica, Victoria, and Angela. Their constant love and support is the firm ground that I stand on in all my endeavors.

NOTES

INTRODUCTION

xii   *Walking home from a neighborhood bar* Peter Hermann, "1 Killed, 12 Robbed in Violent City Spree," *Baltimore Sun*, November 24, 1999; Michael Ollove, "Tacy's Story," *Baltimore Sun*, December 15, 1999. Downloaded from SunSpot.net January 10, 2001.

xv   *Baron-Cohen proposes an explanation for these and other differences* See Simon Baron-Cohen, *The Essential Difference: The Truth about the Male and Female Brain* (New York: Basic Books, 2003).

xvi   *gender is what's above the neck* See for example Virginia Prince, "Sex vs. Gender," in "Transsexualism: A Perspective" in *Proceedings of the Second Interdisciplinary Symposium on Gender Dysphoria Syndrome*, Donald R. Laub, M.D., and Patrick S. Gandy, M.S., eds., Stanford University Medical Center, February 2–4, 1973. "For those of you who do not know me, I am a male. I was born one and I will die one. I am not a homosexual. I am not a transsexual, but I have lived the last five years as a woman. There is not one thing that any doctor or any surgeon at this symposium could possibly do to improve my gender. Any kind of carving that you might do on me might change my sex, but it would not change my gender, because my gender, my self-identity is between my ears, not between my legs," 21.

xvii   *one cheeky irony of life* Lindsey Berkson, *Hormone Deception* (Chicago: Contemporary Books, 2000), 43.

xxii   *In 2002 alone, twenty-three people in the United States were slain* National Transgender Advocacy Coalition interview with Gwen Smith, creator of "Remembering Our Dead" website, http:www.gender.org/remember/index.html. "I think 2002 is only the 'deadliest year' we have statistics for because of three factors. The media is more willing to report on these cases, we have more avenues to find these stories via the world wide web, and we are more sensitive to these cases within our own community. . . . Rather than thinking of 2002 as being part of an upward trend of murder cases, I paint a somewhat more disturbing picture: maybe 2002 is much closer to the actual per-year number of cases."

xxii *seventeen-year-old Gwen Araujo was dragged into a garage* On June 22, 2004, Judge Harry Sheppard declared a mistrial in the Araujo murder case after the jury foreman informed him that the eight-man, four-woman jury was "hopelessly deadlocked." The jury had deliberated for ten days. Defense attorneys had used a "gay panic" strategy, arguing that their clients (twenty-four-year old Jason Cazares, Michael Magidson, and Jose Merel) were inspired by "passionate rage" when they discovered that Araujo, with whom all three had previously had sex, was biologically male. After bludgeoning Araujo with a can, frying pans, and a shovel, and strangling her, the defendants buried her in the Sierra foothills, and then went out to McDonald's for breakfast.

xxiii *Tyra's story is surprisingly commonplace* Sarah D. Fox, Ph.D., "$2.8 million Award in Tyra Hunter Wrongful Death Suit," *Quill*, December 12, 1998. Retrieved from http://www.gendernet.org/quill/pr000004.htm, February 12, 2003.

xxiii *Nature loves variety* Milton Diamond, plenary lecture at the International Foundation for Gender Education annual meeting, March 21, 2003, Philadelphia, Pa.

One THE HANDS OF GOD

3 *I certify that Chevalier d'Éon* Quoted in Magnus Hirschfeld, *Transvestites: The Erotic Urge to Cross Dress*, trans. by Michael A. Lombardi-Nash (Buffalo, N.Y.: Prometheus Books, 1991), 341–42.

3 *far from being a product of the modern world* See, for example, *Third Sex, Third Gender: Beyond Sexual Dimorphism in Culture*, Gilbert Herdt, ed. (New York: Zone Books 1994); "Mythological, Historical, and Cross-Cultural Aspects of Transsexualism," in *Transsexualism and Sex Reassignment*, ed. Richard Green, M.D., and John Money, Ph.D. (Johns Hopkins University Press, 1969), chap. 1; Part I, "Cultural and Historical Background" in Vern L. Bullough and Bonnie Bullough, *Cross Dressing, Sex, and Gender* (Philadelphia: University of Pennsylvania Press, 1993); and Leslie Feinberg, *Transgender Warriors* (Boston: Beacon Press, 1996).

3 *gender crossing is so ubiquitous* Bullough and Bullough, *Cross Dressing, Sex, and Gender*, 5.

5 *You have served me just as well* Letter quoted in ibid., 337.

5 *The London Stock Exchange took bets on his gender* Marjorie Garber, *Vested*

Interests: Cross-Dressing and Cultural Anxiety (New York: Routledge, 1992), 260.

5 *I am what the hands of God have made me* Letter to the Count de Broglio, February 10, 1775, quoted in Garber, *Vested Interests*, 264.

5 *has always been a reward for bravery on the battlefield* Letter quoted in Hirschfeld, *Transvestites*, 339.

6 *His hand was already slipping under my sheet* Herculine Barbin, *Herculine Barbin: Being the Recently Discovered Memoirs of a Nineteenth-Century French Hermaphrodite*, trans. Richard McDougall (New York: Pantheon, 1980), 68–69.

6 *condemned Abel to "abandonment, to cold isolation"* Ibid., 87.

7 *When that day comes a few doctors will make a little stir* Ibid., 103.

7 *Variety is Nature's way* Milton Diamond, at the annual meeting of the International Foundation for Gender Education, March 21, 2003, Philadelphia, Pa.

7 *The most famous such case* Hart underwent analysis with a Portland, Oregon, psychiatrist, J. Allen Gilbert, who, in 1917, helped Hart obtain a hysterectomy and begin living as a man. In *Gay American History: Lesbians and Gay Men in the U.S.A.* (New York: Thomas Y. Crowell Company, 1976), historian Jonathan Ned Katz identifies Hart on the basis of a paper Gilbert wrote about the case, hails Hart as a lesbian foremother, and harshly criticizes Gilbert for the course of treatment he recommended. In *Sex Changes: The Politics of Transgenderism* (San Francisco: Cleis Press, 1997), Pat Califia takes Katz and other gay historians to task for their tendency to view early transmen such as Hart as self-hating lesbians. "Unfortunately, since Katz's work has appeared in print, other gay and lesbian historians have also promoted the myth that all 'passing women' are lesbian elders. . . . The task of sorting out the dykes from the transgendered men, or at least the task of recognizing that both tendencies are present in the histories of 'passing women,' still remains to be done" (Califia, 155).

9 *gender identity is subject to scrutiny* Jillian Todd Weiss, "The Gender Caste System: Identity, Privacy, and Heteronormativity," *Law and Sexuality* 10 (2002): 131.

10 *Ordinarily, the purpose of scientific investigation* Harry Benjamin, *The Transsexual Phenomenon* (New York: Ace Books, 1966), 5.

11 *I'm not a girl, I'm not a girl* Author interview with "Brad" [source requested anonymity for family reasons], San Francisco, Calif., August 31, 2001.

11 *first employees of the city of San Francisco to take advantage of the new policy of insurance reimbursement* On Monday, April 30, 2001, the Board of Supervisors passed a measure making the city the first in the nation to pay for

its transgendered employees' surgical and medical needs related to sex correction. The coverage does not extend to cosmetic procedures, only to
hormones, genital reconstruction, and hysterectomies and mastectomies
for FTMs. Employees must work for the city for a year to become eligible
for the benefits. If using a doctor within the city's health network, employees have to pay 15 percent out of pocket; if using a doctor outside the network, employees are responsible for 50 percent of the costs. An article by
Margie Mason for the Associated Press said that the city had identified fourteen transgendered employees out of its thirty-seven thousand workers.
Margie Mason, "Sex-Change Benefits Approved in San Francisco," Associated Press, April 30, 2001. Brad told me, "In the city there are thirteen of
us. Half of those have already had the surgery; out of the other seven, three
don't want surgery. So I would say that there are only four people. Hello?
There are not going to be droves of people coming out here. There aren't
that many city jobs, and you've got to wait a year anyway. This year
they've got one point seven million dollars set aside for the thirty-five surgeries they thought were gonna happen. They said that they overesti-
mated, because they wanted to err on the side of more, but they are way
overestimating."

12 *a recent needs assessment survey* Jessica Xavier, "Final report of the Washington Transgender Needs Assessment Survey," Washington, D.C., Administration for HIV and AIDS, District of Columbia Department of
Health.

14 *the prevalence of SRS in the U.S. is at least on the order of 1:2500* Lynn Conway, "How Frequently Does Transsexualism Occur," available online at
http://www.lynnconway.com.

14 *A group of researchers in the Netherlands* P.L.E. Eklund, L.J.G. Gooren,
and P. D. Bezemer, "Prevalence of Transsexualism in the Netherlands,"
British Journal of Psychiatry 152 (1988): 638–40.

14 *"gender identity disorders" are probably far more common* Weiss, "Gender
Caste System," 129 (n. 9).

15 *Gunter Dorner, a German endocrinologist* G. Dorner, F. Gotz, W. Rohde, et
al., "Genetic and Epigenetic Effects on Sexual Brain Organization Medi-
ated by Sex Hormones," *Neuroendocrinology Letters* 22 (2001): 403–409.
See also G. Dorner, I. Poppe, F. Stahl, et al., "Gene and Environment-
Dependent Neuroendocrine Etiogenesis of Homosexuality and Transsexualism," *Experimental and Clinical Endocrinology* 98, no. 2 (1991): 141–50;
G. Dorner, "Neuroendocrine Response to Estrogen and Brain Differentiation in Heterosexuals, Homosexuals, and Transsexuals, *Archives of Sexual
Behavior* 17, no. 1 (February 1988): 57–75; G. Dorner, "Sex Hormone De-

pendent Brain Differentiation and Sexual Behavior," *Experimental Brain Research* suppl. 3 (1981): 238–45; G. Dorner, F. Docke, F. Gotz, et al., "Sexual Differentiation of Gonadotrophin Secretion, Sexual Orientation and Gender Role Behavior," *Journal of Steroid Biochemistry* 27, no. 4–6 (1987): 1081–87.

Dorner has published extensively on the organizational effects of hormones on the brain, and possible implications for sexual orientation and transsexualism. Earlier in his career, Dorner's theories on the somatic basis of homosexuality and gender variance were considered reactionary, but since 1987, the biological school has rebounded. "By the early 1980s, endocrinological theories of sexual orientation seemed to have reached a low point of credibility, and those who still espoused them were considered the 'bad guys' who were on a mission to eliminate homosexuality by a technical fix. In Dorner's case the label was well deserved." Simon LeVay, *Queer Science: The Use and Abuse of Research into Homosexuality* (Cambridge and London: MIT Press, 1996), 120. Later, in a discussion of Dorner's hypothesis that prenatal stress might play a role in the development of homosexuality in men, LeVay says that "to give Dorner his due, his theory does have one thing going for it: it is based on a solid body of research conducted on animals." *Queer Science*, 164.

15 *the flip side of the postmodern "performativity" argument* See Judith Butler, *Gender Trouble: Feminism and the Subversion of Identity* (New York: Routledge, 1999) and *Bodies That Matter: On the Discursive Limits of Sex* (New York: Routledge, 1993).

16 *many of these chemicals can disturb development of the endocrine system* World Health Organization, "Global Assessment of the State of the Science of Endocrine Disruptors," retrieved from http://www.who.int/pcs/ emerg_site/edc/global_edc_TOC.htm, July 31, 2002.

16 *Some . . . argue that the buildup of these endocrine-disrupting chemicals* See Theo Colborn, Dianne Dumanoski, and John Peterson Myers, *Our Stolen Future* (New York: Dutton, 1996).

16 *Animal research has also shown that DES and other estrogenic chemicals* See J. A. McLachlan, R. R. Newbold, and B. Bullock, "Reproductive Tract Lesions in Male Mice Exposed Prenatally to Diethylstilbestrol," *Science* 190 (1975): 991–92; R. R. Newbold, B. Bullock, and J. A. McLachlan, "Mullerian Remnants of Male Mice Exposed Prenatally to Diethylstilbestrol," *Teratog. Carcinog. Mutagen.* 7 (1987): 377–89; W. B. Gill, G. F. Schumacher, M. Bibbo, et al., "Association of Diethylstilbestrol in Utero with Cryptorchidism, Testicular Hypoplasia and Semen Abnormalities," *Journal of Urology* 122 (1979): 36–39; J. A. Visser, A. McLuskey,

M. Verhoef-Post, et al., "Effect of Prenatal Exposure to Diethylstilbestrol on Mullerian Duct Development in Fetal Male Mice," *Endocrinology* 139 (1998): 4244–251.

17 *The moderators of an online discussion group* Scott Kerlin and Dana Beyer, M.D., "The DES Sons Online Discussion Network: Critical Issues and the Need for Further Research," unpublished paper, August 2002.

17 *There are millions of us who were exposed to DES* Author interview with Dana Beyer, Bethesda, Md., September 27, 2002.

18 *there is no more psychopathology* This was noted as early as 1973. "The psychodynamic histories of transsexuals do not yield any consistent differentiation characteristics from the rest of the population." Marie C. Mehl, Ph.D., "Transsexualism: A Perspective" in *Proceedings of the Second Interdisciplinary Symposium on Gender Dysphoria Syndrome,* ed. Donald R. Laub, M.D., and Patrick S. Gandy, M.S., Stanford University Medical Center, February 2–4, 1973, 15.

18 *transsexuality is "a part of human variation"* Author interview with Rusty Moore, New York City, July 1, 2001.

18 *Somewhere the hormones that are secreted either by the brain* Author interview with Beyer.

19 *an anomaly or mutation is not in itself pathological* Georges Canguilhem, *The Normal and the Pathological* (New York: Zone Books, 1991), 137.

19 *There's an idea that people have subconsciously inculcated* Author interview with Susan Stryker, San Francisco Calif., September 4, 2001.

Two THROUGH SCIENCE TO JUSTICE

30 *Plato was acquainted with . . . "Mixed beings"* In Niels Hoyer, ed., *Man into Woman: An Authentic Record of a Change of Sex* (New York: E. P. Dutton and Company, 1933), 112. ("Niels Hoyer" was a pseudonym for Ernst Ludwig Harthern Jacobson.)

31 *Paragraph 175* Paragraph 175 of the German penal code, inherited from an earlier Prussian code, made sex between men a felony punishable by imprisonment for up to six months. "Paragraph 175 was no dead letter. It was actively enforced by police surveillance, by entrapment, and by the use of informers. About 500 men were imprisoned under paragraph 175 each year." LeVay, *Queer Science,* 17.

On the other hand, Christopher Isherwood wrote, "The Berlin police 'tolerated' the bars. No customer risked arrest simply for being in them. When the bars were raided, which didn't happen often, it was only the boys who were required to show their papers. Those who hadn't any or were wanted for some crime would make a rush to escape through a back door or window as the police came in." Christopher Isherwood, *Christopher and His Kind* (New York: Farrar, Straus and Giroux, 1976), 30.

31 *a strange million-headed city like a cuirass* In Hoyer, *Man into Woman*, 125.

31 *Berlin, in Hirschfeld's time* Erwin J. Haeberle, ed., *The Birth of Sexology: A Brief History in Documents* (Washington, D.C.: World Association for Sexology, 1983), 10.

32 *During the early years of the twentieth century* Charlotte Wolff, *Magnus Hirschfeld: A Portrait of a Pioneer in Sexology* (London, Melbourne, New York: Quartet Books, 1986), 52.

32 *A couple of times I was invited to accompany Hirschfeld* Harry Benjamin, "Reminiscences," address given at the Twelfth Annual Conference of the Society for the Scientific Study of Sex, November 1, 1969. Archiv fur Sexualwissenschaft, http://www2.hu-berlin.de/sexology/GESUND/ARCHIV/REMINI.HTM, 9/10/2001.

33 *Berlin's "famous decadence"* Isherwood, *Christopher*, 29.

34 *It was a place of education* Isherwood, *Christopher*, 18.

34 *By sexual intermediaries we understand manly-formed women* Hirschfeld, *Transvestites*, 215.

35 *Whether erotic transvestism is a rare and exceptional phenomenon* Ibid., 141.

35 *My sex life is not so great* Ibid., 109.

35 *As a rule I only cross-dress* Ibid., 62.

36 *When I put on a woman's dress* Ibid., 29.

36 *I myself, as a child, took every opportunity* Ibid., 84.

36 *I cannot report anything of much importance* Ibid., 95.

37 *In most of the cases we can trace the urge back to their early childhood* Ibid., 143.

37 *The transvestites that we have come to know* Ibid., 141.

37 *The pre-sexological era of modern sex research* Haeberle, *Birth of Sexology*, 15.

38 *Hirschfeld was a eugenicist* Wolff, *Magnus Hirschfeld*, 250.

39 *women betray their manly mixture* Hirschfeld, *Transvestites*, 222.

41 *The nineteenth century had cherished a belief* Elaine Showalter, *Sexual Anarchy: Gender and Culture at the Fin de Siècle* (New York: Viking 1990), 8.

41 *Often compared to a flower* Patricia Marks, *Bicycles, Bangs and Bloomers: The New Woman in the Popular Press* (Lexington: University Press of Kentucky, 1990), 1.

41 *The New Woman, who appeared as if by magic* On the eve of the twentieth century, the French historian Michelle Perrot observed, "The image of

the New Woman was widespread in Europe from Vienna to London, from Munich and Heidelberg to Brussels and Paris." Showalter, *Sexual Anarchy*, 38.

42 *"detrimental to the health and morals" of women* Ann Heilman, *New Woman Fiction: Women Writing First Wave Feminism* (New York: St. Martin's Press, 2000), 121.

43 *an avant-garde of male artists, sexual radicals and intellectuals* Showalter, *Sexual Anarchy*, 11. See also Sally Ledger, *The New Woman: Fiction and Feminism at the Fin de Siècle* (Manchester and New York: Manchester University Press, 1997): "The New Woman materialised alongside the decadent and the dandy, and although they had surprisingly little in common, they were repeatedly linked in the flourishing periodical press of the 1890s. The New Woman and the decadent writers both overtly challenged the dominant sexual codes of the Victorian era" (5).

44 *In each person there is a different mixture of manly and womanly substances* Hirschfeld, *Transvestites*, 229.

44 *In a radical departure from earlier medical practices* LeVay, *Queer Science*, 26.

44 *Abraham published an article reporting the surgeries* Felix Abraham, "Genitalumwandlungen an zwei mannlichen Transvestiten" [Genital reassignment on two male transvestites] *Zeitschrift fur Sexualwissenschaft und Sexualpolitik* 18 (1931): 223–26 in *International Journal of Transgenderism* 2, no. 1 retrieved from http://www.symposion.com/ijt/ijtc0302.htm 9/20/2001.

45 *I remember the shock with which Christopher first realized* Isherwood, *Christopher*, 15.

45 *Some of the doctors to whom he went thought him neurotic* Norman Haire in Hoyer, *Man into Woman*, vi.

45 *agreed that Andreas [Einar] was probably an intermediate sexual type* Ibid., vii.

46 *"'Why have I been sent here?' he wondered"* Ibid., 51.

46 *By means of a thousand penetrating questions* Ibid., 52.

46 *The first operation, which only represents a beginning* Ibid., 134.

47 *I feel like a bridge-builder* Ibid., 250.

48 *All that I desire is nothing less than the last fulfilment* Ibid., 275.

48 *You must sympathize with me in my desire for maternity* Ibid., 280.

48 *an abyss of suffering* Ibid., 286.

48 *Paralysis of the heart put an end to her short young woman's life* Ibid., 287.

49 *Weeds never die* Wolff, *Magnus Hirschfeld*, 198.

49 *Homosexuals as Speakers in Boys' Schools* Haeberle, *Birth of Sexuality*, 38.

49 *Some have argued that the institute's files* Benjamin, "Reminiscences." "Hirschfeld never returned to Germany after his world tour. The Nazis

had come to power. Some of the prominent ones had been patients of Hirschfeld. That is why his records and books and his Institute were destroyed so promptly."

50 *The German academic community became totally absorbed in socialization theory* Author interview with Simon LeVay, Los Angeles, Calif., September 7, 2001.

Three THE BOMBSHELL

62 *I looked into a sea of faces* This account of Christine Jorgensen's life is a summary based on her memoir *Christine Jorgensen: A Personal Autobiography,* published in 1967, and reprinted by Cleis Press in 2000. I also spoke with a few people who had known Jorgensen at various points throughout her life, most notably Joanna Clark (Sister Mary Elizabeth), an early transactivist who was Jorgensen's friend and neighbor in Southern California. The first person to serve in the United States armed forces as both a man and a woman; founder of AEGIS, the first and most comprehensive source of AIDS information on the Internet; and author of one of the early legal texts for transpeople—Clark truly deserves to be the subject of a book in her own right.

63 *Dolly and I were surrounded* Jorgensen, *Christine Jorgensen,* 5.

63 *Grandma was always my champion* Ibid., 16.

63 *A little boy wore trousers* Ibid., 8.

63 "'*Mom,' I asked, 'why didn't God make us alike?'*" Ibid., 9.

64 *After World War Two, there was the creation of this really rigid gender system* Author interview with Stryker.

64 *Mrs. Jorgensen, do you think this is anything for a red-blooded boy* Jorgensen, 14–15.

64 *Instead of assimilating into a group* Ibid., 20.

64 *I tried to find some solace in books* Ibid., 25.

65 *time when I would have an important place behind the cameras* Ibid.

65 *I wondered if my new associates would notice* Ibid., 28.

65 *I wanted to be accepted by the army for two reasons* Ibid., 30.

65 *couldn't help comparing myself with the boys in my group* Ibid., 31.

66 *During the months in the service* Ibid., 33.

66 *I awaited a miracle to release me* Ibid., 35.

66 *Christine Jorgensen lived with my mother and father* Author's personal communication, Peggy Stockton McClelland, June 7, 2001.

67 *His hips were wide like a woman's* Paul de Kruif, *The Male Hormone* (New York: Harcourt, Brace and Company, 1945), 94.

68 *for purely scientific purposes* Ibid.

68 *The boy's thyroid gland began to grow* Ibid., 95.

69 *In five days he had four hot flashes* Ibid.

70 *They crowed. They battled. They chased hens enthusiastically* Ibid., 54.

70 *symptoms of underdevelopment or even retrogression passed away* Ibid., 52.

70 *the female implanted with the male gland will always be a male* Ibid., 56.

71 *He came to America quite by happenstance* Author interview with Christine Wheeler, New York City, February 11, 2002.

71 *I was greatly impressed with his sex changes* Erwin J. Haeberle, "The Transatlantic Commuter: An Interview with Harry Benjamin," *Sexualmedizin* 14 no. 1 (1985). Retrieved from http://www2.hu-berlin.de/sexology/GESUND/ARCHIV/REMINI.HTM, 9/10/2001.

72 *Every year during the 1920s* Benjamin, "Reminiscences."

72 *Benjamin felt that Steinach was a genius* Author interview with Wheeler. See also Chandak Sengoopta, "Tales from the Vienna Labs: The Eugen Steinach–Harry Benjamin Correspondence," *Favourite Edition,* Newsletter of the Friends of the Rare Book Room, New York Academy of Medicine 2 (Spring 2000).

73 *Freud admitted that he, too, had undergone the Steinach operation* Benjamin, "Reminiscences." As did the poet William Butler Yeats and scores of other men who "had recourse to the operation in the belief that it would 'rejuvenate' them physically and mentally." Sengoopta, "Tales," 1. "Benjamin was diligent beyond belief in spreading his master's word but soon held back because of Steinach's wrath and unfair imputations."

73 *Broadly speaking, the Steinach Operation strengthens the endocrine system* Harry Benjamin in the introduction to Paul Kammerer, *Rejuvenation and the Prolongation of Human Efficiency: Experiences with the Steinach Operation on Man and Animals* (New York: Boni and Liveright, 1923).

73 *This study group, which began meeting in 1916* Charles Ihlenfeld, in "Memorial for Harry Benjamin," *Archives of Sexual Behavior* 17, no. 1 (February 1988): 3.

74 *Harry believed that the urine of young men* Leah Cahan Schaefer in "Memorial," 13.

74 *Still determined to find some cure or satisfactory compromise* Jorgensen, *Christine Jorgensen,* 73.

75 *Once out of the store, I headed for the car* Ibid., 77.

76 *the present wonder is not that intersexual conditions occur* Victor Cornelius Medvei, ed., *A History of Endocrinology* (Lancaster, Boston: MTP Press Ltd., 1982), 406.

76 *The great feeling of listlessness and fatigue* Jorgensen, *Christine Jorgensen,* 79.

77 *after pouring out "the whole story of my perplexing life"* Ibid., 92.

78 *There are several questions about the interaction of the hormone* Ibid., 93.

78 *Thus began a period in my life* Ibid., 96.

79 *Miraculously, the complex I'd had for years* Ibid., 98.

79 *The hormone tablets were discontinued for several weeks* Ibid., 101.

79 *I felt you could not be cured, psychologically* Ibid., 103.

79 *which her doctors were alternately calling "genuine transvestism" and "psychic hermaphroditism"* Christian Hamburger, Georg K. Sturup, and E. Dahl-Iversen, "Transvestism: Hormonal, Psychiatric, and Surgical Treatment," *JAMA* 152, no. 5 (May 30, 1953): 391–96.

79 *To return to my old way of life* Jorgensen, *Christine Jorgensen,* 104.

80 *As you can see by the enclosed photo* Ibid., 107.

80 *I admit the question didn't take me by surprise* Ibid., 110.

80 *Nature has made a mistake, which I have corrected* Ibid., 115.

80 *Filled with a kind of unknown dread* Ibid., 128.

81 *To me that message was a symbol of a brutal and cruel betrayal* Ibid., 128.

81 *Kinsey had never seen a case like this* Haeberle, "Transatlantic Commuter," 4.

81 *after reading about "operative procedures that feminized men"* Lean Cahan Schaefer and Connie Christine Wheeler, "Harry Benjamin's First Ten Cases (1938–1953): A Clinical Historical Note," *Archives of Sexual Behavior* 24, no. 1 (February 1995): 79.

   Note: Although "Barry" was Benjamin's first "immediately recognizable" transsexual patient, Benjamin had earlier encountered other individuals in his practice whom he later admitted were probably transsexual as well. Schaefer and Wheeler call Otto Spengler—a patient of Hirschfeld's whom Benjamin met in the twenties and began treating for arthritis in 1938—his first transsexual patient. In the introduction to Green and Money's *Transsexualism and Sex Reassignment,* Benjamin recounts the story himself, describing Otto Spengler as "an elderly transvestite . . . separated from his wife . . . who had his home together with his business establishment. He lived there completely as a woman." This patient had read about the "newly discovered female hormone, Progynon" and asked Benjamin if use of the hormone would enlarge his breasts. "With some hesitation I agreed to investigate, and after a few months of parenteral therapy, a mild gynecomastia was produced to the infinite delight of the patient and with emotional improvement." In this introduction Benjamin also notes his encounters with two medical students in the thirties whom, in retrospect, he believed to be transsexual persons. Because none of these persons requested sex reassignment surgery, they would not be considered "true transsexuals" if the typology Benjamin later developed were used.

82 *Benjamin's first inclination was to send the boy to a psychiatrist* Author interview with Wheeler.

82 *He invited me for drinks at the Sulgrave Hotel* Virginia Allen in "Memorial," 26–27.

83 *The papers here are full of the Jorgensen case* Schaefer and Wheeler, "Harry Benjamin's First Ten Cases," 86.

83 *encountered a mountain of mail* Christine Jorgensen in "Memorial," 24–25. Jorgensen spoke to the assembled guests by telephone from her home in California.

84 *The transsexual (TS) male or female is deeply unhappy* Benjamin, *Transsexual Phenomenon*, 13–14.

85 *the three-to-one estimate of Christine Jorgensen's physician* Christian Hamburger, "The Desire for Change of Sex as Shown in Personal Letters from 465 Men and Women," *Acta Endocrinologica* 14 (1953): 361–75.

85 *Like male-bodied transsexuals* Benjamin, *Transsexual Phenomenon*, 149.

86 *Fifty years ago, when I was a medical student in Germany* Benjamin, *Transsexual Phenomenon*, 118.

86 *facilitating another kind of "passing"—from Jewish to German* See Sander L. Gilman, *Making the Body Beautiful: A Cultural History of Aesthetic Surgery* (Princeton, N.J.: Princeton University Press, 1999). "The key visual stereotype of the Jew that had to be unmade was the feature nineteenth-century scientists labeled 'nostrility.' At the close of the nineteenth century, the size and shape of the Jew's nose were signs that everyone, including Jewish physicians, associated with the Jew's character and permanent visibility within society. The means to change the nose, and perhaps the character, was supplied by Jacques Joseph (1865–1934), a highly acculturated young German Jewish surgeon practicing in fin de siècle Berlin. Born Jakob Joseph, he had altered his too-Jewish name when he studied medicine in Berlin and Leipzig. Joseph was a typical acculturated Jew of the period, and he understood the cultural signification of marks of honor and dishonor" (122).

86 *Benjamin "understood that you couldn't separate the body from the mind"* Author interview with Wheeler.

87 *Treating the gender dysphoric person* Schaefer and Wheeler, "Harry Benjamin's First Ten Cases," 74.

88 *a genial old paternalist* Author interview with Stryker.

88 *a number of patients went into prostitutional activities* Benjamin, *Transsexual Phenomenon*, 131.

89 *Leslie Feinberg describes a series of such encounters* Leslie Feinberg, "I Can't Afford to Get Sick," in *Trans Liberation: Beyond Pink or Blue* (Boston: Beacon Press, 1998), 79–80.

89 *Without her courage and determination* Benjamin, *Transsexual Phenomenon*, viii.

90 *As you know, I've been avoiding publicity* Schaefer and Wheeler, "Harry Benjamin's First Ten Cases," 86.

Four MEN AND WOMEN, BOYS AND GIRLS

102 *When I got to the carnival in Stroud* Hedy Jo Star, *My Unique Change* (Chicago: Specialty Books, 1965), 26.

102 *To use the Pygmalion allegory* John Money and Anke Ehrhardt, *Man and Woman, Boy and Girl* (Baltimore and London: Johns Hopkins University Press, 1972), 152.

103 *Money's research thus combined radicalism* In a 1995 article in the *Quarterly Review of Biology,* Professor Milton Diamond described Money's theory as "psychosexual neutrality at birth" to clarify the distinction between Money's view and his own. Diamond believes that humans are "predisposed psychosexually at birth" and that behavior is ultimately the result of an interaction between this predisposition and environmental influences. Milton Diamond, "A Critical Evaluation of the Ontogeny of Human Sexual Behavior," *Quarterly Review of Biology* 40 (1965): 147–75.

103 *the presence of undescended testicles was proof that the girl was* really *a boy* See Alice Domurat Dreger, *Hermaphrodites and the Medical Invention of Sex* (Cambridge Mass.: Harvard University Press, 1998). See also Susan J. Kessler, *Lessons from the Intersexed* (New Brunswick, N.J.: Rutgers University Press,1998).

103 *In 1948, Murray Llewellyn Barr, a Canadian geneticist* Murray Barr and Michael Bertram, "A Morphological Distinction between Neurones of the Male and Female and the Behavior of the Nuclear Satellite during Accelerated Nucleoprotein Synthesis," *Nature* 163 (1949): 676–77. See also M. L. Barr, "Some Notes on the Discovery of the Sex Chromatin and Its Clinical Application," *American Journal of Obstetrics and Gynecology* 112, no. 2 (January 15, 1972): 293–96.
     The inactivation of one X chromosome in female cells occurs early in embryonic development, between days twelve and sixteen, and the X chromosome that is inactivated is determined randomly. The inactivated chromosome coils and condenses, forming the "Barr body," which is used to determine chromosomal sex.

104 *It was as a graduate student in the Harvard psychological clinic* John Money, *Gendermaps: Social Constructionism, Feminism, and Sexosophical History* (New York: Continuum, 1995), 19. "This case set me on an academic course

that would lead to a Ph.D. dissertation on 'Hermaphroditism: An Inquiry into the Nature of a Human Paradox,' which allowed me to spend several hours interviewing the youth in question. At that time he was 17 years old. Diagnostically, his case was classified, according to the terminology of the era, on the basis of the presence of two undescended testes and no ovarian tissue, as one of male pseudohermaphroditism with the testicular feminizing syndrome, nowadays known as the androgen insensitivity syndrome."

104 *It pointed clearly toward the principle of a discontinuity* Ibid.

105 *The term "gender role" was conceived "after several burnings of the midnight oil"* Ibid., 20–21.

105 *In this more fully articulated definition* J. Money, J. Hampson, and J. Hampson, "An Examination of Some Basic Sexual Concepts: The Evidence of Human Hermaphroditism," *Bulletin of the Johns Hopkins Hospital* 97 (1955): 302.

106 *instinctive masculinity and instinctive femininity are present* Ibid.

107 *there was considerable evidence that visible genital anomalies* Ibid., 307.

108 *Once imprinted, a person's native language* Ibid., 310.

108 *By the time that Money and the Hampsons published their next paper* J. Money, J. Hampson, and J. Hampson, "Imprinting and the Establishment of Gender Role," *Archives of Neurology and Psychiatry* 77 (1957): 333–36.

109 *Before contemporary medical interventions* John Money, *Sex Errors of the Body and Related Syndromes*, 2nd. ed. (1968; repr., Baltimore, London, Toronto, Sydney: Paul Brookes Publishing Co., 1994), 6. Diamond and others have pointed out that in his Ph.D. dissertation in 1951, Money expressed a point of view wholly at odds with his later insistence on the devastating psychological effects of anomalous genitalia. In the 1951 dissertation, Money marveled at the psychological resilience and emotional stability of the intersexual patients he encountered. Yet four years later at Johns Hopkins, he described extreme emotional suffering and confusion in a similar group of individuals. Without an explanation by Money, it is hard to account for this rather extreme shift in his interpretation of various data.

109 *I think that many other binaries were structured by that binary* Author interview with Stryker, September 2001.

111 *I remember them removing my penis when I was five* *Hermaphrodites Speak!* videocassette produced by the Intersex Society of North America. Available by contacting ISNA at its website, http://www.isna.org.

111 *We're now seeing plenty of people* Author interview with Paul McHugh, M.D., Baltimore, Md., June 2002.

112 *Money had an idea, a real hypothesis* Author interview with Ben Barres, M.D., Ph.D., Stanford, Calif., August 2001.

113 *In a 1999 paper, Reiner indicates that his data show* W. G. Reiner, "Assignment of Sex in Neonates with Ambiguous Genitalia," *Current Opinions in Pediatrics* 4 (August 11, 1999): 363–65. See also W. G. Reiner, "Gender Identity and Sex Reassignment: A Reappraisal for the 21st Century," *Advances in Experiental Medicine and Biology* 511 (2002): 175–89.

114 *Besides the rounding out of my hips and the slenderness of my legs* Hedy Jo Star, *My Unique Change*, 13.

114 *my "sissiness" was really inborn femininity* Ibid., 24.

114 *The first couple of years on the road* Ibid., 53.

115 *Red was a normal man with a normal sexual desire* Ibid., 78.

115 *My face was covered during the examination with a sheet* Ibid., 80.

116 *I was disappointed that I couldn't have the operation immediately* Ibid., 83.

116 *The hormone shots had done wonders* Ibid., 89.

117 *The studies that we have made would all indicate* Ibid., 91.

117 *I didn't feel any malice towards the doctors* Ibid., 93.

118 *early in 1962, a friend referred her to a doctor in Chicago* Ibid., 117.

118 *the operation is extremely complex* Ibid., 121.

118 *Since the change and my adjustment to it* Ibid., 127–28.

119 *By the early sixties, Money had met Benjamin* "Memorial," 16.

119 *Aaron Devor . . . has been researching Reed Erickson's life* See Aaron H. Devor and Nicholas Matte, "ONE Inc. and Reed Erickson: The Uneasy Collaboration of Gay and Trans Activism, 1964–2003," *GLQ: A Journal of Gay and Lesbian Studies* 10, no. 2 (2004): 179–209; Aaron H. Devor, "Erickson Education Foundation," in *The Encyclopedia of Lesbian, Gay, Bisexual and Transgender History in America* (New York: Charles Scribner's Sons, 2003); Holly Devor, "Reed Erickson (1912–1992): How One Transsexual Man Supported ONE," in Vern Bullough, ed., *Before Stonewall: Activists for Gay and Lesbian Rights in Historical Context* (New York: Haworth Press, 2002), 330.

120 *the name of the Erickson Educational Foundation (EEF) came up from time to time* Telephone interview with Aaron Devor, Ph.D., June 10, 2002.

122 *Dr. John Money, psychologist at Johns Hopkins* Harry Benjamin in Money and Green, *Transseuxalism and Sex Reassignment*, 7.

122 *for a number of months, maybe even years* John Colapinto, *As Nature Made Him: The Story of the Boy Who Was Raised as a Girl* (New York: HarperCollins, 2000), 36.

124 *The press release announcing the opening of the Johns Hopkins Gender Identity Clinic* Issued on November 21, 1966.

124 *at "my instigation it had been formally named the Gender Identity Clinic"* Money, *Gendermaps*, 24.

124 *The former ... resented its parsimonious approach to patient care* See for
example Dallas Denny, "The Politics of Diagnosis and a Diagnosis of Politics: The University Gender Clinics and How They Failed to Meet the
Needs of Transsexual People," *Chrysalis Quarterly* 1, no. 3 (1991): 9–20.

125 *The Johns Hopkins transsexual program* "Memorial," 16.

125 *The surgeons were saying to me* Author interview with Paul McHugh, Baltimore, Md., June 2002.

125 *The Meyer study* Jon K. Meyer and Donna J. Reter, "Sex Reassignment:
Follow-Up," *Archives General Psychiatry* 36 (August 1979). Other follow-
up studies include Michael Fleming, Carol Steinman, and Gene Bocknek,
"Methodological Problems in Assessing Sex-Reassignment Surgery: A
Reply to Meyer and Reter," originally published in *Archives of Sexual Behavior* 9 (1980): 451–56, available online at http://www.symposion.com/
ijt/ijtc0401.htm; K. Jarrar, E. Wolff, and W. Weidner, "Long-Term Out-
come of Gender Reassignment in Male Transsexuals," *Urologe A* 35, no. 4
(July 1996): 331–37; J. Rehman, S. Lazer, A. E. Benet, et al., "The Reported
Sex and Surgery Satisfactions of 28 Postoperative Male to Female Transsexual Patients," *Archives of Sexual Behavior* 28, no. 1 (February 1999):
71–89; P. Snaith, M. J. Tarsh, and R. Reid, "Sex Reassignment Surgery—
A Study of 141 Dutch Transsexuals," *British Journal of Psychiatry* 162
(May 1993): 681–85; C. Matekole, M. Freschi, and A. Robin, "A Con-
trolled Study of Psychological and Social Change after Surgical Gender
Reassignment in Selected Male Transsexuals," *British Journal of Psychiatry*
157 (August 1990): 261–64.

126 *Critics have noted that* Michael Fleming, Carol Steinmen, and Gene Bock-
neck, "Methodological Problems in Assessing Sex-Reassignment Surgery:
A Reply to Meyer and Reter," originally published in *Archives of Sexual
Behavior* 9 (1980): 451–56, available online at http://www.symposion
.com/ijt/ijtc0401.htm

128 *There are far too many fags and TVs* Patricia Morgan (as told to Paul Hoffman), *The Man-Made Doll* (Seacaucus, N.J.: Lyle Stuart, Inc., 1972),
112–13.

In an article published in the *Western Journal of Medicine*, May 1974,
Dr. Norman Fisk of the Stanford Gender Identity Clinic describes the
physical and emotional effects of "chop shop" surgery:

> All too often we see rather pathetic examples of patients who have
> acted impulsively or injudiciously and have sought surgical sex con-
> version by means which they consider to be most expedient. It is
> well known that this particular group of patients are extremely vul-
> nerable to easy exploitation by charlatans and quacks. The tragic

results are seen in persons who have had inadequate surgical operations and are not able to perform sexually either with ease or, in some instances, at all. These people represent a rather disparate and intensely frustrated and desperate group who require, when possible, expert surgical revision of procedures previously poorly done. Ofttimes the flagrant exploitation of these patients also includes participation in illicit markets for sex steroids, silicone injections and rather poorly performed ancillary surgical cosmetic procedures. It is for these reasons that it is critically important for reputable and responsible physicians to recognize the medical legitimacy of gender disorders and, where possible, to attempt either to successfully treat such patients or to refer them to those who can.

Norman Fiske, "Gender Dysphoria Syndrome—the Conceptualization That Liberalizes Indications for Total Gender Reorientation and Implies a Broadly Based Multi-Dimensional Rehabilitative Regimen," *Western Journal of Medicine* 120 (May 1974): 386–91.

130 *Back in those days, they used to say* Author interview with Beyer.

132 *Hopkins's cachet with transsexual people* Author's personal communication, Jessica Xavier, June 25, 2002.

133 *In June 1997, Milton Diamond and Keith Sigmundson* Milton Diamond and H. K. Sigmundson, "Sex Reassignment at Birth: Long-Term Review and Clinical Implications," *Archives of Pediatrics and Adolescent Medicine* 151 (March 1997): 298–304.

134 *Diamond had participated in animal experiments* Milton Diamond and W. C. Young, "Differential Responsiveness of Pregnant and Non-Pregnant Guinea Pigs to the Masculinizing Action of Testosterone Propionate," *Endocrinology* 72 (1959): 429–38. See also M. Diamond, "Androgen-Induced Masculinization in the Ovariectomized and Hysterectomized Guinea Pig," *Anatomical Record* 157 (1963): 47–52; M. Diamond, "Genetic-Endocrine Interaction and Human Psychosexuality," in M. Diamond, ed., *Perspectives in Reproduction and Sexual Behavior* (Bloomington: Indiana University Press, 1968), 417–44. For a complete list of Diamond's publications, go to http://www.hawaii.edu/PCSS/bibliography/bib1960.html.

134 *lots of older literature that clued us in* See Diamond's review, "A Critical Evaluation of the Ontogeny of Human Sexual Behavior," *Quarterly Review of Biology* 40 (1965): 147–75.

134 *Subsequent experiments by the researcher Roger Gorski and colleagues* R. A. Gorski, J. H. Gordon, J. E. Shryne, and A. M. Southam, "Evidence for a Morphological Sex Difference within the Medial Preoptic Area of the Rat Brain," *Brain Research* 148 (1978): 333–46; M. Hines, L. S. Allen, and R. A.

Gorski, "Sex Differences in the Subregions of the Medical Nucleus of the Amygdala and the Bed Nucleus of the Stria Terminalis of the Rat," *Brain Research* 579 (1992): 321–26; L. S. Allen, M. Hines, J. E. Shryne, and R. A. Gorski, "Two Sexually Dimorphic Cell Groups in the Human Brain," *Journal of Neuroscience* 9 (1989): 497–506.

136 *In* Transsexualism and Sex Reassignment Money, "Psychological Aspects of Transsexualism," in Green and Money, *Transsexualism and Sex Reassignment,* 112.

137 *In postmodern social constructionist theory* Money, *Gendermaps,* 136.

139 *the studies carried out by Simon LeVay* L. S. Allen, M. Hines, J. E. Shryne, and R. A. Gorski, "Two Sexually Dimorphic Cell Groups in the Human Brain," *Journal of Neuroscience* 9 (1989): 497–506; W. C. Chung, G. J. De-Vries, and D. F. Swaab, "Sexual Differentiation of the Bed Nucleus of the Stria Terminalis in Humans May Extend into Adulthood," *Journal of Neuroscience* 22 (2002): 1027–33; J. M. Goldstein, L. H. Seidelman, N. J. Horton, et al., "Normal Sexual Dimorphism of the Adult Human Brain Assessed by in Vivo Magnetic Resonance Imaging," *Cerebral Cortex* 11 (2001): 490–97; J. N. Zhou, M. A. Hoffman, L. J. Gooren, D. F. Swaab, "A Sex Difference in the Human Brain and Its Relation to Transsexuality," *Nature* 378, no. 6552 (November 1995): 68–70 (available online at http://www.symposium.com/ijt/ijtco106.htm); Frank P. M. Kruijver, Jiang-Ning Zhou, Chris W. Pool, Michel A. Hoffman, Louis J. G. Gooren, and Dick F. Swaab, "Male-to-Female Transsexuals Have Female Neuron Numbers in a Limbic Nucleus," *Journal of Clinical Endocrinology and Metabolism* 85, no. 5 (2000) 2034–41.

139 *Of course, the very idea that the brain is sexed* See, for example, "Sexing the Brain" in Anne Fausto-Sterling, *Sexing the Body: Gender Politics and the Construction of Sexuality* (New York: Basic Books, 2000).

139 *Like it or not, we are living in a sexual revolution* John Money and Patricia Tucker, *Sexual Signatures: On Being a Man or a Woman* (Boston, Toronto: Little, Brown and Company, 1975).

Five LIBERATING THE RAINBOW

151 *We were led out of the bar* Sylvia Rivera, "I'm Glad I Was in the Stonewall Riot," in Feinberg, *Trans Liberation,* 106–7.

152 *Yet the backlash itself* The persistence of violent homophobia among cultural conservatives in the United States is given chilling expression in this e-mail received by the writer Andrew Sullivan two days after the 2004 presidential election:

I wonder if you noticed that yesterday all eleven states that considered the question of gay marriage voted to ban it. ALL ELEVEN. I think this sends a very clear message—true Americans do not like your kind of homosexual deviants in our country, and we will not tolerate your radical pro-gay agenda trying to force our children to adopt your homosexual lifestyle. You should be EXTREMELY GRATEFUL that we even let you write a very public and influential blog, instead of suppressing your treasonous views (as I would prefer). But I'm sure someone like yourself would consider me just an "extremist" that you don't need to worry about. Well you are wrong—I'm not just an extremist, I am a real American, and you should be worried because eleven states yesterday proved that there are millions more just like me who will not let you impose your radical agenda on our country. (Downloaded from http://www.andrewsullivan.com on November 4, 2004.)

153 *Some came from the homophile movement* See Karla Jay, *Tales of the Lavender Menace: A Memoir of Liberation* (New York: Basic Books, 1999), 77.

153 *Hopeful (but not certain) that something was going to happen* Ibid., 80.

153 *young, white and unemployed* Ibid., 78.

153 *Sylvia Rivera, a Latina street queen* Ibid., 79.

154 *I had never met a real drag queen before* Ibid., 80.

154 *The general membership is frightened of Sylvia* Martin Duberman, *Stonewall* (New York: Plume, 1984), 235–36.

155 *a bunch of stoned-out faggots* Dudley Clendenin and Adam Nagourney, *Out for Good: The Struggle to Build a Gay Rights Movement in America* (New York: Touchstone, 1999), 49.

155 *The more daring activists who had sprung forward* Ibid., 54.

155 *She would throw herself into every meeting* Duberman, *Stonewall*, 238.

156 *Back then, we were beat up by the police* In Feinberg, *Trans Liberation*, 106.

156 *Their first home was the back of a trailer truck* Duberman, *Stonewall*, 251–52.

156 *Marsha and I had always sneaked people into our hotel rooms* In Feinberg, *Trans Liberation*, 108.

157 *There was always food in the house* Ibid.

157 *It is possible for all homosexuals* Clendenin and Nagourney, *Out for Good*, 75.

157 *Huey decided that we were part of the revolution* In Feinberg, *Trans Liberation*, 108.

157 *When attacked by a GAA man* Duberman, *Stonewall*, 238.

158 *was being seized by drag queens as their holiday* Clendenin and Nagourney, *Out for Good*, 169.

158 *O'Leary was challenged by Lee Brewster* Ibid., 172.

158 *We liberated them. They owe us* Rally and march for Amanda Milan attended by the author, New York City, June 2001. I met and spoke briefly with Sylvia Rivera at the rally, intending to interview her formally at a later date. She passed away before I was able to do so. David W. Dunlap, "Sylvia Rivera, 50, Figure in Birth of the Gay Liberation Movement," *New York Times,* February 20, 2002.

159 *the guilt-ridden commentary* Dale Carpenter, "The Myth of a Transgender Stonewall," "Outright" (column), *The Texas Triangle,* downloaded from http://www.txtriange.com/archive/1022/viewpoints.htm.

160 *Since May, I've been the food director* Sylvia Rivera in update to radio program "Remembering Stonewall," downloaded from http://www.sound portraits.org/on-air/remembering_stonewall/update.php3.

160 *I am proud of myself for being there that night* In Feinberg, *Trans Liberation,* 109.

161 *there was this very strong association formed between gender nonconformity and homosexuality* Interview with Simon LeVay, Los Angeles, Calif., September 2001. "The idea of the congenital invert sums it up better than anything, the idea that people like gays and lesbians were pretty much like we now call transsexuals. My guess is that part of the reason for that misconception was that only a very small fraction of gays and lesbians came to public attention, and they were probably the more gender-nonconformist. You come across in the literature about the Mollies and so forth, in the eighteenth century—these very gender-noncomformist gay men who formed their little societies and had their pubs where they met and it's clear that they dressed as women. And there were probably other homosexual men and women who never came to public attention, and so there was this very strong association formed between gender nonconformity and homosexuality. And then I think that there was a kind of overcorrection in that since the Second World War in the gay and lesbian community there's been an almost excessive denial between homosexuality and gender nonconformity. However, I think there is a connection and I think that the evidence is particularly good for childhood."

161 *Gender issues stood at the forefront of the radical challenge* Joanne Meyerowitz, *How Sex Changed: A History of Transsexuality in the United States* (Cambridge and London: Harvard University Press, 2002), 232.

162 *the Cockettes, a group of singing, dancing, gender-fuck hippies* Susan Stryker was the first person to mention the Cockettes to me. Two years later, the feature-length documentary *The Cockettes,* by David Weissman and Bill Weber, was released. The film was a nominee for Best Documentary at the Independent Spirit Awards and winner of Best Documentary, Los Angeles Film Critics.

162 *They were people who brought together clashing styles* Author interview with Stryker, September 2001.

162 *Many of us believed that the best way to eliminate the male/female divide* Jay, *Tales*, 82.

163 *a novel that reflects hir experience* Feinberg prefers the use of non-gender-specific pronouns (hir, sie) and usage in these paragraphs reflects hir preference.

163 *One day I came home from work* Leslie Feinberg, *Stone Butch Blues* (Ithaca, N.Y.: Firebrand Books, 1993), 135–36.

164 *As much as I loved my beard as part of my body* Ibid., 222.

164 *strangers had raged at me for being a woman who crossed a forbidden boundary* Ibid., 244.

164 *the real Feinberg was denied medical treatment* Feinberg, *Trans Liberation*, 2.

165 *In May 1958, the* Sunday Express *of London* Liz Hodgkinson, *Michael, Née Laura: The Story of the World's First Female to Male Transsexual* (London: Columbus Books, 1989), 137.

165 *Proud of being a woman* Mario Martino. *Emergence: A Transsexual Autobiography* (New York: Crown Publishers, 1977), 246.

166 *For me, some of the hardest people to come out to* Author interview with Ali Cannon, San Francisco, Calif., September 4, 2001.

166 *It was really hard* Author interview with Tom Kennard, San Francisco, Calif., September 5, 2001.

167 *bitchy, catty, dykey, frustrated, crazy* Morgan quoted in Jay, *Tales*, 113.

167 *I will not be your "nigger" any longer* Del Martin quoted in Clendenin and Nagourney, *Out for Good*, 96.

167 *called on feminists to cut their ties with men* Clendenin and Nagourney, *Out for Good*, 90.

168 *for lesbians, the best thing that emerged from the Lavender Menace* Jay, *Tales*, 145.

168 *Man-hating . . . is an honorable and viable political act* Morgan quoted in Clendenin and Nagourney, *Out for Good*, 166.

169 *All transsexuals rape women's bodies* Janice Raymond, *The Transsexual Empire: The Making of the She-Male* (Boston: Beacon Press, 1979), 104. For a response to Raymond, see Sandy Stone, "The Empire Strikes Back: A Post-Transsexual Manifesto," in *Writing on the Body: Female Embodiment and Feminist Theory* (New York: Columbia University Press, 1997), 336–59.

169 *Raymond and McHugh echo each other in characterizing transsexualism as "an ideology"* Raymond, *Transsexual Empire*, 5.

169 *and comparing sex-reassignment surgery to a lobotomy* Ibid., 131.

169 *it is biologically impossible to change chromosomal sex* Ibid., 126.

169 *Masculinity and femininity . . . are social constructs* Ibid., 3.

169 *The transsexual has not been adequately conditioned* Ibid., 132.

170 *We know that we are women who are born with female chromosomes* Ibid., 114.

170 *Transsexualism is thus the ultimate . . . conclusion of male possession* Ibid., 30.

171 *Female-to-male transsexual people . . . have been assimilated into the transsexual world* Ibid., 27.

171 *The Transsexual Empire is ultimately a medical empire* Ibid., 119.

171 *One hypothesis that is being tested* Ibid., 140.

173 *I have a newspaper article in my files* Author interview with Stryker, September 2001.

174 *John Ronald Brown, "presented himself as the champion of transsexuals"* Meyerowitz, *How Sex Changed*, 271.

175 *He was exceedingly handsome* Jan Morris, *Conundrum* (New York: Harcourt, Brace, Jovanovich, 1974), 155.

175 *What Erickson did on a small scale* Author telephone interview with Aaron Devor, June 10, 2002.

176 *When the first HBIGDA conference was going to be held* Author interview with Jude Patton, June 21, 2003, Philadelphia, Pa.

177 *HBIGDA recognized the rise of private practitioners* Meyerowitz, *How Sex Changed*, 273.

Six CHILDHOOD, INTERRUPTED

192 *I wonder what my parents imagined would happen to me in a mental hospital* Daphne Scholinski, *The Last Time I Wore a Dress* (New York: Riverhead Books, 1997), 6.

192 *Defining a mental disorder* Herb Kutchins and Stuart A. Kirk, *Making Us Crazy: DSM—The Psychiatric Bible and the Creation of Mental Disorders.* (New York: Free Press, 1997), 27.

193 *As early as 1956, the psychologist Evelyn Hooker* Evelyn Hooker, "The Adjustment of the Male Overt Homosexual," *Journal of Projective Techniques* 21 (1957): 18–31; Evelyn Hooker, "Male Homosexuality in the Rorschach," *Journal of Projective Techniques* 22 (1958): 33–54.

193 *The deletion of homosexuality from the manual* See "The Fall and Rise of Homosexuality," in Kutchins and Kirk, *Making Us Crazy*, 55–100, a discussion of the political activism and internal debate in the American Psychiatric Association that led to the deletion of the diagnosis.

194 *DSM is the psychotherapist's password for insurance coverage* Kutchins and Kirk, *Making Us Crazy*, 12.

195 *"transsexualism" first appeared as a diagnostic category* American Psychi-

atric Association, *Diagnostic and Statistical Manual of Mental Disorders,* 3rd ed. (Washington, D.C.: American Psychiatric Association, 1980).

195 *due to inexperience and naïveté* Norman Fisk, M.D., "Gender Dysphoria Syndrome: The How, What, and Why of a Disease," in *Proceedings of the Second Interdisciplinary Symposium on Gender Dysphoria Syndrome,* eds. Donald R. Laub, M.D., and Patrick S. Gandy, M.S., Stanford University Medical Center, February 2–4, 1973, 8. The symposium was sponsored by the divisions of Urology and Plastic and Reconstructive Surgery at the Stanford School of Medicine. Laub, a surgeon, and Fisk, a psychiatrist, were the primary architects of the Stanford Gender Identity Clinic. See also D. R. Laub and N. Fisk, "A Rehabilitation Program for Gender Dysphoria Syndrome by Surgical Sex Change," *Plastic and Reconstructive Surgery* 53, no. 4 (April 1974): 388–403. For a consumer's perspective on the Stanford program, see Dawn Levy, "Two Transsexuals Reflect on University's Pioneering Gender Dysphoria Program." Levy describes the experience of Sandy Stone and Jamison Green in the program. Stanford Online Report. Downloaded on July 18, 2001, from http://www.stanford .edu/dept/news/report/news/may3/sexhange-53.html.

195 *We avidly searched for those patients who, if admitting to homosexual behavior at all* Fisk, "Gender Dysphoria Syndrome," 8.

196 *intensely and abidingly uncomfortable in their anatomic and genetic sex* Ibid., 10. Fisk admits that "the vast majority of patients who qualify for primary diagnosis of gender dysphoria syndrome, as opposed to transsexualism, are people who themselves rush to embrace the diagnosis of transsexualism." He attributes this to the fact that "both homosexuality and transvestism are still affectively experienced by many of our patients and their families as painful and inexcusable moral perversions or fetishes," implying that a diagnosis of transsexualism was not, at that time, perceived in the same manner by the patients themselves or their families (14). See also Laub and Fisk, "Rehabilitation Program"; and Norman M. Fisk, "Five Spectacular Results," *Archives of Sexual Behavior* 7, no. 4 (1978).

196 *In 1994, the diagnosis of transsexualism was deleted* American Psychiatric Association *Diagnostic and Statistical Manual of Mental Disorders,* 4th ed. (Washington, D.C.: American Psychiatric Association, 1994).

197 *a strong and persistent cross-gender identification* Diagnostic criteria for gender identity disorder of childhood, from *Diagnostic and Statistical Manual of Mental Disorders,* 4th ed. (American Psychological Association, 1994).

198 *Behaviors that would be ordinary or even exemplary for gender conforming boys and girls* Katharine Wilson, Ph.D., "Gender Identity Disorder in Children," http://www.gidreform.org, 3.

198 *Recent revisions of the DSM* Katherine Wilson, Ph.D., "The Disparate
Classification of Gender and Sexual Orientation in American Psychiatry,"
presented at the 1998 Annual Meeting of the American Psychiatric Association," retrieved from http://www.gidreform.org, March 31, 2001; Katherine Wilson, Ph.D., "Gender as Illness: Issues of Psychiatric Classification,"
in *Taking Sides—Clashing Views on Controversial Issues in Sex and Gender,*
E. Paul, ed. (Guilford, Conn.: Dushkin McGraw-Hill, 2000), 31–38. Retrieved from http://www.gidreform.org. See also Justin Cascio, "Bias in
Writings on Gender Identity Disorder," retrieved from *TransHealth.com* 1,
no. 4 (Spring 2002). http://www.trans-health.com/Iss4vol.1/research
.htm.

199 *boys diagnosed with GID in childhood* "The most extensive and detailed of
199 prospective studies was carried out by Richard Green, a psychiatrist at
UCLA. In his study, about four-fifths of the markedly effeminate boys became rather conventional homosexual or bisexual men, one boy became a
transsexual man, and the remainder became heterosexual men. . . . Thus
the association between childhood gender nonconformity and adult homosexuality is well established, especially in men," LeVay, *Queer Science,*
98, discussing Richard Green, *The "Sissy Boy Syndrome" and the Development of Homosexuality* (New Haven: Yale University Press, 1987).

This conclusion has been disputed more recently by some clinicians who
treat children and adolescents, for example, Peggy T. Cohen-Kettenis,
Ph.D., Department of Child and Adolescent Psychiatry, University
Medical Center, Utrecht, Netherlands. "Our data show that GID in childhood is associated with more than just one long-term trajectory. Continu-
ation of GID into adolescence by no means seems to be a rare exception.
We believe that treatment should be available for all children, regardless of
their eventual sexual orientation, and should depend only on the severity
of suffering experienced by the child." In the Netherlands, adolescent children are eligible for hormone treatment if they meet the clinic's criteria.
Cohen-Kettenis notes that of seventy-four children referred to the clinic
before the age of twelve, "17 intensely gender dysphoric adolescents
applied for sex reassignment. . . . Of the 17, 3 adolescents have started
cross-hormone treatment." Peggy T. Cohen-Kettenis, "Gender Identity
Disorder in DSM?" Letter, *Journal of the American Academy of Childhood
and Adolescent Psychiatry* 40, no. 4 (April 2001): 391.

199 *American psychiatric perceptions of etiology, distress, and treatment goals for
transgendered people* Wilson, "Disparate Classificiation," 9.

199 *No single group has gone more unnoticed by society* Gianna E. Israel and
Donald E. Tarver II, M.D., *Transgender Care: Recommended Guidelines,*

Practical Information and Personal Accounts (Philadelphia: Temple University Press, 1997), 132.

200 *If there is any cure for children or youth with gender-identity issues* Ibid., 137.

200 *Parents with resources large or small will spend their last penny* Ibid., 134.

200 *Because gender-identity conflicts are still perceived as a mental health disorder* Ibid.

201 *or . . . out on the streets* A study of homeless LGBT youths published in the *American Journal of Public Health* in 2002 concludes that "homeless youths who identify themselves as members of sexual minority groups are at increased risk for negative outcomes" such as "greater vulnerability to physical and sexual victimization, higher rates of addictive substance abuse, more psychopathology, and riskier sexual behavior in comparison with homeless heterosexual adolescents." Bryan N. Cochran, Angela J. Stewart, Joshua A. Ginzler, and Ana Mari Cauce, "Challenges Faced by Homeless Sexual Minorities: Comparison of Gay, Lesbian, Bisexual, and Transgender Homeless Adolescents with their Heterosexual Counterparts," *American Journal of Public Health* 92, no. 5 (May 2002): 773–77.

201 *Children with gender issues frequently are regarded as unruly or disruptive* Israel and Tarver, *Transgender Care*, 135.

201 *People were really mean to him at school* Jeremiah Hall, *The Advocate*, November 22, 2002.

201 *I had no friends* Author interview with Alyn Liebeman, Philadelphia, Pa., March 21, 2003.

203 *Because isolation and ostracism are key components of transgender youth experience* Israel and Tarver, *Transgender Care*, 133.

204 *skipped over hope, joy, love and anything else positive* Scholinski, *The Last Time*, 93.

204 *wore Toughskin jeans with double-thick knees* Ibid., 46.

204 *Linda opened her purse* Ibid., 104.

205 *They got to be afraid of me* Ibid., 107.

205 *Genderqueer kids present an ideal profile for sexual predators* Riki Anne Wilchins, *Read My Lips: Sexual Subversion and the End of Gender* (Ithaca, N.Y.: Firebrand Books, 1997), 130.

205 *The second time I was over, the man kept his hand on my shoulder* Scholinski, *The Last Time*, 132–33.

206 *100 percent . . . had been physically abused or beaten as children* Wilchins, *Read My Lips*, 24.

206 *such abuse "appears not as an anomaly"* Ibid., 305.

206 *I was being physically abused at home all the time* Author interview with Brad.

207 *I'd walk up to him close enough so that his angry face was all I could see* Scholinski, *The Last Time*, 2.

207 *I didn't mind being called a delinquent* Ibid., 16.

208 *She held up cards with a picture of a policeman* Ibid., 30.

208 *Daphne presents a tomboyish appearance* Ibid., 56.

208 *Drug addiction offered itself to me like a blanket of forgiveness* Ibid., 86.

209 *I sneaked a glance, and it was a jolt* Ibid., 119.

209 *Donna wanted me to walk skittery, like a bird* Ibid., 124.

209 *I still wonder why I wasn't treated for my depression* Ibid., 197.

210 *The limited evidence suggests that individuals are given DSM diagnoses* Kutchins and Kirk, *Making Us Crazy*, 260.

211 *the designation of Gender Identity Disorders as mental disorders is not a license for stigmatization* Harry Benjamin International Gender Dysphoria Association, Standards of Care, http://www.hbigda.org/soc.html.

212 *DSM is a red herring* Author interview with Beyer.

212 *There's all this empirical data, exceptional data, data that doesn't fit their [psychiatric] theory* Author interview with Christine Johnson, Philadelphia, Pa., May 13, 2002.

213 *High rates of polycystic ovary syndrome* Hartmut A. G. Bosinski, Michael Peter, Gabriele Bonatz, Reinhard Arndt, Haren Heidenreich, Wolfgang G. Sippell, and Reinhard Wille, "A Higher Rate of Hyperandrogenic Disorders in Female-to-Male Transsexuals," *Psychoneuroendocrinology* 22, no. 5 (1997): 361–80; A. H. Balen, M. E. Schachter, D. Montgomery, R. W. Reid, and H. S. Jacobs, "Polycystic Ovaries Are a Common Finding in Untreated Female-to-Male Transsexuals," *Clinical Endocrinology* 38, no. 3 (1993): 325–29.

213 *Researchers currently view PCOS as a developmental disorder* D. H. Abbott, D. A. Dumesic, and S. Franks, "Developmental Origin of Polycystic Ovary Syndrome: A Hypothesis," *Journal of Endocrinology* 174 (2002): 15.

213 *Just because something is in the DSM doesn't make it a real disease* Author interview with Paul McHugh, Baltimore, Md., June 17, 2002.

214 *I think that it . . . should not be in the DSM* Author interview with Ben Barres, Palo Alto, Calif., August 2001.

214 *To the extent that it is in the DSM, I don't think that it should be applied* Author interview with Anonymous, New York City, July 22, 2001.

216 *If you talk to post-op transpeople, most are what you would call conservative on this question* Author interview with Chelsea Goodwin, New York City, July 2001.

216 *My fear is that it [the GID diagnosis] will get thrown out of the DSM* Author interview with Wheeler.

218   *To our knowledge this is the first transgender marriage case in the U.S. in which
      extensive medical evidence* Shannon Minter, press release by National Cen-
      ter for Lesbian Rights and Equality Florida, February 21, 2003. A Florida
      appeals court ruled the Kantaras marriage null and void in July 2004, send-
      ing the custody case back to family court. Further appeals are expected.

219   *Basically, we know squat about our community* Author interview with Julie
      Maverick, Baltimore, Md., May 1, 2002.

220   *Transgendered people commonly receive substandard . . . medical treatment*
      NTAC request for funding, unpublished personal communication, Julie
      Maverick.

220   *LGBT patients face many barriers to adequate health care* See Hope Vander-
      burg, "Are LGBT Patients Receiving Adequate Healthcare?" conference
      summary, American Medical Students Association Fifty-first Annual Con-
      vention, March 28–April 1, 2001. Retrieved from http://www.medscape
      .com/Medscape/M . . . 07.01.vand/mms0507.01.vand-01.html on 5/14/01.

220   *rates of HIV infection among male-to-female transsexuals in cities* See Jes-
      sica Xavier, Washington Transgender Needs Assessment Survey, and The
      Transgender Community Health Project, published by the San Francisco
      Department of Public Health, February 1999, available at http://hivinsite
      .ucsf.edu/InSite. See also "HIV-Related Tuberculosis in a Transgender
      Network—Baltimore MD and New York City 1998–2000," *Morbidity
      and Mortality Weekly Reports* 49, no. 15 (2000): 317–20. "A Plague Unde-
      tected," a news article by Nina Siegal published in *Salon*, March 2001, cor-
      relates high rates of HIV infection among trans communities in a number
      of cities to needle-sharing in black-market hormone use. Siegal quoted
      Jason Farrell, executive director of the Positive Health Project, an AIDS
      outreach program in New York City, as saying, "Due to the lack of track-
      ing, there might be an epidemic out of control and we don't know about it,
      nor do we have the resources to address it if we need to." Siegal also quotes
      Dr. Paul Simon, a medical epidemiologist at the Los Angeles County De-
      partment of Health Services, who helped conduct a survey of 244 male-to-
      female transsexual people in 1998 and 1999. Simon and his colleagues
      found that 22 percent of those studied were HIV-positive. "That's as high
      as what we were seeing among gay and bisexual men in the 1980s at the
      peak of the epidemic. It's a very high rate of HIV infection." Retrieved
      from www.salon.com on April 9, 2001.

220   *In this culture, and in most of the civilized word today, research data is used*
      Author interview with Kit Rachlin, Washington, D.C., February 16, 2002.

225   *As more young transsexuals push to begin transitioning at a younger age* Maria
      Russo, "Teen Transsexuals: When Do Children Have a Right to Decide

Their Gender?" *Salon*, August 28, 1999. Dowloaded from http://www .salon.com/health/sex/urge/1999/08/28/transexualteens, April 9, 2001.

Seven FEAR OF A PINK PLANET

240 *Developments in the last decade* Christine Johnson, "Endocrine Disrupting Chemicals and Transsexualism," unpublished paper, available online at http://www.TransAdvocate.org.

242 *Yes, there seems to be a great deal of discomfort in the media* Author's personal communication, Christine Johnson, November 13, 2001.

244 *a workshop on endocrine disrupters in February 2002* Test Smart Endocrine Disrupters Workshop, Fairfax, Va., February 25–26, 2002.

244 *DES was first synthesized . . . in the laboratory of Sir Charles Dodds* E. C. Dodds and W. Lawson, "Oestrogenic Activity of Certain Synthetic Compounds, *Nature* 141 (1938): 247–49.

245 *Seven published papers subsequently reported* Roberta J. Apfel, M.D., and Susan M. Fisher, M.D., *To Do No Harm: DES and the Dilemmas of Modern Medicine* (New Haven: Yale University Press, 1984), 23.

245 *A larger, controlled study* W. J. Dieckmann, M. E. Davies, L. M. Rynkiewicz, et al., "Does the Administration of Diethylstilbestrol During Pregnancy Have Any Therapeutic Value?" *American Journal of Obstetrics and Gynecology* 181, no. 6 (December 1999): 1572–3.

246 *DES became a routine part of the quality care that practitioners gave their middle-class patients* Apfel and Fisher, *To Do No Harm*, 25.

247 *Methyl groups are entirely derived* Sandra Blakeslee, *New York Times*, October 6, 2003.

247 *DES also feminizes these patients* Apfel and Fisher, *To Do No Harm*, 41.

247 *A fact sheet on DES* The reference to transsexual changes was removed from the online version of the NTP fact sheet in 2003. However, the reference to "transsexual changes particularly in utero" remains in the dictionary. Diethylstilbesterol entry, in J. Buckingham and F. Macdonald, eds., *Dictionary of Organic Compouds*, 6th ed. (New York: Chapman and Hall, 1996).

247 *the fetus probably becomes sensitized to all estrogens by DES exposure* Apfel and Fisher, *To Do No Harm*, 46.

248 *If the timed sequence of hormone signals is disrupted* Berkson, *Hormone Deception*, 89.

248 *The term* default sex *has such a passive ring to it* Natalie Angier, *Woman: An Intimate Geography* (New York: Anchor Books, 1999), 43.

249 *began during weeks 5 and 6 of fetal life* Apfel and Fisher, *To Do No Harm*, 47.

249 *probably underestimates the number of* in utero *exposures* Berkson, *Hormone Deception*, 64.

249 *In April 1971, a paper published in the* New England Journal of Medicine A. L. Herbst, H. Ulfelder, D. C. Poskanzer, "Adenocarcinoma of the Vagina: Association of Maternal Stilbestrol Therapy with Tumor Appearance in Young Women," *New England Journal of Medicine* 284, no. 15 (April 15, 1971): 878–81.

251 *This despite the existence of a 1939 editorial in the* Journal of the American Medical Association Anonymous, "Estrogen Therapy: A Warning," *JAMA* 113, no. 26 (1939): 234.

251 *lobbied for research funding to study its effects* Not until 1992 did the National Institutes of Health convene a meeting on the long-term effects of DES. Shortly afterward, Congress passed the DES Education and Research Amendment, which provides funding for research and for a public and physician education campaign.

251 *DES was one of the prime movers behind the nascent women's health movement* Author interview with Dana Beyer, September 2002.

252 *For a very long time, we've been battling with the forces* Author's personal communication, Scott Kerlin, September 7, 2002.

252 *says social scientist Scott Kerlin* Kerlin is currently a counselor in private practice in Kingston, Ontario. From 1998 to 2000 he was a lecturing professor in social sciences and human development at Washington State University.

253 *I've gotten advance looks at the CDC materials* Author's personal communication, Scott Kerlin, September 12, 2002.

253 *DES exposure causes imbalances in fetal hormone levels and impairment of normal functioning in hormone receptors* See Robert Bigsby, Robert E. Chapin, George P. Dayston, et al., "Evaluating the Effects of Endocrine Disrupters on Endocrine Function during Development," *Environmental Health Perspectives* 107, supp. 4 (August 1999): 613–18. See also John Travis, "Modus Operandi of an Infamous Drug: Mutant Mice Provide Clues to How DES Wreaked Havoc in the Womb," *Science News*, February 20, 1999, retrieved from http://www.sciencenews.org_sn_arc99/2_99/bob2.htm, April 12, 2003.

253 *Hypospadias . . . and urethral meatal stenosis . . . have also been noted in DES sons* N. M. Kaplan, "Male Pseudohermaphroditism," *New England Journal of Medicine* 261 (1959): 641–44; D. Hoefnagel, "Prenatal Diethylstilbestrol Exposure and Male Hypogonadism," *The Lancet* 7951 (January 17, 1976): 152–53.

For a recent study on increased risk of hypospadia in DES grandsons (sons of DES daughters), see H. Klip, J. Verloop, J. D. van Gool, M. E.

Koster, C. W. Burger, and F. E. van Leeuwen, "Hypospadias in Sons of Women Exposed to Diethylstilbestrol in Utero: A Cohort Study." *The Lancet* 359 (2002): 1102–7. See also H. Klop, J. Verloop, J. D. van Gool, M. E. Koster, C. W. Burger, and F. E. Leeuwen, "Increased Risk of Hypospadias in Male Offspring of Women Exposed to Diethylstilbestrol in Utero." *Paediatric and Perinatal Epidemiology* 15, no. 4 (2001): A19.

254 *The DES Sons Online Network was also formed to expand awareness* Scott Kerlin and Dana Beyer, M.D., unpublished paper, Scott Kerlin personal communication with the author.

254 *About 50 percent of our two hundred people . . . exhibit some form of gender variance* Dana Beyer responding to questions after a presentation at the International Foundation for Gender Education conference, March 22, 2003, Philadelphia, Pa.

255 *In July 2004* "The vast majority of individuals whom I have allowed to join the [DES Sons] network had either 'confirmed' (i.e., directly through medical records access or indirectly through personal conversation with mother or other family members) or 'strongly suspected' (i.e., all evidence points in that direction, but medical records access and/or contact with mother not possible) prenatal DES exposure. However, a few (less than fifty since the network was formed) who had no way of confirming their exposure were also permitted to join in order to assist them with unanswered questions. (It is estimated that 50 percent of all DES-exposed XY males have never been told of their exposure.)" Scott Kerlin, personal communication with the author, July 9, 2004.

255 *It seems that the entire focus of any ongoing "cohort" tracking* Author's personal communication, Scott Kerlin, September 12, 2001.

255 *the goal of the DCCS is to determine whether the health risk of cancer* Centers for Disease Control, http://www.cdc.gov/DES.

255 *not only increased incidence of hypospadias but also "lower ratings"* I. D. Yalom, R. Green, and N. Fish, "Prenatal Exposure to Female Hormones," *Archives of General Psychiatry* 28 (April 1973): 554–61.

256 *A study published in 1992 by researchers at the Kinsey Institute* J. M. Reinisch and S. A. Sanders, "Effects of Prenatal Exposure to Diethylstilbestrol (DES) on Hemispheric Laterality and Spatial Ability in Human Males," *Hormones and Behavior* 26, no. 1 (1992): 52–75.

256 *this subject, as I don't need to tell you* Personal communication, Pat Cody to Scott Kerlin, June 8, 2001.

256 *Since we cannot create fresh studies of DES in humans* Author's personal communication, Scott Kerlin, September 10, 2002.

257 *In 2001, the researcher Niels Skakkebaek and colleagues* N. E. Skakkebaek,

E. Rajpert-De Meyts, and K. M. Main, "Testicular Dysgenesis Syndrome: An Increasingly Common Developmental Disorder with Environmental Aspects," *Human Reproduction* 5 (July 2001): 972–78.

258 *the biological plausibility of possible damage to certain human functions (particularly reproductive and developing systems)* World Health Organization, "Global Assessment of the State of the Science of Endocrine Disrupters," retrieved from http://www.who.int/pcs/emerg_site/edc/global_edc_TOC.htm, July 31, 2002.

259 *It is somewhat ironic that two synthetic chemicals* John McLachlan, "Environmental Signaling and Endocrine Disruption," *Endocrine Reviews* 22, no. 3 (2001): 323.

259 *Reviewers considered the work metaphysical* Sheldon Krimsky, *Hormonal Chaos: The Social and Scientific Origins of the Environmental Endocrine Hypothesis* (Baltimore and London: Johns Hopkins University Press, 2000), 13.

260 *The higher the dose, the greater is the expected effect* Krimsky, *Hormonal Chaos*, 13.

260 *The authors of a 2000 paper* "It is also the case that the environmental endocrine hypothesis resides at the boundary of endocrinology and toxicology, challenging the common wisdom of both fields. For example, Crews et al. outlined some of the salient points that distinguish environmental endocrine disruption from other toxicological approaches. They contrast the 'traditional toxicological approach,' which utilizes a carcinogenic model or acute toxicity, with the 'endocrine disrupter approach,' which relies on a developmental model and delayed dysfunction." McLachlan, "Environmental Signaling," 320, referencing D. Crews, E. Willingham, and J. K. Sipper, "Endocrine Disrupters: Present Issues, Future Directions," *Quarterly Review of Biology* 75 (2000): 243–60.

260 *In 1990 . . . Theo Colborn published the results of an extensive literature search* T. Colborn, A. Davidson, S. N. Green, et al., *Great Lakes, Great Legacy?* (Washington, D.C.: Conservation Foundation, 1992).

261 *studies on what he called "the positioning effect"* F. vom Saal and F. Bronson, "Sexual Characteristics of Adult Female Mice Are Correlated with Their Blood testosterone Levels during Prenatal Development," *Science* 208 (1980): 597–99; F. S. vom Saal, W. Grant, C. McMullen, and K. Laves, "High Fetal Estrogen Concentrations: Correlation with Enhanced Adult Sexual Preferences and Decreased Aggression in Male Mice," *Science* 220 (1983): 1306–9.

261 *Colborn, vom Saal, and other researchers began sharing data* T. Colborn, F. S. vom Saal, and A. M. Soto, "Developmental Effects of Endocrine Disrupt-

ing Chemicals in Wildlife and Humans, *Environmental Health Perspectives* 101 (1993): 378–83.

261 *Together, the two wrote a paper, published in the British medical journal* The Lancet R. M. Sharpe and N. E. Skakkebaek, "Are Oestrogens Involved in Falling Sperm Counts and Disorders of the Male Reproductive Tract?" *The Lancet* 431 (1993): 1392–95.

262 *Additional research funds to study different components* Krimsky, *Hormonal Chaos,* 57.

262 *Is it a coincidence that since the introduction of chlorinated pesticides* Johnson, "Endocrine Disrupters."

263 *Clearly researchers knew that sexual developmental changes were observed with DDT . . . as early as 1950* H. A. Burlington, V. F. Lindeman, "Effect of DDT on Testes and Secondary Sex Characteristics of White Leghorn Cockerels," *Proceedings of the Society for Experimental Biology and Medicine* 74, no. 48051 (1950): 48–51. See also R. M. Welch, W. Leven, and A. H. Conney, "Estrogenic Action of DDT and Its Analogs," *Toxicology and Applied Pharmacology* 14 (1969): 358–67.

263 *When I saw the words "endocrine disrupter" a lightbulb went off in my head* Author interview with Christine Johnson, Philadelphia, Pa., May 13, 2002.

264 *he acknowledged that 45 percent of his patients had hypogonadism* Benjamin, *Transsexual Phenomenon,* 53, 75. Actually, Benjamin estimated that 40 percent of his patients showed signs of hypogonadism. In the chapter titled "The Etiology of Transsexualism," he states: "A possible endocrine cause of transsexualism has been investigated in a few cases with great thoroughness. Beyond a few suspicious findings, no definite proof has yet been found. It may or may not have an endocrine significance that among my 152 male transsexuals, nearly 40 percent were found to have more or less distinct signs of a degree of sexual underdevelopment (hypogonadism). . . . In such a condition, the pituitary as well as the gonads may be at fault with, of course, an inborn reason behind it." Benjamin's shrewd guesses are not too far off the mark, judging from recent discoveries about the effects of EDCs.

264 *Scott Kerlin recently uncovered a provocative lead* Personal communication with the author, July 29, 2004. References H. Benjamin, "Should Surgery Be Performed on Transsexuals?" *American Journal of Psychotherapy* 25, no. 1 (January 1, 1971): 74–82. Also, H. Benjamin and C. L. Ihlenfeld, "Transsexualism," *American Journal of Nursing* 73, no. 3 (March 1, 1973): 457–61.

265 *They can recount exactly where they were and what they were doing* See, for example, Morris, *Conundrum,* 15. "I was three or perhaps four years old when I realized that I had been born into the wrong body, and should re-

ally be a girl. I remember the moment well, and it is the earliest memory of my life. I was sitting beneath my mother's piano, and her music was falling around me like cataracts, enclosing me as if in a cave. . . . What triggered so bizarre a thought I have long forgotten, but the conviction was unfaltering from the start."

265 *My former career was in the insurance industry* NTAC listserv (ntacmembers@yahoogroups.com) Tuesday, March 19, 2002.

266 *Wonderful! For years I lived just ½ mile from a lot of those settling ponds* Ibid.

267 *These include fish, frogs, and alligators* Author interview with Maverick. See also: D. M. Fry and C. K. Toone, "DDT-Induced Feminization of Gull Embryos, *Science* 213 (1981): 922–24; L. J. Guillette, T. S. Gross, G. R. Masson, et al., "Developmental Abnormalities of the Gonad and Abnormal Sex Hormone Concentrations in Juvenile Alligators from Contaminated and Control Lakes in Florida," *Environmental Health Perspectives* 102 (1994): 680–88; T. Hayes, K. Haston, M. Tsui, A. Hoang, C. Haeffle, and A. Vonk, "Atrazine-Induced Hermaphroditism at 0.1 ppb in American Leopard Frogs (*Rana pipiens*): Laboratory and Field Evidence," *Environmental Health Perspectives* 111, no. 4 (April 2003): 568–75.

268 *the concept is ahead of the science* Author conversation with James Yager, Ph.D., Baltimore, Md., May 31, 2002.

268 *estrogens are considered reversible cellular signals* McLachlan, "Environmental Signaling," 333.

268 *when a gene programmed to respond to estradiol at puberty is misprogrammed* Ibid., 335.

269 *McLachlan points to one interesting example* McLachlan, referencing J. R. Tanner, "St. Anthony's Fire, Then and Now: A Case Report and Historical Review," *Canadian Journal of Surgery* 30 (1987): 291–93.

269 *individuals exhibiting the bizarre symptoms of St. Anthony's fire* J. McLachlan, "Environmental Signaling," 335.

270 *More people are coming around* Author interview with Milton Diamond, Philadelphia Pa., March 21, 2003; Milton Diamond, "Pediatric Management of Ambiguous and Tramatized Genitalia." *Journal of Urology* 162 (1999): 1021–28.

271 *what is gender-specific behavior* H. F. Meyer-Bahlburg, J. F. Feldman, P. Cohen, and A. A. Erhardt, "Perinatal Factors in the Development of Gender-Related Play Behavior: Sex Hormones versus Pregnancy Complications," *Psychiatry* 51, no. 3 (1988): 260–71. See also Hestien Vreugdenhil, Froukje M. E. Slijper, Paul G. H. Mulder, and Nynke Weisglas-Kuperus, "Effects of Perinatal Exposure to PCBs and Dioxins on Play Behavior in Dutch Children at School Age," *Environmental Health Perspectives* 110, no. 10 (October 2002): 593–98; D. E. Sandberg, J. E. Venn, J. Weiner, G. P.

Beehler, M. Swanson, and H. F. Meyer-Bahlburg, "Hormonally Active Agents in the Environment and Children's Behavior: Assessing Effects on Children's Gender Dimorphic Behavior Outcomes," *Epidemiology* 14, no. 2 (March 2003): 148–55.

271 *the subject of essential sex differences in the mind is clearly very delicate* Baron-Cohen, *Essential Difference*, 1.

272 *Systematizing and empathizing are wholly . . . different processes* Ibid., 3.

273 *Diagnoses of autism, like those for gender identity disorder, have been rising steadily over the past few decades* "The U.S. Department of Education reports a 900 percent increase in cases of autism since 1992. On C-Span exhausted, terrified, furious parents vent their hopeless wrath during congressional hearings investigating claims that Big Pharma has ignored for years their belief that pediatric vaccinations precipitated their child's acquisition of autism. Is the mercury-based preservative contained in the vaccine—thimerosal—overwhelming the baby's premature immune system? . . . Sensing the inevitable, bills exonerating vaccine manufacturers from liability snake their way through Congress. The most notorious of which, a rider, Mickey Finn'd at the 11th hour into the density of the Homeland Security Bill under cover of smallpox, attempted to exempt Eli Lilly from any and all damages related to vaccine complaints. The provision's author? Senate Majority Leader Dr. Bill Frist, R-Tenn. Uncovered by public watchdogs, it has since been removed from the bill." Scot Sea, "Planet Autism," *Salon*, September 27, 2003. Available online at http://www.salon.com/mwt/feature/2003/07/27/autism/index.html.

Two interesting (though unrelated) facts are buried in this excerpt—mercury is a known endocrine disrupter, and the Eli Lilly Company was also one of the primary manufacturers of DES.

277 *The navy discharged me in '74* See "A Life of Service: Sister Mary, Whose Past Has Seen Many Painful Twists and Turns, Now Brings Comfort to Others with the World's Most Comprehensive Web Site on AIDS and HIV," Jean O. Pasco, *Los Angeles Times* (Home Edition), December 1, 1997; "Sharing the Word on AIDS Technology: Patients and Others Can Count on Sister Mary Elizabeth's Electronic Bulletin Board in San Juan Capistrano to Provide Extensive Information for Free," Leslie Berkman, *Los Angeles Times* (Orange County Edition), April 18, 1994; "There Is Still a Prayer for New Religious Order," Lynn Smith, *Los Angeles Times* (Orange County Edition), November 14, 1988; "Vows Repudiated: Bishop Blocks Transsexual Nun's Order," Lynn Smith, *Los Angeles Times* (Orange County Edition), January 8, 1988.

ANSWERING THE RIDDLE

288 *denied his claim of discrimination and request for damages* In the ruling against Oiler, the Louisiana court noted that "the words of Title VII do not outlaw discrimination against a person who has a sexual identity disorder, i.e., a person born with a male body who believes himself to be a female, or a person born with a female body who believes herself to be male; a prohibition against discrimination based on an individual's sex is not synonymous with a prohibition based on an individual's sexual identity disorder or discontent with the sex into which they were born. The dearth of legislative history on section 2000e-2(a) (1) strongly reinforces the view that the section means nothing more than the plain language suggests." Title VII of the Civil Rights Act adopted in 1964 provides protection from discrimination on the basis of sex.

289 *In 1989, I became aware* Phyllis Randolph Frye, "Transgenders Must Be Brave while Forging This New Front on Equality," keynote address at the Georgetown Journal of Gender and the Law Fifth Annual Symposium, Washington, D.C., February 27, 2002.

291 *scientists are being cautioned not to use hot-button words . . . such as "gay"* An article published in the *New York Times* on April 18, 2003, described the challenges faced by applicants for federal grants under the Bush administration. "Scientists who study AIDS and other sexually transmitted diseases say they have been warned by federal health officials that their research may come under unusual scrutiny by the Department of Health and Human Services or by members of Congress, because the topics are politically controversial. The scientists, who spoke on condition that they not be identified, say they have been advised they can avoid unfavorable attention by keeping certain 'key words' out of their applications for grants from the National Institutes of Health or the Centers for Disease Control and Prevention. These words include 'sex workers,' 'men who sleep with men,' 'anal sex,' and 'needle exchange,' the scientists said." Erica Goode, "Certain Words Can Trip Up AIDS Grants, Scientists Say," *New York Times*, April 18, 2003.

SELECTED BIBLIOGRAPHY

The following books and articles were helpful to me in understanding various aspects of the subjects discussed within these pages. Journal and magazine articles previously cited in the notes are not included in this list; book titles are duplicated in both lists. This is far from being a definitive bibliography of all the titles, both scholarly and trade, available on these topics.

Angier, Natalie. *Woman: An Intimate Geography.* New York: Anchor Books, 1999.

Apfel, Roberta J., and Susan M. Fisher. *To Do No Harm: DES and the Dilemmas of Modern Medicine.* New Haven: Yale University Press, 1984.

Baron-Cohen, Simon. *The Essential Difference: The Truth about the Male and Female Brain.* New York: Basic Books, 2003.

Benjamin, Harry. *The Transsexual Phenomenon.* New York: Ace Books, 1966.

Berkson, Lindsey. *Hormone Deception.* Chicago: Contemporary Books, 2000.

Bornstein, Kate. *Gender Outlaw: Of Men, Women and the Rest of Us.* New York: Vintage Books, 1995.

Brevard, Aleshia. *The Woman I Was Not Born to Be: A Transsexual Journey.* Philadelphia: Temple University Press, 2001.

Bullough, Bonnie, Vern L. Bullough, and James Elias. *Gender Blending.* Amherst, N.Y.: Prometheus Books, 1997.

Bullough, Vern L., and Bonnie Bullough. *Cross Dressing, Sex, and Gender.* Philadelphia: University of Pennsylvania Press, 1993.

Butler, Judith. *Bodies That Matter: On the Discursive Limits of Sex.* New York: Routledge, 1993.

———. *Gender Trouble: Feminism and the Subversion of Identity.* New York: Routledge, 1999.

Califia, Pat. *Sex Changes: The Politics of Transgenderism.* San Francisco: Cleis Press, 1997.

Canguilhem, Georges. *The Normal and the Pathological.* New York: Zone Books, 1991.

Clendenin, Dudley, and Adam Nagourney. *Out for Good: The Struggle to Build a Gay Rights Movement in America*. New York: Touchstone, 1999.

Colapinto, John. *As Nature Made Him: The Story of a Boy Who Was Raised as a Girl*. New York: HarperCollins, 2001.

Colborn, Theo, Dianne Dumanoski, and John Peterson Myers. *Our Stolen Future*. New York: Dutton, 1996.

Cromwell, Jason. *Transmen and FTMs: Identities, Bodies, Genders and Sexualities*. Urbana and Chicago: University of Illinois Press, 1990.

de Kruif, Paul. *The Male Hormone*. New York: Harcourt, Brace and Company, 1945.

DeVor, Holly. *FTM: Female to Male Transsexuals in Society*. Bloomington: Indiana University Press, 1997.

Diamond, Milton. *Perspectives in Reproduction and Sexual Behavior*. Bloomington: Indiana University Press, 1968.

Dillon, Michael. *Self: A Study in Endocrinology and Ethics*. London: William Heinemann Medical Books, Ltd., 1946.

Docter, Richard. *Transvestites and Transsexuals: Toward a Theory of Cross-Gender Behavior*. New York: Plenum Press, 1988.

Dorner, Gunter. *Hormones and Brain Differentiation*. Amsterdam: Elsevier, 1976.

Dreger, Alice Domurat. *Hermaphrodites and the Medical Invention of Sex*. Cambridge, Mass., and London: Harvard University Press, 1998.

Duberman, Martin. *Stonewall*. New York: Plume, 1994.

Ekins, Richard, and Dave King. *Blending Genders: Social Aspects of Cross-Dressing and Sex-Changing*. London and New York: Routledge, 1996.

Ellis, Havelock. *Man and Woman: A Study of Human Secondary Sexual Characters*. London: Walter Scott, 1897.

Fausto-Sterling, Anne. *Sexing the Body: Gender Politics and the Construction of Sexuality*. New York: Basic Books, 2000.

Feinberg, Leslie. *Stone Butch Blues*. Ithaca, N.Y.: Firebrand Books, 1993.

————. *Trans Liberation: Beyond Pink or Blue*. Boston: Beacon Press, 1998.

Foucault, Michel. *Herculine Barbin: Being the Recently Discovered Memoirs of a Nineteenth-Century French Hermaphrodite*. Translated by Richard McDougall. Pantheon Books: New York, 1980.

Garber, Marjorie. *Vested Interests: Cross-Dressing and Cultural Anxiety*. New York: Routledge, 1992.

Gilman, Sander L. *Making the Body Beautiful: A Cultural History of Aesthetic Surgery*. Princeton, N.J.: Princeton University Press, 1999.

Green, Richard. *The "Sissy Boy Syndrome" and the Development of Homosexuality*. New Haven: Yale University Press, 1987.

Green, Richard, and John Money. *Transsexualism and Sex Reassignment*. Baltimore: Johns Hopkins University Press, 1969.

Haeberle, Erwin J. *The Birth of Sexology: A Brief History in Documents*. Washington, D.C.: World Association for Sexology, 1983.

Heilman, Ann. *New Woman Fiction: Women Writing First Wave Feminism*. New York: St. Martin's Press, 2000.

Herdt, Gilbert, ed. *Third Sex, Third Gender: Beyond Sexual Dimorphism in Culture*. New York: Zone Books, 1994.

Hirschfeld, Magnus. *Transvestites: The Erotic Urge to Cross Dress*. Translated by Michael A. Lombardi-Nash. Buffalo N.Y.: Prometheus Books, 1991. Originally published as *Die Transvestiten* (Leipzig: Max Spohr, 1910).

Hodgkinson, Liz. *Michael, Née Laura: The Story of the World's First Female to Male Transsexual*. London: Columbus Books, 1989.

Hoyer, Niels. *Man into Woman: An Authentic Record of a Change of Sex*. New York: E. P. Dutton and Company, 1933.

Isherwood, Christopher. *Christopher and His Kind*. New York: Farrar, Straus and Giroux, 1976.

Israel, Gianna E., and Donald E. Tarver II, M.D. *Transgender Care: Recommended Guidelines, Practical Information and Personal Accounts*. Philadelphia: Temple University Press, 1997.

Jay, Karla. *Tales of the Lavender Menace: A Memoir of Liberation*. New York: Basic Books, 1999.

Jorgensen, Christine. *Christine Jorgensen: A Personal Autobiography*. San Francisco: Cleis Press, 2000.

Kammerer, Paul. *Rejuvenation and the Prolongation of Human Efficiency: Experiences with the Steinach Operation on Man and Animals*. New York: Boni and Liveright, 1923.

Kates, Gary. *Monsieur d'Éon Is a Woman: A Tale of Political Intrigue and Sexual Masquerade*. New York: Basic Books, 1995.

Katz, Jonathan Ned. *Gay American History: Lesbians and Gay Men in the U.S.A.* New York: Thomas Y. Crowell Company, 1976.

Kessler, Susan J. *Lessons from the Intersexed*. New Brunswick N.J.: Rutgers University Press, 1998.

Krimsky, Sheldon. *Hormonal Chaos: The Scientific and Social Origins of the Environmental Endocrine Hypothesis*. Baltimore and London: Johns Hopkins University Press, 2000.

Kutchins, Herb, and Stuart A. Kirk. *Making Us Crazy: DSM—The Psychiatric Bible and the Creation of Mental Disorders*. New York: Free Press, 1997.

Laub, Donald, and Patrick Gandy. *Proceedings of the Second Interdisciplinary Symposium on Gender Dysphoria Syndrome*. Stanford, Calif.: Division of Reconstructive and Rehabilitation Surgery, 1973.

Ledger, Sally. *The New Woman: Fiction and Feminism at the Fin de Siècle*. Manchester and New York: Manchester University Press, 1997.

LeVay, Simon. *Queer Science: The Use and Abuse of Research into Homosexuality.* Cambridge and London: MIT Press, 1996.

Marks, Patricia. *Bicycles, Bangs and Bloomers: The New Woman in the Popular Press.* Lexington: University Press of Kentucky, 1990.

Martino, Mario. *Emergence: A Transsexual Autobiography.* New York: Crown Publishers, 1977.

Medvei, Victor Cornelius, ed. *A History of Endocrinology.* Lancaster, Boston, The Hague: MTP Press Ltd., 1982.

Meyerowitz, Joanne. *How Sex Changed: A History of Transsexuality in the United States.* Cambridge and London: Harvard University Press, 2002.

Money, John. *Gendermaps: Social Constructionism, Feminism, and Sexosophical History.* New York: Continuum, 1995.

Money, John. *Sex Errors of the Body and Related Syndromes* (2nd ed.). Baltimore, London, Toronto, Sydney: Paul Brookes Publishing Co., 1994 (1st ed. 1968).

Money, John, and Anke Ehrhardt. *Man and Woman, Boy and Girl.* Baltimore and London: Johns Hopkins University Press, 1972.

Money, John, and Herman Musaph, eds. *Handbook of Sexology.* Amsterdam, London, New York: Excerpta Medica, 1977.

Money, John, and Patricia Tucker. *Sexual Signatures: On Being a Man or a Woman.* Boston, Toronto: Little, Brown and Company, 1975.

Morgan, Patricia (as told to Paul Hoffman). *The Man-Made Doll.* Secaucus, N.J.: Lyle Stuart, Inc., 1972.

Morris, Jan. *Conundrum.* New York: Harcourt, Brace, Jovanovich, 1974.

Namaste, Viviane K. *Invisible Lives: The Erasure of Transsexual and Transgendered People.* Chicago and London: University of Chicago Press, 2000.

Raymond, Janice. *The Transsexual Empire: The Making of the She-Male.* Boston: Beacon Press, 1979.

Rees, Mark. *Dear Sir or Madam: The Autobiography of a Female to Male Transsexual.* London: Cassell, 1996.

Roberts, Mary Louise. *Disruptive Acts: The New Woman in Fin de Siècle France.* Chicago and London: University of Chicago Press, 2002.

Scholinksi, Daphne. *The Last Time I Wore a Dress.* New York: Riverhead Books, 1997.

Showalter, Elaine. *Sexual Anarchy: Gender and Culture at the Fin de Siècle.* New York: Viking, 1990.

Spry, Jennifer. *Orlando's Sleep: An Autobiography of Gender.* Norwich, Vt.: New Victoria Publishers, 1997.

Star, Hedy Jo. *My Unique Change.* Chicago: Specialty Books, 1965.

Stone, Sandy. "The Empire Strikes Back: A Post-Transsexual Manifesto," in *Writing on the Body: Female Embodiment and Feminist Theory.* Ed. by

K. Conboy, N. Medina, and S. Stanbury. New York: Columbia University Press, 1997, 337–59.

Thompson, Raymond (with Kitty Sewall). *What Took You So Long? A Girl's Journey to Manhood.* London: Penguin Books, 1995.

Thurman, Judith. *Secrets of the Flesh: A Life of Colette.* New York: Knopf, 1999.

Turner, William B. *A Genealogy of Queer Theory.* Philadelphia: Temple University Press, 2000.

Wilchins, Riki Anne. *Read My Lips: Sexual Subversion and the End of Gender.* Ithaca, N.Y.: Firebrand Books, 1997.

Wolff, Charlotte. *Magnus Hirschfeld: A Portrait of a Pioneer in Sexology.* London, Melbourne, New York: Quartet Books, 1986.

Woolf, Virginia. *Orlando.* London: Vintage Books, 1992; first edition Hogarth Press, 1928.

INDEX

A NOTE ABOUT THE AUTHOR

Deborah Rudacille is a science writer at John Hopkins University. She is the author of *The Scalpel and the Butterfly: The Conflict Between Animal Research and Animal Protection*. She lives in Baltimore.

A NOTE ON THE TYPE

Pierre Simon Fournier *le jeune,* who designed the type used in this book, was both an originator and a collector of types. His services to the art of printing were his design of letters, his creation of ornaments and initials, and his standardization of type sizes. His types are old style in character and sharply cut. In 1764 and 1766 he published his *Manuel typographique,* a treatise on the history of French types and printing, on typefounding in all its details, and on what many consider his most important contribution to typography—the measurement of type by the point system.

Composed by Stratford Publishing Services, Brattleboro, Vermont
Printed and bound by Berryville Graphics, Berryville, Virginia
Book design by M. Kristen Bearse